Buying & Selling a Home
For Canadians

FOR
DUMMIES®
4TH EDITION

Buying & Selling a Home
a Home
For Canadians

FOR

DUMMIES®

4TH EDITION

by Tony Ioannou and Sarah Daniels

John Wiley & Sons Canada, Ltd.

Buying & Selling a Home For Canadians For Dummies® 4th Edition

Published by
John Wiley & Sons Canada, Ltd.
6045 Freemont Blvd.
Mississauga, ON L5R 4J3
www.wiley.com

Library and Archives Canada Cataloguing in Publication Data

Ioannou, Tony

   Buying and selling a home for Canadians for dummies / by Tony Ioannou, Sarah Daniels. — 4th ed.

Includes index.
ISBN 978-0-470-96402-6
978-0-470-95197-2 (ebk), 978-0-470-95196-5 (ebk), 978-0-470-95195-8 (ebk)

        1. House buying—Canada.   2. House selling—Canada.

I. Daniels, Sarah, 1964– II. Title.

HD1379.I52 2011   643'.120971   C2010-907651-6

For general information on John Wiley & Sons Canada, Ltd., including all books published by Wiley Publishing Inc., please call our distribution centre at 1-800-567-4797. For reseller information, including discounts and premium sales, please call our sales department at 416-646-7992. For press review copies, author interviews, or other publicity information, please contact our publicity department, Tel. 416-646-4582, Fax 416-236-4448.

Wiley also publishes its books in a variety of electronic formats. Some content that appears in print may not be available in electronic books.

Printed in the United States

2 3 4 5 BRR 15 14

WILEY

About the Authors

Tony Ioannou is currently a senior associate and manager with Dexter Associates Realty in Vancouver, and has been interviewed many times in the Vancouver and national media about the state of the real estate market and the industry in general.

Tony obtained his real estate licence in 1984, and has consistently been a top-producing salesperson with NRS Block Bros., and with Dexter Associates Realty since 1990. In 1990, he obtained his agents (managing brokers) licence, but continues to enjoy working as a residential real estate sales person primarily on the West Side of Vancouver. He has also worked as a division director for the Real Estate Board of Greater Vancouver, sits on a number of industry committees, teaches a real estate course to new real estate agents, and speaks to the public about real estate at seminars and shows.

Sarah Daniels is currently a realtor who works in association with her brother, Philip DuMoulin, at Bay Realty Ltd in the Greater Vancouver area.

Sarah obtained her real estate license in 2003 following a long career in Vancouver in both radio and television. She began her real estate career at Hugh and McKinnon Realty Ltd. before joining Bay Realty Ltd in 2006. She is the author of *Welcome Home: Insider Secrets for Buying or Selling Your Property* and appears regularly on Global BC's noon news commenting on real estate trends. Sarah also continues to write for local publications, as well as emceeing local events.

Authors' Acknowledgements

Thanks to copy editor Andrea Douglas, production editor Lindsay Humphreys, and technical editor Elizabeth Spivak of Prudential Sadie Moranis Realty.

Publisher's Acknowledgments

We're proud of this book; please send us your comments through our online registration form located at `http://dummies.custhelp.com`. For other comments, please contact our Customer Care Department within the U.S. at 877-762-2974, outside the U.S. at 317-572-3993, or fax 317-572-4002.

Some of the people who helped bring this book to market include the following:

Acquisitions and Editorial

Acquiring Editor: Robert Hickey

Copy Editor: Andrea Douglas

Production Editor: Lindsay Humphreys

Technical Editor: Elizabeth Spivak, Prudential Sadie Moranis Realty

Editorial Assistant: Katey Wolsley

Cartoons: Rich Tennant (`www.the5thwave.com`)

Cover photo: ©istock/sjlocke

Composition Services

Senior Project Coordinator: Kristie Rees

Layout and Graphics: Joyce Haughey, Vida Noffsinger

Proofreaders: John Greenough, Lisa Stiers

Indexer: Claudia Bourbeau

John Wiley & Sons Canada, Ltd.

Deborah Barton, Vice President and Director of Operations

Jennifer Smith, Publisher, Professional & Trade Division

Alison Maclean, Managing Editor, Professional & Trade Division

Karen Bryan, Vice-President, Publishing Services

Publishing and Editorial for Consumer Dummies

Diane Graves Steele, Vice President and Publisher, Consumer Dummies

Kristin Ferguson-Wagstaffe, Product Development Director, Consumer Dummies

Ensley Eikenburg, Associate Publisher, Travel

Kelly Regan, Editorial Director, Travel

Composition Services

Debbie Stailey, Director of Composition Services

Contents at a Glance

Table of Contents

Introduction

$\mathcal{B}$uying or selling a home is an incredibly enormous undertaking, but at the same time it shouldn't be the cause of shortness of breath, dizziness, or an extended hospital stay. However, it does involve some of the most important financial decisions you'll ever make, as chances are your home is the biggest asset you'll ever own. But it's not so bad — especially with this book in hand. Armed with information about everything from mortgages to heating systems, you can calmly face the real estate world and see how it works. With this book, you get to know what fixed rate, open term mortgages are. You find out just how important a home inspection can be. And most important, you discover what your priorities are, and how to match them with a home — a home of your own.

If you're considering buying a home, you've come to the right place! Self-promotion aside, we tell you what you need to think about before making that huge decision, how to make your choices in a realistic and informed way, and how to avoid unexpected problems, crumbling foundations, and street parking.

If you're selling, we share all kinds of information about what your buyer expects from you, how to get the most money for your home, and how to manage the details so you don't overlook anything. If you're thinking about selling your home yourself, you can find lots of tips to help you out. Selling your home is a long, intense process that many people do as a full-time job; we try to help you see whether you're really up for that kind of do-it-yourself challenge.

Buying a new home or leaving an old and cherished one involves a lot of decisions and considerations. In this book, we outline them all, and help you move on to your new home, wherever that may be.

About This Book

Some of us are buyers, some of us are sellers, and some of us are both at the same time. We divide the book into easy-to-use parts: Read the first half if you're looking to buy a home, and the second half if you're trying to sell one. Actually, read both halves: It'll help you get inside the head of the person on the other side of the contract, and what they may be thinking! We cover diverse topics like mortgages, shopping for a new home, and assembling your selling team — your real estate agent and lawyer. Wherever you start reading, we guarantee you can find information that's useful and easy to absorb. We do our best to keep it simple, but sometimes you just can't get around using the A-word (amortization).

If you're on the fence about whether you're ready to be a homeowner, read this book. We go through the pros and cons of both buying and renting, and explain the financial benefits that can be yours from investing in your own home. If you already have a home, this book is a great refresher course on how to handle all the details involved in choosing a new home. If this is your first time on the home-buying market, we take you through all the key decisions to make and the steps to take to get yourself into the right home at the right price.

Selling your current home is often a very tough decision, and we don't ignore the fact that you may not feel completely ready to slap a "for sale" sign on the front lawn. This book helps you determine whether you're ready to say goodbye to your present home. If you've already made up your mind to move on to a bigger and better (or a smaller and less expensive) home, we take you through the nuts and bolts of getting your home sold. We include pointers on working with a selling agent, or handling the sale yourself. Everything from writing your listing, to making your home irresistible to buyers, to negotiating the best selling conditions — it's all here.

How This Book Is Organized

Each part of this book focuses on a specific stage in the buying or selling process. Buyers and sellers are concerned with some of the same things, like the price of the home in question. We investigate your buying and selling options from each point of view separately. For example, you'll approach the negotiating table quite differently if you're buying a home than if you're selling. You may find it helpful to read up on your "opponent's" probable tactics, or you may just want to focus on your own questions and concerns. Either way, we've got plenty of information for you.

Part I: Deciding to Buy

This part looks at making the decision to buy a home. We start with the basic question "Is now the right time?" and provide guidelines to help you answer it truthfully. Next, you need to take a cold, hard look at your finances, to see what you can truly afford to buy. We give you all the tools necessary to paint a realistic financial picture. Then you need to think about mortgages, and understand the different financing options. Finally, it's time for some soul searching: what kind of home is right for you?

Part II: Discovering Your Perfect Home

When it comes to actual house hunting, you're going to need a list of priorities to make sure that when you do make an offer on a property, it really is

the right home for you. In this part, we help you choose the right professionals to help you buy a home — not to mention keep you informed, safe, and
sane. Then you need to prioritize what you want in a home into a usable set
of criteria. Armed with this list, it's time to go shopping. We tell you how to
look for potential homes and evaluate the homes you see. And before you
start shopping for new living room furniture, we provide a dose of reality
by letting you in on all sorts of potential problems you may not notice right
away when you're touring prospective houses, and what to look for (and in)
as you investigate.

Part III: Getting the House You Want

This part deals with the paperwork involved in buying a home. This is where
you find all the information you need on making offers (just what do all those
conditions in the sale contract mean?), terms, and negotiating tips . . . everything you need to close the deal. Professional home inspections, surveys, and
new-home warranties are also covered in this part. Speaking of paperwork,
we put together a moving timeline starting two months (yes, two months)
before you move all the way through to the blissful day after. Read up! It's
time to get organized.

Part IV: Deciding to Sell

Again, it's decision time — but now it's from the seller's perspective. In this
part, you figure out whether the timing's right to sell your home. Depending on
market conditions and your budget, staying put and renovating may make more
sense. And what about the money? How much can you get for your home? And
(an often-overlooked point) how much will it cost you to move? We also suggest
ways to balance the selling of one house with the buying of another, focusing on
what to do with your mortgage and on timing the closing properly.

Part V: Preparing Yourself and Your House to Sell

This part gives you advice on how to get your home ready for potential buyers.
We include all the information you need to find the right real estate agent for
you — or to decide that you want to be your own real estate agent and market
and sell your house yourself. More paperwork is involved on the selling side
of the equation than on the buying side. This part outlines sale contracts,
commissions, and disclosure statements. We also take a look at inspections
and appraisals from the seller's point of view, so that you can make sure your
home is ready to sell. Finally, we offer tips on advertising your home to potential buyers — whether you're selling with an agent or on your own.

Part VI: Sealing the Deal

It's time to face more paperwork (but this book makes it much more bearable). This part covers offers and counteroffers, as well as transferring deeds and titles. Turn to the last chapter in this part for advice on negotiating from the seller's side of the table.

Part VII: The Part of Tens

Here are extra tidbits we just couldn't fit into the body of the book. Of special interest is the section on regional home-buying concerns; Canada is a large and diverse country, and each region and province has some little quirks and peccadilloes you may want to read up on. We also provide some helpful tips for condominium owners, and some valuable maintenance advice to help you protect the value of your real estate investment.

Icons Used in This Book

As you read through this book, you'll see a few icons lurking on the left-hand side. Here's a guide to what they mean:

Extra-helpful information to help you survive in the real estate jungle.

A heads-up about potential problems and pitfalls in your path.

Reminders of important information that you don't want to lose sight of in your home hunt or purchasing pursuit.

Places where you may want to look deeper and ask for further information. We don't have the space to explain everything, you know. . .

Definitions of terms, technical information, and stuff that you don't necessarily need to know but may want to anyway.

Part I
Deciding to Buy

The 5th Wave   By Rich Tennant

"I'm well aware that we ask for a lot from our home mortgage applicants, Mr. Harvey. However, sarcasm is rarely required."

In this part . . .

When will you be ready to buy a home? What kind of home should you buy? What neighbourhoods should you look in? Whose help should you enlist? How are you going to come up with the cash?

Why are you panicking? Relax, kick back with a cup of tea, and read this first part. You won't actually find the answers to these questions, but you will find advice on how to figure out the answers for yourself.

Chapter 1

Looking to Buy a Home?

. . . .

In This Chapter

▶ Becoming a homeowner — what's in it for you?

▶ Deciding if you're ready to buy

. . . .

Dorothy said it best: There's no place like home. You may be a jet-setting entrepreneur or a stay-at-home parent, but we're willing to bet where you live is your most cherished space. You need a place to wind down, to relax, and to rejuvenate. Whether you own or rent (or mooch off your parents), the place you call home is the foundation of your life.

We all want our homes to be perfect — even though our definitions of perfect change over time. Maybe as a teenager, your perfect bedroom was all black with huge speakers in every corner of the room. Twenty years, three children, two dogs, and a father-in-law later, your idea of perfect is an ensuite bathroom with a rain shower head and a jetted bathtub — not to mention a lock on the door. We all need a living space that can adapt to our changing needs and wants, and, of course, what better way to have that living space than to own it?

The idea of owning a home can be scary. After all, if anything goes wrong or needs to be fixed, you're responsible. Your water pipes may freeze and break, your basement may flood, or your electrical system may need a complete overhaul. People can put thousands of dollars into their homes for renovations, and thousands more for emergency repairs. And then there's daily upkeep, seasonal maintenance, taxes . . . but ask homeowners, and they'll invariably tell you that taking the plunge is worth it.

Even though owning your home can dictate how much money you have for other things and leave you constantly worrying about finances, researching and planning will help you stay in control. You can and should decide how much home you can afford, and that's why this section of the book is geared toward getting you the home you want — at a price that doesn't leave you eating peanut butter sandwiches three times a day for the next 20 years. After all, you want your home to complement your lifestyle, not overrun it. You want enough money left over to create that ensuite bathroom you've dreamed of.

Joys of Ownership

We probably don't even need to write this section. If you're reading this book, the idea of owning obviously appeals to you. But as a helpful reminder, we point out some of the advantages of owning a home.

✓ **More stability; less stress.** Stability is a wonderful thing — it means that there will be less on your mind. Moving, according to some, is the third most stressful activity in life (after death and divorce). Owning a home means you don't have to worry about moving from one rental apartment to the next, about how much rent will go up next year, about what happens if the landlord decides to sell the place, or even about keeping the landlord happy enough so that you can re-sign the lease. Home owning also means that you acquire a major investment, which will make you feel more secure when thinking about the future.

✓ **The home is yours.** It's yours to do with what you want! You can change even the small things you don't like: the dripping faucets, the ugly shag rug, and the shower head that goes only as high as your belly button. And all your time, effort, and money go into your investment, not someone else's. You no longer have to deal with landlords not fixing things, or spending small amounts of money when they do. Of course, many building owners and managers out there respect their tenants and respond quickly to the tenants' and the building's needs. However, good landlords are hard to find, and chances are that your house or apartment simply won't be their priority; their own homes will.

✓ **Your sense of community deepens.** Even if you're more anti-social than Mr. Scrooge, owning a home encourages you to appreciate the surrounding community. After all, protecting the value of your property requires you to protect the general area, too. You may start grudgingly by organizing a neighbourhood protest against your local park being turned into a dump site (which would mean horrible things for your investment), but hopefully, you'll start to actually like your neighbours. Belonging to a community can be a wonderful feeling. We recommend that you buy a home in an area where the majority of residents own the properties they live in — homeowners tend to care more about the neighbourhood than tenants do.

✓ **You're a better person.** Or, at least, people think you are. Home ownership often translates to people thinking wonderful things about you: You're mature, you're dependable, and you're stable. And paying your mortgage on time every month does wonders for your credit rating. (And with banks encouraging direct withdrawal payments, paying on time is really easy to do.)

Making an investment

Although mortgages may be uppermost in your mind, buying a house isn't just a financial investment. It's a lifestyle investment. What and where you buy will ultimately dictate how you will live. Bought a fixer-upper with the intention of doing all the renovations yourself? Five years later, you may still be devoting all your time and money to it. Bought a home in the distant sub-urbs, but work in the heart of the city? You may spend more time in heavy traffic than at home. On the other hand, maybe you've become a gourmet cook because your wonderful kitchen deserves to be used constantly, and the once-rec-room, now-home-theatre means you can host a big Grey Cup bash every year.

You may have to make sacrifices when you buy a home — but you can make them informed sacrifices. You'll have to do some creative brainstorming to imagine the upsides and downsides of various features of the home you're considering. For instance, you may buy a house on a corner lot, knowing that you'll have a lot of snow shovelling and leaf raking to do. However, you may not mind these tasks too much because you decided before you bought the house that its unobstructed south-facing kitchen windows and big garden were well worth the effort.

✔ **You can benefit financially.** Even with a mortgage that may seem over-whelming, there are definite advantages to owning a home. Think of a mortgage as a forced savings plan, in which you (usually) cannot skip a deposit or withdraw money, and each payment gives you a slightly bigger part of your asset. Home ownership is also generally considered a good investment — one that grows over time. Another great thing about investing in a home is that if it's your principal residence, you don't pay tax on the amount you earn. The increase in your home's value, similar to other types of investments, is called a *capital gain*. On other invest-ments, you would normally pay tax on these gains, but you're exempted from paying this tax if the capital gain is on your principal residence. (More on capital gains in Chapter 15.)

Should You Buy Right Now?

Although you may think researching real estate markets and waiting for the right time to buy are the only ways to get a good deal, your personal situa-tion is what should really determine your decision to buy. Are you able to pay your mortgage, utilities, taxes, insurance, and whatever maintenance comes up, not only for the next year but also for the next 5, or 25? (We show you how to get a picture of your financial situation in Chapter 2.)

Are you willing to remain in the same place for the next five years? Considering the closing costs involved whether you're a seller or a buyer (more on closing costs in Chapter 2), be prepared to keep your home for at least a few years. Avoiding having to sell your home quickly is a good idea, because chances are you'd have to sell at a lower price. So even if the market is at an all-time low and interest rates are way down, buying a home could be a huge mistake if you're in the middle of a career change or planning a move to Luxembourg in a year.

Maintaining a house requires a big commitment — of both time and money. Each season presents a list of chores to maintain your home's integrity and efficiency. Overlooking the overflowing eaves or the leaky roof may lead to significant water damage; neglecting your furnace can cause hundreds of dollars in repairs to it and your frozen home. There are many situations in which a little neglect can transform into expensive repairs and sometimes irreversible damage, resulting in huge losses when it's time to sell. And don't forget that all sorts of little things that you may not have expected, such as a broken major appliance, can happen. It's the "nickel and dime" effect — and you may feel as if that's all you have left! Putting away a bit of money every month in a maintenance fund will help make those occasional big-ticket (or constant low-cost) expenses a bit easier to stomach.

Knowing your finances

Home buying is an investment. Although it is cheaper in the long run to buy than to rent, that initial outlay of cash is enough to send anyone's heart racing. You'll need to take a careful look at your current expenditures in order to evaluate your readiness to take on mortgage payments and home maintenance. Chapter 2 helps you determine whether you're financially ready to buy.

Knowing where your money goes now is a crucial first step. Suppose that after you've accounted for what you spend on food, clothes, transportation, and vacations, you still have a $15,000 surplus. You're not really sure where it went last year, but figure it should be all the cushion you need to cover the new costs of being a homeowner. If your pipes freeze and you need to call in a plumber, you don't want to discover that you've already spent most of that $15,000 surplus on gifts for your friends and family, as well as regular rounds of drinks for all your pals down at the local pub.

Have a plan for the future, too. Know what you want to spend on RRSPs. You may have kids and want to contribute to their education; tuition is only going up. Being clear on where you want your financial life to be in five years, and in ten years, will help you make smart decisions now about how much to put into a down payment and how much to carry in monthly mortgage payments.

Don't buy your dream home without leaving enough money to replace the 25-year-old couch that you picked up when you first moved out on your own.

Comparing renting to buying

Owning your home instead of renting almost always makes more sense in the long run, especially if you settle in one area. The biggest advantage of owning over renting is that your monthly payments are an investment (and they'll eventually cease!). The most common complaint about buying a home is having to pay the mortgage, and more specifically, the interest on the mortgage. You can live with your parents until you've made enough money to buy a home outright, but your parents may not want to live with you for that long!

Renting your home instead of owning it does have advantages, and there are times in your life when owning isn't the best option for you. One of the biggest reasons to buy a home is for stability, but if you like a flexible lifestyle, a home may be a burden to you. Owning a home is a serious commitment, so if your priorities aren't geared to making regular mortgage payments or having a permanent address, renting may be better for you.

If you're in one of the following situations, you may want to wait a while to buy a home:

- ✔ **Having financial woes:** Although you can leap into home ownership with as little as a 5 percent down payment, you still have to come up with that amount. And you'll have to be prepared to make those regular mortgage payments for what may seem like an eternity, not to mention all the other costs of being a homeowner. Getting a mortgage also may be tricky if you've neglected other loans, or have significant debts.

- ✔ **Living in transition:** You haven't decided to live in one place. Saddling yourself with a chunk of property and debt if you think you're really going to want to spend the next year island hopping around Greece is not the best move.

- ✔ **Lacking job security:** If you end up relocating for employment, you may have to get rid of your home in a hurry. If you don't have a reliable or steady source of income, lenders may not be willing to authorize a mortgage, because you can't guarantee you'll have more freelance work in the coming years.

- ✔ **Dealing with space uncertainty:** Although you can't really predict having triplets, there's no sense in buying a two-bedroom bungalow if you're pretty sure that your brother-in-law's family of seven and their three dogs will move in with you for an unspecified amount of time. Unless this is your way of ensuring they can't live with you, you may find you have to change houses sooner than you'd like. If you are considering setting up a home office or starting a home-based business in the future, make sure you have a spare bedroom or room in the basement to expand.

✔ **Facing a bad housing market:** Generally speaking, you should focus on your own situation rather than the real estate market. But there may be a time when interest rates skyrocket and yet homes sell for twice as much as their listing prices — in these circumstances, it's probably better to wait until the market cools down to buy a home. If a monthly cost analysis shows that buying a home would be 20 to 30 percent more than renting a comparable home, think twice about buying. (We show you how to analyze monthly costs in Chapter 3.)

✔ **Waiting for the gravy train:** You and your friend are opening a new high-end spa in a trendy downtown neighbourhood, and you need some start-up capital. You decide to invest all your savings in the business instead of in real estate. If your spa turns out to be a successful business that you end up turning into a franchise, you may be able to buy an estate in the south of France instead of a bungalow in the suburbs.

Considering home-owner concerns

You may be skeptical about the complications of buying a home. However, the many different kinds of homes and ownership of homes mean you don't have to let your hatred of raking leaves and mowing the lawn stop you from owning. The following are the most common reservations about home owning:

✔ **Unexpected costs:** One of the main arguments for renting is that you know what your monthly costs are, and they don't change. When you own a house and the furnace breaks down, you have to fix it. But consider that when you rent, your landlord may not get around to fixing things right away, or he may be in Florida for the holidays and you may be stuck in the cold for a while. Although living in the same building as your landlord may guarantee some things are fixed in a hurry, your concern about a missing screen on your bedroom window may not be her priority. And maybe she likes the house at 18 degrees Celsius during the winter and 30 degrees in the summer. Sometimes paying the money to get things fixed is worth the hassle, but if you pay for a repair in your rented home, you may never see that money again.

So, though the responsibility for repairs in your home will fall on your own shoulders, the main point is that you have the control. And with a mortgage, you know from the beginning how much you'll be paying each month for the length of your mortgage; with renting, it's hard to get that guarantee.

✔ **Extra work:** Don't like doing lawn work, shovelling snow, or fixing leaks? Your partner or child refuses to do your dirty work for you? Instead of renting to avoid such chores, you may prefer to buy a condominium where someone else takes care of the maintenance. If you buy an apartment-style condo, you won't even have a sidewalk to worry about!

Keep in mind that when you move into a new home, you'll have new rates for some monthly expenses, like utilities (heating, hydro, water). You may be taking on new costs such as property taxes and home and garden maintenance. New homeowners should also prepare for the worst by ensuring they have reserve funds for emergency repairs. Make sure you have enough monthly income left over after your mortgage payments to cover these costs, as well.

Adding up the costs of home owning

Okay, so you want a better idea of exactly what kinds of costs a new homeowner faces? Here goes.

✔ **Maintenance:** You may have a high-maintenance relationship or a low-maintenance relationship with the home you buy. Be sure your finances can handle the costs of regular repairs. Also, keep an emergency fund for unexpected repairs, and contribute to it on a regular basis. If you dip into it to help pay your way to Tahiti, that's your call, but be aware that if your basement is flooded when you return, you may not have the cash to pay a plumber.

✔ **Insurance:** You will need proof of fire and extended coverage insurance before you can finalize the purchase of your new home, because the property itself is the only security against the loan. If your new home burns down . . . well, you understand. Insurance costs vary, depending on your deductible, the value of your home and its contents, and the type of coverage you get, as well as each insurer's rates. Shop around for an affordable policy that covers you for the replacement of your personal property and grants you a living allowance if your home is destroyed. Getting a policy with public liability insurance is also a good idea because it protects you if someone is harmed on your property. (You can find more on insurance in Chapter 11.)

✔ **Utilities:** When you buy a home, you assume all the heating, cooling, water, and electricity bills for the property. If you live in the colder, draftier parts of this country, you already know that heat is the most important utility there is. And if you've ever rented a house and paid the hydro bill separately for electric heat, you've already been walloped by the biggest utility bill you've ever experienced. If the house you're buying is new, you'll probably pay less for utilities because of better insulation and construction quality. If you're buying a resale home, ask the owners for copies of their utility bills so you can figure out average heating costs. In Chapter 8, we go over the costs and benefits of various heating systems commonly found in Canadian homes.

✔ **Taxes:** Property taxes are calculated based on your home's assessed value and the local tax rates. Unfortunately, property tax rates can fluctuate yearly, and they vary from region to region. Some real estate listings will state the amount of the previous year's taxes for the property being sold. When you're looking at homes, find out from the selling agent or the owners what the previous year's taxes were. If you need a high-ratio mortgage to buy a new home, your lender may insist that property tax installments be added to your monthly mortgage payments. (See Chapter 3 for more details on high-ratio mortgages.)

✔ **Condo fees:** The great thing about living in a condo is that someone else looks after all the pesky maintenance and landscaping stuff. The flip side is you have to pay for it in your condo fees. In addition to your mortgage payments, condo fees alone can cost as much as rent in a decent apartment.

Understanding the market

The housing market fluctuates, experiencing both strong and weak periods. History has shown, however, that the market will rise in the long run. So don't focus too much on waiting for the "right time" to buy. Predicting how the market will go is nearly impossible, and if you wait around forever for the market to be perfect, you'll waste tonnes of potential investment money on rent! Generally speaking, after you buy your first home you'll continue to own it for years to come, and its value will increase. Your personal situation is what really matters, because that will determine whether you'll have to sell the home in a hurry — or whether you can really afford to buy in the first place.

Having said all this, chances are you still want to know how the market works, because there are periods when it's best to be a buyer (and conversely, times when it's best to be a seller). You can see what the current market is like by checking out the prices in the local paper and asking your real estate agent how the current market compares to the past 12 months. Your agent can tell you how homes have been selling in the past year, what the *median sales price* was (the median sales price is the actual middle price between the highest and lowest selling prices, not the average price), and usually even how long homes were on the market, price adjustments, the types of homes sold, and their neighbourhoods.

A good overall economy naturally produces a stronger market with more people looking to buy. Chances are, of course, there will be more sellers, because with more money, owners may decide to "trade up" and buy bigger homes. A strong economy also produces more construction and housing developments, opening up the market to more new homes.

To understand the housing market, there are a few terms and effects that are good to know about.

- **Buyer's market:** Ideally, the best time to buy is during a *buyer's market*, when many sellers want to sell but few buyers are looking to buy. Homes take longer to sell, so buyers can take more time to make decisions. To sell a home in this market, sellers have to list at aggressively competitive prices, and sometimes even offer other incentives, such as *secondary financing*. (See Chapter 3 for a discussion of financing options.) If you have to sell your home during a buyer's market, the good news is that you're able to take advantage of these same conditions when you go to buy a home for yourself!

- **Seller's market:** The opposite of a buyer's market is a *seller's market*. Few homes are on the market, but buyers are plentiful, which results in fast home sales at prices close to, or even above, the listing prices. Some homes sell even before they're listed. Because of the rise in sales, some owners may decide to take on selling their homes themselves. In a seller's market, buyers have less negotiating power and less time to decide, and may even find themselves in a bidding war. So if you're buying in a seller's market, be prepared to make quick decisions. Have all your homework done and your financing arranged. (See Chapter 2 for details on mortgage pre-approval.)

- **Seasonal influences:** Winter in Canada is notorious for being cold and unpleasant virtually everywhere except the south coast of British Columbia. People don't like to venture out much, unless it's for necessities like groceries, hockey games, or skiing. Besides, who wants to look for a home when they're busy buying gifts for the holiday season? Frostbite aside, the winter months also tend to be slower for the real estate market because people with children don't like to move during the school year. A lot of properties aren't on the market simply because sellers know their homes look best in the summer with the flowers, the leaves, and the sunshine. This means there's a good possibility that the homes on the market at this inhospitable time of year must be sold, so you may find a good bargain. You just may have to deal with snowdrifts and –40-degree temperatures on moving day. In large cities, however, weather may not be an influence at all. So if you see a home you love in downtown Toronto in January, don't assume it's a fire sale.

- **Interest rates:** If you need a mortgage to purchase your home (lucky you, if you don't!), you'll find that interest rates make a big difference in how much home you can afford. When interest rates are high, fewer buyers tend to be in the market for a new home. You can see the logic: A 4.5 percent interest rate on a $200,000 mortgage loan will cost you approximately $9,000 in interest in one year, while the same $200,000 loan at a 7 percent interest rate will cost you about $14,000 in interest! Different types of mortgages can increase or decrease your interest rate from what banks consider the current standard. Have a look at Chapter 3 for more information.

Chapter 2

Understanding Your Finances

. . . .

In This Chapter

▶ Investigating your finances

▶ Increasing your down payment with the Home Buyers' Plan

▶ Calculating what size mortgage you can get

▶ Getting a pre-approved mortgage

▶ Adding up your closing costs

▶ Preparing for unexpected home-buying costs

. . . .

*W*hen you decide to enter the world of home ownership, it's time to take a cold, hard look at your finances. Budgeting may be something that you're well acquainted with — or it may be the area of your life in which you subscribe to the old saying "ignorance is bliss." Whatever the case, we've got all the information here to allow you to buy your next home with confidence!

Armed with a clear (and honest) picture of your financial situation, you're ready to look at more specific costs associated with buying a home, like getting a mortgage. We help you figure out what amount of a mortgage your bank is likely to give you — and encourage you to get your mortgage pre-approved before you start home shopping. The chapter wraps up with a look at closing-day costs, such as insurance and legal fees and land transfer taxes, so you know exactly what to anticipate before the seller hands you the keys. Trust us, we've been there! Just when you think you're ready to move in, you face a few last expenses that can really add up.

Getting Up Close and Personal with Your Finances

Although it can be depressing to compare your less than Trump-like income to your substantial expenses, you'll be even more down in the dumps if you can't make your mortgage payments on your new home. In assessing what amount of mortgage you're eligible for, your lender takes into account only those debts you have to pay. So, if you can't imagine your life without the monthly spa and hairdresser appointments at that high-end salon, or if your restored (and constantly maintenance-challenged) vintage automobile is as important to you as the food you eat, you'd better take that into account when you tabulate what you can actually afford — because the bank won't. Take a look at Table 2-1: After you deduct your total monthly expenses from your total monthly income, the remaining amount is what you can afford to pay toward your mortgage each month — and that amount should include a buffer for issues like emergency repairs, taxes, and other items that may crop up.

Table 2-1	Monthly Budget Worksheet
Monthly Amount	
Net income after taxes	_____
Partner's net income after taxes	_____
Other income: investments, gifts, annuities, trust funds, pensions, etc.	_____
Total Income	_____
Monthly Expenses	
Investments	
RRSPs	_____
Education funds	_____
Other	_____
Debts	
Credit cards	_____
Lines of credit	_____
Student loans	_____
Other loans/debts	_____
Transportation	
Auto loan or lease payments	_____
Insurance	_____

Monthly Amount	
Registration	_____
Repairs/maintenance	_____
Fuel	_____
Parking	_____
Public transit	_____
Household Costs	
Groceries	_____
Laundry/dry cleaning	_____
Utilities	_____
Hydro/electricity	_____
Water	_____
Gas	_____
Home insurance	_____
Electronics	_____
Telephone	_____
Cell phones/wireless devices	_____
Cable television	_____
Internet	_____
Health	
Medication	_____
Monthly Amount	
Glasses/contacts	_____
Dental/orthodontics	_____
Therapist	_____
Special needs items	_____

(continued)

Table 2-1 (continued)

Miscellaneous	
Life insurance	_____
Education	_____
Tuition fees	_____
Books/supplies	_____
Daycare	_____
Entertainment	_____
Restaurant meals	_____
Vacations	_____
Clothing/accessories	_____
Recreation/sports	_____
Membership fees	_____
Equipment	_____
Pets	_____
Gifts	_____
Other	_____
Total Expenses	_____
Calculate Maximum Monthly Mortgage Payment	
Total income	_____
Minus total expenses	_____
Equals Your Maximum Monthly Mortgage Payment	_____

Before you even think about mortgage costs, you need to determine how much of a down payment you have to purchase a property. This lump sum is your initial amount of equity you're putting into the purchase — the balance of the purchase price will be financed through your mortgage. At the present time in Canada, a down payment of 5 percent is the minimum required for the purchase of a primary residence. Even if you have a lump sum of cash (or money from an RRSP — we address that in the next section) to use as a down payment, you'll need to set money aside for your closing costs.

Boosting Your Down Payment: The Home Buyers' Plan

If you're a first-time buyer (or you haven't owned a home as your principal residence in the past five years), you can take advantage of the federal government's Home Buyers' Plan (HBP). Basically, the plan lets you put the money in your RRSP toward a down payment on a home, and the best part is that you aren't penalized for the withdrawal. You don't even pay income tax on the money, unless you don't repay the RRSP loan within a certain amount of time. The plan lets you borrow up to $25,000 from your RRSP toward the down payment, and a maximum of two buyers can participate and purchase a home together. (If your partner or relative, say, has an RRSP of his own, he can also withdraw up to $25,000, for a possible total of $50,000.) Of course, you do have to follow certain conditions:

- ✔ You must sign a written agreement that you are buying or building a home in Canada.

- ✔ You must have the money in your RRSP for at least 90 days before the withdrawal.

- ✔ You have to repay the amount of the withdrawal within 15 years.

- ✔ You must repay at least ¹⁄₁₅ of the amount you owe each year.

- ✔ You will use the new home as your "principal place of residence," or main home.

- ✔ You have to be a resident of Canada.

Talk to your lender or lawyer to see if this plan is a good option for you. You can also check it out online at the Canada Revenue Agency Web site, `www.cra-arc.gc.ca` (click on "Individuals" and then "Homeowners").

Determining What Size Mortgage You Can Carry

After you figure out your maximum monthly mortgage payment (refer to the previous section), you may realize that you qualify for a larger mortgage than you initially considered. At this point, you're faced with two scenarios: what you can comfortably afford and what amount you can absolutely financially stretch yourself to in order to buy your dream house. Lenders will be more than happy to give you a larger mortgage if you can afford the payments, but you should decide what monthly payment amounts comfortably fit within your budget. You don't want to be saddled with a large mortgage and not be able to afford some of the creature comforts of life.

Financial institutions have two typical approaches to determine how big a mortgage they're willing to give you. One method involves calculating your *Gross Debt Service (GDS) ratio*. This ratio is calculated as the percentage of gross annual or gross monthly income needed to cover all housing-related costs (including principal and interest payments on your mortgage, property taxes, hydro, water, and heating, and half the monthly condo fees, if applicable). It should not be more than approximately 32 percent of your gross annual or gross monthly income. The other method is to calculate your *Total Debt Service (TDS) ratio*. This ratio is calculated as the percentage of gross annual or monthly income required to cover all your housing-related costs *plus any other debts* (for example, student loan, car, and credit card payments). This figure should be no more than 40 percent of your gross annual or monthly income.

You can use a calculation like this one to determine your Gross Debt Service (GDS) ratio:

Gross monthly income (pre-tax):	$6,000
Multiplied by 30% available for housing:	$0.3 \times \$6,000 = \$1,800$
Minus estimated monthly property taxes ($200):	$\$1,800 - \$200 = \$1,600$
Minus estimated hydro, heating, and water costs (and half the monthly condo fees, if applicable):	($200)
Monthly income available for mortgage payments:	$1,400
(Figures are approximate and have been rounded.)	

Your GDS ratio can be a very misleading guide in deciding what size mortgage you can carry, however, particularly if you have a lot of other debts. This is when knowing your Total Debt Service (TDS) ratio comes in handy. You can use this method to calculate your TDS ratio:

Gross monthly income (pre-tax):	$6,000
Multiplied by 40% available for housing and other debts:	$0.4 \times \$6,000 = \$2,400$
Minus current monthly debt payments ($400 for car payment, $200 for credit cards, $150 for student loan):	$2,400 − $400 − $200 − $150 = $1,650
Minus estimated monthly property taxes ($200):	$1,650 − $200 = $1,450
Minus estimated hydro, heating, and water costs (and half the monthly condo fees, if applicable):	($200)
Monthly income available for mortgage payments:	$1,250

As you can see, the Total Debt Service presents a much more accurate picture of what is left over to spend on housing.

Online, you can find several calculators that total your GDS and TDS ratios automatically when you fill in a table. See the Appendix for our list of Canadian mortgage resources available on the Internet. You'll also find lots of good advice on the Web about financing sources to consider and options to bargain for when you're negotiating a mortgage. See Chapter 9 for more information on using the Internet.

Using GDS and TDS calculations can help you determine a reasonable price range for a new home, but they factor in only the official debt you carry — not the other obligations you may prefer to forget about. So remember to factor in your other costs, which you can work out in the Monthly Budget Worksheet, earlier in this chapter (Table 2-1).

Getting a Head Start with a Pre-approved Mortgage

Before even thinking about looking for a new home, speak with your lender or mortgage broker about getting *pre-approved* for a mortgage. The process is quick and simple, and the good thing is that it costs you nothing and can save you valuable time — as well as possible home heartbreak. You'll know exactly how much you have in your budget, because the process is exactly the same as applying for an actual mortgage. However, with today's rapidly shifting lending rates and qualification requirements, you should stay in constant touch with your representative even after getting pre-approved: What was true three months ago may not apply today!

Getting an online estimate of the mortgage you qualify for is very easy (see Chapter 3 for more information), but it's just that — an estimate. Until you provide your mortgage broker or lender with the necessary documents and go through the actual pre-approval process that we outline here, you aren't pre-approved.

Similar to applying for an actual mortgage, when you apply for pre-approval you answer questions and provide documents based on your financial position, debt load, and credit history. (Details about the mortgage process appear in Chapter 3.) There is usually a fixed time period (from 30 to 120 days) for which lenders will offer a certain size mortgage at a specific interest rate, and they will confirm this in writing. The advantages to being pre-approved are as follows:

- **You know your price limit.** Before you set your heart on the mansion up the road, it's a good idea to know your financial limitations.

- **Your offers are taken more seriously by sellers.** Sellers prefer to accept an offer from someone who has started to arrange financing. After all, there's a chance the buyer who has not yet been pre-approved may not be able to get financing at all. These days, smart agents will not even take a client out to look at properties until she has her financing sorted. Getting pre-approved takes the worry out of qualifying well in advance.

- **You're protected from any rise (and can take advantage of any drop) in interest rates.** As long as you close your sale within the time period of the pre-arranged mortgage (typically, from 30 to 120 days), you can rest assured that your mortgage will be at the rate stated in your pre-approval even if bank interest rates have risen since you initially obtained the pre-approval.

Even with pre-approval, you still have to secure the mortgage after you've negotiated the buying of a home. Your final mortgage approval is subject to a full check of your finances and an appraisal of the market value of the property you want to buy. But pre-approval means most of the paperwork has been done beforehand, which speeds up the process significantly.

If you're applying for a _high-ratio mortgage_ (your down payment amounts to less than 20 percent of the purchase price of the home you're buying), you're also subject to the approval of the _Canada Mortgage and Housing Corporation_ (CMHC), a federal Crown corporation that administers national housing programs and insures mortgages under the provisions of the National Housing Act. Your application for CMHC approval can't be processed until you have an accepted "offer to purchase" contract from your seller. (See Chapter 10 for details concerning contracts of purchase and sale.)

Just because you're pre-approved for a mortgage doesn't mean you can make an unconditional offer to buy a home. Write into your offer to purchase contract a "subject to financing" clause (a very common procedure) so that you have at least a couple of days to complete your mortgage approval. A mortgage is a contract; it's a legally binding document, and you must uphold it. Make sure you know what you're getting into. Read all the details, and ask your lender to explain anything you don't understand. You're trying to buy a house here, not make a deal with the devil.

Anticipating the Closing Costs

The last big hurdle in the home-buying process is *closing* — when you complete all the paperwork and sign off on all the documents needed to purchase your new home. At this time, you also finalize all the really boring details that need to be covered when you buy a house. For example, the property has to be transferred into your name, obviously enough; but first, your lawyer must check that no one else has any claims against the house or property. You may have municipal taxes to pay, land transfer taxes to pay, accounts to settle with the previous owners, mortgage details to finalize, and so on. (We walk you through closing day in Chapter 13.)

 Each one of the closing day items outlined in this section costs you money. You don't want to find yourself short of cash on that final important day. Speak to your mortgage broker, lender, or realtor to get a good ballpark estimate of your closing costs. Nobody needs a surprise on closing day.

Deposit and down payment

You are generally required to pay a deposit of at least 5 percent of the purchase price of the house, and you may pay it in stages, or all at once. Your first offer on a house may include an initial deposit, which can be as little as $500 or $1,000, depending on real estate practices in your area. You pay this deposit with a regular or certified cheque, payable to your real estate agent's brokerage. Generally, this amount is deposited only after your offer has been accepted. The deposit, which is a negotiated amount, is held in your real estate agent's trust account. If you aren't using an agent, your lawyer usually holds your deposit in trust.

When all conditions in your agreement of purchase and sale have been settled (see Chapter 10 for information on these items), you increase the deposit, often to around 5 percent of the purchase price, although this amount is negotiable. Every province is different, however. In some provinces, there is a one-time deposit of approximately 5 percent. This deposit may be handed over with the initial offer, or may be collected when all subjects are removed. Again, the deposit increase is payable to the real estate agent's brokerage by certified cheque or bank draft and is held with the earlier deposit in the real estate agent's trust account. In some provinces, having a one-time deposit held in trust by the listing agent is common. In other provinces, the deposit is held by the buyer agent's brokerage. The deposit forms part of the down payment — you pay off the balance of the down payment on the closing date (also known as the completion date). A certified cheque or bank draft payable to your lawyer or notary public is the most common way to pay the balance of your down payment. Your lawyer will advise you of the exact amount you have to bring in and the preferred method of payment.

If you make a small down payment (perhaps 5 percent on an affordable house), the amount of the deposit your real estate agent holds may also represent the total down payment. In this case, your agent's brokerage will convey the money to your lawyer or notary for you. Remember, many closing costs will be above and beyond this 5 percent down payment, so make sure you are well aware of what those costs will be.

Three key closing fees

To sew up your mortgage deal, you need financing, insurance, and a good lawyer. Of course, lining up all of these details costs money, so get ready for further costs at closing time.

Financing fees

If you use the services of a mortgage broker, the lender will probably pay the brokerage fee. However, if you have had past financial difficulties, you may be required to pay this fee yourself; it will likely be as much as 2 percent of the total mortgage. Ask early in the process what to expect.

Keep in mind that if you're breaking one mortgage — or blending a mortgage and renegotiating more favourable terms — you may face some penalties. Make sure you are well aware of those costs.

Insurance fees

If you have a high-ratio mortgage, you must obtain mortgage loan insurance. Insurance costs range between 1 percent and 4.75 percent of your total mortgage amount. (This surcharge can be ever changing. Find out more from your mortgage broker or lender.) For convenience, you can incorporate your insurance fee into your monthly mortgage payments. You may have to pay taxes on your insurance as well: In some provinces, GST and/or HST are charged.

An application fee may be payable on your mortgage loan insurance. The fee can range from $75 to $235, depending on whether an appraisal is required. You can find more on mortgage insurance in Chapter 3.

Legal fees and disbursements

You need a lawyer (or a notary, if you are buying in Quebec) to review the offer to purchase, perform a title search, draw up your mortgage documents, and tend to the closing details. Your lawyer also takes care of any reimbursements owed the previous owner (for items such as prepaid hydro and water bills, and property taxes). All other utilities, such as phone, cable, and non-prepaid hydro, are read at the time of closing and billed to the appropriate parties. You can find more information on the role of the lawyer, and how to find one, in Chapter 6.

You pay only the applicable portion of the expenses from the date that you take possession of the home you're buying. (If you're buying a resale condo, and the condo fees are prepaid, they, too, will be pro-rated.) How much all these fees will cost depends on how complicated your deal is, but you can count on about $500 to $2,000 to cover legal fees. The pro-rated fees for property taxes, condo fees, and any other prepaid expenses will be outlined in the Statement of Adjustments prepared by your lawyer. You can find more on Statements of Adjustments in Chapter 11.

Appraisals, surveys, inspections, and condominium certificates

Here are four more items that you may have to pay for before closing day:

- ✔ **Appraisal:** You'll probably need to get an appraisal for your lender. An *appraisal* is an independent confirmation that a home's purchase price is of fair market value. If you ask nicely, you can probably get your lender to pay for the appraisal. A basic appraisal fee is about $150 to $250, but that figure goes up if you're buying a large home or a home located in a neighbourhood with very little turnaround. Appraisals are done on a comparison basis, so if there's nothing to compare with, more work is involved, hence the higher fee. (See Chapter 6 for more on appraisals.)

- ✔ **Survey:** The Land Titles Office, or your lender, may require an up-to-date survey in order to approve your mortgage. A *survey* verifies the boundaries of your property and ensures that there are no encroachments either by you onto your neighbour's property or vice versa. The price of surveys varies widely, depending on the location and type of property. Your real estate agent can give you an idea of what to expect. (We talk more about surveys in Chapter 12.)

  In some provinces, the cost of a survey can be avoided by purchasing *title insurance*. Title insurance protects property owners from survey errors or defects that would've been revealed had an up-to-date survey been done. The cost of title insurance in most cases is less than that of a new survey, but if you're purchasing property with the idea of building, you'll want a survey regardless.

- ✔ **Inspection:** Take our advice: Get a professional home *inspection* done on the home you're going to buy. An inspection is a report on the presence and apparent condition of the structural and operational systems of a home. (See Chapter 12 for details.) The cost of an inspection ranges from $250 to $750. If your property is very large or unusual in its construction, count on a higher fee. If you're moving to a rural area where wells or septic tanks are involved, get separate inspections for the septic tank and/or field and the system itself. Also, have the well tested for water potability (basically, is it drinkable?), supply, and pressure. These separate inspections can be pricey, but to pass on them can be expensive and cause future inconveniences (unless you don't mind using an outhouse in the winter, or waiting for a water truck to deliver to you every two weeks. . .).

✔ **Condominium certificate:** If you're buying a condo, you'll need a document confirming the seller has fulfilled all obligations to the condominium corporation. This information is contained in a document variously known as the *condominium certificate, estoppel certificate, information certificate, Form F,* or *status certificate,* to name a few of its incarnations. Ask your real estate agent what the local alias is. This certificate and its supporting documents will cost you from $50 to $100, although if you're buying in Quebec, you don't need it (*c'est bon, non?*).

Taxes

Of course, your new home-owning adventure wouldn't be complete without taxes. Get ready for these additions to your closing costs, too:

✔ **Property tax:** As we mentioned earlier in this chapter, if the previous owners of your new home paid any property taxes in advance, the tax paid is pro-rated to the closing date and you have to reimburse the sellers. The reimbursement you make is called an *adjustment.* (See Chapter 11 for more information on adjustments.) When you take possession of your new home, all bill payments become your responsibility.

✔ **Land transfer tax/deed transfer tax:** Depending on where you live, you may also have to pay a transfer tax. The calculation and applicability of this tax varies across Canada. The provinces with a transfer tax are British Columbia, Manitoba, Ontario, Quebec, New Brunswick, Newfoundland and Labrador, Prince Edward Island, and Nova Scotia (though rural Nova Scotia is exempt, as is all of Alberta and Saskatchewan).

Your real estate agent or lawyer can tell you what to expect. Generally, the amount of the transfer tax works out to between 1 and 5 percent of the purchase price of your home, sometimes calculated on a sliding scale. Some provinces will waive part or all of the provincial transfer tax for first-time buyers.

✔ **Harmonized Sales Tax or the Goods and Services Tax:** If you're buying a newly built house (that is, you're the first one to live in it — no prior owners), you may pay 5 percent GST on the price, or, if you live in

British Columbia, Ontario, Quebec, Nova Scotia, Newfoundland and Labrador, or Prince Edward Island, you'll be subject to *Harmonized Sales Tax*. The HST is (basically) the combination of both the provincial and federal sales tax. For instance, in British Columbia, the HST is 12 percent. These taxes also apply if you purchase a house that has been substantially renovated.

Depending on the province and the price point of the home you're purchasing (among other things), you may be entitled to a tax rebate. Don't forget to find out how and when to apply for any rebates before you purchase. Every province's rules are different, so speak to your realtor or lawyer for details.

Don't forget that you will pay GST or HST on all services for all parties concerned: your lawyer, your listing agent, your inspector, your appraiser, and so on.

Little Extras You May Not Have Considered

We don't have to tell you that Canada is a big country. Especially if you're moving from one province to another, keep the following points in mind:

- ✔ **Local oddities:** Ranging from the obvious to the unexpected, there are probably as many obscure local closing costs in various parts of Canada as there are regional accents. Your real estate agent and/or lawyer can advise you on which of the following may apply to your purchase: garbage/recycling charges, diking fee (if the area is below sea level), meter hookup, tree planting, education development fees — the list goes on. If you're buying a resale house, the fees are pro-rated to your closing date.

- ✔ **Moving costs:** Do some research to arrive at a reasonable budget for your move. Of course, the exact amount will vary depending on how much stuff you have to move, how far you have to move it, and how much you're willing to move on your own. Expect moving rates to be higher at the end of a month or during the summer, because these are high-traffic times for moving companies. Try to plan ahead. Make some calls to request moving cost estimates. A higher moving estimate with a guarantee may end up being the better way. Often moving companies will charge considerably more than the original quote they supplied to get your business. Ask others for referrals. If you decide to rent a van or truck, reserve it in advance.

- ✔ **Utility charges:** Be prepared to pay connection fees for hooking up your telephone, cable, and hydro, and don't forget getting your mail redirected by the post office (this costs about $30).

Chapter 3

Your Mortgage Options

. . . .

In This Chapter

▶ Keeping interest payments low

▶ Deciding which type of mortgage you need

▶ Understanding mortgages

▶ Checking out your mortgage options

▶ Insuring your mortgage

▶ Insuring yourself

▶ Choosing a mortgage broker or lender

▶ Getting information from your lender

▶ Knowing what information you must provide

. . . .

*I*n recent years, your mortgage options have blown wide open. In this chapter, we introduce you to some of the finer points of mortgage options so that you can personalize your mortgage to fit your needs. We explain the various kinds of mortgages available and explore the options. Knowing the main features and benefits (and possible drawbacks) of every option helps you choose the right kind of financing so that you can afford your new home.

Of course, when you know what kind of mortgage you want, there's the small matter of actually getting it. We give you advice for smooth sailing through the financing process: who to talk to, what questions to ask, and what you'll need to tell them about yourself. This chapter helps you secure the mortgage you need with the terms you want.

Your Mortgage Mission

Your mission, if you choose to accept it, is to get the best mortgage for your personal situation while paying the least amount in interest. Use these strategies to keep your interest payments low:

✔ **Make as large a down payment as you comfortably can.** The larger your down payment, the smaller your loan (principal), and the less interest you'll have to pay. (First-time homebuyers can use funds from their RRSPs to help boost their down payments; refer to Chapter 2 for more information.)

✔ **Arrange to pay back the loan as quickly as possible.** The longer the *amortization period,* the life of the loan, the more interest you'll pay.

✔ **Commit to making weekly or biweekly payments.** This payment schedule allows you to pay off the principal more quickly and therefore pay less interest on it.

✔ **Make extra payments whenever you can.** For example, when you get a cash bonus at work, win the lottery, inherit billions, or patent the software that will dawn a new era of bug-free programming, immediately put money toward your mortgage.

✔ **Make sure your mortgage allows you to prepay principal.**

Even if you can't take advantage of these tricks, you don't have to bid your dream home goodbye. If you've done the research — and the math — you're sure to find a mortgage that fits.

Types of Mortgages

Mortgages break down into two types based on the amount of the down payment and, therefore, the amount of risk the lender is assuming by advancing you the money.

Conventional mortgages

A *conventional mortgage* covers not more than 80 percent of the purchase price of a house or condominium or the property's appraised value, whichever is lower. (See Chapter 6 for more information on home appraisals.) So if you want to buy a $200,000 house, you need a $40,000 down payment (20 percent of the purchase price) if you're applying for a conventional mortgage.

High-ratio mortgages

High-ratio mortgages account for between 80 and 95 percent of the purchase price of a house or condominium or the property's appraised value, whichever is lower. If you purchase a property with a down payment of less than 20 percent, your mortgage will need to be insured by Canada Mortgage and Housing Corporation (CMHC), Genworth Financial, or AIG United Guaranty.

The insurance protects the lender if you default on your mortgage. An insurance premium ranging from 1 to 4.75 percent of the mortgage amount, predetermined by a sliding scale, will be added to your mortgage and incorporated into your payment schedule. You may also have to pay an extra premium if you take out a variable rate mortgage. We talk more about mortgage insurance later in this chapter, and of course, your lender or mortgage broker can answer all your questions, too.

A full list of the high-ratio mortgage limits, plus a wealth of other mortgage and real estate information, is available at the CMHC Web site at www.cmhc-schl.gc.ca.

Mortgage Basics and Jargon 101

One cool thing about getting a mortgage (unlike a computer, for example) is that every element has a clear purpose. When you sit down with a pen and paper and calculator, or simply open your spreadsheet program on your computer and start plugging in numbers, it all starts to make sense really, really quickly. Every mortgage has five chief elements, which we explore in this section.

Mortgage principal

The total amount of the loan you get is called the *principal*. So if you need to borrow $150,000 to buy a house, then your principal is $150,000. The principal will become smaller and smaller as you pay off the loan.

Interest

Interest is the money you pay a lender in addition to repaying the principal of your loan — a sort of compensation so your lender profits from giving you a loan. The *interest rate,* calculated as a percentage of the principal, determines how much interest you pay the lender in each scheduled payment — the cost of borrowing the money.

People like to buy property when interest rates are low because they can either buy a more expensive house than if the rates were higher or pay off the mortgage more quickly. For example, at a 5 percent interest rate, a $100,000 principal would cost you approximately $5,000 in interest each year. At a 7 percent interest rate, you would pay approximately $7,000 a year — that's a difference of $2,000 a year that would go to paying off your principal in the low-interest-rate scenario rather than being gobbled up by interest.

Each lender will have subtle differences in how much extra money you may put against the principal (prepayment options), with different payment schedules offered. And most important, they'll give you a discount on the posted rates if and when you convert your mortgage to a longer, fixed rate. Do your research before you commit to a mortgage — you have lots of options out there.

The way your lender adds up the interest you owe has a big impact on the amount of interest you pay over the life of the mortgage. If interest is *compounded,* or added, to your balance owing every day, you'll pay more over the lifetime of the mortgage than if interest is compounded semi-annually. Most mortgages are compounded semi-annually, but your lender may offer you other options.

Fixed rate mortgage

Because interest rates rise and fall, some times are better than others for taking out a mortgage. To give yourself some stability, you can choose a *fixed rate mortgage* that allows you to lock in at a specific interest rate for a certain period of time (*mortgage term*). If interest rates are rising, you may want to lock in at a fixed rate so you know what your monthly costs will be over the term of your mortgage. When a mortgage term expires, you can renegotiate your interest rate and the length of time (term) that you will make payments at the new rate.

As you shop for mortgages, you can see that each lender specifies a certain interest rate for a certain term: Under most market conditions, the lower the fixed interest rate, the shorter the time period you can lock in to pay that rate. However, a longer term, fixed rate mortgage allows you to put a dent in your principal before facing the possibility of an increase in your monthly payments. Take a look in the financial pages of the newspaper or mortgage rate Web sites on the Internet, and you'll see a chart of mortgage rates that will look something like Table 3-1. The fixed rate mortgages in Table 3-1 range from six months to six years.

Fixed rate mortgages are offered with a variety of options, such as different prepayment options and weekly, biweekly, or monthly payment schedules, so make sure to talk to several lenders (or a mortgage broker) to see who offers the most competitive interest rate and terms.

Table 3-1	Mortgage Rates							
Banks	**Variable Rate**	**6-month**	**1-yr**	**2-yr**	**3-yr**	**4-yr**	**5-yr**	**6-yr**
Banks "R" Us	3.50	4.65	3.90	4.05	4.20	4.35	4.50	4.67
Mr. Bank	3.45	4.70	4.40	4.60	4.90	5.10	5.25	5.75
Mortgage Trust	3.50	4.65	3.95	4.25	4.30	4.50	4.75	5.25

Variable rate mortgage

A *variable rate* mortgage is usually set up with a one- to six-year fixed term and the interest rate fluctuates with the market. If you, the borrower, see that interest rates are starting to rise, you can usually lock in to a fixed rate for the balance of the mortgage term. The first option you see in Table 3-1 is a variable rate mortgage.

Not all variable mortgages are created equal, however. If you want to lock in to a fixed rate for the balance of the mortgage term, some banks may charge a penalty to lock in the mortgage. Make sure you know of any restrictions or penalties you may face if you decide to lock in during your mortgage term.

The interest rates of variable rate mortgages vary from lender to lender, but most are offered in some relation to the *prime rate,* which is the interest rate that banks charge their most creditworthy borrowers (that is, the big corporate clients). Rates for variable mortgages usually vary from half a percentage point below prime to half a percentage point above prime. Borrowers should also make sure that they're comparing the same prime rate — some lenders will list a variable rate mortgage at half a percentage point above the well-recognized and respected Bank of Canada prime rate, while another lender will offer a rate one-quarter of a percentage point below the "Bank of Bumpf" prime. This figure may be an elevated prime rate, which of course means the lender's supposed lower rate is no bargain at all.

Variable rates are not for everyone — you'll need to keep track of interest rates to make sure you lock in your mortgage rate before interest rates rise. A bit of a gamble is involved, but the payoff can be a lower interest rate if you're prepared to watch interest rates and monitor when to lock them in.

Changing from a variable rate mortgage to a fixed term during the life of your mortgage doesn't make good sense. If rising rates are causing you concern and you switch, you'll be switching into a much higher interest rate and payment. With variable, you're in for the long haul or not at all.

The choice between a variable and a fixed rate mortgage is also a lifestyle decision. With a variable rate, you can usually buy more of your home with a smaller payment and save interest costs, but if you tend to look in the paper each week and worry about rising rates, think again. You may lose all your interest savings to the medical costs associated with interest rate stress!

If you use a mortgage broker, or get to know your bank manager very well, she may call or e-mail you to let you know that a jump in interest rates is looming. If you get that call, you can then decide if you want to lock in the balance of your variable mortgage or float with the fluctuations in interest rates. Any rise in rates may be temporary, so you'll have to decide (with the input of your lender or mortgage broker) whether or not to lock in your rate. You'll soon determine how well you handle stress, uncertainty, and risk. Also, find out about escape options. If you pay out this mortgage early (before the third anniversary), what penalty will be charged?

Blended payments

Mortgages are set up so you get a huge chunk of cash to buy your home and then you repay the money in regularly scheduled payments. In effect, each mortgage payment you make is split: One portion goes toward paying off the principal, and the other portion goes toward paying off the interest. Hence, *blended payments.*

Every time your lender compounds the interest you owe on your loan, your monthly blended payment changes. As you pay down your principal, the actual amount of your payment doesn't change, but the portion of the payment that goes toward the principal increases and the amount that goes toward interest slowly decreases.

If your mortgage is $100,000 (with a 5 percent interest rate compounded semi-annually) to be paid over a period of 25 years, your monthly payments will be approximately $585. Table 3-2 illustrates this.

Table 3-2	Breakdown of Blended Payments		
Timeline	*Your Monthly Payment of $585*		
	Principal	*Interest*	*Balance Principal*
1 month	$168	$417	$99,895
6 months	$171	$413	$98,982
1 year	$176	$409	$97,938
5 years	$2,517	$4,498	$88,580
10 years	$3,231	$3,784	$73,924
20 years	$5,321	$1,694	$30,977

You can see that as you pay down the principal, the distribution of your payments changes. Gradually you begin paying more money toward the principal than toward the interest you owe to your lender.

The more frequently you make mortgage payments, the faster you pay down your principal — which means that the more quickly you eliminate your mortgage, the less interest you pay. Payment schedules can be arranged monthly, semi-monthly, biweekly (every two weeks)', or weekly. Arrange with your lender to make payments as often as you can reasonably manage. If you can make weekly payments rather than monthly ones, you'll save thousands of dollars over the lifetime of the loan. Table 3-3 illustrates how making more frequent payments can really whittle down the time it takes to repay a mortgage.

Table 3-3	Mortgage Payment Frequency Comparison	
Calculations for a 25-year $200,000 mortgage at 5 percent interest, compounded semi-annually		
Payment Options	*Monthly Payments*	*Years to Repay Mortgage*
Monthly	$1,169	25
Biweekly	$609	20
Weekly	$339	19

Amortization period

The *amortization period* of your mortgage is the length of time on which the calculation of your monthly payments is based. The advantage of a longer amortization is that the monthly payments are smaller and therefore more manageable. The disadvantage is that the longer the amortization, the longer you carry a principal and, therefore, the more you pay in interest. And interest really adds up. Currently, the longest amortization period available in Canada is 30 years, as of March 18, 2011. You can see in Table 3-4 that the total interest on a 25-year amortization is almost double what you'd pay for a 15-year amortization.

Table 3-4	Amortization Payment Comparison		
Calculations for a $150,000 mortgage at 5 percent interest, compounded semi-annually			
Amortization	*Monthly Payments*	*Total Paid*	*Total Interest*
15 years	$1,186	$214,000	$64,000
20 years	$990	$238,000	$88,000
25 years	$877	$263,000	$113,000

Mortgage term

A *mortgage term* is the specific length of time you and your lender agree your mortgage will be subject to certain negotiated conditions, such as a certain interest rate. Terms usually range from 6 months to 10 years, but occasionally a lender will offer a 15- or 25-year term.

At the end of the term, you generally have the option to pay off your mortgage in full or to renegotiate its terms and conditions. If interest rates are ridiculously high, you'll probably want to negotiate a shorter term, then arrange a longer term when rates are more favourable. If rates are on their way down or very low, a variable rate — which allows you to lock in when you want — may be the way to go. At the end of your mortgage term (or before, if you are refinancing), you can transfer your mortgage to another lender.

If you are refinancing, or renegotiating, the terms of your mortgage before the end of your mortgage term, you very likely will incur penalties. However, if the rate you'll receive after renegotiating is much more competitive, those one-time costs may well be worth it!

Mortgage-a-rama: All the Nifty Options

Depending on how much of a down payment you can make, you'll be eligible for either a conventional or a high-ratio mortgage. If you can bankroll a conventional mortgage, then you have at least 20 percent of the money needed to buy a new home. If your savings leave you with a down payment that's less than 20 percent, then you qualify for a high-ratio mortgage.

No matter which financial position you find yourself in, you still have a number of mortgage options to choose from. You may even want to consider not getting a mortgage at all, and going with a line of credit instead. In this section, we consider each of these options.

Payment options: Open, closed, or in between?

Before you sign on the proverbial dotted line, you need to know your mortgage payment options: open mortgages, closed mortgages, or mortgages that offer something in between. Whichever option you choose affects how much money you pay over the lifetime of the loan and the flexibility of the terms. Some mortgages allow you to pay off your principal in lump sums as you wish and prepay your principal without any penalties. Other mortgages allow you to prepay only once a year on the anniversary date of the mortgage, or there may be no possibility of prepayment at all.

Different financial institutions offer a range of mortgages involving different degrees of flexibility for prepayment. Even most closed mortgages have some prepayment options. You can make specified maximum prepayments, usually between 10 and 20 percent, once a year either on any payment date or on the anniversary date of the mortgage, and in some cases you can increase each payment. You're charged a penalty if you pay down more.

Open mortgages

If you have an *open mortgage*, you can pay it off in full or in part at any time with no penalty. By chipping away at your principal early, you can save crazy amounts of money in interest. Of course, every penny you save in interest is a penny that doesn't get into your lender's hot little hands — which is why the average fixed interest rate quoted for an open mortgage is 0.4 to 0.6 percent higher than a closed mortgage for the same term.

The majority of open mortgages with a fixed interest rate are available only for a short term. Most variable rate mortgages have a fixed five-year term, but may be open after three years, and as you can see in Table 3-1, variable rate mortgages are usually offered at a lower rate.

An open mortgage is a good choice if you're going to move again soon, if interest rates are expected to plummet, or if you're expecting a huge cash windfall once oil is discovered in the scrubland you bought near Medicine Hat. This kind of mortgage is good for the short term when rates are high, and it can usually be converted to a closed mortgage at any time.

Closed mortgages

The advantage of signing on to a closed mortgage for a term, or specified period of time, is that you'll typically get lower interest rates and you'll be able to budget for fixed, regular payments. The downside is that if you need to move before your term is up, or if you have extra cash, such as an income tax refund, that you'd like to put toward paying off a large portion of your principal, you may pay a penalty for this privilege.

Most closed mortgages give the borrower the ability to prepay 10 to 20 percent of the outstanding balance without penalty, often on the anniversary date of the mortgage.

In some cases, there may be restrictive conditions that will make getting out of your mortgage an expensive proposition. You may face a prepayment penalty (Chapter 16 has more information about paying off your mortgage early and the possible penalties) or rate differential fee if you want to discharge the mortgage before the end of the closed mortgage term. Read the fine print, and ask lots of questions.

Portable mortgages and blended payments

If your mortgage is *portable,* you can take it with you to your new house. When you get ready to move, you'll be glad you asked about this option, especially if you negotiated great terms or if interest rates have gone up since you locked in to your current mortgage. Even if you're buying a more expensive house, having a portable mortgage is still to your advantage.

For example, if you have a $200,000 mortgage at 6 percent interest and you're in the third year of a five-year term, you can take the mortgage with you to the $375,000 house you want to buy. You'll need an additional $50,000 loan to be added to your principal. If the going rate on new loans is 5 percent interest for a three-year mortgage to match the remaining three years of your five-year term, you'll need to negotiate a blended rate on the new amount. The blended mortgage payment will be composed of two parts: your initial payment toward your $200,000 mortgage plus the second payment toward the additional $50,000 mortgage. Remember that your payment will be the result of "blending" two mortgage rates, and of course, your monthly payment itself will consist of interest and principal components.

Assumable mortgages

When you're buying a house, in addition to contacting financial institutions about mortgages, you may want to ask the sellers if they would allow you to take over their mortgage as part of the price you pay for the house. This option is quick, and it may save you some costs usually associated with setting up a mortgage, such as legal, appraisal, and survey fees.

You may also save money in interest payments if the seller's mortgage rate is lower than what is currently available on the market. Do check the remaining term on the mortgage, and discuss this option with your real estate agent or your real estate lawyer.

Having an *assumable mortgage* on your home means that when you want to sell it, you can have a qualified buyer assume the mortgage. This option is a great incentive if you have good terms and conditions, and it saves the buyer time finding financing and money setting it up. Most mortgages are assumable as long as the buyer can qualify for the mortgage amount.

You can still expect to go through some financial examination even if you're assuming the seller's mortgage. The lender will want to ensure that you meet the mortgage requirements. See "The Information Game: What Your Lender Wants from You" later in this chapter for more on supplying personal and financial information to your lender.

Vendor (seller) take-back mortgages (VTB)

A less common type of mortgage, especially when the housing market is going strong, is the *vendor take-back mortgage*. This type of mortgage is sometimes used if a seller is anxious to move, for example, or if the market is really sluggish, or if a seller is looking for a good investment after he gets his equity out of his house. In each case, the seller may offer to lend you the money for your mortgage. Sellers may offer you lower rates than big financial institutions will, and they won't require the appraisals, inspections, survey fees, and financing fees you expect to pay a traditional lender.

A vendor take-back mortgage can get very complicated, so you'll want to have your lawyer draw up the papers to guarantee that everything is in order. Some sellers will sell buyers a mortgage and then pass it on to a mortgage broker to handle instead of dealing with it personally.

Builder/developer interest rate buy-down

If you're in the market for a new home, you may find builders and developers willing to offer mortgages with an *interest rate buy-down*. This arrangement may take the form of a vendor take-back mortgage where the builder/developer will lend you the money, or more commonly, the builder may buy down the interest rate of the mortgage you're getting from a bank — usually by 2 or 3 percent. This mortgage option explains those newspaper ads for projects and subdivisions for sale with 3 percent mortgages.

The goal of the interest rate buy-down is to sell real estate. Buy-downs help buyers who are having trouble qualifying for a mortgage at current rates, or allow buyers to qualify for larger mortgages and therefore buy more-expensive properties in the development. Keep in mind, however, that these mortgages are typically not renewable, meaning that after the term is up, your mortgage rate, and therefore your monthly payment, is likely to climb significantly.

After your first mortgage term with an *interest rate buy-down* is up, you need to negotiate new terms, and if you've borrowed the money from the builder or developer, you need to find a new lender — usually a bank. Naturally, your lender will do an appraisal of your property. You're expecting this. What you're perhaps not expecting is that your new lender may appraise your one- or two-year-old house at several thousand dollars less than the price you paid for it. Here's why this happens: Builders want to offer reduced interest rates as an incentive to buyers. However, they're still protecting their bottom lines, so to compensate for offering lower interest, they incorporate the cost of the buy-down into the price of the house itself. This practice means you pay a larger principal on the builder's inflated price of the house.

The solution? Don't borrow the money from the builder or developer in the first place. Arrange a mortgage with a financial institution, and ask the builder or developer to buy down the interest with your lender. This way, you can take advantage of the deal on the interest rate and you still have the option to renew your mortgage with your lender at the end of the term. Another option is to take your mortgage at market rates and ask the builder to lower the selling price accordingly.

"Can I have a mortgage with that, please?" Like car dealers, sellers can really sweeten the deal by helping you put the financing in place with assumable mortgages, vendor take-back mortgages, and builder/developer interest rate buy-downs — options that can save you a lot of money. But buyer beware: Read the fine print, and consult with your agent and lawyer before accepting any seller's mortgage offer — it might just be too good to be true.

Line of credit

Buying a property using a line of credit instead of a conventional mortgage is increasingly common, and it works a bit like a credit card. You'll need to make a minimum monthly payment, but that payment covers only the interest — it won't pay down the *principal,* or the amount of the loan. Anything else you pay beyond that monthly payment is up to you. To reduce the outstanding balance of the line of credit, however, you must pay more than the minimum monthly payment, or the principal won't be reduced.

The benefits of the line of credit are

- ✒ Lower monthly payments (should you choose to pay just the minimum)
- ✒ Total flexibility paying off the outstanding balance of the loan — with a regular mortgage, you can't change your monthly payments at will

The downsides of buying with a line of credit are

- ✒ At the minimum payment, no reduction in the outstanding balance
- ✒ Rate fluctuates with prime, meaning that it's not fixed (for example, at the prime rate or 0.25 percent or 0.50 percent over prime)

If you're someone whose income fluctuates with occasional high-income months, this option may be right for you. To qualify, you need to have a higher down payment (at least 25 percent) and a very good credit rating. Determining if a line of credit is something that will work well for you, as opposed to a conventional mortgage, will take some time and analysis with your bank or mortgage broker.

High-Ratio Mortgage Insurance

If you have a down payment of less than 20 percent (but more than 5 percent) of the purchase price of your house, then you're eligible for a high-ratio mortgage. However, lenders will require you to have mortgage insurance so that their risk is protected. The lender arranges high-ratio insurance.

Qualifying for high-ratio mortgage insurance

Many buyers have high-ratio mortgage insurance coverage through the Canada Mortgage and Housing Corporation. (See the Appendix for a list of provincial CMHC offices across Canada.) Currently, there are two other high-ratio mortgage insurers: Genworth Financial and AIG United Guaranty (the latter does very little Canadian business because of the financial difficulties experienced by its U.S. parent company). However, CMHC is the granddaddy of the group and does the vast majority of the business. All institutions have four standard eligibility requirements:

- ✔ The home you're buying will be your principal residence.

- ✔ The home you're buying is in Canada.

- ✔ Your *Gross Debt Service (GDS) ratio* is not more than approximately 32 percent. In other words, the total you spend on housing (including principal and interest, property taxes, heating, and 50 percent of condo fees) isn't more than approximately 32 percent of your gross (pre-tax) household income. (See Chapter 2 for help in determining your GDS ratio.)

- ✔ Your *Total Debt Service (TDS) ratio*, including any car loans, student loans, and credit card debt, isn't more than 40 percent of your gross (pre-tax) household income. (See Chapter 2 for details on calculating your TDS ratio.)

Determining the cost of high-ratio mortgage insurance

The premium for high-ratio mortgage insurance is typically 1 to 4.75 percent of the mortgage amount, determined by a sliding scale. Changes in recent years regarding high-ratio mortgage insurance have been frequent. Make sure you discuss the implications with your mortgage broker or lender. (Insurance premiums are also different for those who are refinancing.) You may also expect a surcharge for amortizations greater than 25 years.

Be sure to ask about incentives for you, the borrower, if you buy an energy-efficient home or borrow money to make more energy-saving renovations to an existing home. You may qualify for as much as a 10 percent refund on your mortgage loan insurance premium.

Other Mortgage Insurance: Life and Illness

Mortgage life insurance guarantees your mortgage will be paid in full if you die. Some lenders offer this insurance and will add the premium to your mortgage payments. Shopping around through an insurance broker for the best rates is still a good idea, though. You may want to get insurance coverage for all parties responsible for the mortgage (for example, if your home is in your name and your spouse's, both of you should be insured).

The lender may offer insurance where it will pay off the balance of your mortgage upon your death, commonly referred to as *declining balance insurance*. However, you may also want to consider regular term insurance. The premiums are comparable to declining balance insurance, but this policy covers you for the full amount of your mortgage should you pass away — not just the outstanding balance.

In addition to mortgage life insurance, some lenders offer *critical illness insurance*. This insurance usually covers certain serious illnesses only — the main three being cancer, heart attack, and stroke — but many people want the security of knowing their mortgage will be paid off, or close to it, not only in a case of death but also if they get really sick. This type of coverage is an add-on, so you can't get it independently of life insurance. Whether this option is right for you depends solely on you and your insurance preferences, but make sure you ask the right questions before deciding. Find out exactly what illnesses are covered, if you need to take a medical exam, and exactly what the extent of your coverage would be.

Going Mortgage Hunting

For the longest time in Canada, if you wanted a mortgage, you went down to the local bank, spoke to the manager or loans officer, filled out the forms, and waited patiently. Eventually you would be told whether you qualified or not, and what interest rate you would pay. In most cases, the rate that was posted in the window was the rate that you would get. But with the surge in real estate transactions in recent years, and the advent of the Internet as a virtual font of information, things have changed.

Now, when you go hunting for a mortgage, you'll find that the whole process is more transparent. Major banks and lenders often post all their rates, and mortgage brokers also post rates from the lenders that they deal with.

Because of all the information available online, in newspapers, and on the news, everyone is able to access the best rates available to them, with no worries about getting stung with a rate higher than expected.

You may find all of the information to be a bit overwhelming, and may want to turn to a professional to help you wade through it. In that case, you need a mortgage broker, and we discuss just what they do and how to find one. If you want to go it alone, we've got you covered, too.

Enlisting a mortgage broker

These days, more and more Canadians are using a mortgage broker to help them organize the financing of their home purchase. A *mortgage broker* is a licensed lending professional who represents several different lenders, and usually offers more loan options than a commercial bank.

Mortgage brokers can work independently, or they can work for the lending arm of a major bank. In the latter case, those brokers represent the lending products of their bank alone, but don't be deterred — they may well be able to get you superior rates and terms. Independent mortgage brokers often use many different lenders, including banks with in-house mortgage brokers. Independent brokers also have access to some innovative broker-only lenders that may even offer more attractive rates and features.

Understanding how a mortgage broker works

A mortgage broker is basically your representative with lenders, and does all the dirty work for you. Essentially, you provide the broker with the information required to qualify for a mortgage (that's a little further on in this chapter, in the section, "The Information Game: What Your Lender Wants from You"), and your broker takes care of the rest.

A broker helps you navigate the bumps you may encounter in qualifying for a mortgage. If you have any little glitches on your credit history, your broker can help fix them. For example, you may think that the store credit card with a $25 balance you forgot to pay three years ago is no big deal, but it may have become a very big deal on your credit report. Your broker can help you clean up that spill.

When you work with a mortgage broker, your credit history is pulled only once. Why is this important? Consider this: Say you decide you're going to be hands-on, and you go to five major Canadian banks to apply for a mortgage. At every bank you approach, you fill out an application and the bank pulls your credit report. Every time your report is requested, your credit score is negatively affected. In the eyes of the credit bureau, every request for your credit information is an application for money, and it affects your overall score. Of course, you aren't really applying for five separate mortgages, or car loans, or credit cards, but the credit police don't know that.

After your broker helps you sort through any credit issues, she can pre-approve you for a mortgage, helping you set your budget for the property you want to purchase. You can also talk to your mortgage broker about amortization rates and payment frequency, determining the best options for you. (Refer to "Mortgage Basics and Jargon 101" for more on these terms.)

Finally, armed with your information and your needs, your broker can find you the rates, terms, and conditions that will work best for you. Generally, mortgage brokers are not tied to just one lender (unless you are using a bank's in-house mortgage specialist), so they can provide options from many lenders. Another plus? They get to do all the arm twisting with lenders and fight the good fight for you, so if you aren't a confrontational type who likes to negotiate, you're off the hook!

Finding a mortgage broker

The best way to find a good mortgage broker can often be by asking friends who have recently purchased a home, or by asking your agent. After all, your agent wants to sell you a home, and a good mortgage broker helps to do just that! Your agent will probably have several mortgage brokers to recommend who will work hard for you.

Just as licensing rules for real estate agents are different throughout Canada, there are differences for mortgage brokers, too. All mortgage brokers in Canada must be licensed, however, so make sure you are dealing with a licensed specialist.

If you're determined to remain with the financial institution that you have been with, you may want to deal directly with their in-house mortgage specialists.

Seeking out mortgage brokers online

How do you tell if an online mortgage broker is a reputable and upright business, or just an ex-con with some Web skills? The mortgage broker's site can offer you a couple of clues:

✔ The company should be a registered member of the Canadian Association of Accredited Mortgage Professionals (CAAMP) (www.caamp.org).

✔ The site should offer a company profile, with thorough and easy-to-understand text on the mortgage broker process. The site should also feature a list of preferred lenders. The longer this list, and the more major banks whose names you recognize, the better — this shows that the broker has a good business relationship with many clients and can cast its nets wider to find you the best deal.

Many mortgage brokers also work out of local offices of national companies, so you may have to go through a national site to find a local mortgage specialist. You may be asked to fill out an online form with contact information such as your e-mail address, street address, and phone number. At this stage, give only the information that is necessary to get in contact with the mortgage broker — you don't need to give private information to anyone over the Internet.

If the site you're visiting starts asking for private information (such as account numbers and credit information), leave the site immediately — you may have stumbled across a bogus company pretending to be a helpful lender.

Searching on your own

Of course, you can always apply for a mortgage the old fashioned way: by yourself. Many trust companies, credit unions, and *caisses populaires* (cooperative financial institutions similar to credit unions) don't deal directly with mortgage brokers, so you may want to approach them individually, if they're who you want to do business with. Don't be afraid to negotiate!

If you've decided that DIY is the way you want to go, in many cases you can contact the lender directly (if it's a major bank or credit union). Other lenders may be accessible only through mortgage brokers. Don't be afraid to network. Ask friends who have recently bought or sold a home where and how they got their financing and if they were satisfied.

As with most things these days, the Internet is your go-to place for rates and information. By going to your favourite search engine, you can search "mortgage rates in Canada" and get a whole host of results to compare. You must be diligent though: Rates are constantly changing, so in order to get that great rate you see guaranteed, you'll need to act fast.

In the following section, we investigate just what you'll see at most lenders' Web sites, and discuss what applying for a mortgage online is like.

Cool tools

Just how much can you really do on your bank's Web site? We went to some major Canadian bank sites and came up with the following handy tools (some had more, and some had less, so surf around!):

✔ **Canadian housing prices:** A list of average housing prices in major Canadian cities.

✔ **Glossary of financial terms:** You can look up home- and mortgage-related gobbledygook online.

✔ **"How much you can afford" calculator:** An estimate of how much you can afford to shell out on a monthly basis to pay down your mortgage.

✔ **Mortgage calculator:** A breakdown of what your mortgage payments would be on different payment frequencies and different mortgage plans.

✔ **Mortgage personality profile:** Well, it doesn't ask you for your favourite colour, but this tool does indicate what type of mortgage may be best suited to your financial personality — whether you keep track of interest rates, how long you plan to own your house, and so on.

✔ **Net worth calculator:** If you know your assets from your liabilities, you can calculate your net worth online in minutes.

✔ **Personal budget calculator:** The math is done for you.

Online calculators are an awful lot like, well, regular calculators: They're only as accurate as the numbers you plug in. Don't start house hunting based on the results if what you've typed in is what you think your income is after tax, or what your remaining student debt is, give or take a few thousand. These calculators work best as indications only, even with the most spot-on information.

You'll find that some online calculators won't present you with a very realistic picture. Just because they say that, according to the information you've entered, you can carry a $200,000 mortgage, that doesn't mean you'd have any money left over for other expenses. Remember, the calculator is just a computer program that has absolutely no need to have a social life, buy its kids shoes, or get the car fixed.

Online mortgage pre-approval

Ready to go for that mortgage pre-approval? Well, most bank Web sites provide an online pre-approval application. You may want to proceed the old-fashioned way: Putting your coat on, grabbing your financial files, and visiting the bank. If you'd rather pour yourself a stiff drink and go through the motions in the comfort of your own home, access your bank's 24-hour, 1-800 service number, where you can usually be pre-approved over the phone.

You can go ahead and apply for pre-approval online, but here's why we mention it last:

✔ No one is on the other side of the desk or the phone helping you through. This means that you're your own financial adviser, and must have a very good idea of your financial capabilities and the type of mortgage you want and can afford.

✔ About one-third of the way through your online application, after you've plugged in all the relevant numbers and the whirring central bank computer is happy enough with your down payment to proceed, you'll get a proposed pre-approval amount. You may be tempted to jump up from your computer, yell "Whoopee!" and get yourself another stiff drink — er, Shirley Temple — to celebrate. But this is not your final answer! This amount is a conditional pre-approval, based on the truth of the numbers you've provided, pending a credit check, and so on. The online application will walk you through all of those conditions in the steps to come, you can be sure.

So before visions of Tudor mansions start dancing in your head, use this tip to keep you grounded: Keep in mind that when your virtual bank offers you these numbers, you haven't even given your name yet! What kind of lender would give you money at this stage? No one. Take a deep breath, and keep typing and clicking through right to the bitter end. And, as we mention in Chapter 2, even if you have a pre-approved mortgage, you should still make any offer "subject to financing" because your lender will usually require at least an appraisal before granting you a mortgage.

To get an absolutely firm pre-approval, you'll have to provide detailed income and debt verification. Without this verification, your online pre-approval is only an indication of what you may be able to afford — it isn't a guarantee that you'll be able to get the mortgage amount that you determined through your online pre-approval process.

At some point in the online pre-approval, your bank will put a "disclaimer" screen in front of you. Read it. Print it out. Keep it. Read it again. You get the picture. . .

Online credit checks

If you're a little foggy on your credit rating, you can easily access it on the Internet — but be extra careful about where you go. In Canada, Equifax (www.equifax.ca) is the pre-eminent and most trusted consumer source for credit information. On their Web site, you can see your credit report for around $15 and have access to it online for 30 days. If you type "online credit check Canada" into your search engine, you'll come up with a whole truckload of sites, some of which are legit and some of which are e-villains — although the word "wizard" in the domain name does give you a pretty big warning sign.

Questioning Your Lender

Just because you're the one requesting money doesn't mean you can't ask questions. Lenders profit from your business, so don't be afraid to bring up your concerns. You should expect to be answered directly, in a courteous manner, and you should reply to your lender's questions in kind. Keep a list, and have paper with you to use in meetings or on the telephone so that you can be sure to cover all the bases.

Stay cool and calm as you chat with prospective lenders. Remember, you're shopping for a mortgage, not begging for one. Keep this list handy to be sure you ask the right questions:

- **What is your name, title, and phone number?** Start with the basics.

- **Do you comply with all the provisions of Canada's privacy legislation?** In case you're wondering if your information will be kept confidential, don't worry. In Canada, the *Privacy Act* and the *Personal Information Protection and Electronic Documents Act* (PIPEDA) are two federal laws that forbid lending institutions (and other businesses) from disclosing your private information. For more details about privacy legislation, you can visit `www.priv.gc.ca/index_e.cfm`.

- **What mortgage types and terms do you have available?** Do you have any that are specifically designed for my situation? Many major banks have special offers for first-time homebuyers, for example.

- **What are your current mortgage rates?** Compare the rate offered for closed mortgages to the rate offered for open mortgages. An open mortgage gives you more flexibility and can save you money, but usually has a higher interest rate than a closed mortgage, as we explain earlier in this chapter.

- **How are you making your mortgages competitive with other lending institutions? Are any discounts or cash-back options available?** Some lenders lower their interest rate a bit if you ask nicely or show them lower rates from the competition; other lenders offer you a percentage off your mortgage up front — usually between 1 and 3 percent as a cash-back program — to help you with your closing costs.

- **What mortgage fees do you charge? Is there a mortgage application fee?** Make sure you know what kind of costs your lender expects you to cover.

- **Do you pre-approve mortgages? Is there a fee for this?** Most institutions do not charge a pre-approval application fee.

- **How long will it take to process my loan request? After it's approved, how long should I allow before I close the deal?** When you set your closing dates for the purchase of a new home, the schedule for your transfer of funds is crucial. Know what to expect.

✔ **How is the interest compounded?** Most lenders compound interest semi-annually (every six months). Ask if your lender offers any other compounding options that may save you money.

✔ **Can I convert from a variable to a fixed rate mortgage?** As we explain earlier in this chapter, if you choose a variable rate mortgage, you're vulnerable to fluctuations in the current interest rate. When interest rates rise, you must make higher mortgage payments; when rates fall, you pay less. You'll want to have the option to convert your variable rate mortgage to a fixed rate mortgage if interest rates begin to climb significantly.

✔ **What are my payment options?** As we detail earlier in this chapter, to save yourself a lot of money in the long run, you should make payments as often as you can — weekly is best.

✔ **Can I pay off the mortgage early? Is there a penalty for this? Can I pay down some of the principal without penalty? How much a year?** You'll probably want the option to make an extra lump-sum payment toward your mortgage principal at least once or twice a year to help you save on the interest.

✔ **Is mortgage life and critical illness insurance available with your mortgages? Will they cover both my partner and me?** You'll want to protect your family members in case something happens to you. But check the cost. A separate insurer may offer lower insurance premiums for the same coverage.

✔ **If my credit rating is not acceptable at this point, what can I do to improve it? Or what options do I have?** Be prepared: Any lender who offers mortgages will check your credit rating.

The Information Game: What Your Lender Wants from You

No matter who you use to secure your mortgage, you'll always have to provide the same sort of information. Don't take it personally. Even Donald Trump has to fill out this kind of paperwork and answer these types of questions when he's looking to finance his next mega project. Consider yourself in good company!

Tell us about yourself

Mortgage brokers or lenders will ask you to fill out an application when you apply for a mortgage. They'll ask about your financial status and employment, as well as your personal information and history. Expect questions like these:

- ✔ **What is your age, marital status, and number of dependants? Where do you work? What is your position? How long have you been with the company? What is your employment history?** Unless you're self-employed, you'll probably need a letter from your employer confirming your position with the company. If you're self-employed, bring your tax assessments (not your tax returns) from the past two years to confirm your earnings.

- ✔ **What is your gross (pre-tax) family income?** You may need proof of income, like a T4 slip or, if you're self-employed, personal income tax returns. You'll also be asked to show proof of other sources of income, such as from pensions or rental property.

- ✔ **What do you currently spend on housing? If you're a homeowner, what is the current market value of your house?** You may have to provide copies of your rental lease agreement for the apartment or suite you're renting, or a copy of your current mortgage.

- ✔ **Do you have funds for a down payment?** The lender wants to ensure that your down payment will be available when you need the money to close on your purchase. The lender will want to see where your down payment is coming from — is it sitting in the bank, or will it be coming from your beloved Aunt Bibi in the near future?

- ✔ **What assets do you have, and what is the value of each one?** You can include vehicles, properties, and investments.

- ✔ **What liabilities do you have?** You can include credit card balances, car loans, student loans, and lines of credit.

Your mortgage broker or lender will also ask for your consent to do a credit check. A credit check may give you a good or bad credit rating, depending on your financial history. We recommend you contact a credit-reporting agency, such as Equifax Canada or your local credit bureau, to obtain a copy of your credit report. (See the sidebar "Online credit checks" in this chapter.) Examine it in detail. If you find inaccurate or outdated information in the report, you can have those items corrected or removed to make your credit rating as glowing as it can possibly be. See the Appendix for contact information regarding Equifax Canada, not to mention (but we'll mention it again) many other useful resources dealing with home buying and selling.

Let's have it in writing, please: The paperwork

For the most part, banks or mortgage brokers can pre-approve your mortgage over the phone. You may have to fax them the required paperwork, and in return, they'll fax you a written confirmation outlining the terms of your mortgage pre-approval. Often, you won't meet your banker until you receive the sellers' acceptance of your offer to purchase their home and you're ready to seal the deal by finalizing all the financing.

Getting all the papers together for a mortgage is just the beginning of a long paper shuffle you'll be doing until you finally get the keys to your new home. Be prepared with the following documents when you find yourself with an accepted offer to purchase a property:

- ✔ Copy of a recent appraisal for the home you're buying (if requested — the bank may already have ordered it for you)
- ✔ Copy of the property listing
- ✔ Copy of the Agreement of Purchase and Sale (for a resale house)
- ✔ Plans and cost estimates if you're buying a new house (construction loans only)
- ✔ Certificate for well water and septic system (if applicable)
- ✔ Condominium financial statements (if applicable)
- ✔ Survey certificate
- ✔ Property disclosure statement (signed by both parties) or condominium certificate (if applicable)
- ✔ Copy of Title

Chapter 4

Finding Your Kind of Home

. . . .

In This Chapter

▶ Finding the right fit — what type of home is for you?

▶ Dealing with neighbours

▶ Earning a little extra: Basement suites, duplexes, and triplexes

. . . .

*T*he home that you choose to live in is a reflection of your lifestyle and personality. Although you may think you have only a few basic housing options to choose from, many homes on the market are a mixture of two or more types. The variety available is impressive, so you should have a good idea of what you're looking for in advance.

In this chapter, we help you out by listing some common advantages and disadvantages of the different home types. It's up to you to think long and hard about your individual situation and what makes sense for you. If you're the type of person who likes to hop in the shower at 6:00 a.m., crank up the stereo, and sing at the top of your lungs, you can probably eliminate an apartment-style condominium as an option. On the other hand, if you would rather cut off your own toes than rake leaves or shovel snow, owning a condo with a year-round maintenance crew may be right up your alley. Of course, sometimes your budget or your preferred location is the deciding factor as to whether you live in a detached property or in a condominium or townhome. You may have to adjust your lifestyle to your bottom line.

Houses: So Many Choices . . .

Most people have a strong preference for either apartment-style condominiums or houses. Chances are, you already know which is more to your taste (if not, start thinking about it right now). Even if you've decided you want a house to call home, you have additional considerations. Do you want a new house? A resale house? A duplex? A semi-detached or a fully detached house?

Ask yourself what's most important to you when it comes to your living space. Decide which kinds of homes are acceptable before you start looking seriously, and tell your agent what your priorities are and which types of houses best suit your needs and tastes.

Location may determine what you can afford — for example, a semi-detached (half-duplex) in the best part of town or a detached home in a good but not great part of town. Set your priorities, and determine what you really want. Chapter 6 guides you through this decision-making process.

Pros and cons of buying a brand-new home

Say you've decided that you must have everything fresh and new in order to be happy with your home-buying purchase. You can buy new in two ways: Buy a vacant lot and build your house yourself or buy a new home that's already been finished by a builder or developer. Either situation has some major advantages and disadvantages.

Good reasons to buy new

If you're in the market for a new home as opposed to a resale house, you probably have a pretty clear idea of why. Here are the key advantages of buying a new house:

- ✓ **Safety standards:** Your house will meet the most recent standards in safety and energy efficiency — saving you money in the long run. Your home will probably also be more technologically up to date, which means you don't have to do any major rewiring to get your high-speed Internet, or run phone lines from the bedroom to the basement.

- ✓ **Choice of materials:** You get to see the builder's specs, so you know exactly what you're getting — construction materials, operating systems, and so on.

- ✓ **New Home Warranty Program:** You should be eligible for a new homeowner's comprehensive warranty that covers defects in materials and construction, and may also cover building code violations and major structural defects. Check the *New Home Warranty Program* (NHWP) in your province. You can find more information on the NHWP in Chapter 12.

- ✓ **Newness:** You won't have previous wear and tear on the structural components, operational systems, or appliances, assuming, of course, you don't buy used appliances for your new home.

- ✓ **Possible tax savings:** In many provinces, you may have to pay a land transfer tax or a deed transfer tax when you purchase a home. The calculation and applicability of this tax varies across the country, and in some cases those building their own homes receive a break: You may pay the transfer or deed tax on the value of the land only, and not the finished value of the home. But don't get too excited, prospective handy-people: Taxes make an unwanted appearance in our con list as well . . .

✔ **Modern construction:** Improvements in home-building techniques and technology over the years may mean you're getting better-quality construction. You also get a home designed with contemporary needs in mind (in other words, you get big closets!).

When your new home is finished, the builder will take you on one last tour before you take possession of the house — allowing you to see for yourself that everything contracted has been done properly. But keep in mind that this tour in no way replaces a professional inspection. See Chapter 12 for more information on inspections.

Difficulties of buying new

If you're buying in a newly developed neighbourhood, chances are the finished house will not look exactly like the promotional material. Even a new house in an established neighbourhood may not look exactly like the artist's rendering that first caught your eye. You may encounter several other potential drawbacks when buying a new home:

✔ **Lack of services:** The surrounding neighbourhood may not yet be equipped with accessible public transportation, schools, groceries, shopping, or other amenities that are standard in an established area.

✔ **Distance:** New subdivisions and lots are generally found outside of densely populated regions, so you may not be able to build or buy a new house in the urban area of your choice.

✔ **Uncertainty about your neighbours:** You won't know in advance what the neighbours are like. Will they be organizing all-night street dances every time there's a full moon? This uncertainty may be particularly true in an apartment-style condo if a number of the suites are sold to investors who will rent them out.

✔ **Taxes:** Property taxes may be higher in a newly developed area that requires roads, schools, sewers, and so on. Also, you likely have to pay up to 5 percent GST or 13 percent HST on the purchase of a new home. (On the upside, in many cases you may be eligible for a rebate. Refer to Chapter 2 for more information on GST or HST on new houses.)

✔ **Fixed prices:** If you're buying in a development, the price of the homes is usually not negotiable and you may have to go through the developer's agent.

✔ **Timing:** You may end up constantly scanning the news about the latest construction strike because it has an impact on the finishing date of your home.

✔ **Construction inconvenience:** You may have to put up with noise and dust created by the continual construction in the area.

✔ **Undeveloped landscape:** You may move into your home and find that you're surrounded by mud fields and a giant dirt heap with no sidewalks or lawn anywhere in sight. With time you can, of course, add your own landscaping, but lush greenery will take a while to create.

You can minimize the stress of added expenses by anticipating that they will crop up and by doing your research. Make sure you fully understand all the costs associated with building — get a *detailed* breakdown of all estimated costs from your builder so you know exactly what is covered and what is optional or extra. The contract to build a house includes a lengthy specification list that can run 10 to 15 pages. Everything down to the towel racks should be outlined. If you're doing the building yourself, make up your own specification list.

As for delays in the building process, you can't really do much if the porcelain tiles or sleek German faucets don't arrive on time. And if Mother Nature decides she doesn't want you to move in until one year from next September, well, you'll just have to wait. Have a contingency plan in the event that your new home is not fit for habitation on time.

The upside and downside of building it yourself

So, you've been glued to every home-building, home-fixing, home-staging, and home-arranging show that has aired in the last several years, and you figure that through osmosis you are, indeed, "Canada's Next Awesome Home Builder." Well, we have a reality check for you: These shows are heavily edited. Here are some things to consider before trying to frame your home:

✔ **Making it exactly what you want:** You get to choose and/or design the actual structure and components of your home — the building materials, the position on the lot, and so many other features. In a nutshell, you get what you want. However, if you're in a position to buy land in a new subdivision, do be aware that many have *building schemes* attached, meaning that the homes built within that area must meet certain size and architectural standards. So, if you think that you're going to build a mini replica of the Taj Mahal, think again. Even exterior paint colours can be part of that building scheme. This also applies to infill housing in established urban neighbourhoods. Check zoning bylaws first for size allowed, setbacks to property lines, etc. And be prepared for unhappy neighbours if you do something very different from surrounding homes.

✔ **Scheduling and planning risks:** Delays and extra expenses are practically guaranteed. As with renovating, building almost always costs more than you think it will initially and it almost always takes longer than you first estimate.

When building your own home, keep a "reserve fund" or be sure that you can access further funds should the need arise — you don't want to create delays by not having the money to complete the building after it's begun. We suggest padding your building budget by an extra 10 to 15 percent, just in case.

Country living in a new home

If you're planning to build a fabulous ranch house so far away from civilization that you forget the rest of the world exists, keep these extra considerations in mind:

- **Electricity and phones:** Bringing in phone and hydro lines may cost you extra. (Nowadays, alternative energy sources are available that may be more amenable to country life, such as wind-powered generators. The popularity of this renewable and emission-free method has been rising steadily in recent years, and it is capable of powering a house equipped with all the usual energy-efficient appliances.)

- **Water:** Water quality may be an issue, and you may have to spring for a proper filtration system. If you have to drill a new well, and if that well is particularly deep, you may be looking at some big costs.

- **Extra taxes:** If you're in a relatively isolated and unincorporated area, services such as road maintenance and schools may be supported by a small population base, requiring a higher per capita tax burden to maintain even a minimal level of services.

- **Garbage:** As with any home in the boondocks, new or resale, garbage and recycling pickup may be unavailable.

- **Snow removal:** You may need to organize and pay for snow removal yourself, or with others who share your road.

- **Sewage and plumbing:** Building a septic system or hooking up to a sewage line can be extremely expensive and may require substantial preliminary work (researching the water table and underground water flows). In Chapter 8 we cover all the details to ensure your septic system is in acceptable condition.

Resale houses

Suppose you don't feel like dealing with the hassle of building a new home, and new houses or subdivisions don't appeal to you. Fortunately, there are plenty of resale houses on the market. (Whether these are in your favourite region is another question.) You can expect some of the following perks from buying one of these pre-existing beauties:

- **Convenience:** The neighbourhood amenities, like public transportation, schools, parks, shopping, groceries, and so on, will already be established.

- **Luxuries:** Extras that would put a serious strain on your wallet to build or buy new (such as a swimming pool, satellite dish, hot tub, custom cabinetry, or a finished basement) may come with the house.

- **Character:** Older homes may have unique or antique-quality features that give them character and add to the potential resale value.

- **Tax savings:** You don't pay GST/HST on the purchase of a resale home (unless substantial renovations were done, in effect making the house "count" as new).

- **Landscaping:** Lawns and gardens will probably be well established.

- **Immediate readiness:** You can move into a resale home right away in most cases. Things like light fixtures and carpeting are already installed, and usually what you see is what you get. With a good inspection, there should be few surprises after you move in. In a new home, what you picture in your mind may not be the reality when building is complete.

Every rose has its thorn, too — sometimes more than one. Balancing off the advantages listed above, you may have to deal with some of the following difficulties:

- **Less energy efficiency:** Older houses are often (but not necessarily) less energy efficient, utilities may cost more, or upgrades may be needed in the not-too-distant future.

- **Repairs needed:** Previous wear and tear on the house may make maintenance more expensive.

- **Decor challenges:** A used home may not feel like your own until you redecorate.

- **Space constraints:** Older homes are often smaller than newer ones: Hallways, rooms, and closets can sometimes feel like they were meant for Smurfs rather than the average-sized Canadian; many basements won't have even 6-foot-high ceilings.

- **Modern updates needed:** Minor renovations or repairs may be necessary to accommodate your lifestyle, or to meet new safety or building codes.

- **Structural concerns:** You have no say in the layout or what building materials are used, so you may not be entirely satisfied with the structure of the home.

- **Tax:** Land transfer tax and/or deed transfer tax may apply to the purchase, depending on your location. Talk to your agent or lawyer about this.

Absolutely prefabulous

We're talking about prefab homes, which are also called manufactured homes, and have they ever come a long way from your cousin Lurleen's double-wide trailer. The term *prefab* means the home is prefabricated in a factory, delivered, and then set up on your property. If the description reminds you of eating chicken fingers in Sunnyvale with your neighbour Bubbles — think again. You should know that there's a whole movement toward modern, attractive, already built housing for people who don't want to wait through a year and a cold Canadian winter (which can slow down construction) for their new house to be built. Plus, they look really cool.

If your dream house has an indoor pool, or you live with your mother-in-law, prefab probably isn't for you. These homes tend to be small, about the size of a one-bedroom apartment, but the largest ones can have several rooms and two storeys. Also, smaller doesn't necessarily mean cheaper. When you factor in the costs of construction, assembly, installation, and delivery, a prefab costs about the same as a house constructed the old-fashioned way.

No matter what prefabs are used for — a main home, a vacation home, or an addition on an existing house — what's great about them is that they're eco-friendly. Off-site assembly means the manufacturers use only the amounts of material needed, so there's hardly any construction waste. Some prefabs are made with renewable materials like bamboo flooring and earth-friendly products like non-toxic paint and built-in water-saving fixtures. Many models are created to make the most of natural light, with lots of windows to keep electricity costs down.

When you buy a prefab, you do need land on which to plunk down your house. Because the shipping costs are quite high, you may not be able to park a prefab on a mountain peak, but it can be delivered by truck, train, or even helicopter. When the house arrives, the site has already been prepared for the home's installation with hookups for power, water, sewer, and phone/cable. And the prefab home already includes systems for plumbing, heating, and electricity that will be connected to the services at the site. You choose any extra features, like ceiling fans and light fixtures, cabinets, and, in some cases, furnishings.

If you don't own land of your own, you can lease or rent a pad in a subdivision or park that is set up for prefab homes. You have to be very careful with terms and conditions of any lease for a pad for your home — make sure you're very clear about monthly fees, what services are included, and the details of any renewal option for your pad lease. You can also plunk down your home in a gated community that's designed specifically for prefab homes. In these communities, you buy a small plot of land and pay a monthly maintenance fee to cover your part of the shared expenses, just like owning a condo. These communities offer a higher level of security, plus the added security of owning your piece of land rather than leasing it. Be sure to investigate the community's culture to see if it's right for you. Because many of these communities have age restrictions for residents, they're quieter and more suitable for adults than small children.

You can visit www.thehomeboys.com to see some of these cool, modern abodes. Chic, simple, environmentally responsible — and you don't have to worry about tornadoes blowing your house away.

Move right in, or fix it up: The right resale home for you

Like most significant questions, the answer to whether buying a fixer-upper is a good idea is "That depends." Most resale homes can be put into one of three categories: move-in condition, "handyman special," or adequate condition (meaning somewhere in between).

Ready to move in

Houses in move-in condition are exactly that — ready for you to drag the furniture up the front steps and then settle in. A house in move-in condition may have been repaired or renovated to bring it up to tip-top shape. Buyers pay more for a premium house — but many prefer a lower price and the chance to do upgrades their way, rather than a higher price and lots of sparkling new designer cabinetry that's totally at odds with their taste. Nothing is worse than a house with a new $20,000 custom kitchen tiled from floor to ceiling in colours you can't stand. With a move-in-ready home, chances are you won't have the ability to build any new equity (meaning you may find it difficult to add value to the property).

Needs care and attention

A handyman special is a house that is cheaper because it needs some work — anything involving a plumbing tune-up to a major overhaul can fall into this category.

A handyman special is potentially a bargain if and only if the defects are fixable — and fixable within a reasonable budget. For instance, if the defects include structural damage resulting from the use of the dwelling as a *grow-op* (a home that's been converted in order to cultivate marijuana plants, mushrooms, or other drugs), don't even consider purchasing it. The moisture and chemicals used to pull off a successful grow-op can lead to wood warping and harmful mould growth, and the odour is practically impossible to eliminate. Many municipalities that have had issues with grow-ops (or any other illegal drug operation for that matter — meth labs in homes are equally destructive) will require the home to be inspected before it's declared fit for humans again. Additionally, insurance companies won't touch these properties with a 10-foot pole unless this inspection has been done, so you may not be able to get a mortgage on a home that has been used in the mass production of illegal drugs. Check with your municipality, your insurance company, and your lender before you proceed with a home that has this scarlet letter attached!

Assuming that the problems are fixable and the property's value can be increased, if you're an electrician, plumber, or carpenter, for example, involving yourself in this sort of venture may be worthwhile — *if* you have the time. But, whatever tasks you don't have the skill, expertise, or time to manage yourself, you'll have to pay someone else to handle. You'll be financially responsible for materials, labour, tax, and other expenses, which can get very expensive, very quickly.

For first-time homebuyers, who generally have enough trouble finding money for the down payment, investing in a house that needs a lot of work may be a bit of a stretch. But don't be discouraged from buying one of the cheaper houses on the block — that's *always* a smart move, because the value will be affected positively by the more expensive neighbouring houses. Remember, not everything in the home has to be done all at once: A lot can be accomplished cosmetically with a bit of paint and some elbow grease.

Many people buy houses that badly need renovation to fix them up and then sell them for a profit. If you plan to sell the house in the future, be careful — if your upgrades result in the house becoming the most expensive on your street, you won't recoup the money you put into renovating.

Ask your agent, or investigate on your own, the price range of houses in your vicinity. If your $200,000 house is the cheapest on the block and the most expensive house is $560,000, you may be in a good position to renovate and sell for a profit. But if you pay $200,000, do major renovations, and then ask for $400,000 — while every other house on the block is valued around $275,000 — you're in trouble. If you aren't using an agent, an appraiser can use comparable current listings and recent sales to help you determine market value in your area.

Don't renovate your house beyond the property value your neighbourhood can support. A two-storey Georgian-style home would look pretty weird in a trailer park. Get detailed estimates of how much your intended renovations will cost — then compare the money you'll put into your home (buying costs + renovation costs) to the neighbouring home values. For example, a starter home in an area that's up and coming doesn't need to have $10,000 worth of granite countertops in the kitchen. Those counters most likely won't reflect the price point of the neighbourhood, and that money may be better spent on big-ticket items like a furnace, a roof, or windows. Alternatively, you can figure out how much you can spend on renovations without going over the average value of homes in your area, and then find out what improvements you can get for that much money. Will that budget be enough to turn the house into the dream palace you intended? If not, don't buy it. If you're buying with the intention of reselling, will that budget be enough to upgrade so that the new selling price will make you a profit? If not, don't buy it.

Your average resale home

Most resale houses fall into the category of adequate condition — houses that are in good condition structurally and are certainly livable, but will need to be recarpeted, repainted, or redecorated to become *your* home. Don't be afraid to tackle cosmetic changes — in fact, expect it. Although having to make structural, plumbing, or electrical repairs to your new home is cause for worry, basic finishing changes are par for the course. Putting a fresh coat of paint here and there, or refinishing the hardwood floors, is most often a worthwhile expense. If you're uncertain what everything will cost, make your offer subject to receiving and approving a contractor's or architect's estimate before committing to the purchase.

Your Neighbours: How Close Is Too Close?

Whether you're buying new or resale, you need to think about your neighbours and how much room you'd like in between your home and theirs. Varying degrees of "attachment" exist — the five most common are the following:

- **Single-family detached:** *A single-family detached* house sits by itself on its own lot. Ownership includes the entire structure and the lot. The owner or owners are responsible for all repairs and maintenance, property taxes, and associated costs.

- **Semi-detached:** *Semi-detached* houses are joined by a shared wall, but the structure as a whole (that is, both units) is independent of other houses on the street. Ownership includes your half of the structure and land, and you're responsible for all the costs and work associated with that half.

- **Link houses or carriage houses:** *Link houses* or *carriage houses* share a common foundation and a garage — usually separated into two garages that share a common wall — that provides a joint access route to the backyard. Often these houses share a basement wall so that they seem detached to passersby. Ownership and responsibilities are similar to those for semi-detached houses.

- **Rowhouses or townhouses:** *Rowhouses* or *townhouses* share a common wall on one or both sides. You may have full ownership of a townhouse, although in some cases, townhouses are condominiums. Often, a group of independently owned townhouses has a housing association that collects dues and handles some of the maintenance for the whole row.

- **Apartment units or condos:** *Apartment units,* also known as *condos,* are in low-rise or high-rise buildings that usually offer a secure entrance, elevators, and shared common areas — and lots of neighbours. We talk more about condos in Chapter 5.

Obviously, the closer your house is to your neighbours, the more exposed you are to potential noise and disturbances. Remember, sound doesn't travel in only one direction. Your neighbours' teenagers may drive you insane with loud music and frequent parties, but what sounds from your house drive them crazy? If your two dogs spend their days howling for you to come back from work, preventing the writer next door from completing her screenplay, you have a problem. If you can show your neighbours consideration, they'll probably show you the same respect.

Also, if you buy a home built close to your neighbours, the yard is generally quite small — which can be a good or a bad thing, depending on how you feel about yard work. You'll limit your options to expand your living space. Detached houses are easier to renovate.

Home Owning as an Investment

Investing in real estate has become extremely fashionable. But unlike some other fads, putting your money into the real estate market can make excellent short-term sense *and* see you through in the long run. Though your return on your real estate investment isn't as exciting as the stock market can be during exuberant times, it's a far sight better and more reliable than a slumping, sluggish market.

This section just touches on this topic; if you're really interested in becoming a real estate mogul, check out *Real Estate Investing For Canadians For Dummies* by Douglas Gray and Peter Mitham (Wiley).

Before purchasing property for investment, consult your financial planner, guru, psychic — whomever you trust — to make sure it fits into your long-term plans and any tax-related concerns.

Not all properties are purchased as a principal residence. Lending requirements now stipulate that a secondary or income property in many cases will not qualify for Canadian Mortgage and Housing Corporation (CMHC) financing, which means you need to have a minimum 20 percent down payment on the property. Lenders also take into account property taxes, maintenance, and insurance, so factor these in if you plan to purchase an investment property.

Many homebuyers may need the revenue from a basement suite to help them afford their dream house. Local bylaws and regulations regarding basement suites vary: Check with the local authorities before buying a house with a secondary suite. Check with your bank if you'll be relying on the revenue from a basement suite. Some banks will consider the rent from a basement suite as income, even if the basement suite is illegal. You may be able to qualify for a higher mortgage if you purchase a primary residence with a rental suite. Lenders will typically credit approximately 50 percent of the annual expected income from the property, giving you a chance to look in a higher price range.

A property with two legal suites is called a *duplex,* and three suites is a *triplex.* In a duplex, one of the units can be the owner's residence, and the other a rental unit. Depending on the circumstances you have arranged with your lender, the owner can rent out both units and the duplex can be a rental property, with the rent from both units helping to pay the mortgage. Duplexes are usually detached houses, but can occasionally be semi-detached (townhouses) as well. The owner of the duplex is responsible for all expenses and maintenance associated with the structure and lot (minus, of course, whatever costs are picked up by the tenants). If the owner intends to live in one of the units, financing the purchase of a duplex should be similar to the purchase of a single home, although some banks may require a higher down payment (and high-ratio CMHC insurance may not be available) for a duplex or triplex. As mentioned before, lenders will consider the rent from legal suites (and sometimes from unauthorized suites) as income, which will help buyers qualify for a mortgage they couldn't otherwise afford.

Obviously, the advantage of owning a duplex is that it will provide additional income via your tenants' rent. Buying a duplex can be a good long-term investment too — the income generated by the rental unit can increase the resale value of the property. The potential profit from renting will depend on location. Before you buy a duplex, find out what average rents are in the area.

Buying a half-duplex where each half of a building is owner-occupied is also possible. Half-duplexes can be side by side, top and bottom, or front to back to form a two-unit apartment building, with many of the maintenance costs split between the two owners.

Talk to a lawyer about the legalities of buying a rental property. If the rental suite currently has tenants, you need to know where you stand. Confirm what your rights are according to the Residential Tenancies Act in your province. Find out what the local market will bear for a suite in a duplex. Make sure the home has been registered as a duplex, to ensure renting out part of the house is legal. Just because the previous owner rented out the basement doesn't mean it was allowed. The Blue Pages in the phone book will list the phone number for the provincial Tenancy Branch, which can answer any questions about tenant and landlord rights and the paperwork necessary to comply with the provincial legislation.

Buying a duplex — or any other property that will have tenants — doesn't often go as swimmingly as planned. Most people don't realize how much work, or how expensive, it is to be a landlord. Don't take the responsibility lightly. If your tenant's toilet springs a leak, you have to look after it, or if they're late with the rent, you have to deal with the financial strain.

Your financial adviser can tell you how owning a rental property will affect your income taxes — both now and when you sell. If you claim part of a home's rental income as personal income and write off part of your home expenses, this may affect your claim to principal residence tax exemption should you realize a profit when you sell the house. (See Chapter 15 for details on the tax benefits of the principal residence exemption.)

Part II
Discovering Your Perfect Home

In this part . . .

Close your eyes (okay, don't really close your eyes 'til you've finished reading the rest of these instructions), lean back, put your feet up, and picture your ideal home. Maybe it's a century-old Victorian manor with turrets and a coach house. Maybe it's a modernist square, with kilometres of skylights and orderly gardens. Maybe it's a condo with a view of the park, a huge balcony, on-site tennis court, and bowling alley. Got a good picture of it? Excellent. Take a mental snapshot — that's probably the only way you're going to see that home.

Yes, most of us have to settle a bit. But if you're old enough to buy a house, you're probably familiar with the fine art of compromise by now. This section will help you prioritize what you need, what you want, and what you'd be really lucky to find. After you've figured that out, you'll find advice on where to look and what to look for, as well as tips on discriminating between real and imagined benefits, obvious and not-so-obvious drawbacks.

Chapter 5

All About Condominiums

. . . .

In This Chapter

▶ Considering condominiums

▶ Weighing your options: New, previously owned, and conversions

▶ Looking at the condominium corporation and the condominium certificate

▶ Joining a co-op

. . . .

*Y*ou're a social butterfly and love being surrounded by others; you love the convenience of having the gym a short elevator ride away; you love the security of a 24-hour doorman; you love the spectacular view from the 27th floor; and you love not having to worry about yard work. If all of these things describe you, well, you're a condo dweller through and through.

To lots of people, the word *condominium* is associated with living in the equivalent of a beehive: you're just one of the little worker drones in cookie-cutter accommodations. That notion is simply not true, and in this chapter, you discover why. "Condominium" refers *only* to a type of ownership, *not* to a type of architecture. Condo owners have sole ownership of their individual units (which could be townhouses), and they share the right to use common areas with other unit owners.

In British Columbia, condominiums are often called *strata units,* especially in listings and legal documents. This name traces back to 1967, and comes from all the way down under. Before 1966, B.C. lacked condominium legislation, so, seeing a need for one, the province simply adopted New South Wales's. This legislation was called "The Strata Titles Act of New South Wales, Australia." In 1980, B.C. changed the name to the Condominium Act, but the term *condominium* was not used once within the Act itself. Then, in 2000, the act governing condominiums in B.C. was changed to the Strata Property Act. So if you're on the West Coast you'll hear "strata title" and "strata unit" an awful lot.

Weighing the Ups and Downs of Condo Living

Whether you buy into a *new condominium corporation* (the organization responsible for the condominium's upkeep) or an established one, there are several advantages to condo living:

- ✔ **Greater security:** Some condominium residences have a 24-hour concierge to screen visitors to the building. In a modern condominium complex, you can expect security cameras and coded passes for access to the building, elevators, garage, and amenities.

- ✔ **Low maintenance:** You have less outside maintenance to do — no house painting in the blistering summer sun for you! Never again will you muck out an eavestrough (or argue with your partner over who will do it). In most cases, yard work is also a thing of the past for a new condo owner.

- ✔ **Amenities:** Much like a university residence, a condominium complex may feature on-site amenities such as a convenience store, gym, laundry and dry-cleaning facilities, swimming pool, and sometimes even a putting green! (Keep in mind though, the more amenities, the higher your monthly condo fees will be!)

- ✔ **Sense of community:** Ideally, you'll find that a condominium has an interactive community of people living within it. Although you may not get along with everyone at the condo meetings, you'll likely discover a supportive group of residents who make you feel at home.

Before you start rubbing your hands together anticipating your carefree lifestyle as a condominium owner, let us bring to light a few of the downsides as well:

- ✔ **Less autonomy:** You can't always do exactly what you like — you may not be able to hang bright curtains in your windows, blast the radio on your balcony, or accept the little kitten your friend brings for your birthday.

- ✔ **Unpleasant restrictions:** You may have to accept inflexible rules or disagreeable decisions made democratically by your condo corporation. You may be forced to compromise on rules governing the conduct of condo owners, or issues regarding the building structure or facilities (for example, if everyone in the condo complex but you votes in favour of erecting a 20-foot-tall gold statue in the lobby, you're stuck paying for your share of the cost regardless).

- ✔ **Proximity to neighbours:** Your home will be very close to your neighbours, and you may not get along with them — but you'll still share a business and managerial role with them in the condominium corporation.

✔ **Maintenance concerns:** You must depend on the condominium corporation (and the management company they hire, in most cases) to handle building repairs and to be financially responsible with your maintenance fees. For example, you may feel your building needs a new roof, and that putting it off will be more costly in the long run. The condo corp may feel otherwise. Your neighbours will need to agree with you in order for that new roof to proceed.

✔ **Financial risk:** You share responsibility for large, unexpected repair bills — for example, if your condo springs an ominous leak.

When you buy your condo, it'll become your own neighbourhood, just like if you had a house on a little street in the 'burbs. Often the owner of the condo unit is the person who lives there, but in some buildings renters occupy many of the units. Ask the property manager or your real estate agent for the renter/owner ratio before you buy. Owners who live in their condos tend to be much more hands-on as neighbours, and concerned with the upkeep of the property, including the common areas. Just think of the first place you rented: the dirty dishes in the sink, the scrapes in the wall from where you accidently smacked the door — and all the other things that you may have taken better care of if they had belonged to you.

Mondo Condos

Just like any shopping expedition, you've got a variety of choices when it comes to picking what condo is right for you, and a lot of it comes down to your own individual taste and lifestyle. In this section, we explain some of your options and discuss their pros and cons.

Shiny and new

Maybe you've entered the witness protection program and are creating a whole new life, and need a brand-new home to match . . . or maybe you're just attracted to the idea of owning a completely new unit. While we can't really comment on the witness protection thing, we can say that you're not alone when it comes to wanting a newly built condo. These days, in many Canadian cities, condo buildings seem to be springing up everywhere. You can buy a condominium from the developer months, or even years, before the building is finished.

Each province has individual New Home Warranty Programs to protect you, the condo/homebuyer, in case the developer is unable to follow through with the transaction, or if the developer is not around to fix problems that occur during the warranty period after the building is finished. In the Appendix you can get the contact information for the New Home Warranty Program for your province.

Look into what warranty the developer is offering, and see if warranties have been honoured willingly in the developer's other projects.

The good stuff

People always rave about new-car smell, but it doesn't hold a candle next to the scent of a brand-new condo. And that's not the only reason why you may be interested in buying new:

- ✔ **You're starting from scratch (or unscratched, actually).** New condominiums have never been lived in before, and the idea of starting with a blank canvas is very appealing. You get unscratched floors, a brand-new bathtub, and blank walls to do up any way you want. Plus, you don't have to deal with a previous owner leaving junk behind.

- ✔ **You're in charge of the details.** Most developers offer a variety of colour schemes and flooring choices, as well as upgrades to personalize your condo. The beauty is that you make all the decisions, and your home is already just the way you want it on the day you move in.

- ✔ **You're a modernist.** If it's a brand-new building and things like appliances are included, you'll get a new fridge and stove, and an up-to-date washer and dryer, so you won't have to deal with leaky, noisy, old appliances that weren't well maintained. The developer may have a standard appliance package, or you may want to upgrade to something really super — you know, some fridges have built-in televisions . . .

- ✔ **You get to create condo culture.** Remember when you changed schools in grade ten mid-year, and you found it hard to fit in because everyone already had their own groups of friends? Well, with a new condo, everyone is new and you have the chance to be a founding member of the condo's "culture," if you will. You attend the condo meetings from the start and feel more like an important part of the community, instead of the new kid on the block.

The not-so-good stuff

Now, we don't want to frighten you away from buying a new building, but we do want to help you to be as informed as possible before you make this massive purchase. You should know about a couple of possible detriments to buying a new condo.

Condo corporation concerns

When you buy new, you face some uncertainty about the stability of a new corporation — you cannot be sure that you'll have the best property managers or a competent board of directors. If the corporation is mismanaged or, worse, has insufficient funds, you're in serious trouble should your condo building require repairs, renovations, or upgrades.

If any repairs aren't covered by the developer's warranty (or the provincial New Home Warranty Program), the condo fees the owners in a new building pay may be raised to cover any financial shortfalls. In this situation, unit owners may even be forced to foot the entire bill, and the resale value of the unit may be drastically reduced.

Delayed move-in dates

You've bought your condo, you've picked out all its special features, and of course, you can't wait to move in. You set the move-in date at the time of purchase, so you've given notice on your apartment, eager to shake off the shackles of renting once and for all . . . or so you think. Just when everything is all set, you get a letter from the developer pushing your move-in date back another three months. "Is this legal?" you ask yourself.

Well, yes, it is legal. In your agreement of purchase and sale (see Chapter 10 for more information and a sample agreement), the developer probably included a clause that gives him or her the right to delay the date of occupancy, which is a real problem if you've already turned your life upside down anticipating the original move-in date. Before you sign anything, be sure you're aware of such a clause in your contract. Always read the fine print, because the small details you'll find there may extend your move-in date beyond what you (and the developer) are expecting.

The clause in the agreement of purchase and sale that deals with move-in dates usually says something like this: *"If the condominium unit is not ready for occupancy on the specified completion date, the developer may, by written notice to the buyer or the buyer's solicitor, extend the completion date at any time and from time to time as required to any date determined by the developer, by which time the developer expects the condominium unit will be ready for occupancy and a separate title for the condominium unit issued."*

Legally, with such a clause, developers have the right to extend the date of occupancy, as long as they provide buyers with sufficient notice, which varies depending on which province you call home and what you have agreed to in your contract.

We hope you never have to face delayed occupancy, but it does make you understand why your mother always told you to wear clean underwear. In other words, it's best to be prepared. If you're moving out of a rental, you may be able to extend your lease a bit or continue month to month. Check with friends or relatives, just in case you need a temporary place to stay, and budget some extra cash for any temporary living expenses (room rental, motel). Make a list of storage companies where you could keep your stuff until the suite is ready. Not being able to move into your condo isn't the ideal situation, but having a plan B (or even C) helps make things a lot easier.

The developer is required to give you sufficient notice if your date of occupancy needs to be extended. If no clause exists in your contract to delay your move-in date, or you haven't received proper notice that your condo won't be ready when the time comes, each province has homeowner legislation to protect you in such a case. Knowing your rights is always important.

When you initially visit a condo development or speak with the developer or his or her representatives, find out what the anticipated date of occupancy is and then consider whether or not it's realistic. Sometimes, depending on the type of development you're interested in, the occupancy date can be years away. Something else to keep in mind: If the condo won't be ready for occupancy for two years, will your life still fit that condo? If you're in your 20s (or any age, really), a lot can happen in two years. You may be single when you sign the purchase contract, but married with a baby on the way when the condo is finished!

Your real estate agent can offer valuable advice in this area, too. If the developer swears up and down that everything will be ready in four months but digging hasn't even started yet, be careful. If the developer says three to four weeks, plan to stay where you are or make alternative arrangements — the suite and the building probably won't be ready that soon. (And you may want to rethink the purchase. Here's someone who obviously has no ability to budget or schedule time!) If, say, the building is at the drywall stage and the developer anticipates you'll be moving into the unit in six to eight weeks, this timeline is much more realistic.

The whole building has to be ready before you can move in — the developer needs to get an *occupancy permit* for the entire building from the local town, municipal, or city government. Even if your own suite is ready and finished, you can't move into the building until an occupancy permit indicates that the entire building is safe, and the elevators, sprinklers, and emergency systems are all working. The one variation from this rule may occur in a phased townhouse development, where a *partial occupancy permit* may be issued to cover different phases of a project as they're finished.

Condo assignment sales

What if that beautiful condo development you've been lusting after is all sold out, even before anyone's moved in? Not to fear, all is not yet lost. You may be able to buy a unit in the development through an *assignment sale,* the resale of a condo unit before the building is finished. Assignment sales usually involve three major players:

- The developer
- The original buyer (*the assignor*)
- A second buyer (*the assignee*) who buys the unit from the original buyer

Lofty aspirations

Lofts have become quite popular among city dwellers, and believe it or not, not every person who owns one is a tortured artist. A *loft* is just a specific style of condominium (assuming we're talking about lofts you buy, not lofts you rent), and the same general pros, cons, and considerations apply. The difference between what's marketed as a loft and what's marketed as a condo has to do with architectural style and, potentially, how "finished" the living space will be when you purchase it.

Lofts have open floor plans and typically high ceilings, often with exposed pipes and beams, and large windows that let in plenty of natural light. Many are in older buildings and warehouses that have been converted into residential units — if you're looking at a converted building, make certain that the structure is sound, safe, and reasonably efficient (and read more about conversions later in this chapter). Some "hard" lofts have no internal walls at all; other "soft" lofts have three or four walls.

Lofts can come equipped with as many features and facilities as traditional condominium complexes. On the other hand, you can purchase "raw" lofts that are devoid of appliances and sometimes even plumbing. A raw loft gives you the freedom to finish the space to best suit your lifestyle and taste, but it also means that extra work, time, hassle, and money have to go into your living space before you can actually start living there.

Whether loft living is for you greatly depends on your lifestyle and taste. Clearly, if you're at all opposed to sound travelling from one end of your living space clear across to the other, a loft is not for you. You may also want to rethink buying a loft if you need the creature comforts of an established neighbourhood. Many lofts can be in "transitional" neighbourhoods that aren't traditionally residential, and the area may lack services and amenities such as a grocery store or a place to rent DVDs. Getting a litre of milk at 8:00 p.m. may take a long hike or drive.

If you're thinking about buying a loft as an investment property, keep in mind that, like any trend, their popularity may not stand the test of time. If loft living goes out of fashion as quickly as it came in, you may find it's a difficult property to unload.

An assignment sale occurs when the assignor transfers the contract and all its terms to the person (you) who wants to buy the unit and become the new owner. Essentially, the original buyer (the assignor) will "flip" the contract to the assignee. When the building is finished, you're granted title (it's not like being knighted, but it's still pretty cool) to the property, which means it's officially yours.

Permission from the developer (in writing, of course) is always required for an assignment to take place. The assignee is buying the contract to purchase the condo, and it's a legal deal, with paperwork and money exchanges and some tricky jargon thrown in, so you'll definitely need a lawyer and an experienced real estate agent to make sure you get it all right.

The assignor isn't off the hook for the sale until the assignee closes on the purchase of the condo as specified in the original contract. If the assignee doesn't complete the sale as specified in the original contract, the assignor is, in most cases, still liable for any damages suffered by the developer.

Not all new developments allow their condos to be assigned — the contract may contain a clause between the original buyer and the developer denying the buyer permission to assign the contract to a subsequent buyer during the construction period.

Assignment listings are very often not listed on the Multiple Listing Service (MLS) system because the assignor doesn't own the unit (the developer still owns it) and Real Estate Boards across Canada usually require the owner to sign a listing form. An assignment listing can be listed on MLS only if the developer consents, but many developers don't want an already-sold property to be re-listed, because it may be in competition with units that the developer has not yet sold. (For more on MLS listings, see Chapter 8.)

Questions to ask when buying new

Some new condominiums are up for sale long before they're built. Earlier in this chapter we talk about the possible financial risks of dealing with a new corporation, but what about the risk of buying something before it's even finished? You may find the model suite or a slick photograph to be pretty seductive, but be sure to get the hard facts about your future condo before you hand over any money. Here are some questions to ask:

✔ **Who are the people in my neighbourhood?** Chances are, if the brochure shows groups of elderly people playing canasta and mentions the excellent on-site medical facility, and you're 28 years old with a dog and a brand-new barbecue, you may be looking at the wrong development.

✔ **Where will the heating vent, air-conditioning vent, and electrical boxes be placed?** You don't want a vent smack dab in the middle of the living room wall. If these systems are in the wrong spots, the look of your living space can be seriously affected.

✔ **Will my walls be soundproof or paper-thin?** Because you'll be living so close to your neighbours, finding out about the quality of the building materials and if any provisions have been made to ensure privacy is important.

✔ **What options do I have?** Can you choose light fixtures, countertops, or cupboard handles specifically for your unit? What appliances are included, and do you have any choice as to what kinds?

✔ **How big is my condo, really?** Do the floor plan measurements include both inside and outside walls, or do they represent the actual floor space? A foot or so can make a big difference when you're trying to fit that L-shaped couch into your new place.

✔ **How's my view?** Although you can't see your exact view before construction is completed, know which way your unit will face, which floor you'll be on, and what'll be outside your window. Looking at the same neon billboard every day gets pretty old, pretty fast. Many developers have photos of the anticipated view from the unit — and these aerial pictures can give you a great idea of the view, and how the view and outlook varies from floor to floor. (Keep in mind that if a new high-rise goes up right beside you, all bets are off.) If you're looking at a lower-floor unit, ask where the garbage cans are going — you don't want to be admiring the smelly dumpsters from your living room.

✔ **What's in it for me?** Does the purchase price include a parking spot? Will there be a pool or a rooftop garden? Do you have to pay extra for a storage locker? Find out exactly what you're getting, and confirm everything in writing so you're not surprised later on.

Previously enjoyed

We admit it; we're biased: We think that buying from an established condo corporation is the safest way to go. Buying resale may not be as flashy as buying a brand-new unit, but it's definitely got its advantages, which we discuss. However, because we're nothing if not fair, we also talk about the downsides.

The ups

When you buy from an established condo corporation, you're buying into a building with a documented history. An established condo corporation has a track record you can look to for assurance that the property managers have unit owners' best interests at heart. You have a chance to review how the building's run and maintained before you decide to buy a suite. You have access to minutes of the building meetings to see how the corporation has responded in the past when repairs were necessary or emergencies arose. You can find out how well the reserve fund has been maintained, how well the governing body has responded to owners' requests for upgrades, and if condo fees have increased or are about to increase because of planned renovations.

Most of this information about a condo's history will be provided by the listing agent if you show serious interest in the condo. You should always make an offer subject to your approving the building's records and so on to get everything you need (for more on "subject to" offers, see Chapter 10). Having all this information ahead of time provides peace of mind, knowing that you're making a sound investment.

Besides having the condo corporation's history readily available for you to investigate, you should consider a resale condo for other reasons:

✔ **You may save a little money.** Like anything, you pay a premium for new. So the privilege of owning a new unit costs a little more than a similar resale (previously owned) unit. Plus, the biggest saving of all: You don't pay GST or HST on resale housing . . . yippee!

✔ **You can see the whole picture before deciding to buy.** As children, we're taught to "use our imaginations," but that's not really the best course of action when you're investing in a home. Because a resale condo is already built, you can check out the view and the size of your space and see how well the grounds are maintained, and you won't get any last-minute surprises after you move in.

✔ **You won't have to wait.** Very particular circumstances notwithstanding, the move-in date you establish with the previous owner will stick, because you don't have to worry about construction delays or labour problems with a condo that already exists.

✔ **You can find out the condo's history.** Ask current owners what they like and don't like about the building. Find out if they've experienced problems in the past, and how well management handled these situations. If someone says everything's great except that the hot water hasn't worked for three weeks, you may want to think things over.

✔ **You can know in advance if you'll fit in.** Chat with your potential neighbours and find out what kind of people live in the building. No, you won't like everyone, and, shockingly, not everyone will like you, but find out if you at least have similar lifestyles and want the same things for the condo corporation.

✔ **You know the rules in advance, as well.** For example, when purchasing brand new, no rental restrictions may initially apply. You may find that a lot of the buyers purchased their units as an investment, and you may end up with neighbours that are all renters. A resale unit will more likely have more concrete restrictions on things like rentals, so if you want to live with other owners who have a vested interest in the property, resale may be the way to go.

The downs

Resale sounds pretty good, doesn't it? Just consider a few things before you make the big decision:

✔ **You're no Martha Stewart.** If decorating or, rather, redecorating isn't your thing, know that you'll probably have to face it with a resale condo. You may possibly think the seller's electric pink bathroom with a duck-shaped shower head is gorgeous (or hilarious), but more likely you'll want to make the room your own, which takes a bit more time than when you start off with completely blank walls.

✔ **You may need to make some upgrades.** Although the unit will have been inspected, you may find that the stove doesn't have all the bells and whistles you need for your famous fusion cooking, or that the shower head doesn't have the right water pressure, so you'll have to upgrade. Even if you're happy with what you've got, the fixtures and appliances may be reaching the end of their lifespan. For example, if the toilet or ceiling fan breaks down, you'll have to pay for the repair or replacement when you own the suite.

✔ **You're not covered by your province's New Home Warranty Program.** The program applies to new homes only — it doesn't apply to properties already built, although the balance of the warranty will transfer to second owners if they buy the unit in the warranty period.

Newly converted

Somewhere in between old and new, conversion condominiums give you a little bit of both. These condos are residential buildings that were once something other than a condo. Some are former apartments that switched over to condo status, some are ex–office buildings. But others have had pretty interesting past lives as schools, churches, warehouses, or factories, and may be perfect for you if you're looking for a cool and unusual home.

You may also like a conversion because in some cases the building exists in an area, such as a warehouse district, that offers you an amount of space that would normally be out of your price range if it were built in the hot and trendy condo neighbourhood. Ah, the joys of gentrification . . . the transition of commercial and industrial areas into residential neighbourhoods. These new neighbourhoods may not be for everyone, but if you're overcome by the pioneering spirit, a funky conversion in a non-residential area may offer you more bang for your buck.

Although you may love the idea of living in a building with history, you need to think about the practical impact that old exterior will have on your unit. All the internal parts of the building will be new (the developer usually has to gut the old building and create the new units within its shell), but the outside may not offer you everything you want in a home, especially if the building is older. If it's an old church that's been converted, you may not get as many windows and balconies as you would in a new building.

If you're keen to buy a conversion condo, have the building inspected to make sure major renovations won't be needed shortly after you move in (see Chapter 19 for information on inspections). A qualified home inspection can check that the quality of the construction and design are good and functional and won't lead to major problems down the road.

Buying a *pre-sale* (the building is not yet built) conversion condo opens you up to some risks. Your only chance to do a building inspection will be after the building is finished — but by that time, you've already committed to buy the suite. And because the condominium corporation won't have had time to build up a decent reserve fund, condo fees can potentially skyrocket if important repairs are needed. Also, not every province's New Home Warranty Program covers conversion condos, because they're considered "old" on the outside even if they're new on the inside. Be sure to check with the warranty program in your province before you buy.

Owning Your Piece of the Condominium Corporation Pie

When you buy a condo, you're buying an interest in the condominium corporation and the common, shared property of the condominium complex. As a unit owner, you have some say in how the condominium corporation, sometimes called *the strata corporation* in B.C., conducts itself. The corporation has a board of directors, a president, and a treasurer (the terminology will vary from province to province) who are elected by the owners in the building. Usually, ownership of one unit equals one vote.

Although the board of directors is composed of condominium unit owners, boards often hire professional property managers to act under their supervision. The corporation has a legal obligation to hold regular meetings that all unit owners can attend. Having information about how the corporation is run is your right, but taking an active role in this process is your responsibility also.

Establishing your expenses: The condominium certificate

When you own a home, you're responsible for all improvements and repairs to your property. Things are less straightforward with a condominium, so a document is needed to clear up who's on the hook for what. The *condominium certificate* lays out exactly which expenses are the responsibility of the condo corporation, which fall to individual owners, and which will be shared by all unit owners. The condominium certificate also outlines the financial status of the condominium corporation.

The certificate will tell you what your monthly condo fees will be for shared expenses, what your individual unit costs will be, and what the financial status of the corporation is — especially regarding the reserve fund. A *reserve fund* is money put away by the corporation for any repairs or upgrades that become necessary. Usually, a portion of your monthly condo fee goes into this fund. Having a well-maintained reserve fund is crucial.

The condominium certificate will usually tell you if the condo corporation is involved in any legal proceedings, and may outline how many units in the building are rented and how many are owner-occupied.

The condominium certificate will also show if the seller has paid all the fees. If the seller hasn't paid the condo fees, provisions exist for any unpaid fees to be paid upon the sale of the unit. Your real estate agent or lawyer can advise you on how to proceed with your purchase, but make sure you don't get stuck with any of the seller's liabilities.

Before buying into an existing building, review a current condominium certificate prepared by the condominium corporation or the property manager acting on behalf of the building. If you're buying into a new building, in lieu of an existing condominium certificate, you have the right to ask the developer for a copy of the proposed condominium certificate (if one is available) or a *full disclosure statement* or *prospectus*. This document should contain a proposed budget and outline a number of features for the new development. (If no proposed budget exists, get out as fast as you can!) Have this document reviewed by a lawyer before agreeing to purchase a unit.

Living by the rules: condos and condon'ts

In addition to the financial details of ownership, the condominium certificate lays out the bylaws that are the code of conduct for residents. The certificate stipulates how many units can be rented, and whether pets are allowed, vamong other things.

Bylaws for new condos

For a new development, the new owners will establish a new set of bylaws and regulations when the building has transferred from the developer to the individual owners. Your province's legislation regarding condominiums should form the basis of the bylaws. The advantage of buying a unit in a new building is that you can have a say in the formation of the new bylaws and rules and regulations.

You have to assume that the proposed rules will be enforced. But as with any rules, the bylaws are good only insofar as they are enforced. When you decide to buy a new condominium, you have no way of knowing who will buy in that complex and how the rules will change in accordance with the other residents' tastes and demands. On the other hand, the proposed bylaws may not change after you move in, but they may not be enforced by the corporation or, more important, by the other residents.

If a big selling point with you is the proposed bylaw stating that there will be "quiet hours" after 10:00 p.m., you have no guarantee that this will be enforced. If some residents ignore the rule and other residents don't seem to care (or are kind of hard of hearing), you may simply have to put up with noise all night long. Even if residents get up in arms over the ill conduct of a few, complaints may fall on deaf ears — you can't be sure the governing body will be receptive. In all provinces getting rid of a problem tenant is possible, but removing a problem owner is very difficult.

Bylaws for established condos

In a well-established complex, many uncertainties about the rules disappear. You can go to the complex and talk to the present owners. We suggest you make several visits to any new home you're considering buying. You can call the property managers for the building to see if they have any insight into the building and the running of the complex in general. Find out how any complaints about bylaw violations have been received and handled, what rules are enforced, how often or drastically the bylaws have been changed, and so on. All this adds up to a better understanding of the lifestyle in the complex and how many compromises you'll have to make while living there. Often, you can discern a lot of this information by reading the minutes of the board meetings: You can see what issues have been brought up and, by following the minutes from meeting to meeting, how those issues were addressed. Finding out just how quickly owners' concerns are dealt with can give you an idea of how proactive the building is when it comes to solving problems.

Visit the condo complex more than once when you're doing your research. Go at different times of the day and night to get a real feel for the atmosphere. An agent may have you drop by at the best time for showcasing the unit, so you may end up with an inflated opinion.

Living Co-operatively

Two different kinds of co-ops exist: *market co-ops* and *non-market (subsidized) co-ops*. Although the units in a market co-op are for sale, those in a non-market co-op are for rent only and cannot be sold. In this book, because we're all about buying and selling, we focus on market co-ops. Co-operative housing is often thought of as synonymous with low-income housing, but this simply isn't the case.

Co-operative living is something of a compromise between house living and condo living. Co-ops retain the community feel of a condo complex but with greater control over living space. In a market co-operative, owners don't own a unit itself; rather, they jointly own, with the other members of the co-op, the *co-operative corporation*, which is the corporation that owns the structures and land that form the co-op. Owners are assigned shares in the company based on the size of their unit — and these shares are the owner's "equity" in their unit. As a shareholder in a co-op corporation, you're entitled to occupy one of its units. The lease you have on the unit is different from a rental lease — it gives you the legal and exclusive right to occupy that unit (so long as all the stated obligations to the co-op corporation are met), and it gives you the right to participate in governance of the co-op. Take note: Whereas in a condo complex you have the option to participate, in a co-op you're *expected* to put in the time and effort required to take your share of responsibility for the governance of the community. In fact, in a market co-op you must be approved by the board of directors (made up of other elected owners) before buying in. When you buy in to a condo, you approve the building. When you buy in to a co-op, the building approves you.

Finding a bank that will finance the purchase of a co-op unit may be tricky, but not impossible. The equity in the suite is the assigned shares in the corporation, and many banks won't accept these shares as collateral for a mortgage. Therefore, co-ops are both harder to buy and harder to sell. Co-ops will generally appreciate as the market moves up (or depreciate as it slides down), but because any potential buyer may have difficulty securing a mortgage, co-ops tend to have lower market values than equivalent freehold condos.

Considering the co-op's pros

You may be inclined toward buying a co-op rather than a condominium because of the following reasons:

- ✔ **More bang for your buck:** The price will be lower, so you should get a larger unit for your money than you would get in a conventional, freehold condominium.

- ✔ **You're not just buying, you're joining:** In contrast to condominium corporations, many non-market co-ops are non-profit organizations.

- ✔ **You have lower costs:** Monthly fees are typically less in a co-op compared to those of a condo (and monthly fees are set by a vote of the co-op members).

- ✔ **You perform less maintenance than with a house:** As with a condo, some of the maintenance and yard work won't be your responsibility.

- ✔ **Your opinion counts:** Your views will probably have greater weight in a smaller co-operative community than in a larger one.

- ✔ **You have some influence over who lives there:** As a co-op member, you have a say in who is allowed to purchase shares in the co-op corporation (and, therefore, who your neighbours will be) if you sit on the board of directors.

Weighing the co-op's cons

Some serious disadvantages to co-operative living should also be considered:

- ✔ **Member approval controls the community:** Selling the right to your unit requires that your buyer be approved by the co-op community.

- ✔ **Limited choice of areas:** You may not be able to find a co-op in the neighbourhood you want.

✔ **Financial arrangements:** Getting financial backing for the purchase of a co-op is often more difficult than with a condo, and mortgage rates are often higher.

✔ **Community commitments:** Being a participating member of the co-op community takes time and effort.

✔ **Participation in the upkeep of the co-op:** Some maintenance and yard work *will* be your responsibility.

✔ **Regulations:** Often, the codes of conduct for members of a co-op are similar to those of condo owners, and these codes may be restrictive.

✔ **Group finances:** If another member of the co-op goes broke, you may be affected.

Chapter 6

Home-Buying Help

You're taking a really big step when you decide to purchase a house. Fortunately, lots of experienced people are around to help. Do yourself a favour and pick a good team. Don't be afraid to ask a lot of questions and shop around until you find professionals you have confidence in and you can relate to. In this chapter, we talk about some of the key players on your home-buying team:

✔ Your real estate agent

✔ Your appraiser

✔ Your lawyer

Understanding the Agent's Role

Lots of real estate agents will want to work with you. Make sure you find one you want to work with. You will rely on your agent for information and advice about your specific situation. Your agent deals with the sellers, negotiates for you, and advises you throughout the process. When you pick an agent to work with, you want to make sure that you're a good fit, personality-wise.

Buying a house without the right team behind you is a lot like playing hide-and-seek . . . blindfolded. So, when you decide to work with an agent, here are some of the key qualities to look for:

✔ **Knowledge:** Your agent must be familiar with the neighbourhoods you like and the style and price range of house you are looking for. So if you want to buy a condo in Toronto, you probably won't want to rely on that agent friend of yours in Ottawa.

✔ **Experience:** Your agent should be someone who has worked with clients like you before, who knows how to help you buy the house you want for a fair price, and who can anticipate problems before they come up.

✔ **Time:** Your agent must be willing to spend time to give you the support and direction you need . . . when you need it. If you place a call to your agent and don't hear back within 24 hours (but preferably much less!), you may not get the service you need.

✔ **Contacts:** Your agent should have a list of colleagues and advisers to call in when you need financial advice or assistance, legal work, appraisals, and so on.

✔ **Ethics:** Your agent should always have your best interests in mind. If you feel uncomfortable with something your agent says or does, you may want to move on.

✔ **Established broker/office manager:** Your agent relies on the backup of a respected and well-connected broker who is often also the office manager. If a serious problem arises, you'll rely on this indispensable person too.

✔ **Multimedia skills:** Your agent should be able to search listings on the Internet and be readily available via e-mail, or even text.

Figuring out your relationship with your agent and the broker/manager

We know, you thought you had your work cut out for you just understanding the relationships you already have in your life. Well, the relationships among you, your agent, and the agent's broker can be no less confusing. But help is on the way! In this section, we take you through the ins and outs of what an agent and a broker do, and then talk a bit about the different types of agents out there.

✔ **Real estate agent (also sometimes referred to as salesperson, Realtor representative, or sales representative):** Subcontracted by the broker to work on behalf of the buyer or seller, or, occasionally, both.

✔ **Broker or managing broker/nominee:** Legal "agent" who works on behalf of the buyer or seller, or both; usually serves as an office manager overseeing daily operations, and also reviews all transactions.

When you decide to work with a real estate agent, you are effectively engaging the services of the agent's broker as well, regardless of whether you meet that individual. The broker is the person you can turn to if things go terribly, terribly wrong and your agent can't manage the situation. A skilled broker is able to call in favours if bureaucratic roadblocks or procedural questions arise, or if your home purchase spirals into one of the rare legal disputes that can happen when closing a real estate deal.

Note: Some real estate agents also have the qualifications to legally call themselves brokers, but they tend to use the more commonly understood term of *agent* or even *representative*. In many provinces, a broker's (or managing broker's) licence requires additional training and testing and a licence designation beyond that of a salesperson. With this extra education, an individual can own a brokerage or run an office (be the "nominee" for the office) and ensure that the salespeople and all of the office's trust accounts adhere to the requirements of the provincial Real Estate Act.

A broker or brokerage company, and by extension a real estate agent, may be a seller's agent or a buyer's agent. In some cases, real estate agents working for the same broker will represent both the seller and the buyer in a deal. Although each party has its own real estate agent, because both agents work for the same broker or legal agent, the situation is referred to as *dual agency*. The agent that you are working with to find a home may show you a property that is listed with his or her office. If you buy that property, you will have to agree to enter into a limited dual agency agreement. For more on agency relationships, see Chapter 17.

Another term you will encounter is *Realtor*. This term is a trademark of the Canadian Real Estate Association (CREA). Only brokers and real estate agents who are CREA members may use this term to describe themselves professionally. Extensive training and continuing education are required. Realtors also follow a very strict Code of Ethics and Standards of Business Practice, designed to protect *your* best interests.

The rules and regulations governing agency relationships vary a bit from province to province. Ask your local real estate board or your provincial real estate council for specifics. In general, agency relationships break down as follows.

Seller's agent

When real estate agents are *seller's agents,* they owe full loyalty to sellers and must give them all information and take every action to obtain the highest price and best conditions of sale for them. Don't expect the seller's agent to tip you, as a buyer, off to the fact that a seller is anxious to move and will probably accept $10,000 less than the asking price. And if you meet a seller's agent at an open house, be discreet. If you say that you're going to put in a bid on the home at $10,000 less than the asking price, but you're willing to pay full price in order to get into the neighbourhood, the seller's agent is legally obliged to disclose that information to the seller. Remember the one point in your favour: The seller's agent also has a legal obligation to tell you, the buyer, if he knows of any serious problems with the home being sold. Expect honest, complete answers to your inquiries.

Buyer's agent

Surprise, surprise — a *buyer's agent* works in the best interests of buyers. Even though your buyer's agent's commission is usually paid out of the seller's proceeds from the sale, her legal and ethical duties are to you. Your buyer's agent should keep your personal and financial information confidential. If the sellers let slip that they're going through a messy divorce and want to sell the house as soon as possible, your buyer's agent will share this information with you. She'll also let you know if she finds out that the sellers are willing to accept a lower price. Your buyer's agent will be able to look at comparable properties and advise you on how much is reasonable to offer on the homes you're considering. A buyer's agent negotiates the best deal possible on the buyer's behalf, ideally the lowest price and best conditions for the buyer.

If you want to purchase a home that is "For Sale by Owner," don't be afraid to bring in an agent to represent you in the purchase. Just because the seller wants to go it alone doesn't mean you have to. You may be responsible for paying the agent a standard fee or a commission (if you cannot get the seller to absorb the cost), but having a professional prepare the paperwork, as well as having access to info about comparable properties, may give you huge piece of mind.

Dual agency

If both the buyer's and the seller's agents work for the same broker or brokerage company, this is called *dual agency*. One company is brokering a deal between two parties, and it legally represents both sides. This situation can open up a number of conflict-of-interest concerns.

To head off any problems, the broker is legally obliged to tell you and the seller that he (or his company) is representing both the buyer and the seller. Ask the broker to explain clearly what the implications are for the sale negotiations. You will be asked to accept the dual agency situation in writing. If you're unsure what to do, contact your local real estate board for clarification. Although both agents may work out of different offices and not know each other, if they work for the same company they must also acknowledge in writing that they are in a dual agency situation.

Suppose you haven't chosen an agent and you go to an open house and absolutely love the house. What do you do? Remember that the agent holding the open house works for the seller. If you're comfortable with that agent, you can ask her to represent you, and enter into a limited dual agency agreement. However, if you aren't comfortable with the agent or the concept of a dual agency relationship, you can scramble and find another agent to work with you as your buying agent. You don't have to work with the agent holding the open house unless you want to.

No matter who you talk to — the agent, your Uncle Wayne who referred you to the agent, the senior broker where the agent works, or the agent's most recent clients — don't be shy, and don't let things slip because you don't want to offend anyone. There are no stupid questions! Face it, you'll feel a lot worse if you don't ask, and not asking will cost you in the long run. You don't purchase a home every day, but your agent probably assists a bunch of buyers every month. You're trusting your real estate agent to help you make the biggest single investment of your life, so ask away!

Choosing an agent

When you choose a real estate agent, look for someone who will work hard for you. Someone who asks questions to clarify what you need and what you want is kilometres ahead of someone who tries to *tell* you the same information. The best agent will be curious about you, your family, your finances, and your future plans. Someone who asks questions and listens to your answers will serve you far better than someone who takes charge and tells you what you want. Your agent should respect your time and independence; a good agent will provide you with all the information you need, and give you room to make your own decisions. The best client–agent relationship happens when the agent and buyer have similar temperaments in terms of enthusiasm, sense of humour, and energy level.

Select an agent who works primarily in the community or area where you want to live. Real estate agents have in-depth knowledge of neighbourhoods, selling prices, schools, property taxes, utility rates, local amenities, and civic issues.

Choose a full-time agent over one who works part-time. The real estate market changes constantly, and part-time agents just won't be able to keep up with new listings and market activity. A full-time agent not only stays more in touch with the market but also is more familiar with the paperwork involved.

Be sure that your agent is familiar with the variety of Web sites and agent-driven marketing tools, such as the Multiple Listing Service (www.realtor.ca). New multimedia tools are available, it seems, almost monthly to realtors, so you want to work with someone who is tech savvy and can set you up with such tools as automated searches, in which properties that meet your criteria are automatically e-mailed to you. Using the latest technology will save you all sorts of time and make your home hunting that much more pleasurable.

Hunting for an agent online

The Web can be a great help in your search for an agent. First, you can access real estate Web sites to find someone who's right for you; if you're a seller, look through the agency's home listings online to find the person representing homes that are similar to your own. Then, when sizing up prospective agents, look for one who is comfortable working with the Internet and other electronic tools. He or she can access MLS listings on the Web and e-mail them to you, saving you many phone messages, trips to the agent's office, and fruitless home visits.

Real estate agents and cyberspace connect in very useful ways. To find an agent, you can visit any major real estate agent's office online, through his or her company's Web site. There, you'll often find the agent's bio (outlining his real estate specialties), images of properties he is currently representing, and information about recently sold homes so you can see initially if the two of you will be a match. In addition to listings, these sites often feature helpful information on moving, financing, and the neighbourhood you're interested in.

Even the coolest-looking, most impressive Web site shouldn't be used as a replacement for real contact with your potential agent. Meet with agents to know if they have the right personality to work with you and to make sure they understand exactly what you want. E-mail is great, but e-misunderstandings can happen to even the most careful writer. (Can you tell if we're being sarcastic right now? We're not, but you get the point.)

Many real estate agents' sites feature a *home tracker* tool, where you enter in the vital statistics of your dream home (including price range) and are e-mailed when a home goes on the market fitting that description. If you're an e-mail junkie, this may be how you'd like your agent to keep you informed about new listings that she has found for you. This virtual relationship will keep you on top of any new listings that meet your criteria, and can save you hours of visiting homes that sound good over the phone but look absolutely nothing like what you want in person. Keeping in touch with your real estate agent via e-mail can be a lot more convenient (and a lot less intrusive) than playing telephone tag, receiving numerous faxes for every new listing, or going on multiple useless home visits.

If you're a wired person and want an electronic relationship with your agent, make sure that he or she is Net savvy — and if you want quick answers to your questions, make sure the agent has ready access to e-mail, either via a computer or smartphone. Just because an agent has a Web site doesn't mean that she or he knows how to use e-mail efficiently.

Taking referrals into account

If possible, use an agent recommended by a friend, relative, business associate, or someone else you trust. If the agent provided good service to that person, chances are you'll get good service too.

Speaking to a head broker at a major real estate company may be extremely helpful. Even if you're moving cross-country, chances are the broker will have a list of contacts for agents working in particular areas, as well as agents who deal with particular types of properties. Search the Internet too; www. realtor.ca is an excellent site that is linked to all real estate boards across Canada and can help you get a feel for prices and neighbourhoods anywhere in the country. Through this site, you may also find an agent active in an area you want to check out. If you live close to the neighbourhood that you are scouting, a casual drive around may reveal the signs of agents who work in the area and are selling the type of property you're interested in buying.

After you have the names of a few agents, arrange to meet with them. Ask each of them to bring a record of all the houses they've listed and sold in the past year. This way, you can verify what kind of homes, neighbourhoods, and price ranges are most familiar to each agent. You'll also figure out quickly whether you get along with the agent. Remember that an agent with good people skills will not only be nicer to work with but also represent you well to sellers and be an effective negotiator when the time comes to make an offer.

Interviewing the agent's clients

Some agents will have a list of clients you can talk with to try to determine if you'll be compatible with the agent. If you decide to talk to your agent's clients, try asking some of the following questions:

✔ First and foremost, did the agent show you what you were looking for? Were the choices in the right price range, with the right features, in the right neighbourhood?

✔ Did the agent act with honesty and integrity when asking for or providing you with information? Were you told what information would be confidential and what the agent needed to disclose?

✔ Did the agent work to your schedule and have time for all your questions? Time to take you to showings? Did the agent return your calls promptly, with helpful answers?

✔ Was the agent able to explain things in simple terms for you, or did he or she use legalese and jargon that went over your head?

✔ Did the agent treat sellers with respect and good manners if present during showings?

✔ Do you feel the agent advised you well on writing the contract and determining time frames?

✔ Do you feel the agent negotiated a good deal for you?

✔ Will you call the agent again when you're ready to sell your home?

✔ Is there anything else I should know about this agent or the agent's company?

Asking the right questions, making the right choices

You're interviewing potential agents for the job of helping you find a home. While it's not actually time for you to get revenge for every job interview you went on that went badly, you can ask these questions when you're interviewing prospective agents. An experienced, reliable agent will have no problem with being put in the hot seat.

✔ **How long have you been an agent? Do you work full time?** The longer your agent has been in the business, the more you benefit from the wide range of experience. However, you don't want to work with someone who is resting on his laurels, either. That eager and hardworking agent with three years of experience may be a perfect fit for you.

✔ **Who do you represent?** Some agents prefer to work on behalf of buyers, and some prefer to work on behalf of sellers.

✔ **How many clients do you have right now, and will you have the time to work with me?** A good agent has an established client list and will be working with a number of buyers and sellers at any time. If you're looking for a specific type of property (for example, a condo with a water view), is the agent working with other people looking for the exact same type of property, and will that create a conflict?

✔ **Do you use online search tools?** Knowledge of the Multiple Listing Service is an essential tool in the home search process, as is access to other agent-driven Web sites and other tech tools that will make your search that much more productive.

✔ **How many agents work in your office?** Are you working in an active and vibrant office that is up to date on market activity and is aware of new listings as they come on to the market?

✔ **Does your office have an active and attentive manager/broker?** You need to know you have someone to turn to if you and your agent need help with a particularly complicated or unusual circumstance.

✔ **Will any responsibilities in my home search be delegated to someone else?** You want to know that you're going to receive the agent's personal attention. Many busy agents have assistants to whom they will refer potential buyers — make sure you get to work with the agent you are choosing.

✔ **What neighbourhoods/types of homes do you specialize in?** You probably already know the kinds of properties you're interested in, and you want your agent to be an expert in that particular field.

✔ **What price range do you deal in primarily?** You have a budget, and you need an agent who's skilled at working within that money range.

✔ **How many people have you helped buy a home in the past year?** You want an active agent who's successful in the current real estate market.

✔ **How many people have you helped sell a home in the past year?** Knowing the stats on your agent never hurts, but the best agent for you doesn't necessarily have the highest number of sales.

✔ **Can you refer me to real estate lawyers, mortgage brokers, inspectors, or appraisers if I need their services?** Any agent with some experience will have a few contacts that you can capitalize on.

✔ **Do you have a list of client testimonials that I can look at?** Read over what former clients have to say about your agent. If your agent doesn't have testimonials to read, contact former clients about their experiences.

Making your agent work for you

Explain your home-buying requirements to your agent. Bring along your list of household and neighbourhood priorities (see Chapter 7). When the agent knows your needs, tastes, and budget, the fun really starts — you go on tour. Your agent will show you around various homes and neighbourhoods until you decide you've found the one you want. At the same time, your agent may help you remove some blinders that you don't realize you have on by expanding your horizons into other neighbourhoods or even styles of homes.

When you're ready, your agent will present your offer to the sellers. Your real estate agent will help you negotiate the sale terms and conditions and then firm up the deal for you.

To facilitate the whole sale process, your agent should give you referrals (if you need them) to other professionals, including real estate lawyers, appraisers, financial advisers, lenders, contractors, and inspectors. (She should refer you to a couple of each, to ensure favouritism isn't a factor.)

A good agent will be adaptable and creative in order to meet your needs. If you can't visit a house in person, you may be able to arrange for an online virtual tour, or if you're planning a cross-country move, your agent may be able to provide a video tour of some homes.

Unless you are looking in two vastly different areas, we recommend working with one agent only. Most agents have access to the MLS system, as well as other realtor tools, so if you're using more than one agent, you'll see overlap in the properties they find for you. Pick the agent that you feel you can trust and has the time to work with you, as opposed to casting a net and using many agents. You'll always find that you get better service.

Reading the signs

Most real estate agents are hard-working, responsible professionals who do everything they can on your behalf. If your agent doesn't fall into this category, you'll probably notice on your own pretty quickly, but just in case, we've compiled this handy list of warning signs that point to poor agents:

- They never point out any problems with the houses they show you. In fact, they stand around playing games on their smartphones, or making personal calls to their bookies.
- They swear up and down that the foundation isn't crumbling, even though your two-year-old has kicked in the corner.
- They show you only houses that are being listed by their company, and when you ask to see other listings, they're uncooperative.
- They show you only mansions when you're in the market for a semi-detached.
- They make you feel pressured or bullied or, even worse, foolish.
- They can't answer basic questions about construction or mechanical systems.

If your real estate agent is (a) too busy, (b) too pushy, or (c) too clueless, end the relationship!

You're in the driver's seat — your agent is supposed to be guiding you into a great deal, not over the edge of a cliff. If you signed a brochure (an acknowledgement of the buyer–agency relationship, not a contract), it doesn't bind you to that agent forever. Call the local and provincial real estate board for advice on your particular situation. If you signed a buyer's contract with the agent that stipulates you'll pay a finder's fee to the agent if he finds you a house (as opposed to the usual sharing of the commission paid by the seller), make sure the contract has a termination date or a release clause if you want to terminate that agreement. Often, however, the agent you work with won't ask you to sign an agreement. You want to work with someone you trust, and who trusts you.

Don't commit to anything you don't feel comfortable with. You want to buy a house, and you want the process to be as pleasant and hassle-free as possible.

Who Needs an Appraiser, and Why?

If you've enlisted the help of an agent to buy a home, then you probably don't need an appraiser (but keep reading — this is good stuff), because part of your agent's job is to perform a property evaluation for you before you submit an offer. Your agent will provide you with a market overview, and then determine where the home you're looking at is situated, price-wise, within the market. With that knowledge, you can go ahead and make an offer to the seller that is within a reasonable range for the value of the home.

Now, if you're buying a home but not using an agent, or if the home you're buying is a private sale (For Sale by Owner), an appraiser is an excellent resource. Hey, car buyers have used car guides to help them determine whether a certain car make and model is a good deal, so it's only right that homebuyers have a similar resource (albeit in much less portable human form). As a buyer who doesn't have an agent to help you determine the market value of the home in question, you want an appraisal done so you'll know where to start bidding and when to stop, and to confirm that the offer you make is fair market value. If you're super-familiar with the market and totally confident that the asking price is fair, this is a service you won't need. Most people, however, will need the help.

In most cases, your lender will use an appraisal to help determine the amount of the mortgage you are entitled to, based on the appraised value of the home you're buying. The lender is using your new house for collateral for the mortgage, and the bank will want an appraisal to make sure the offer you have on the house is fair market value.

Your mortgage lender will probably insist that its appraiser conduct the assessment of the home you're buying . . . even if you have done your own appraisal before submitting an offer. If this is the case, you have no say in the choice of the appraiser. But chances are the lender's appraiser is both quali- fied and experienced. After all, a financial institution depends on the apprais- er's expertise to decide whether to lend out hundreds of thousands of dollars.

Bear in mind that if your lender orders the appraisal, you likely won't receive a copy. Ask to see a copy of the appraisal if possible because chances are you'll pay the fee for it. (More on appraisal fees later in this section.)

What is an appraisal?

An *appraisal* is an evaluation of a home's worth, so you'll know that the seller is asking a fair and reasonable price. When you pay a professional for an appraisal of a house, you get an unbiased, informed assessment. The appraiser looks at the property and makes an assessment based on the home's size, features, amenities, and condition, as well as recent sales of comparable homes in the neighbourhood. Remember, what determines the value of a home isn't just the home itself, but what's around it as well. Things like noisy train tracks or a garbage dump near a home, even a great home, can change the value.

Appraisal reports must contain the purpose of the appraisal, the legal description or identification of the property examined, a listing of *encumbrances* (any financial charges owing against the property), and an analysis of the best use of the property.

The most common method of appraisal is the CMA, which is short for *comparative market analysis* (although sometimes it stands for *competitive market analysis* or *current market analysis*). To determine a property's value through a CMA, the appraiser compares the home you're considering buying to other homes in the same neighbourhood that are comparable in size, features, and amenities.

What will the appraiser look for?

The appraiser scours the house and the neighbourhood. In particular, appraisers look at the following:

- ✔ **Size, age, and condition of the house:** Does the home need repairs now or in the near future? Have upgrades, refinishing, or renovation work been put into the home recently? (This part of the appraisal tends to focus on kitchens and bathrooms.)

- ✔ **Operating systems:** Do the heating, air conditioning, plumbing, and electrical systems all function properly?

- ✔ **Amenities:** What kind of luxury features does the home possess, such as a pool, wine cellar, hot tub, solarium, or four-car garage?

- ✔ **Neighbourhood characteristics and immediate surroundings:** What does the yard back onto? Which way do the windows face? Are schools, shopping, and transit services nearby? Is the home within what's considered a safe neighbourhood?

> ✔ **Special or unique features of the home:** Is it a designated heritage home, or is it situated on a ravine lot with a stunning view?

Appraisers are required to do only a visual inspection, but they may probe further. This means the appraisal process can vary in length, from a quick walk-through to an hours-long inspection. If you're requesting a *very* small mortgage or have great assets and collateral securing your mortgage, the appraiser may even do a *drive-by appraisal,* a quick confirmation that the home is still standing and appears to be of fair value.

If you're looking at buying a condo, you should be warned that an appraiser may not be aware of the status of the condominium corporation, and so may not take this into account (for more about condominium corporations, refer to Chapter 5). If you get to meet the appraiser, make sure you ask him if this has been factored into the assessment. If the appraisal is being ordered through your lending institution, make sure the lender is aware of any factors that may not be readily evident, and make sure the bank notifies the appraiser of these pertinent details that can affect the appraised value of the property. Maybe the current owners are asking $50,000 less than the appraised/fair market value because they want to unload their leaky condo before a huge repair bill comes in. Make sure the appraiser has as much information as possible (everything you know, he should know!) to determine market value.

Note: Depending on who orders the appraisal (private or bank), results can vary. Bank appraisals for mortgage purposes sometimes do not accurately reflect the desirability of the home and often appear lower in value.

What do I look for in an appraiser?

Chances are good that you won't have to choose your appraiser — your lender will probably handle that for you. If the responsibility does fall to you, make your choice based on more than just the appraiser's Web appeal. Consult your lender to see who they recommend. Any appraiser recommended by a lending institution should be fully qualified and accredited.

Certification is what you look for in an appraiser, plain and simple. An independent appraiser should have an AACI (Accredited Appraiser Canadian Institute) or CRA (Canadian Residential Appraiser) designation. Make sure you ask to see your appraiser's credentials.

Reputation is also key — work with someone you can trust. Ask any friends who've bought homes recently for their suggestions, or contact the *Appraisal Institute of Canada (AIC)* for a list of certified independent appraisers in your area.

The Appraisal Institute's Web site (www.aicanada.ca) has a Find an Appraiser feature that works in two different cases. First, if you need an appraiser but have no idea where to start or who to look for, never fear. Simply enter the criteria for your specific situation; for example: Canmore, Alberta, Single Family Rural, and Appraisal Review. When you submit the information, the Web site will provide you with a list of accredited appraisers in your area who best fit your needs. You'll also get all the necessary contact information, including phone numbers, e-mail addresses, and Web sites, if they have one. Second, if you've been given the name of a top-notch appraiser (your great-aunt's neighbour's babysitter says they're fabulous) but you're not sure how to contact them, the AIC Web site can help you with that as well. Just enter the last name of the appraiser into the search box, and if they're in the database, you'll get that much-sought-after contact info.

The AIC Web site has a lot of information about the value of renovations in real estate, which may interest you when looking at potential homes. Check out Renova, an interactive feature that gives you rough estimates of what different types of renovations are worth. Maybe the seller sounds convincing, but you don't really think that scrubbing the kitchen floor qualifies as a kitchen upgrade, do you?

Low appraisals and high offers

If your $350,000 offer has been accepted and *then* your bank's appraiser determines the home is worth only $325,000, the bank may not give you the mortgage you need, especially if you're asking for a high-ratio mortgage (meaning you have less than a 20 percent down payment). If you run into this financing difficulty, you can try to do some serious negotiating with the seller to lower the home's price. Or, if you have pre-approval for the $350,000 mortgage, you may need to cough up a larger down payment to reduce the risk your lender is taking by giving you a mortgage.

If you're concerned about the value of the home you want to buy, you can add a *"subject to appraisal"* clause to your purchase offer. This clause means that your offer is subject to the buyer receiving and approving the appraisal for the subject property on or before a specified date. This condition is for the sole benefit of the buyer.

Adding this "subject to appraisal" clause to your home purchase offer gives you some protection from paying too much for the home you're planning to buy. If you're unhappy with the appraised value, you can reconsider your offer. If you suspect that the lender's appraisal radically undervalues the home, talk with your real estate agent to make sure the appraiser knows all the pertinent details about the subject property. The appraiser simply may not be familiar with the area where the home is located. Express your concerns to your lender — you should be able to obtain information on the appraiser's background and experience. If you're certain that the appraiser doesn't know your market well, you may be able to have a reappraisal conducted at no cost.

For more information about offers and "subject to" clauses, see Chapter 10.

How much can I expect to pay?

The price of an appraisal varies depending on how difficult a job it is for the appraiser. If there have been many recent sales in the neighbourhood and the home doesn't have scores of out-of-the-ordinary features, the assessment will be straightforward and cheaper. You can expect to pay anywhere from $200 to $500 for an appraiser's services.

You may be able to work out an agreement with your mortgage lender to pick up the appraisal cost. Ask your agent about writing into your offer to purchase that it is (1) subject to financing, but also (2) subject to the buyer (you) receiving a satisfactory appraisal. (See the "Low appraisals and high offers" sidebar in this chapter, as well as Chapter 10 for details on adding conditions to your offer.) This clause will help you make sure that your house "appraises out" — you don't want to carry a mortgage on what you thought was a $500,000 home when it's appraised at only $375,000.

How a Lawyer Fits into the Picture

A good lawyer or notary is like an insurance policy: If you ever need one, you'll really be happy you got one. You will definitely need a lawyer or notary to *close* the transaction, that is, to handle the final mortgage paperwork and title transfer. In some cases, like if you're buying or selling a home due to divorce or separation, or if tax issues are involved, you may want your lawyer to review your documents. In these cases, you may want to make any offer subject to having your lawyer or notary review all paperwork.

What a real estate lawyer does for you

Besides needing a lawyer to check all the niggling little legal bits near closing time, you may find a lawyer can be indispensable early on in the deal as well. He or she is there to protect your rights and to make sure every part of the contract is A-okay. In the following sections, we explain what a lawyer does during two crucial times in the home-buying experience.

B.C. (before closing)

The *contract of purchase and sale* (sometimes called the *agreement of purchase and sale*) is the legal document you and your agent use to make an offer to purchase a home, and you need to be sure it's drawn up correctly. If your real estate agent has many years of experience drawing up home purchase offers, you may feel confident that she can write an offer and present it to the sellers without a lawyer's scrutiny. Don't take chances. If you have any concerns, ask your agent to add a subject clause to the offer that gives your lawyer a chance to review the agreement of purchase and sale after the sellers have accepted your offer but before all the conditions of sale (the "subject to" clauses) are removed. You'll likely have to stipulate a short 24- or 48-hour time period for the legal review, or the seller may object to this condition. (See Chapter 10 for more information on the contract of purchase and sale and adding conditions or "subject to" clauses.)

The agreement of purchase and sale is a legally binding contract. A lawyer may be able to give you valuable input before you sign your agreement or before you remove your conditions and commit to buying the house. Damage control is often less effective and more costly and time-consuming than prevention. Yes, everyone makes mistakes. But if it's your *lawyer's* mistake, at least your lawyer is insured, which in turn protects you.

If you're buying a newly built home, you'll use your builder's agreement of purchase and sale, and it will be quite different from the standard form found in your province or region. No two builders' contracts are alike; they tend to be lengthy documents and often contain details that favour the builder. Have your lawyer or notary or agent advise you which clauses to remove before you sign, and which to clarify with the builder/seller.

A.D. (after the deal)

After you sign the offer, your lawyer or notary handles the final mortgage and closing paperwork. Your lawyer furnishes the following important services:

- ✔ **Title search:** Your lawyer checks that the sellers of the home are the registered owners of the property and that any claims registered against the property (any debts or liens, for example) are cleared before the title is transferred to you.

- ✔ **Conveyancing:** Your lawyer prepares and reviews all documents needed to transfer the ownership of the new home, and ensures you get valid title (the deed) to the property.

- ✔ **Application of title insurance:** If necessary, your lawyer gets insurance that protects you and the lender in the event of any problems with the title or zoning of the property.

- ✔ **Survey review:** Your lawyer confirms the survey is accurate and valid, and investigates any encroachments or rights of way on the subject property.

- ✔ **Assessment of builder commitments:** If you're buying a new property, your lawyer can ensure that the builder provides everything you're entitled to receive and that your new house has a valid occupancy permit from the local city or municipality.

- ✔ **Tax investigation:** Your lawyer checks to see if any municipal taxes are owing if you're buying a resale home, or determines if you or your builder is responsible for paying GST if you're buying a newly built home.

✔ **Land transfer tax/deed transfer tax:** Your lawyer calculates the amount of transfer tax that you must pay (if applicable in your province).

✔ **Fees payable to seller:** Your lawyer tallies the *adjustments* (the amounts you owe the seller to compensate for prepaid utility bills, property taxes, rental income [if any], and other service fees paid in advance). Every region has different issues that may need adjusting at closing.

✔ **Mortgage paperwork:** Your lawyer draws up your mortgage documentation if the bank allows him to do this, which is usually the case. (In some rare cases, the bank will want their lawyer to draft the mortgage documents.)

Where to find a lawyer or notary

Look for someone who specializes in real estate law. In most of Canada, this will be a lawyer or possibly a notary; in Quebec, you will hire a notary. Friends, neighbours, or relatives who have recently bought or sold a home are a good source of recommendations. Your real estate agent, broker, or lender will also have contacts among local lawyers or notaries and should be able to give you the names of several real estate specialists to choose from. You can also find legal associations on the Internet.

As you've probably guessed by now, a simple search for "lawyer" and "Canada" — or a keyword for your region — won't do you a whole lot of good. You'll get gazillions of hits for lawyer Web sites, lawyer directories, lawyer-finder services, and the like. Remember, self-promoting Web sites are iffy in terms of reliability, and many of the Web sites won't even apply to where you live. Do you really want to sift through all these hits?

Although we don't recommend finding a lawyer on the Internet by using the "eeny, meeny, miney, moe" (catch a legal beagle by the toe) method, the Web can be a useful tool for checking out leads you're given. You may want to snoop out whether that guy whose name you were given by the owner of the Mike's Mart is really a former attorney general.

The place to start your search for a reliable lawyer is within a self-regulated organization, whose members must be trained professionals and meet set standards. If you have a lead for a lawyer in your area, the best use of your Internet time will be spent visiting the Federation of Law Societies of Canada (www.flsc.ca). Acting as a blanket forum for the whole country, the Federation provides links to all the provincial and territorial Law Societies' Web sites. Most of these sites allow you to do lawyer lookups for the current members of that province's Law Society.

Another excellent site for verifying the status of lawyers is www.Canadianlawlist.com, a searchable online database that boasts listings for 55,000 lawyers and 19,000 law offices. Simply set the Areas of Practice setting to Real Estate, and within seconds you'll be looking at a comprehensive list of lawyers in your region.

When you get the name of a lawyer you're thinking of using, you can always enter his or her name in a search engine like Google to see what shows up. For example, the lawyer may have her own Web site, which will give you more information, or you may find out she is being nominated for "Lawyer of the Year." On the downside, your search may also bring up stories about her sordid past — googling (yes, it's now a verb) anyone whose name you find online never hurts.

Just because someone's a lawyer doesn't mean that he can handle a real estate transaction for you. Chances are, your best friend's shark of a divorce lawyer is excellent — but he'd be a "shark out of water" when it comes to your contract of purchase and sale.

What to look for in a lawyer or notary

Find someone who speaks your language. As you interview lawyers and notaries, pay attention to how open they are to your questions and how clear their answers are. If they make their fee structures sound complicated, they may not be able to adequately explain the ins and outs of your agreement of purchase and sale or other legal documents involved in the purchase of your home. Choose a lawyer you can understand and who has the patience to explain terms adequately. For all intents and purposes, keep it local, too: If something crops up at the last minute that requires you to head to the lawyer's office, you don't want to be a two-hour drive away.

Don't base your final choice of lawyer or notary only on price. More experienced lawyers will often charge higher rates but get more done in less time, saving you money in the long run. Also, keep in mind that you are hiring a lawyer to give you peace of mind. A competent lawyer or notary should be able to explain every step of the transaction to you in clear and simple language regardless of whether the firm occupies a flashy corporate office tower or a modest street-level suite.

Before you hire a real estate lawyer, make sure you know a bit about what you're getting into. Consider the following sections as guidelines for the questions you ask.

Local real estate experience

Tenancy laws, title registration procedures, and local property regulations can all change periodically. A local real estate lawyer or notary is up to date on all regional laws and probably has good connections with the enforcing bodies. These two questions are key:

- ✔ How many years have you specialized in real estate law?
- ✔ How long have you worked in this region or city?

Fees and disbursements

We're sure you already know that a lawyer's fees can be positively heart-stopping. Because you can't skip the cost of a lawyer (though your heart's probably skipped several beats by now!), you'd better know how much to budget to cover legal expenses. Start by making these inquiries — and write down the answers:

- ✔ How do you structure your fees?
- ✔ Do you provide free estimates of cost?
- ✔ If I opt for a flat fee, what services are included?
- ✔ Under what foreseeable circumstances might I require additional services?
- ✔ When and how will you let me know if the fees go above the amount estimated?
- ✔ How much do you recommend I budget for disbursements?
- ✔ What taxes are applicable to the fees?

When you're searching for a lawyer, ask the ones you interview for references. Take the names and telephone numbers of some recent clients (if possible). If you found lawyers' or notaries' names using the phone book or a professional association, asking for references is especially important. Call the lawyer's references to see what they have to say.

Hello, I'm calling regarding . . .

For those of you who feel nervous about speaking to complete strangers as you're checking references, keep this list handy. Try asking a lawyer's former clients the following:

- ✔ Were you satisfied with your lawyer's services?
- ✔ Did you find any surprises in the final bill for your lawyer's services and disbursements?

- ✔ Did you feel your lawyer adequately explained to you the implications of all the decisions you made and documents you signed?
- ✔ Is there anything else about this professional or the services provided that I should know?

Chapter 7

Prioritizing Your Needs

Before you start going to open houses or calling an agent to take you out looking at homes, decide what you're actually looking for. Consider these three criteria: what you *want,* what you *need,* and what you can *afford.*

If you looked at our financial advice in Chapter 2, you probably already know the price of the home you can afford. (If not, we recommend you take a look.) The trick is to fit the home you need and want into your financial plans. Remember, this home doesn't have to be the last one you ever live in: You may get some of what you're looking for now, and even more in five years when you decide to move on. You have to prioritize and be prepared to leave at least some (and potentially most) of what you *want* by the wayside, without sacrificing much of what you really *need.* This chapter helps you organize your thoughts so that you can make a home purchase that has the right features and location for you.

What's Right for You Now

We all want the perfect home: white picket fence, manicured lawn, and tennis court. Or maybe your dream home has a 1,000-square-foot deck complete with hot tub, built-in barbecue, and surround-sound party speakers. If you're self-employed, maybe a suitable home office space is at the top of your list. Or maybe you're tired of mowing in July and shovelling in January, so your ideal space is an apartment-style condo in the heart of downtown Lunenburg.

Whatever your current dreams, chances are your life will be different 20 years from now, with new priorities. You may not need that office space as much as another parking space when your spouse *finally* learns to drive. But you can't really predict 20 years down the road, so don't sweat it, and focus on the foreseeable future.

Considering your foreseeable future

One of the first things you need to decide is how long you expect to stay. Your requirements will be very different if you plan to live out your days in your new home than if you're looking to turn around and sell it for a (hopefully) quick profit. But because the quick resale is a risky — and usually unprofitable (don't get us started) — idea, we assume you're settling in for at least the next five years.

In addition to what you think you need now, consider the potential for change in your future. Though you can't plan for everything that can possibly happen in the next ten years, your next few years should be visible. If you're just married and starting out, think about the possibility of having children somewhere down the line. Parenthood may be *way* down the line, but will it be before you're ready to move again? If so, buying that swanky one-bedroom, two-level loft may not be the smartest choice for you.

If you're heading toward retirement, think about the difficulties you may encounter as you get older. Will you still be able to climb the stairs to the third-floor master bedroom in ten years? That large back garden may be great for the grandkids, but who is going to mow the lawn and do the weeding? Maybe a place with a park down the street can fit the bill instead.

You have a lot to keep in mind when you start to prioritize. Make one list of your current priorities, and another one of your expected future needs. Consider both lists as you shop for your home.

Saving space for change

Chances are, the main reason you're thinking about a move is the potential for an expanding family. Whether your new family members are a baby (or two), a mother-in-law, or those two Irish Wolfhounds you adopted, you may need more room in the future to accommodate change.

So, if you admit that the possibility of sharing your space at some point exists, looking for a home with an extra room, or a basement or attic that can be converted when the time comes, is a good idea. In the meantime, of course, you can use that space as a home theatre or extra storage (shoes, anyone?).

If some flexibility — whether in the form of another bedroom or a basement full of potential — isn't built into your home, you may find yourself moving again faster than you think, and certainly faster than you'd like.

Knowing What You Want

So many elements make up a home that often deciding which ones are most important to us is hard. You may take many things for granted when you have them (like huge closets for shoes!), but don't forget to make a record of those (sometimes) small items that make all the difference in your satisfaction with where you live. For example, if you walk to work, living on a steep hill may be a great workout in the spring and summer but a dangerous and slippery slope in the winter.

Part of knowing what you want is knowing what you don't want. *I don't want to mow grass,* for example, is a good start. Or, *I don't want a basement where my shoulders hit the ceiling.* You will always find things you don't like about your current home and other people's homes, whether those things are the lack of water pressure, the windows not opening wide enough, or the lack of street parking. If a certain deficiency is going to drive you crazy, you need to avoid it so that it doesn't ultimately affect your use and enjoyment of your home. By identifying your pet peeves, you can zero in on what you're looking for.

You can't always get what you want

Prioritizing the features that you absolutely can't live without in a home alongside those that may sound nice but that, at the end of the day, you don't really need will stand you in good stead when your agent starts showing you houses. When push comes to shove, you'll be willing (and able!) to compromise. And you just may find that you get what you need.

Liz was going through a divorce and needed to find a property with three bedrooms for her two children, a garage, and adequate storage. She also wanted to stay relatively close to her ex, who was going to stay in the matrimonial home, and near the schools that the children were attending.

Liz and her agent found a great home with loads of potential well within her budget, but she decided she really didn't want to renovate after all. Then her agent found her a more expensive property, all updated and in the same neighbourhood, but Liz thought the bedrooms were a bit too small and didn't like the street the home was on. On the third try, her agent showed her a fully renovated home, right on budget, with good room sizes and on a nice street. But Liz decided the home was a bit too far away from where she wanted to be, and that she needed a home with a sunny back garden.

Liz's agent told her that it was time to prioritize. Each home had features that appealed to Liz, so she needed to figure out which features were the most important. After a bit more tire kicking, Liz realized she really liked house number three: She would just have to accept a new location and a little less sunshine.

Focusing on your needs

We all know what we'd like in our ideal home. The features of your dream home provide a good starting point for your search; most of us judge potential homes with our standards of perfection in mind.

Try to keep your mind focused on your home-buying needs. You shouldn't let your emotions overrule practicalities. (See Chapter 9 for the dangers of falling in love.) Even though you really want the home with the incredibly landscaped backyard, reminding yourself that the rest of the house just doesn't meet your basic needs will help you overlook the cosmetics. Face it: You're in Canada, and depending on where you live, that back garden will be unusable for six months of the year (or more!).

If you're a first-time buyer, remember you're just that — buying for the first time. Chances are, you'll sell your home in five to ten years, and trade up to a bigger one. So don't worry if you can't buy your absolute dream home in the perfect neighbourhood right now. Instead of trying to buy a home with seven bedrooms for the 12 kids you plan to raise, realize that you can live comfortably right now with a four-bedroom home with a fenced-in backyard at a reasonable price. You may not like the idea of buying a smaller "starter home," but it puts you in a better position to buy a bigger home down the road without sacrificing vacations, evenings out, and hockey lessons to your mortgage. Nobody wants to be house poor! What you can afford will probably never match your ideal, but with a little bit of flexibility, you can find a home that suits you until child number eight comes along.

Making the list

Because you're probably going to be making compromises, keeping focused on your basic needs and not giving them up too quickly, while being aware of where you can be flexible, is important. Here are some of the things you'll need to consider:

- **Location:** Perhaps the most obvious factor . . . where do you want to live? After you have been pre-approved for a mortgage, you'll have a good idea of what you can afford, which may determine where you will end up living. For example, you may be able to purchase a cool two-bedroom condo in the city or a four-bedroom family home out in the suburbs, both in the same price point. Either way, you'll have lots of options.

- **Type of home:** What type of home best suits your needs? If you have a habit of falling down the stairs and breaking your toes, you may think about buying a bungalow or an apartment-style condo. Or, perhaps you're thinking about a detached home, what with your talented family of violinists and all. (If you're curious about what different types of homes exist out there, have a look at Chapters 4 and 5.) If your tastes run to modern architecture, you won't want to look at century-old Victorian-style homes.

- ✔ **Exterior:** What do you need outside? Is there enough room for the Great Dane to do laps? Do you need fencing around your yard to keep the kids in? Do you need a sunny yard to garden in, or are you more of a herbicidal maniac? Like to throw summer parties? Then you'll probably want that sunny yard bricked in or covered with a large deck. Or maybe you need a lot of pavement on which to park your three cars, two motorcycles, and RV.

- ✔ **Kitchen:** What do you need in a kitchen? If you have a big family, you probably want an eat-in area and an automatic dishwasher. If you're a professional cook, counter space and large appliances may be your priority. The presence of appliances may not be the deciding factor, but room to install them is.

- ✔ **Bathrooms:** How many do you need? If you're looking for anything with more than one storey, bathroom location is important, too. Is there one on the ground floor, or do you have to send your guests up to the one between your kids' rooms? If you like to take long, relaxing bubble baths on Sundays, you won't be interested in a home with only stand-up showers.

- ✔ **Bedrooms:** How many bedrooms are you looking for? Do you need an extra one for a home office or frequent house guests? If you're just starting out and you may be having children in the not-so-distant future, count them in when calculating your needs. If your children are finally off to college and moving out, you may want fewer bedrooms.

- ✔ **Renovations:** Are you willing to do them? If the home has all the bones that you're looking for — the neighbourhood works, the room sizes are great, you love the garden and the two-car garage — but it hasn't been updated since 1982 (hey, who doesn't love an entire house finished in a dusky pink colour scheme?), are you willing to do the work? You may find that a bit of elbow grease gets you exactly what you want.

- ✔ **Other considerations:** How small is *too* small for your bedroom? For your kitchen? Will stairs be a problem for anyone in your household, now or in the future? Do you need a finished basement for your home office, your home theatre, or your kids' playroom?

Use Table 7-1 to organize the features you need or want in a new home. Complete the chart by considering what is absolutely essential to your needs, and what you'd really like to have (but that you *could* live without).

For some items in the chart, like a dishwasher or a fireplace, it's a simple yes/ no proposition. A fireplace may be "nice to have," but is it really "essential"? You decide.

Choosing features in a home isn't all sunshine and roses. You may think you want a corner lot with a big yard, but have you bargained for the snow shovelling, leaf raking, and lawn mowing that go with it? How about the settling foundation and structural decay of your dream Victorian mansion? We're not saying you should change your mind about what you want, but when you set your priorities, think about the drawbacks of maintenance and repair that go along with the benefits of home owning.

Table 7-1	Home Priority List	
	Essential Need	*Nice to Have*
Type of Home		
Detached, semi, etc.	_____	_____
Victorian, modern, etc.	_____	_____
Number of storeys	_____	_____
Interior		
Size (m² or ft²)	_____	_____
Number of rooms	_____	_____
Living Room		
Size (m² or ft²)	_____	_____
Open concept/separate dining room	_____	_____
Fireplace	_____	_____
Flooring	_____	_____
Ceiling height	_____	_____
Kitchen		
Size (m² or ft²)	_____	_____
Condition	_____	_____
Eat-in area	_____	_____
Fridge	_____	_____
Stove (gas?)	_____	_____
Dishwasher	_____	_____
Large kitchen cupboards	_____	_____
Accessible kitchen cupboards	_____	_____
Countertops	_____	_____
Flooring	_____	_____

	Essential Need	*Nice to Have*
Bedrooms		
Number	——————	——————
Walkout to balcony	——————	——————
Closet in each room	——————	——————
Flooring	——————	——————
Main Bedroom		
Size (m^2 or ft^2)	——————	——————
Ensuite bathroom	——————	——————
Walk-in closet, south-facing window, fireplace, or other special feature	——————	——————
Flooring	——————	——————
Bathroom		
Number of bathrooms	——————	——————
Size (m^2 or ft^2)	——————	——————
Location(s)	——————	——————
Shower/tub/whirlpool tub	——————	——————
Flooring	——————	——————
Sunroom/Den/Home Office		
Size (m^2 or ft^2)	——————	——————
Location	——————	——————
Flooring	——————	——————
Family Room		
Size (m^2 or ft^2)	——————	——————
Location	——————	——————
Flooring	——————	——————
Hallways		
Width (m or ft.)	——————	——————
Linen closet	——————	——————
Coat closet near main entrance	——————	——————
Flooring	——————	——————

(continued)

Table 7-1 *(continued)*

	Essential Need	Nice to Have
Basement		
Size (m² or ft²)	_____	_____
Finished	_____	_____
Basement/in-law apartment	_____	_____
Washer/dryer	_____	_____
Freezer	_____	_____
Heating (oil, gas, etc.)	_____	_____
Flooring	_____	_____
Other		
CAC (central air conditioning)	_____	_____
Central vacuum	_____	_____
Finished attic	_____	_____
Property will accommodate expansion	_____	_____
Water view	_____	_____
Security system	_____	_____
New windows	_____	_____
Sliding glass doors	_____	_____
Natural light	_____	_____
Exterior		
Frontage (size and direction facing)	_____	_____
Brick/siding/wood/stucco	_____	_____
Roofing material (slate, cedar shake, asphalt shingles)	_____	_____
Parking		
Garage	_____	_____
Carport	_____	_____
Space	_____	_____
Private/shared driveway	_____	_____
Street parking	_____	_____

	Essential Need	*Nice to Have*
Yard		
Size of lot (m² or ft²)	_____	_____
Shed	_____	_____
Deck/patio/porches	_____	_____
Fenced enclosure	_____	_____
Swimming pool	_____	_____
Established landscaping	_____	_____
Landscaping/garden space	_____	_____
Sunlight	_____	_____

Can you afford to be picky? You should be picky if you don't like where the washroom is, or how the stairs are in the middle of the living room. For all intents and purposes, these are things you either can't change or won't want to attempt to change because the costs involved are prohibitive. Don't be picky if you don't like the doorknobs. Even central air can be installed later for less than, say, tearing down a wall or two to open up the dining room. Make concessions on small things you can fix or change yourself later on. Try to use your imagination: Sometimes fresh paint and flooring can turn drab into fab!

What's Close to Home

When identifying your home needs, you focus on both the home's interior and exterior elements. However, the neighbourhood your home is located within is a very significant concern. You may be able to renovate a bathroom in your house, but you can't just move the bus stop in front of your sidewalk or force the fire department to move several blocks away. Your location can affect the way your home value appreciates or depreciates — the old saying, "Location, location, location," isn't an exaggeration.

Consider the specific location of your desired home, as well as the general area. Living three streets away from train tracks may be fine for you, but being across the street from them is absolutely unthinkable. Or maybe you like a certain neighbourhood, but don't want to live on the busy main drag.

What about local amenities — those pesky little details like a grocery store, bank, or pharmacy? If you drive everywhere, then perhaps you don't need amenities close by. On the other hand, if you don't have a car, having some of these places within walking distance may be important, and you'll want to be close to public transportation services.

A neighbourhood isn't only a particular location; it's a type of environment. Look at the characteristics of the areas you like best. Do you like a dense community with people and activity? Or does a secluded location appeal to you? Do you like to see Christmas decorations up in the middle of November, or would you rather not see any at all? Do you want plenty of trees, playgrounds, and parks? Or are sleek high-rise condominium towers near the theatre district more your style?

Think about your family's needs. If your family is athletic, you may want to be near a community centre or a soccer field. If you have children, check out the local schools and find the boundaries (if any) for the *catchment areas*. A catchment area is the geographical area that outlines the boundaries of the neighbourhood that qualifies for admission to a certain school. Maps of school catchment areas are available from local school boards. If you want junior to go to that special French immersion academy, you'd better make sure the location of the house you're considering allows him to attend that school.

You and your favourite hangouts

Okay, they may not be your *favourite* hangouts, but they are where you spend most of your days: the office for you, and schools for the little ones. How far away are you willing to live from where you work? Don't forget that there's added expense if you're moving farther away (more gas, more wear and tear on your vehicle), as well as more stress (longer travel time, more traffic). Having said that, what you need and where you want to live may not always fit in the same budget. That four-bedroom detached home close to work may be two or three times more expensive than the home that is a 45-minute train ride away.

Try to do a test drive or transit ride from your potential neighbourhood to your workplace during rush hour. How long does it take you? How is the traffic on the new route, or the service of the bus or subway? Your initial reaction to the commute will tell you whether you're making a good move.

If you're a parent, think about transportation challenges for the kids too. Can you let the little ones walk to school, or will they need to take a bus or get a drive from you? Is there a nursery or daycare conveniently near to your commuting route? But don't choose location based on work alone. Jobs change, your preference to a neighbourhood might not. Consider where you want to be when you are *not* at work, then how far you are willing to drive for it.

Neighbourhood concerns

If you buy a home at a bargain price because there are train tracks through the backyard, chances are you'll have to list it at a lower price when it comes time to sell and you'll have to wait longer to sell because you'll need to find someone else who is willing to accept those train tracks.

You may find that your relatively quiet community during the day becomes the equivalent of an outdoor nightclub once it gets dark, as teenagers congregate at the park across the street. Make sure your potential neighbourhood suits your needs during the day, in the evenings, and on weekends. Find out what you can't see just by looking. Word of mouth can also be a huge factor in your decision.

- ✓ **Safety:** Consult the local police stations and community papers for statistics on neighbourhood crime.

- ✓ **Emergency services:** Check for the proximity of fire stations, police, and hospitals. Not only will these services make you feel safer if they're close by, but they can also help reduce your insurance costs by reducing the risk of burglaries or total destruction in a fire.

- ✓ **Local information:** Check community newspapers to assess how much of a community the neighbourhood really is, and to discover important information on major construction and housing or commercial developments, as well as any potential rezoning in the area.

- ✓ **Owner statistics:** Ask around to try to determine the ratio of owners to renters in the neighbourhood. More owners mean more commitment to keeping the neighbourhood clean, safe, and happy.

- ✓ **Education facilities:** Visit the local schools. Find out if most of the children in the area attend the local schools, and if not, why. Conversely, many students coming to school from out of the area is a good sign.

  The Fraser Institute publishes annual Report Cards that rank and rate Canada's secondary schools in British Columbia, Alberta, Ontario, New Brunswick, and Quebec. If you're considering buying a home in these provinces, you can visit `www.fraserinstitute.ca/index.asp` and click the Report Cards tab for information on local education providers.

- ✓ **Commercial activity:** Visit the local eateries and businesses. If new ones are moving in and businesses are thriving, it's a sign that the community is growing and that property values may go up by the time you get around to reselling your new home. Lots of "for sale or lease" signs in a nearby commercial area can be a signal of change. The type of businesses in an area also indicates the demographics of the community. Retailers do a lot of market research before choosing a location.

- ✓ **Major construction:** Keep your eyes open for street construction, transportation expansion, or shopping malls and community centres being built — all are signs of a growing community.

- ✓ **Public transit services:** Find out how accessible public transportation is in your area. Easy access increases the value of homes for resale, even if you don't need to use it yourself.

- ✔ **Community affairs:** Attend a neighbourhood meeting to get an idea of how involved residents are in local affairs, as well as what their local concerns are.

- ✔ **Overall contentment:** Talk to the people in the area to find out how happy — or unhappy — they are. You will most likely feel the same way after you move in.

Signs that a neighbourhood is improving

What if you find that perfect neighbourhood, but a few quick inquiries tell you that it's out of your price range? Well, you'll probably have to start neighbourhood hunting again, but now that you know what you're looking for, it should be an easier process. Check out the fringes of your dream area for gems that are close to, but not smack in the middle of, your preferred community. You may be able to find a home in the path of that community's expansion. Or, find yourself a neighbourhood that seems to be up-and-coming. Here are some things to look for when trying to find that diamond in the rough:

- ✔ **Home improvements:** Look at houses in the fringe areas for signs of renovations or improvements. When homeowners spend money to improve their homes, it shows that they are happy enough with the neighbourhood to invest in it. What was once down and out may soon be up-and-coming: Large packs of yuppies roaming the streets are often a good sign.

- ✔ **Real estate activity:** Look for "sold" signs on homes: It means that there are many buyers wanting to live in the area, or a number of sellers who want to leave. Perhaps you'll find several retirees living there who are anxious to make a permanent move to their condos in Florida.

- ✔ **Commercial postings:** Look for signs that shops and restaurants are developing. A healthy area attracts the investment of new business owners. A new Starbucks can be seen as a good sign; a pawn shop . . . not so much.

- ✔ **Major public developments:** New transportation sites can be a stimulus for business and development, and new zonings can indicate the government's interest in investing in the area. New parks and schools can indicate the growth of families in the area.

- ✔ **Attractive exteriors:** Look for well-maintained homes and well-groomed gardens and yards. You can see if the owners care about their homes by the image the neighbourhood projects.

Speaking of improving neighbourhoods, this is often where you may find *flipped homes*, or people actually looking for homes to *flip*. What is a flipped home? Well, it's one of those aforementioned diamonds in the rough that someone has purchased, renovated, and hopes to sell for a quick, healthy profit. You can usually spot a flipped home with the help of your agent: It has been recently purchased and renovated by the seller, often within the space of several months. Your agent has the ability to track the home's history in most cases, so you'll most likely be able to determine what the seller paid for the property and the state the home was in when it was purchased. Expect to see a lot of cosmetic upgrades, like new kitchens and bathrooms, flooring, and paint. Changes to the exterior, like paint and possibly even a new roof, as well as alluring landscaping, gives the property the street appeal to pull in buyers.

Up-and-coming neighbourhoods are often key targets for home flippers because these areas will be attracting many buyers, and because homes in their original condition will be less expensive than their counterparts in more established areas. Flippers also tend to target the type of buyer who wants everything already done — and for many buyers, an essentially all redone home in a neighbourhood that's moving up on the food chain can be an attractive option.

Nothing's wrong with purchasing a flipped home; however, do make sure that the seller has pulled all the appropriate permits necessary and has made all upgrades to code. Just because the home looks all new and shiny doesn't mean you don't need to do an inspection. If anything, be extra careful: You don't want to purchase a flipped home that was done by cutting corners to increase the profits! We discuss flipped homes again in Chapter 9.

If you're thinking of purchasing a home to flip, please use extreme caution! Flipping isn't a sport for neophytes. Many things need to be considered when flipping a home, like budgets, taxes and closing costs, labour, and carrying charges. And, inevitably, the big question: What happens if you can't sell the home? You risk either over-improving a home or under-improving it, based on the neighbourhood, which will affect your ability to sell for the price you want. (We go into a bit more detail about flipping in Chapter 9.)

Your neighbourhood priorities

What's going on outside your home is as important as what's going on inside. Use Table 7-2 the same way as Table 7-1 ("Home Priority List") — to help you form an idea of what qualities in a neighbourhood and a community matter to you.

Table 7-2	Neighbourhood and Location Priorities List		
	Essential	*Nice*	*Not Applicable*
Close To			
Work			
Partner's work			
Schools			
Place of worship			
Family			
Parks, playground			
Daycare			
Shopping			
Public transportation			
Major roads, highways			
Fire station			
Police			
Hospital			
Doctor/dentist			
Public library			
Cultural centres (e.g., theatre)			
Restaurants			
Recreation/health centre			
Public swimming pool			
Ice rink, baseball diamond			
Airport			
Other			
Away From			
Noise			
Traffic, major roads			
Train tracks			

	Essential	*Nice*	*Not Applicable*
Away From			
Hydro corridors	_____	_____	_____
Airport/flight paths	_____	_____	_____
Family	_____	_____	_____
Other	_____	_____	_____
General Location Features			
Established neighbourhood	_____	_____	_____
High property values	_____	_____	_____
Neighbourhood Watch/ neighbours concerned about neighbourhood issues	_____	_____	_____
Good snow removal	_____	_____	_____
Good garbage/ recycling pickup	_____	_____	_____
Quiet street	_____	_____	_____
Picturesque view	_____	_____	_____
Other	_____	_____	_____

Nothing Is Perfect

While home hunting, you'll find that many houses match some but not all your requirements. Or that a house will match all your interior criteria, but won't have parking, or won't be in the ideal neighbourhood. Don't be too narrow in your requirements; remember the difference between what you absolutely need and what you just want to have. The art of buying real estate is making as few compromises as possible while being realistic in your expectations.

Each home is different, and each will have its pros and cons. The home you want may not be in the price range you can presently afford. You may simply not be able to afford Montreal's Westmount area, though you're dying to live there . . . or you may sacrifice your dream home to live in your dream neighbourhood. Theoretically, you can always change your home if it isn't perfect, but there isn't much you can do about the neighbourhood. Keep an open mind when searching for a new home, and make comparisons to help you narrow your list of priorities.

Be flexible. Trust your agent's professionalism — she's likely seen many buyers with similar desires and circumstances. Take her advice and look at the homes she suggests even if you have reservations. Your agent may find a house that's great for you, but that you can't picture until you actually take a tour. Your agent may understand what you want even if you can't express it.

Chapter 8

Home Shopping

In This Chapter

▶ Uncovering homes for sale

▶ Considering foreclosures

▶ Looking at overall style and resale value

▶ Reviewing your priorities

▶ Understanding exactly what you're getting in a new home

▶ Comparing the homes you see and picking a winner

*W*hen you begin your home search adventure, you have to replace the dream home in your mind with the one you can realistically buy. (Unless, of course, you've won the lottery or just inherited a cash windfall, in which case you can probably buy exactly what you like.) But how do you find the right home to fit your budget and your basic needs? You can choose to sit back and leave the searching to your agent, but most of us would like to be more involved in the process. In this chapter, we give you home-hunting tips and suggest ways for you to evaluate the advertised listings and home tours you take so that you can make well-informed buying decisions.

Finding That Perfect Home

If you already have a list of priorities that clearly outlines the features you need and want in a home, and you've done some neighbourhood research (refer to Chapter 7), you probably have a good idea what and where you want to buy. Now you can focus your attention on the real estate market.

These days, you can really get your feet wet in the home-shopping process on the Internet. The Web is a great place to see what homes are out there, check prices, and find out what the price points are in your desired location. Check out the Appendix, where we list Web site after Web site to help your home hunt.

Use your agent

Be open to the expert guidance your real estate agent has to offer. If you hired an agent, let that person match you with a new home. Agents spend hours every day looking at homes, and they have years of real estate experience. A good agent who's in touch with the market may even know about sale properties before they're officially put on the market. (Refer to Chapter 6 for advice on finding an agent.)

Give your agent as much information as you can about what you're looking for, but be open to his advice. If you feel your agent isn't listening to you or isn't providing you with good service, talk about the situation. If you're not able to clear up the problem, you may need to find a different agent.

If you want to live only on one particular block, or in one specific apartment building, you can ask your agent to send out letters to people living there to see if they're considering moving. You may be able to find a property before it hits the market.

Your agent may also have some high-tech tools at his disposal. Depending on where you live and what options your agent has, you may be able to receive automatic e-mail notifications. Your agent can set up online programs that will send you all-new listings that meet your criteria, in the specific area that you prefer. Your agent in many cases can target specific streets, and even blocks. What a time saver! You can narrow down the style of home you're looking for, set minimum values for the number of bedrooms, bathrooms, and interior dimensions — you name it.

Don't limit your search too much: Throw a wider net, and you may find a home that is just right for you that you wouldn't have even known about otherwise.

Neighbourhood watch

These days, the tools that an agent has can make searching your desired neighbourhood for a new home so much easier. But you can still get involved the old-fashioned way by scouring the neighbourhood yourself, looking for new "For Sale" signs, and proceeding accordingly. Agents will tell you that often a home that doesn't seem like a winner online can be a real gem in actuality. So don't necessarily rely on the photos you see; make the effort to look at the home in person — especially if all the other information provided is enticing.

MLS listings

The *Multiple Listing Service* (MLS) can be a useful home search tool. The MLS database contains listings of all homes for sale that are represented by a selling agent. A typical MLS listing gives you a great deal of detail about a given home, including the number and size of rooms, lot size, interior dimensions (square metres or square feet), approximate property taxes, and additional information — details such as "renovated kitchen" or "professionally landscaped." Using MLS is a good way to start your search and familiarize yourself with various neighbourhoods and price points. You can search MLS listings online at www.realtor.ca.

Figure 8-1 shows a sample home listing. Note that a listing contains many important details that can save you, the buyer, wasted trips to see inappropriate homes. The distance to shopping and transit is given, as is information about plumbing, heating, and sewers.

Word of mouth

The more people who know you're buying, the more people will suggest properties to you. Friends may have friends in the area who are thinking of selling. If you talk to people in the neighbourhood you're considering, you may get leads from strangers, too. Neighbours may know who's outgrowing their home or who's retiring to Florida next winter. Don't underestimate the value of word-of-mouth networking.

Don't get so caught up in getting a bargain that you lose sight of what you're buying. If your cousin's neighbour's daughter-in-law's brother is trying to sell a home to you, make sure it's the house you want before you even think about shaking his hand. Don't forget you're trying to buy a home, not make a deal. Never ever engage in oral agreements, even if the price seems right (see Chapter 10). You need a written agreement and the opportunity to do some in-depth investigation before you negotiate the price and terms of sale. An objective assessment of the property value and a professional home inspection must be carried out to ensure you make the right purchase decision.

Read the news

Most cities have free weekly real estate magazines and newspapers that can usually be picked up at real estate offices, street boxes, and convenience stores. These weeklies contain a selection of local residential listings. However, they often promote various real estate agents as much as they promote the listings. In most cases, the real estate weeklies do not present all the homes on the market; they print just the listings of the companies that advertise within them. Some of the weeklies will also rotate ads so that a house will appear every second week. In some areas, two or three real estate weeklies are published, and you would have to read them all to see everything on the market. Be aware that the printed listings are several days old by the time you see them, which may hurt your chances of buying any of the listed homes within the magazine or paper.

The classified sections of local newspapers also have real estate information worth examining — watch for open houses. Often, the advertisements have keywords to clue you in on what the property is like. "Reduced" or "motivated seller" may flag good bargains. Terms like "TLC needed," "fixer-upper," or "handyman special" send strong cautionary signals.

FOR SALE

3234 West 29th Ave, Vancouver

Area:	Vancouver	**Price:**	$1,799,000.00
Sub-area:	Dunbar	**Status:**	Active
Lot size:	55 x 122	**Title:**	Freehold
Taxes:	$6,681.26 (2010)	**Zoning:**	RS-5
Age:	85	**Bedrooms:**	4
Basement:	Unfinished	**Bathrooms:**	3

Construction:	Wood frame	**Sellers interest:**	Owner
Foundation:	Concrete perimeter	**Sewer:**	Municipal
Exterior:	Stucco	**Water:**	Municipal
Roof:	Asphalt	**Renovations:**	Partly
Heating:	Forced air/natural gas		
No of fireplaces:	1 – natural gas		

Features Included: Washer, dryer, fridge, stove dishwasher, garage door opener
Site Influences: Shopping nearby, schools nearby, lane access

Floor	Type	Dimensions
Main	Living room	20 x 14'10
Main	Dining room	16 x 10
Main	Kitchen	12 x 12
Main	Eating area	12 x 12
Main	Family room	14 x 12'6
Above	Master bedroom	13'5 x 12'9
Above	Bedroom	12'4 x 12
Above	Bedroom	11'5 x 11
Above	Bedroom	11 x 10
Basement	Recreation room	25 x 14
Basement	Storage	20 x 14

Total square footage (incl. unfinished basement): 3,270 square feet

Comments: This traditional Dunbar home features cross-hall living room & dining room, and is situated on a generous 55 x 122 lot with beautiful gardens. The principle rooms are very large: 4 bedroom, 3 baths and storage, a bright open kitchen with lots of cabinets. You'll find lots of room for ideas in the unfinished basement with 8' ceilings. This home is central to shopping, Pacific Spirit Park, Vancouver's best schools and UBC while being one of the quietest, premier neighbourhoods in Vancouver. RS-5 zoning permits laneway housing. Plumbing roughed in for basement suite.

Listing Broker: Dummies Realty Inc
Listing Agent: Annie Agent (604) 555-1212
Agent contact: annie.agent@dummiesrealty.ca

Figure 8-1:
This sample listing resembles a typical MLS listing.

Open houses

Often sellers have open houses when they first put their homes on the market, giving you a great opportunity to check them out. You can talk to the seller's agent in person. Find out (if you can) why the sellers want to sell, and how motivated they are to sell. If you don't like the idea of having other people looking at the home at the same time as you, remember you can always make an appointment to see the home again privately. Pay attention to what other potential buyers have to say; they may notice something about the home that you've missed, or have done some productive snooping where you were too shy to look. Listen to their potential plans for the home; they may give you some good ideas.

Don't misrepresent yourself to the seller's agent. If you're working with an agent of your own, be up front about it when talking to the seller's agent at the open house. When an agent spends time and effort on your behalf and then finds out you're working with someone else, you can expect an angry reaction. Don't jeopardize your situation by being dishonest; you may face difficult sale negotiations if the seller's agent is unhappy with you.

In a hot real estate market, you'll find that many properties sell without ever hosting an open house. A home may be listed on MLS and then a few days later the selling agent holds an open house to give other agents an opportunity to view the home, but a public open house just isn't necessary. If you're working with an agent, you may well be able to attend that *agents' open house* in her company — and get a jump on the competition.

Getting Up Close with Foreclosures

Although we aren't going to get into the nitty-gritty of the foreclosure process from the home owner's point of view, suffice it to say that purchasing a foreclosed property takes a certain amount of doggedness and a special type of buyer.

A *foreclosure* is a legal proceeding that bars or terminates the mortgagor's right of redeeming a mortgaged property. Two types of home foreclosures exist, and the process of purchasing a home in foreclosure really depends on which province you live in:

- ✔ **Judicial sale:** A *judicial sale* is conducted under the authority and supervision of the court. In this case, a lender is bound to apply to the court in order to get its permission for selling the foreclosed property.

- ✔ **Power of sale:** In a *power of sale,* the lender sells the property without involving the court. The lender gets the right to sell the home from the mortgage documents or from that province's legislation, which authorizes the power of sale in that particular province in Canada.

In Prince Edward Island, Newfoundland and Labrador, Ontario, and New Brunswick, the power of sale is the primary recovery method for the lender. On the other hand, judicial sales are the way to go in Alberta, Quebec, British Columbia, Manitoba, and Saskatchewan. In Nova Scotia, the main recovery process is known as *mortgage foreclosure and sale* or *mortgage foreclosure,* but it is regarded as a judicial sale because the court is still involved.

When you're buying a foreclosure, either you're buying a home directly from the lender (and its bureaucracy) or the lender has to receive court approval of the offer that you present. Either way, the purchase isn't going to be as simple as dealing with a living, breathing homeowner. Finding out if your offer is accepted can take weeks, and if you have to set a court date, nothing's stopping other interested parties from presenting offers that may be better than the one you submitted originally.

If you're buying a foreclosed home, the previous owners may have been just a wee bit grumpy about losing the roof over their heads. So, you may find damaged walls and floors, or missing appliances . . . heck, you may even find that the toilets are gone — anything's possible. Chances are, if the former owners have been in financial difficulty, they may not have been keeping up with regular maintenance either.

Be aware that the court or lender provides no warranties on the property you're looking to purchase. The purchase is basically an "as is, where is" situation. You can't say to the lender that you'll take the home if they fix the foundation crack: They're not going to. Lenders will proceed only with *clean* offers — offers without conditions. The prospective purchaser must do all due diligence in advance and put forth a subject-free (unconditional) offer. So, you may have to pony up for an inspection in advance and still not get the property.

Savvy buyers can find good deals out there, but be prepared to do lots of homework . . . and waiting.

Sizing It Up: Do You Like the House?

The first thing you think about when you view a home is what it looks like from the outside, or what is known as its *curb appeal.* Do you find it inviting? Can you picture yourself on the lawn? Do you know just where to put your prize rosebushes? Even if the property may look a bit run down right now, will a coat of paint and some sprucing up of the landscaping make a difference?

Style is an important factor too. You may find it difficult to choose what you like from the many styles of home architecture available. Conversely, you may want to steer clear of certain types of homes that just don't float your boat. Perhaps you'll "just know" what's your favourite when you see the house you love. Your gut instincts play a big part in choosing a home. You may just feel that everything comes together perfectly in a certain home: good neighbourhood, close to schools and parks, big yard (but not too big), great floor plan, attractive exterior, ample parking — the whole package.

Consider buying a home the same as making an investment, because it's probably the biggest purchase you'll ever make. Think about the resale value of the home you're buying, and what kind of profit you'll make on your investment. Someday, for some reason, you'll want to sell your home, and hopefully get more than you paid. Factor in the potential that someone else will be buying the home from you eventually, and look for features that will stand the test of time. If the wiring in the Georgian house you're looking at is fine now, think about whether it will still be fine in 5 years, or 20, and consider that you may need to invest in repairs before you can sell again. Will your finances handle the renovations then? Are you prepared to replace the chimney when it crumbles? And what about the roof? Always keep the long-term outlook in mind.

The more homes you see, the easier comparing them and focusing on what you're looking for will be. If you can, stick to the ten-house rule: Visit at least ten homes, including open houses as well as appointments set up with your agent, before you decide to make an offer. You may think this is extreme, but the first set of homes will probably wow you with just their cosmetic charms; after ten wows, you'll have become more critical than "I really like the colour of that bathroom." Keep in mind that if you want a very specific neighbour-hood, it may take years for ten houses to come on the market. You may be faced with a three-house rule instead. However, sometimes when you know, you know. You may fall in love with the first condominium you see, knowing full well that the place has everything that you need and want. If that's the case, you may want to pounce. Your agent can guide you in this decision.

On the other hand, be careful not to see too many homes! You may fall in love with a place, but then think to yourself that there may be something just that much better if you keep looking. Well, if you found your perfect partner, would you keep dating others? (We're hoping you'll say no.) Try not to talk yourself out of a good fit. You'll ultimately drive yourself (and your agent) crazy.

When looking at homes, it makes a great deal of sense for you or your agent to book appointments one after the other. This approach is efficient, and comparing homes is easier when they're fresh in your mind. But try to look at only five or six homes at a time, and take careful note of each home's features. Seeing 15 homes in one day will result in nothing but confusion: Was house number seven the one with the great kitchen, or was that number ten? (Later in this chapter, we discuss making organized records for the homes you view.) Many homes also have *feature sheets* that present detailed information and include a picture. Remember to pick up feature sheets wherever you can to help your recall when you're trying to make decisions later. Your agent should be able to provide you with detailed information sheets as well (often from agent-only information sites).

Look at homes more than once; don't feel you have to make a decision about a home when you first step into it. Unless you're looking in an incredibly strong seller's market, make more than one visit to a home you're seriously interested in, preferably during different times of the day and of the week.

Avoid buying the most expensive home in the neighbourhood. Because home values are influenced by the values of the other surrounding residences, the most expensive homes on the block will have a smaller appreciation than others. After all, if most homes on the street are selling for $225,000, people will probably think twice before making an offer on the home that's listed at $450,000, regardless of how nice it is. Buying the lowest priced house in the best neighbourhood is a strategy worth considering.

I Still Haven't Found What I'm Looking For

If you've looked at what seems like a million homes and you haven't seen any you like, discuss your concerns with your agent. Possibly there has been some miscommunication somewhere, and the two of you are working at cross-purposes. Review your priority list (refer to Chapter 7) together, and talk about why you haven't liked any of the homes you've seen so far.

The problem may be that you have too fixed an idea of what is essential and you need to be more flexible. We can't help but say it again: The home of your dreams may not exist. What you're looking for is a home that's as close as you can get to your ideal, but you're going to have to compromise. The home that may be the right fit may not make your heart race right away, but in the cold light of day it ticks a lot of boxes. Your agent will probably let you know if you're being too picky and may redirect your attention to some homes you've already seen. After you've rethought your priorities, you may have a new appreciation for some homes' advantages. Your agent should also keep you informed if one of the houses you found somewhat interesting has had a price reduction. Suddenly, the house that wasn't quite right can become much more appealing given a $25,000 price reduction.

If you sense your agent doesn't understand what you really want, now may be the time to part ways. Do try to explain to your agent why you feel a change is necessary. Sometimes an agent and a buyer are just not a good fit, and there's no point continuing with a relationship that isn't working. If, however, you have very, very specific criteria, be prepared to wait a long time to find your home. Agents don't have a magic wand that'll be able to make your dream home appear (though we're sure they'd love one). You may have to relax your requirements a little bit, and find a patient agent who understands the importance of your specifications.

All Systems Go

Although you definitely need a professional home inspector to tell you if all the systems in your potential home, such as heating and electricity, are in good condition (refer to Chapter 9), you may be wondering what all these different systems are about, anyway. Knowing the kinds of systems you're buying will help determine what your future home expenses will be, as well as warn you about potentially costly problems you may not notice. Besides, what is a GFCI outlet, anyway, and why is it recommended? You should understand what the difference is between a 60-amp service and a 100-amp service before you get an inspector involved. But good news — after reading this section, you will understand the difference.

Many people rent or lease the hot water tank in their home instead of owning it outright. Ask the seller (or seller's agent) what the status of the hot water tank is; if it's a rental, it may cost you about $10 to $20 a month to continue renting. Also find out how the hot water is heated. Like the home itself, you'll find it more costly if the water tank is heated by electricity, which will probably be the case if your heating system also runs on electricity, or on oil. (Electric heat takes much longer to warm a tank of water than gas- or oil-fired heating does.) One final thing: Check the water tank's capacity — you don't want to run out of hot water every time you shower. On the plus side, a rented hot water tank can easily be exchanged for one with a larger capacity, and if it breaks, it'll be replaced at no cost to you.

Heating systems

Although you get an estimate of what your heating costs will be from your seller's previous bills, it makes sense to know what kind of system you're getting. A poorly maintained furnace with overused filters and clogged ducts will be more expensive to run than a serviced one, regardless of its heating source.

Forced air

A forced air furnace is the most common type of furnace. Fuelled by *natural gas* or *oil* to heat the air, the furnace then pushes warm air up through the house. A properly maintained forced air furnace can be very efficient and economical, but there are different levels of efficiency. Older, conventional furnaces rely on the "hot air rises naturally" idea, which can result in cold basements and warm third floors. This heating system may necessitate ceiling fans on the third floor to circulate the heated air.

Newer, high-efficiency furnaces are, as the name suggests, more efficient than older forced air models and cheaper to run, but they can be relatively expensive to install. In the long run, you can recoup the installation expense through savings on heating bills. High-efficiency furnaces are also very compact; they take up much less space than the older-style forced air furnaces. Many homes can be heated with a high-efficiency furnace that's no bigger than a hot water tank. Any home that already has a high-efficiency furnace installed has at least one solid feature going for it. A forced air furnace can last between 10 and 25 years, and can cost about $2,500 to as much as $10,000 to buy, depending on the level of efficiency you want and the size of the home you are heating.

Hot water

Hot water heating uses radiators, hot water baseboards, or in-floor hot water radiant grids to heat a house or condominium. The hot water is usually heated through a natural gas-, electric-, or oil-fired boiler. A hot water system heats very well, and is controlled through thermostats that control zone valves throughout the system. In older systems, it may be impossible to control the temperature of individual rooms because one thermostat controls the whole house. Also, the valve on above-floor hot water radiators has a tendency to rust.

A standard gas boiler for a hot water heating system may cost around $3,000 and should last anywhere from 15 to 50 years, depending on what type it is. The benefit of hot water heat is there's no dust blown around by a forced air furnace, a great benefit for people with allergies. The hot water system is quieter than forced air and provides a more consistent heat.

If you want to install central air conditioning in a home that has a hot water heating system, you may find it very expensive because you'll probably have to either install new ductwork or install a higher-efficiency system. However, in recent years new air conditioner units that are wall/ceiling mounted on outside walls for venting have become available. These units are very energy efficient (but can be pricey as well). For more information, contact an independent air conditioning expert.

Baseboard heaters

Using baseboard heaters means that there is no ductwork to fill your walls, and each heating unit has its own thermostat, so different rooms of the home can be kept at different temperatures. Hot water baseboards can usually be controlled by a valve on the baseboard, and electric baseboards are controlled by a thermostat dedicated to that baseboard. These heaters can get hot to the touch, so be careful where you place furnishings. This might also be a consideration for parents of young children with curious fingers.

Electric

Due to rising energy costs, electric heating can be very expensive to run (though in some places it may still be cheaper than oil or gas). Heating your home electrically can be done two ways: through baseboards, or using a forced air furnace or hot water boiler (see earlier in this section). Because there is no need for a chimney with electric systems, the efficiency tends to be better, though some people complain that electric systems just don't heat well.

If your property (a new condominium, for example) was designed for electric heat and your property is well insulated, you may find electric heating to be economical and efficient. However, if you're converting a drafty old house to electric heat, your heating bills will be sky-high. Be wary when buying any property where electric heat has been installed if the structure wasn't designed with this kind of system in mind.

Oil

Well, your home won't blow up. That's all one oil furnace owner had to say when we asked her about the advantages of oil furnaces. Oil furnaces were commonplace before the 1970s, but have declined in popularity because they're more expensive than natural gas and require an oil tank that sits in your backyard or takes up room in already overcrowded basements. Some complaints about oil heating include having stinky oil odours in your home if the system isn't working properly, and dirty walls near the tank. If you find a home with an oil tank in the backyard, have it inspected thoroughly before you purchase the house. Despite the move toward natural gas forced air heating systems, many homes still have oil-fired forced air systems, which suggests that they are remarkably reliable.

Supporters of oil heating argue that modern oil furnaces can be the best and cheapest way to heat your home, especially if natural gas lines aren't available in your area. With proper maintenance (you should have it serviced every year), an oil furnace can be quite efficient, though oil has to be delivered in truckloads to your home. Oil can be used to fire a forced air or hot water heating system. An oil-fired furnace can be replaced with a natural gas furnace if gas lines are available in your neighbourhood. Converting from oil to gas may require relining your chimney and installing a better ventilation system.

In many parts of the country, incentive plans exist to convert from oil-fired heating to a more economical natural-gas-fired furnace.

Natural gas

Natural gas is generally more economical than other types of fuel. The catch: You can have it installed only where there are pipelines. The beautiful thing about natural gas is that other appliances that require heat can be bought to run on natural gas, and they tend to be cheaper to run. Many people swear by gas stoves; others love the economical benefits of gas clothes dryers or the option of having a direct line to a barbecue or patio heater. In very rare cases, homes with natural gas heating may have a problem with carbon monoxide, but with proper maintenance (you should have your furnace serviced every year) and carbon monoxide detectors in your home, this shouldn't be an issue. Natural gas can fire a forced air furnace or a hot water heating system.

Oil's well that ends well

When underground or "in-ground" heating oil tanks are abandoned, they pose a major environmental hazard if they aren't decommissioned properly. But that's not the only reason why it's important to investigate before you buy a property. If you find out after you've bought a home that your property includes an abandoned oil tank, you'll most likely incur the cost of removing the tank — which could be substantial. The seller of the home may not know whether a tank is present or not, especially if the home has changed hands many times since the conversion to natural gas (most likely in the 1960s or 1970s).

Most municipalities or utility companies will keep records of when a property converted from oil to natural gas heating, and whether the oil tank was removed at the time of conversion. If there is no record of an oil tank being removed, look for a vent pipe running up the side of the house for no apparent reason. The pipe is a telltale sign that there may be a tank present — vent pipes were required to ensure the oil flowed smoothly from the tank to the furnace. If there's no vent pipe, you can contact a specialized company that searches for in-ground oil tanks. The cost for the initial search is usually $100 to $200.

If the presence of leaking oil is determined, the abandoned tank and any contaminated soil *must* be removed. If the tank has not leaked and it's readily accessible (like in the middle of the front yard), the cost to remove it can be in the $1,500 to $3,000 range.

The absolute worst-case scenario is a real nightmare: The tank had oil left in it when the house converted to natural gas usage, and the tank has since rusted out and has slowly leaked oil into the ground, trickling undetected into the neighbours' yards. At this point, the cost to remove all contaminated soil can be as much as $100,000 or more if the oil has entered the groundwater and adjacent properties.

Propane

Have you heard the news? Propane isn't just for barbecues any more. Many consider propane to be the most convenient and versatile fuel for home heating, and the benefits of using propane are numerous.

First of all, propane goes everywhere. Pressure is used to turn propane gas into liquid, making it very easy to transport, and cheaper too. As an easily portable fuel, it can be used beyond the end of the natural gas mains, and Canada's intricate road and rail network means it can be delivered almost anywhere it is needed — making it an especially smart choice for off-the-beaten-track recreational properties.

Second, we own it! Close to 90 percent of the propane we use is produced in Canada — propane is an abundant homegrown product, right up there with maple sugar candy and half of the stars in Hollywood.

And are you tired of pesky power interruptions? A home served by an individual storage tank, which is constantly topped up, means propane can run virtually uninterrupted.

For the environmentally conscious, propane is less harmful to the environment than other available fuels. To meet pipeline standards, practically all pollutants are removed before propane enters the system. When propane is burned, it meets the U.S. Environmental Protection Agency's clean air emissions standards. In comparison to electricity and fuel oil, propane is generally more efficient, reliable, and clean, and is less expensive.

Heat pumps

Heat pumps work like air conditioners, but as the name suggests, they provide heat as well as cool air. Like a refrigerator, a heat pump compresses and decompresses gases to create or use heat through electricity. Because a heat pump can use more energy than it will produce if the outside temperature is less than 10 degrees Celsius, it works best in conjunction with a central furnace. Again, heat pumps have differing degrees of efficiency, they're very expensive to install (sometimes three times the price of a gas or oil furnace), and they require a larger duct system. Heat pumps are also expensive to maintain, and need yearly service. However, with a heat pump in your home, you don't have to worry about installing a separate cooling system.

Electrical systems

From lighting to cooking, electricity runs most of the important household services you use on a daily basis. You need a reliable and safe electrical system in your home. Be aware of service amps and GFCI — they're two important aspects of a home's electrical system.

Service amps

Electricity comes in three common sizes: 60 amp, 100 amp, and 200 amp. Sixty-amp service is an older electrical standard, usually found in homes with a bit of history. While there isn't anything inherently wrong with 60-amp service, provided the house isn't too large, the bells should still sound in any buyer's mind. Sixty-amp service poses two big problems: First, you may be hard-pressed to find an insurer willing to cover the property, and second, if you ever had dreams of central air conditioning, a dishwasher, or an electric hot water heater, forget them.

Sixty-amp service can't usually handle the demands of anything beyond the usual small appliances, and pushing those limits can increase the risk of fire (which explains our first point). Remember, too, that 60-amp homes were wired before the advent of the power-hungry electric dryer and microwave. Think twice before buying a home with 60-amp service, because sooner or later you'll likely have to upgrade to a minimum 100-amp service. If you want to proceed, be aware that it can cost $750 to $1,500 to bring a house up to 100-amp service, and adjust your offer accordingly.

Older homes may have knob and tube wiring, which also should be upgraded if you are installing 100-amp service. This upgrade will, however, require rewiring most of the house, another expensive proposition depending on the size of the house.

GFCI

GFCI stands for *ground fault circuit interrupter*. You've probably seen them in a hotel bathroom: You know, the outlet with the little red button and the little black button. GFCI is designed for places where water (a very good conductor of electricity) may cause an electric shock and possibly seriously injure a person. GFCI receptacles should be placed in all wet environments, including kitchens, bathrooms, wet bars, laundry rooms, and outdoors. Inexpensive safety measures, GFCI outlets should be installed if the home you buy doesn't already have them.

UFFI

No, we're not talking about Martians; it's insulation we're addressing here. *UFFI,* or *urea formaldehyde foam insulation*, was a popular insulation in the mid-1970s. Unfortunately, when the UFFI foam ingredients weren't mixed properly, the resulting insulation released quantities of formaldehyde gas in homes, causing long-term adverse effects for some people. UFFI was banned in Canada in 1980. However, UFFI may still be in some homes today: The government gave out three times more grants for manufacturing UFFI insulation than the number of rebates that have been applied for to replace it.

If the UFFI in a home was installed properly, it should not break down or pose a risk to you. The Canada Mortgage and Housing Corporation (CMHC) will now insure UFFI-equipped homes. As a safeguard, you may still want to include a clause in your offer to purchase contract, stating that the seller warrants that the home is not insulated with UFFI, but in some provinces the clause is pre-printed in the paperwork. Most sellers will be able to disclose that, to the best of their knowledge, they *are* or *are not* aware of any UFFI in their home.

Septic tanks

Many rural areas aren't serviced by the local municipality's waste management system, and even some urban sites rely on private septic systems to dispose of wastewater. Instead of wastewater flowing through a city sewer system to a treatment site, the septic tank with a leaching bed (also known as weeping tiles or a tile bed) treats the water before it goes back into the soil. The average septic tank requires a space of about 1 square metre (10 square feet). Your septic tank should be at least 1½ metres (5 feet) from your home and 16½ metres (55 feet) from sources of water. The leaching bed should be 30½ metres (100 feet) from sources of water. Sludge collected in the tank should be pumped out every four years. According to the Canada Mortgage and Housing Corporation, minimum tank volumes range from 1,800 litres to 3,600 litres, depending on the province or territory.

The problem with septic systems is that they're not very well regulated by the provincial or federal governments, and so no standard that sellers need to comply with exists. You can get a certificate for the septic system from the home's municipality, but it verifies only the location of the tank and the leaching bed, not its condition.

Don't assume that every rural home has a septic system; ask the seller exactly what kind of waste system is in place. The house can possibly have a holding tank instead. Unlike a septic system, which processes sewage on-site and needs pumping every few years, a holding tank must be pumped every few months. If the home has a holding tank, speak with the seller about the cost of maintaining it.

If you buy a home with a septic system, you should get a plan (either from the owner or the municipality) that shows where the septic tank and leaching bed are located in relation to the house and water sources. Ask about the tank's capacity and when the tank was pumped out last. To ensure the tank was indeed emptied when the seller claims, ask for a receipt of the cleaning, which will confirm the date.

The *drainfield* is the area in the yard directly over the septic system. The drainfield should consist of at least 1¼ metres (4 feet) of native soil between the system and the surface of the yard. When looking at this area, watch for the following problems:

- **Trees or shrubs on the drainfield, rather than grass:** The root systems of trees and shrubs can interfere with the septic system.

- **Pavement, a parked car, a patio, or a building of any kind, such as a garden shed:** These items put undue downward pressure on the septic system, which can crush pipes and prevent the system from working properly.

- **Patches of lush growth, or overly moist soil over the drainfield:** This may be a sign that sewage isn't being processed properly.

- **A bad smell around the yard:** Odour may be a sign that sewage is surfacing, which can pose a major health hazard.

Don't expect a home with a septic system to switch over to a sewer system in the near future, unless there are firm plans for the municipality to do so. Sewer systems are expensive to install, and usually the government will decide it's not worth it. A septic system, however, should last about 30 years, depending on maintenance.

Zonolite/vermiculite insulation — what is it?

Zonolite (also known as vermiculite) insulation is a grey popcorn-like insulation that was blown into home attics and walls for years. The insulation was made from asbestos-contaminated vermiculite ore mined from the 1920s until 1990. Although the mine that was the likely source was closed in 1990, the insulation remains in thousands of homes across Canada. Health Canada says that the best way to prevent asbestos exposure is to leave the insulation undisturbed, but if it is a concern, it can cost thousands of dollars to have the asbestos-contaminated insulation removed.

Well water

Similar to septic systems, a private source of water is used in a home where there are no municipal water lines to supply the residence. The minimum water storage tank you should consider is 40 litres. The main problems with well water are that it can become contaminated and therefore undrinkable, and that if the well dries up you have to do some serious digging.

If you buy a home with well water, ensure that you get a certificate from the seller that guarantees the water to be drinkable. You can determine the quantity of water available as well — you should be able to get a certificate outlining the quantity of available water and the possible lifespan of the well. In some provinces, the seller is obliged to have the water certified by the government before the home goes up for sale. Water is generally tested for bacteria, hardness, and other harmful chemicals. For instance, you may find that there is arsenic in the water. In small amounts, this isn't an issue – but if it's above acceptable limits, you may need to install an expensive filtration system. The well water should be tested annually.

If water becomes contaminated, the municipality sometimes has no choice but to extend a water line up to the area, so a possibility of your water source changing from private to municipal exists. Your property taxes may increase if water services are extended to your property, however.

Stacking Them Up — How the Homes Compare

To help you organize your thoughts as you look at various homes, use the comparison chart in Table 8-1 to record information about the homes you see. Make a copy of the chart, and take it with you when you go to an open house or on a private home tour. Recording all the details makes keeping track of the potential benefits or drawbacks you observe about each home easier.

Table 8-1   Home Comparisons

	Home 1	Home 2	Home 3	Home 4
General Info				
Address				
Type/style of home				
Dimensions (m² or ft²)				
Age of home				
Size of lot (m² or ft²)				
Facilities (applicable to condominiums)				
Asking price				
Property taxes				
Fees (applicable to condominiums)				
Financial reserve fund (applicable to condominiums)				
Overall condition				
Exterior				
Frontage				
Siding				
Condition				
Eaves				
Roof				
Material				
Age				

(continued)

Table 8-1 (continued)

	Home 1	Home 2	Home 3	Home 4
Parking				
Driveway				
Garage				
Number of parking spots (applicable to condominiums)				
Yard				
Condition				
Size				
Landscaping				
Porch				
Deck/patio				
Shed				
Fencing				
Swimming pool				
Special features				
Utilities				
Heating				
Type				
Average annual cost				
Electrical service				
Amps				
Type/age of wiring				
Water				
Municipal/well				
Hot water tank				

	Home 1	Home 2	Home 3	Home 4
Utilities				
Sewers/septic				
Central air conditioning				
Living Room				
Size				
Condition				
Flooring				
Windows				
Dining Room				
Size				
Condition				
Flooring				
Windows				
Kitchen				
Size				
Condition				
Eat-in area				
Flooring				
Windows				
Appliances				
Stove/oven				
Electric/gas				
Condition				
Fridge				
Freezer				
Age/condition				

(continued)

Table 8-1 (continued)

	Home 1	Home 2	Home 3	Home 4
Appliances				
Washer				
Dryer				
Dishwasher				
Freezer				
Microwave				
Attic				
Condition				
Insulated				
Bathrooms				
Number of bathrooms				
Size				
Ground-floor bathroom				
Basement				
Finished				
Size				
Flooring				
Windows				
Separate entrance				
Bedrooms				
Number of bedrooms				
Main bedroom				
Size				
Condition				
Flooring				

	Home 1	Home 2	Home 3	Home 4
Bedrooms				
Closet				
Ensuite bathroom				
Other features				
Bedroom 2				
Size				
Condition				
Closet				
Bedroom 3				
Size				
Condition				
Closet				
Family Room				
Size				
Condition				
Sun Room/Office/Den				
Size				
Condition				
Other Features				
Central vacuum				
Light fixtures				
Fireplace				
Coat closet				
Linen closet				

(continued)

Table 8-1 *(continued)*

	Home 1	Home 2	Home 3	Home 4
Other Features				
Security system				
Soundproofing (applicable to condominiums or townhouses)				
Balcony				
High ceilings				
Kitchen pantry				
Jacuzzi/hot tub				
Sliding glass doors				
Neighbourhood				
Overall				
Police/fire station nearby				
Public transportation available				
Parks				
Schools				
Shopping				
Distance from workplace				
Traffic				
Nuisances				
Other comments				

Chapter 9

This Home Is Great! (Except for . . .)

*Y*our dream home may turn into a nightmare if you don't do your homework to make sure that the home is in (at least) acceptable condition. Try to think like James Bond when you're looking for a home: Have a cool head and an analytic mind. Don't let your heart rule! Sometimes the home that just needs a bit of elbow grease is the right one for you, and not the flashy, staged one that makes your pulse race. Because some things can be remedied for a minimal amount (think: replacing the stove) and others can cost thousands of dollars (think: replacing the foundation), knowing the difference will save you time, money, and stress later.

In this chapter, we discuss what is fixable, what may be a deal breaker, and homes you may want to flag, like foreclosures or flipped homes.

Don't Fall in Love

Most people find home buying a very emotional experience. After all, you're not just making a purchase; you're also choosing a new lifestyle and environment, for at least a few years. Although you must like the home you purchase, you can easily fall in love with a place for the wrong reasons. Don't overlook a home's faults or underestimate its problems simply because the kitchen's to die for, or the view from the master bedroom is spectacular. And don't just dismiss a home because you detest the neon-pink paint job in the bathroom — a wonderful home may be there just waiting to be redecorated.

Minor details can turn into major headaches

Mike and Monique had been searching for the perfect character home in an established neighbourhood. Though they had hoped to find a home with a double garage, their dream home had only a single garage and a driveway so narrow that in order to get one of their vehicles out of the garage, the second one would need to be moved out of the driveway.

Mike and Monique were undeterred — they figured that they could always leave one vehicle on the street if they had to, and went ahead with the purchase. What they didn't realize was that parking in the neighbourhood is restricted to the south side of the street only. Now, consequently, when either Mike or Monique arrives home, all the street parking is invariably taken. What was supposed to be just a minor nuisance has become an ongoing annoyance because one or the other constantly has to move one car to get the other car out of the garage, which is particularly annoying in the long and snowy winter. Adding to the inconvenience is the fact that friends don't like dropping by because they have to park blocks away.

A combination of location and practicality is essential when you're looking for a home that fits your needs. If you're thinking of buying, look at the home more than once. Every neighbourhood has its own activity periods. Visit the area at different times (evening, during the day, weekends) to assess the traffic and noise. Take a walk around. Do you see neighbours outside? Children? Yappy dogs? If you don't like the 'hood, it's not any good.

Reality Check: Can You Fix the Home's Problems?

Part of the evaluation process when looking at homes involves trying to convince yourself, "I can always fix that after I move in." In many cases, that may be true. If you're lucky enough to be a professional contractor with time on your hands, more power to you. But if you're an average Joe or Joanna, you may be biting off more than you can chew. Some things that need fixing are pretty easy to take care of: painting over an ugly wall, or stripping off 20-year-old wallpaper, for example.

Other fixes are just too big to take on, especially if they need to be done immediately after sinking your savings into the purchase of your new home. And remember the sad truth about home renovations: They'll almost always require more time and money than you anticipate. To be on the safe side, add 10 to 20 percent to your renovation cost estimate to cover unexpected difficulties. Expect timelines to run long as well. All it takes is a subcontractor to experience a delay, or that new tile you ordered to ship late, and you can find weeks added on to the renovation process. (For information on finding renovators, builders, and interior designers on the Web, see the Appendix.)

Household cosmetics

You may look like you stepped out of the pages of a French fashion magazine, but Mrs. Olafson, whose 75-year-old bungalow is up for sale, may not share your highbrow tastes. Making cosmetic changes to personalize your home is not a big deal, and you can undertake the expense gradually. Living in a salmon-pink stucco-clad home for a few months until you can afford to repaint the exterior won't kill you.

Many sellers paint their homes in neutral colours to make it easier for potential buyers to visualize the home as they would want it. Of course, not everyone is fond of beige or taupe, so you may encounter a home that requires you to look beyond the shiny turquoise lacquer on its kitchen walls. Then again, if all the appliances, cupboards, and countertops are in shades you find horrifying, you may have a problem, depending on your budget.

A putting-green lawn in a home's front yard can always be landscaped so that you never have to mow. Squeaky planks can usually be fixed with a nail or two (unless you, like many of us, have a hammer phobia). If you're a handy person, you probably won't worry about the sticky closet door. If you're really a do-it-yourselfer, you can rip out that ugly '70s shag carpet and refinish the hardwood underneath — just make sure that there *is* hardwood underneath, and that it's in good condition. Remember that if the hardwood has been refinished once, refinishing it a second time may not be possible — you can end up replacing the floor.

Things you can't change

Accept that you can't change some things about a home, no matter how much you may want to do so. If there's no room for parking, you can't make space that isn't there. You can't make a semi-detached home as soundproof as a fully detached home. If you have to walk through the bedroom to get to the stairs or the bathroom, you've got a problem. You can solve some floorplan problems through renovations, but if you need to tear down walls or relocate your staircase (likely putting you out of the house during renovations and ransacking your child's college fund), you may want to find a home that doesn't require the rebuild.

Location matters are largely out of your control. Unless you put up a mural or demolish the home next door, your large bay window in the dining room is always going to face that large brick wall. The cemetery backing your property isn't likely to move any time soon (and you really wouldn't want its residents to get up and leave, would you?).

Make sure you're legal

If you're considering buying a home with a rental unit, do your homework. Most sellers don't warrant their home's apartments as legal, which means that if you move in and immediately rent the suite, you're putting yourself at legal risk. If anything is unsafe or improperly done, you — the new owner — are legally responsible. Take care calculating how much time and money will go into making that apartment legal. In many cases, basement apartments aren't at all legal, so make sure you check with your lawyer or your local bylaw office before you buy. Municipal zoning may not allow a secondary, legal suite no matter how well it's built. And don't forget the increased cost of insurance that a rental unit may require!

When it's not worth it

Some problems will probably be just too big for you to handle. We're not referring to the long-term renovations you may think of doing later, such as adding a second floor to a bungalow or upgrading the bathroom. We're talking about the kinds of problems you have to deal with immediately — things that take a lot of time and cost a lot of money, usually more than your original estimates.

Our friends Radek and Maya found a wonderful, spacious, completely renovated *legal duplex* (a property with a legal second suite for extra revenue) for a really good price. There was only one catch: The foundation was rotting, a condition discovered by the inspector. The happy couple loved the home so much that they thought they could just have it repaired and take the cost out of the price they'd pay for the home. But because the home was hedged in by the house next door, the estimated cost to fix it — including jacking up the house to do the work, disconnecting and reconnecting the utilities, and re-drywalling the basement — was $50,000. This meant that neither tenants nor owner would be able to live in the home during the repair. The cost of the repair, plus the cost of finding somewhere else to live while it was being done (in addition to putting up the tenants somewhere else), outweighed the good things about the home, so Radek and Maya abandoned the idea of buying it.

If you decide to purchase a fixer-upper of a home, check out your financing options. Most banks will extend lines of credit to ambitious types like yourself. Talk to your mortgage lender.

Many repairs are tempting to try, but you have to be realistic. Things like moving a bathroom or kitchen aren't impossible to do, but the cost can be enormous because the renovation may involve relocating pipes and completely changing the roofline of the home. Ultimately, the price you pay in renovation may not be recouped when you go to sell in the future.

In case you've never done any major renovations to a home, Table 9-1 gives you a rough idea of how much they can cost. As you can see, renovations aren't cheap, so take care when deciding how much you can spend to achieve the results you want.

Table 9-1	**Rough Estimates for Home Repairs and Renovations**
Item	*Approximate Cost*
Bathroom renovation	$5,000 and up (depending on the quality of fixtures and amount of plumbing and electrical work required)
Kitchen renovation	$10,000–$75,000 (or more, depending on the scope of work and quality of materials and appliances)
Furnace — gas, forced air (mid efficiency)	$3,000–$7,000
Central air conditioning, with existing ducts	$2,500–$6,000
Aluminum storm door	$400–$500
Metal insulated door	$700–$800
New roof	$3,000–$50,000 (or more, depending on the roof materials and your home's architecture)
Home rewiring (complete)	$2,500 and up
Hardwood flooring	$6–$12 per square foot
Replace galvanized plumbing	$500–$3,500 (or more, depending on the size of your home and the number of storeys)
Exterior basement door	$6,500–$10,500 (including cutting through concrete foundation and new exterior stairs)

On the Flip Side . . .

There's a new kind of home in town: the *flipped home*. Typically, this home was purchased within the last few months, or maybe slightly longer ago, by an ambitious entrepreneur who figures that he or she can buy a fixer-upper, give it a facelift, so to speak, and then put it back on the market, all tarted up and move-in ready. This investor is looking for buyers who don't want to do anything to the property except move their furniture into it.

Though many flipped homes have been renovated properly and to code, just as many have not. And remember, sellers expect a premium on their investment:

Not only do they have to cover the costs of the purchase and renovations, but they have to cover the carrying and closing costs too. Flippers fully intend to make a healthy profit.

Purchasing a bad flip can cost you a lot of money. If the sellers have done all the renovations themselves and haven't acquired the proper permits, there may be hidden issues that may not be easily detectable in a home inspection, like inadequate wiring, poor plumbing, an incorrectly installed roof — you name it.

Don't be fooled by a cleverly staged home! A flipped home will often be all about the details. How's the paint job? Did the seller cheap out on things like light fixtures and switches? Did the seller go all out in the kitchen but leave the bathrooms looking like they came out of 1985, and now wants top dollar anyway? You need to investigate these things. Fortunately, with the change in market conditions in recent years and the increased savvy of the property-buying public, you won't find as many flipped homes on the market as you may have a few years ago.

If you want to purchase a home that is all done up, you may end up purchasing a flip. Make sure that you know exactly what has been done to the home — your agent should be able to give you an idea of how much the upgrades cost the seller and help you establish the real worth of the home. They will also be able to provide a "timeline" — was that house sold just months ago, and now all "done up" and back on the market? Be aware of your surroundings, as well: Do you really want to purchase the most expensive home on the block? You may be doing just that if you buy a flipped home.

Check It Out: Investigating Your Prospective New Home

After you take a few tours of a home and its surrounding neighbourhood and you decide to narrow down your prospects to the chosen one, it's time to take things a bit more seriously. Now is the time to book that appointment for a good second look. Although we recommend you check the interior and exterior of any home you're buying, remember that your own once-over is no replacement for a professional home inspection done by a certified building inspector (professional inspections are covered in Chapter 12).

If you're flexible about timing, you may want to consider buying a home in the winter. Not only do the homes in some areas tend to be cheaper in winter, but you can also get a better sense of how the home copes with the cold. Is the furnace capable of keeping the home sufficiently warm? At what cost? Check the home for drafts: Are some areas of the home much colder than others?

One common place for drafts is electrical outlets that haven't been sufficiently insulated. Is there snow on the roof of the home? If all the other homes have snow, and the one you're looking at doesn't, the attic is probably not properly insulated, and escaping heat is melting the snow. How well do the eaves work? Chances are, if there are huge icicles hanging at one point in the eaves, they need work. Another great time to check out a home is after a big rainstorm. You may be able to see whether the roof or foundation has leaks that need repair. Basement leaks are difficult to detect during the winter because the ground may be frozen and homes are dry from heating.

Consider all the following items when you make your initial serious inspection. And then if you're really interested in the home, follow up with a qualified building inspector. Don't try to be an expert yourself; always get an experienced, professional opinion.

- ✔ **Foundation:** Check for trees, especially willows, near the foundation. Roots can get into sewers and damage your pipes. Inspect cement cracks for roots. Also, see how far the foundation walls come up — the higher the cement walls for the foundation are, the better protected your foundation is from water damage. The land should slope away from the house to provide proper water runoff.

  If you see poured cement sloping between detached houses, this can be an indication that the residents attempted to prevent water from seeping in. Sometimes this cement helps, but sometimes it doesn't. Have a careful look at the foundation and basement inside. A good home inspector can determine how successful any past repairs were.

- ✔ **Eaves:** Check the condition of the eaves; look for blockages or places where things may overflow. Where the drainpipe ends, check to make sure the runoff is going away from the house.

  Nobody likes to stand outside in stormy weather, but this may be the best time to examine the eaves of a house and to judge their capacity to handle heavy rain or snow. Focus on the areas where the eaves overflow. Does rain build up in a particular area? Building inspectors may be the only people who like heavy rain — every house looks good on a sunny day. When it rains, though, you can see problems with a home that may not otherwise be evident.

- ✔ **Basement:** Look in the ceiling and floor corners for water damage. Use your nose: Does the basement smell musty? Tap any exposed wood foundation; if it's soft or damp, you have a problem. A dehumidifier in the basement may point to a water problem, and you should check it out. In areas where cold is definitely a problem in winter (say, Ottawa), follow the exposed water pipes as much as possible. Are they all insulated? Are there drafts around where you know the pipes run? Ask if the owners have had problems with freezing pipes.

✔ **Electricity and wiring:** Make sure there is at least 100-amp service. Older homes were built with 60-amp service, which just can't handle the demands of an electronic and technologically advanced generation (refer to Chapter 8 for more on electricity). Nobody wants to plug in the toaster and have the house go dark. Insurance companies may not even be willing to insure you until you improve the electrical service, which can cost anywhere from $500–$2,000 or more to upgrade. Watch out for lots of extension cords too; their presence probably means there aren't enough electrical outlets in the home. In older homes, be on the lookout for irregular wiring or unusual phone or cable lines due to former rooming-house situations. Are there enough phone jacks for your five teenagers? Check the dryer and stove outlets, if possible, and flick all the light switches on and off; sometimes light switches are also attached to outlets, rather than to lights. If switch plates and outlet covers have been replaced, don't assume that the wiring behind them has been upgraded or grounded.

✔ **Water pressure:** Turn on the shower or tub and the sink and then flush the toilet. You don't want to be surprised by a sudden loss of hot or cold water while you're taking a shower! Taste the water; it's an added expense if you're always going to be buying bottled because the tap water tastes or smells bad. Fill the tub or sinks, pull the plugs, and watch the drainage speed.

✔ **Effects of water damage:** Always look inside a home at the corners and ceilings (particularly below where plumbing is) for signs of water damage. Make sure you check the closet ceilings, too; chances are whoever fixed the roof and repainted the bedroom ceiling didn't do the closet. If you discover water damage, ask the seller what repairs have been made to address the problem.

✔ **Evidence of pests:** Look for ant traps, mouse traps, roach motels, or other signs of infestations of any kind. Brown stripes in the corners of kitchen cabinets also indicate treatment for cockroaches. These may be temporary or one-time-only problems, but then again, they may not . . .

✔ **Windows:** Check the screens, the window locks, and the glass. Are they single- or double-paned? How secure are the basement windows? If they're an older style, they may not be as energy efficient or as safe as you'd like.

✔ **Attic:** Find out if the attic is well insulated. Heating costs can skyrocket if it isn't, or you'll have the added expense of adding additional insulation yourself.

Make full use of your senses when looking at homes — they can tell you a lot about the atmosphere, and alert you to potential problems. What do you smell, hear, and feel when you approach the house? When you enter different floors and rooms?

Don't be afraid to snoop

Remember not to ignore nooks and crannies when you're inspecting a home. Look inside closets and cupboards for drafts or signs of water damage. Many new homeowners run into problems later that they didn't notice — but should have — when they inspected the home. A common complaint is that the closets are considerably smaller than they remember, or there are no medicine cabinets in the bathrooms or linen closets in the hallway.

Out of shyness or courtesy, you may skip over some details when you're touring a new home — we're Canadian, after all: Intrusiveness isn't our style (we'd like to think so, anyway). But that's no excuse — you really need to know what you're getting into, so don't be afraid to look through everything! The sellers should be prepared for a thorough inspection, so you probably won't encounter mounds of dirty laundry or an avalanche of sports equipment when you open the closets. Open the cupboards too, and check the back of them for drafts or cracks; open the fridge, and see how cool it is; look under the carpet if you're thinking of pulling it up and exposing the hardwood underneath.

Measure the doorways: Can you get your washer and dryer down to the basement? Will your great-grandmother's armoire fit through the door? Also, you may want to consider measuring the sizes of the existing furniture in the home. The measurements will give you a good idea, beyond the actual room sizes themselves, of the scale of furniture the room can handle.

Ask questions!

If the seller's agent is at the home when you make your inspection visit, don't hesitate to ask lots of questions. Prepare a list, and write down the answers. You don't want to rack your brain later trying to remember what the agent said the average hydro bill was. Ask for a *seller's property information statement* (SPIS), also called the *property disclosure statement* (PDS), which provides a seller's disclosure of the home's condition. If the seller is not forthcoming with a copy of the SPIS/PDS, make sure your offer is subject to your receiving, reading, and approving it. Has the home been pre-inspected by a building inspector? Ask about the current owners, the reason why they're selling, what's new about the home, what the neighbours are like, what problems the owners are aware of — the list is endless. Check the zoning department for the municipalities to see if there are any projects proposed that could negatively impact the neighbourhood.

Even if the selling agent can't answer your questions on the spot, you can expect the agent to get back to you. The more you know about the home, the better position you're in when you go to the bargaining table — and the fewer surprises you'll have when you move in.

Has the home been looked after?

Like a car, a home requires preventive maintenance. You want a home that has been taken care of by its previous owners, because past neglect can translate into huge problems later. This concept applies to condominium buildings as well as detached houses. If you can, try to find out about the owners and whether they looked after their home. A big warning sign is absentee owners. If the owners just rent out the home, and don't actually live there, it's probably not as well maintained as it should be. Here are some indications that the present owners are maintaining the home properly:

- **Appliances:** Major appliances like the fridge and stove are well maintained and in good working order.

- **Bathrooms:** The area around the tub or shower has no signs of water damage or mould.

- **Electrical system:** Ground fault connection interrupter (GFCI) outlets are installed in all the necessary areas.

- **Exterior:** The yard(s) is in good condition.

- **Fire safety:** Working smoke detectors and carbon monoxide detectors are in the necessary spots in the home.

- **Foundation:** No cracks exist in the exterior foundation.

- **Furnace:** The seller can provide proof that the furnace has been regularly cleaned and maintained.

- **Overall appearance:** The house doesn't need to be outfitted with all the latest upgrades; pride of ownership will always show through.

- **Porches, patios, external stairs, and railings:** These features are well maintained. The wood isn't rotting, and the cement is even and without cracks.

- **Roofing:** The roof is no more than 10 years old — although some roofs are steel or long-wearing duroid/asphalt that can be good for 50 years or more. Ask about the type of roof the home has, and see if any warranties are in place.

- **Windows:** The windows are well sealed.

Part III
Getting the House You Want

The 5th Wave   By Rich Tennant

"Mr. Johnson, I think we've found your dream home! By the way, how do you feel about ghosts, ancient burial grounds and curses?"

In this part . . .

Yes, we know it's boring and complicated, but paper-work is a huge part of buying a home, so you'd better read this section. Offers, contracts, surveys, closings . . . it's all here for the learning. Then there is the active process of negotiating the terms and conditions you want and closing the deal — when and how you want.

Chapter 10

Let's Make a Deal

After a lot of hard work and pounding the pavement — not to mention all the time spent researching homes and neighbourhoods — the big day has finally arrived. You've found the home that works for you, and now it's time to make it yours. Look in this chapter for advice on making an offer to purchase a home and writing the best possible terms into your sale contract. We explain what the conditions ("subject to" clauses) in your agreement mean — and why you want them in the first place. This chapter tells you what you'll need to know in order to make your purchase and get the home that you want.

Preparing to Make an Offer

As you know from all the time you've spent searching, a home is no impulse buy, so a lot is involved even before you make the offer. We recommend a few steps to take before you put your cards on the table. Waiting another moment when you've finally found that perfect home can be painful, we know, but the time you take on these steps upfront will save you a lot more time and hassle later on.

Get your mortgage pre-approved

If by this stage you haven't spoken to your mortgage broker or lender and had yourself pre-approved for financing, then put this book down and pick up the phone to get the process started. Whether you handle everything over the phone or online with a mortgage broker or walk down to the local lender, this step is crucial and should be taken care of before making any offer. You don't want to fall in love with a home and then find out that you aren't able to finance it.

Pre-approval is a great tactic in the hunt for your dream home — it shows the sellers how serious you are, and more important, it shows you can pay them (refer to Chapter 2 for more information on having your mortgage pre-approved). Indicate to the sellers that you have a pre-approved mortgage. If five offers come in for the home you want after an open house, those that come from people with pre-approved mortgages will move to the top of the pile.

Get to know the local market

Make sure your offer falls in the right price range. Check out neighbouring homes for sale to compare prices. Figure out what to expect. Just as you know you shouldn't be paying $5 for an orange, you should also know the approximate value of the homes that interest you.

Leading up to preparing your offer, your real estate agent should provide you with the area's property statistics, including a list of selling prices versus asking prices of homes recently sold in your prospective neighbourhood. Contrast the original asking prices and the selling prices. The length of time homes spend on the market indicates how much demand there is for homes in the area. If the market is slow for selling, then you may be able to offer a price slightly under the market value. (Slow sales in the neighbourhood can also indicate that comparable homes were overpriced.) On the flip side, if the market's full of eager buyers, you need to be able to compete. Cyclical factors also apply; for example, the market is usually much slower in the winter months because fewer people move in the cold. Urban centres that have low vacancy rates may be an exception to this rule.

Your goal in making an offer is to work toward the lowest reasonable price without aggravating the seller — no small feat. You need to know your stuff. Your offer carries more weight if it matches average selling prices for similar homes and is confirmed by an appraiser's assessment (if you aren't using a real estate agent) or your agent's evaluation of the market. This objective approach helps keep the sellers from getting emotional and digging in their heels. Develop a strategy with your agent for presenting your offer to sellers. Be prepared to point out pertinent sales and comparable houses presently on the market to show your offer is a fair and attractive one.

Keep in mind when preparing to make an offer that statistics are only a starting point; homes aren't created equally. The property next door, or houses that look similar from the outside, won't be exact value matches for the one you want. In the end, only you know what you're willing to pay, and only you know how far you're willing to stretch your dollars.

Get to know the seller

Making a winning offer, believe it or not, has a lot to do with people sense. Take some time to evaluate the possible motivations of your seller. Has the house been on the market for a while? Do you have any idea about the circumstances surrounding the decision to sell? Is the owner buying another house? Has there been a divorce? Is the owner looking to get out soon, or does she have the time to wait for her best price?

You may think that a little getting-to-know-you chit-chat will help you understand what the seller is looking for in a buyer, but don't go too far! If you're too nosy or insensitive ("Gee, there must be a lot of painful memories of your deceased parents in this house, so I'm sure you want to leave as soon as possible") the seller won't want to have anything to do with you. Ultimately, this is a business deal, so you will want to keep it as businesslike as possible and keep personal feelings out of it. No matter how badly they want to sell, a lot of people won't sell to a buyer who they feel is insensitive and acts like a vulture, and they especially won't give that buyer a good deal.

Besides using the excellent manners your mother taught you, you can sweeten the deal you offer by accommodating the seller's time frame if he's in a rush to move, or if he needs some leeway while finding a new home. You may also agree that he can take all the appliances and the drapes.

Get to know your limits

To get to the happy stage of a binding contract, you have to know what you really want and what methods of negotiation will help you get your new home. Do your research and establish your priorities. To help you put things in perspective, take a look at Table 7-1 in Chapter 7 where you rate the features you need and want in a new home. Remember, your home-buying needs are non-negotiable. List your wants in order of importance. Beside each want, indicate the price limit you're willing to pay. Make a list of your "I can't live without this" items and your "I can take it or leave it" items.

After you make your lists, put them aside and take a moment for quiet contemplation to think things over. That way, you can come back to your initial impulses from a fresh perspective. You may find that certain things you think you can't live without may actually become easy sacrifices if you really fall in love with a home. Besides, maybe you'll find that when you listed a humongous kitchen as a must-have it was only because you'd just been watching the Food Network and were feeling really hungry.

If you're absolutely not willing to go above your offer price or negotiate other terms, be prepared to walk away from the deal. Advise your agent that you won't be begging, and have her advise the seller that you're firm with your offer.

Making an Offer

Before you can call any home yours, you have to make an offer to purchase it from the seller, and he must agree to accept your offer. The offer must be made in writing. Just saying, "Hey, I'll give you millions of dollars for your house" won't hold up in court (and if you have a habit of exaggerating, thank goodness for that!). No seller will consider your offer to be serious unless you put pen to paper. Your agent will have all the necessary paperwork required to make an offer. If you don't have an agent, your lawyer can draft the contract for you. Known as a *contract of purchase and sale* or an *agreement of purchase and sale* in some provinces, the contract includes basic terms and phrases that protect both the buyer and the seller.

Although your agent completes the entire contract form, the contract of purchase and sale is considered an "offer" to purchase a home only up until you and the seller come to full agreement on the contract's terms and conditions, and you both meet those conditions acceptably. In some cases, you and the seller will go back and forth several times before you decide on conditions and terms you can both live with. Because much of the contract's legalese can be daunting, in this section we describe the main parts of the contract in plain language. Also, your lawyer or agent will be more than happy to go through it with you and answer any questions you may have.

Go through any contract you sign very carefully. Determine your needs and wants for each item. Write them down if it helps. The common advice for every decision also applies here: Be realistic. If you don't want to go above your offer price, be flexible on other terms.

Figuring out who's who and what's what in your contract

The exact terminology and organization of contracts may vary from region to region, but five elements are basic to every contract of purchase and sale:

- ✔ **Seller:** The seller's full legal name, exactly as it's shown on the current title deed to the house, is written into the contract.

- ✔ **Buyer:** Write in your legal name, exactly as it's shown on your personal identification documents and exactly as it should be shown on the deed. If you and a partner are making a joint purchase, add both full names. Joint purchases can take two forms:

- *Joint tenancy* allows for the "right of survivorship" from one spouse to the other when one dies.

- *Tenancy in common* allows for one spouse's interest in the house to go to that spouse's heirs, not automatically to the other spouse.

✔ **Subject property:** *Subject property* refers to the street address and an exact legal description of the property you're buying. This description may include the lot size, a general description of the home (semi-detached, single-family dwelling with a mutual drive, or other), the specific lot and plan number, and any *easements*. If an easement is mentioned here, it will be acknowledged in more detail in the body of the contract as well. An easement or right-of-way is a specified area of a property that is acquired by another property owner for her benefit. For example, your neighbour's driveway may cross the corner of your property. Because it's her driveway, even though it's technically on your property, she has the right to use that part of your property to park her car. This right is registered on your title, and will be acknowledged in the contract.

✔ **Purchase price:** The *purchase price* is the price you're initially willing to pay. This price will probably change throughout the negotiation; it may go up and down repeatedly. When setting your offer price, keep in mind the additional expenses you'll be incurring, such as land or deed transfer tax, realty taxes, fuel and water rates, legal fees, and insurance costs (these expenses, known as *closing costs,* are described in Chapter 2).

Also allow yourself room to negotiate up. If it's a seller's market (more people looking to buy than homes for sale), you may want to make a higher initial offer right off. We discuss negotiating the price later on in this chapter.

✔ **Deposit:** Your *deposit* is not only part of your down payment but also an indication to the seller of your interest in the house and a sign that you're negotiating in good faith. The initial deposit may be relatively low, but the total deposit may be much more. In some provinces, paying the full deposit upon *final subject removal,* meaning after the deal is firm, is normal. At least 3 to 10 percent of the purchase price is often considered a fair amount for a total deposit, but no hard and fast rules exist. Your real estate agent can advise you what is standard practice regarding deposits in your area. Refer to Chapter 2 for a full discussion regarding deposits.

List the amount of the deposit that is accompanying your offer, and specify that it will be applied to the purchase price of the house on the closing (or completion) of the sale. Normally, the deposit will be held in trust by your agent in a trust account until the completion of the sale. In some provinces, the standard procedure is for the deposit to be held in the listing agent's trust account. You may want to write in that any interest that accrues while the funds are in trust goes to the buyer, and will be paid after completion of the sale.

Note that if you back out of an offer after it has been accepted and all the terms and conditions have been met (that is, the subjects have been removed), you will most likely have to ultimately forfeit your deposit to the vendor and will likely open yourself up to other expensive legal action and possible damages. If you want to try to get out of the deal, you should consult a lawyer and be prepared for bad news.

Understanding terms and conditions ("subject to" clauses)

Most contracts have a blank space where you can write in the specific terms and conditions of your offer. This space is where you build as much safety into your offer as you need. You can make your offer *unconditional,* meaning that you don't require the seller to do anything except agree to the purchase price, deposit, and other terms of the contract. However, we advise that you make your offer subject to some conditions — these conditions will give you some protection from making a bad purchase. As we mention in the next section, if you're pursuing a property that's going to receive multiple offers, you may have to try to satisfy your concerns before making your offer instead of making them conditions.

Conditions are typically worded as "conditional upon" or "subject to" clauses ("I will buy the house, *subject to* financing, *conditional upon* inspection, *subject to* selling my current house," or some other condition). Basically you're saying, in legal terms, "I will buy your house if particular conditions are met (within a set time frame)," such as the following:

- ✔ **Subject to financing:** You'll buy the home if you're able to arrange a suitable mortgage. (Note that some buyers specify the maximum interest rate, the payment schedule, and the monthly payment amount they can consider.)

- ✔ **Subject to selling my present home:** You'll buy the seller's home if you can sell the home you currently own (within a set period of time, such as 30 to 60 days). This usually has an "escape clause" allowing the sellers to continue to market their home and in the event they obtain a second offer satisfactory to them, they agree to give the buyer first right to firm up or release them from the original deal.

- ✔ **Subject to the home's repair:** You'll purchase the home if the seller fixes the leaky roof, or some other substandard feature.

- ✔ **Subject to legal review:** You'll purchase the home provided that your lawyer reviews and approves the contract (usually within a specified amount of time, such as 24 to 48 hours).

- ✔ **Subject to inspection:** You'll buy the home if it passes a professional building inspection.

The home inspection is a chance to review the home before you commit to buying the property. In general, you need to have a reasonable reason not to proceed with your purchase. Therefore, in many provinces the property inspection clause includes a maximum price for repairs that the buyer is prepared to accept before deciding not to proceed with the purchase. This clause prevents the buyer from walking away from a house because a light bulb is burnt out. Also, if the buyer simply changes his mind and no longer wants to buy the property, he won't be able to use the inspection clause to get out of the purchase.

A typical inspection clause with a cost consideration could read like this:

> *This offer is subject to the buyer on or before* [insert date], *at the buyer's expense, receiving and approving an inspection report against any defects whose total cost of repair exceeds $_____* [this amount can be negotiated, but it may be $500 or more] *and which adversely affect the property's use or value.*

This condition is for the sole benefit of the buyer.

- **Subject to survey:** You'll purchase the home if a land survey is conducted or a legal, up-to-date land survey is provided, showing that the home doesn't violate any easements or rights-of-way, and showing the location of any buildings, such as a garage, on the property.

- **Subject to appraisal:** Although your financing is pre-approved, the house is in your price range, and you know you can get a mortgage, you may want to confirm that your offer is reasonable and at fair market value. If you have any doubts, you can make the offer subject to your receiving and approving an appraisal of the subject property.

- **Subject to approving a property disclosure statement:** A *property disclosure statement* is a form that is filled out by the homeowner that asks standard questions regarding the condition of the home and neighbourhood factors which may influence value. If incorporated into the contract, the statement may establish a case against the seller if it can be proven that she knowingly misrepresented the property in question.

- **Subject to bylaw approval:** When purchasing a condominium or townhouse, this condition may be one of several you include. This condition means that your purchase is contingent on agreeing to any and all bylaws affecting the unit in question, which may include rental or pet restrictions.

Specific requirements can also be written in the same area as your conditions, such as the stated requirement that the seller agrees to remove the abandoned car from the garage prior to the completion date. If you don't have enough space on the contract to add all your terms and conditions, they can be written up on *schedule forms,* which are attached to the main body of the contract. Schedule forms (or addenda, or appendices in some provinces) are extra forms that allow you to write as many terms and conditions as are necessary on additional pages that form part of the contract. Make sure that all the schedules you attach are listed on the contract. Keep in mind that when you start negotiating, you may end up adding or removing conditions, and so may the seller. For example, if the seller will not fix the roof, you may agree to remove that condition, but try to deduct the estimated cost of that repair from your offered price.

Don't overdo the conditions. Write a thorough, detailed offer, but make sure you keep your conditions from piling up. Be reasonable. Don't write into your offer that you have the right to inspect the property five times before the closing date — one or two times should suffice.

After you and the seller sign off on all the terms and conditions of your purchase offer, your conditions will (hopefully!) be met. You can then add the paperwork (amendments of waivers or notices of fulfillment, if necessary) to confirm, for example, that the roof has been repaired, that you have secured a mortgage, that you have sold your current house, and so on. After all the conditions are removed, you enter into a binding agreement to purchase and, here's the best part — you've bought your new home.

Competing with multiple offers

In a sellers' market, buyers frequently find themselves in competition to purchase a home. Though this is obviously great news if you happen to be a seller, it can leave prospective property purchasers with a raging ulcer. Generally in these circumstances, a property's asking price and its selling price can be vastly different; the selling price can be well above and beyond what the property was originally listed for.

In a sellers' market, homeowners and their agents sometimes strategize to underprice a property in order to generate a lot of interest — and hopefully a bidding war. Certain types of homes are more likely to benefit from this tactic: in particular, single-family homes in desirable neighbourhoods. For example, if you happen to fall in love with a home in your target area that's completely renovated — with a new roof and furnace, and new landscaping and fencing — impeccably presented, and priced 5 to 7 percent below any comparable home in the area, you may find that you've fallen for a home that's positioned to get multiple offers. Chances are, the seller isn't going to consider offers until a certain date. A typical strategy is to list the property, hold open houses on the weekend so that many prospective buyers can see the home, and then deal with offers several days later.

In multiple-offer situations, logic can go out the window to a certain degree. You need to be prepared to put your best foot forward, and in many cases, do all your homework up front with the chance that you won't get the property in the long run. Ultimately, a seller will want to accept an offer with the best price and conditions. Providing a certified cheque or bank draft with your offer also avoids buyer's remorse in the eyes of the seller and gives them peace of mind to accept your offer. Often the highest bidder changes their mind overnight and doesn't come forward with the deposit money the next day.

Price isn't everything. If you present an offer in which you have no "subject to" clauses (essentially saying that you're willing to enter immediately into a contract) but the price you offer is less than other buyers', you can still end up as the winner. The competition may have to sell another property first (an offer "subject to the sale of"), or perhaps they need to secure financing and want to do an inspection. The seller may be willing to forgo a bit of money in order to accept your offer, which is quick and guaranteed.

Doing your homework

If offers are being withheld until a certain date, you need to get cracking:

- ✔ Make sure that your home financing is secure. You can still include a finance clause in your offer, but if you can avoid it, you'll move up the competition ladder in the eyes of the seller.

- ✔ Ensure that the property title won't offer you any nasty surprises. If any easements or rights-of-way that may affect the property's use or value exist, you'll want to know now. These problems may affect the offer that you plan to present.

- ✔ If possible, do an inspection in advance. You may sweeten your offer again by not including a "subject to inspection" clause if you manage to do an inspection ahead of time and determine that you're happy with the home as is. (Refer to the previous section for more about conditions.)

- ✔ With your agent, look at other homes in the area that sold for more than the asking price. Make some calls to determine how many offers were presented. The same thing applies to the property you're interested in: Are you competing against two other offers, or ten?

- ✔ Figure out the price you're willing to pay. If this is truly your dream home and you've been in this type of bidding war before, you may decide that you're willing to pay a premium to get the home that you want. You'll want to write an offer that you can feel good about; if you lose the home over a mere $1,000, you don't want to be kicking yourself later.

Considering bully offers

A *bully offer* is an offer presented in anticipation of multiple offers. Basically, you're bullying your way to the front of the pack by presenting your offer first, in the hopes that the seller will consider your offer without seeing any other offers that may come forward on the set presentation date. If you're a buyer set on writing a bully offer, try to present as clean an offer as possible, with very few — if any — conditions and a price that will entice the seller to accept.

Get it in writing!

Just like during every other step of the process, don't engage in oral agreements when it comes to the various conditions of your contract. Always put it in writing. If an oral agreement comes up in conversation — "Hey, those are great drapes, would you consider leaving them?" — remember to write it into the contract. Then, and only then, can that portion of the contract become binding. Your offer to purchase a home becomes a binding contract when the seller signs the contract of purchase and sale that contains all your terms and conditions.

Bully offers can be risky. First of all, what if it ends up that you had no competition in the first place? You may have paid an unnecessary premium for the property. That question is one that you'll never know the answer to. You may also risk alienating the seller, who may be put off by such an aggressive strategy. Or, you may be turned away altogether and told to submit your offer on the day that the seller originally selected.

Chapter 11

Signing On to a New Life

In This Chapter

▶ Finalizing details with your home-buying team

▶ Protecting your investment

A fter a lot of work, you and the seller agree on the conditions of the contract of purchase and sale, and then the seller accepts your offer. But just because the offer's signed doesn't mean you can sit back and relax just yet. You have a home inspection to arrange, an insurance company to call, a mortgage to finalize . . . you name it. All this official stuff may not seem that glamorous, but it's vital to your purchase of a home.

This chapter deals with the fine print your lawyer sifts through when closing your deal (don't worry, you'll find no legalese here) and then takes you through the process of getting a mortgage signed off. To finish, we give you the rundown on the different types of home insurance available to safeguard your new investment. We discuss professional surveys, inspections, and warranties in Chapter 12.

Taking Care of the Paperwork

Don't be fooled — there's always *more* paperwork, even after you feel you've got carpal tunnel syndrome from signing and initialing so many forms and documents. In order to take care of the paperwork, however, you'll need help from your carefully selected team of home-buying professionals. So make those calls, schedule appointments, and get things rolling.

Removing conditions

The main reason why you have to see so many people is to take care of the conditions you've written into your offer to purchase. In order for the contract to be binding, every condition — any "subject to" clause that you wrote into the contract of purchase and sale — must be met. If your offer to purchase is "subject to financing," "subject to approval by lawyer," or "subject to roof repair," these conditions must be fulfilled. (For more on conditions, or "subject to" clauses, refer to Chapter 10.)

Give it due process

The time frame for your lawyer's duties will vary, depending on how many days you have until closing. One little piece of advice: Trust in the process. You may have a lot of questions and concerns, but don't panic if the lawyer says he'll do his thing, and will see you again in a month and a half. He'll let you know when he needs anything from you, whether it's a signature, the survey, or your agent's number. Waiting for the day that home is yours isn't easy — especially if you're waiting 90 days to move out of your tiny bedroom in your parents' home — but you have many more things to do before you close, so stop worrying that something may go wrong because you haven't talked to your lawyer in a couple of days.

In most provinces, you sign waivers to confirm that you and the seller have met each of the necessary conditions. Be sure that every condition the seller is responsible for, like fixing the roof, is done — and done properly — before you sign off. Make sure all conditions have been met by the prescribed subject removal date. After all the conditions have been removed, the contract or agreement of purchase and sale is binding. The waivers, or subject removal documents, are prepared by the buyer's agent or the buyer's lawyer if no agent is used.

Paying your lawyer a visit

We recommend you choose a lawyer early in the game if you're undertaking a complex sale or you're not using a real estate agent, so that when you're ready to sign the deal you know exactly who's going to review the paperwork. (Chapter 6 includes tips on how to choose your legal counsel.) Take the contract of purchase and sale to her when the seller accepts your offer.

Ask your lawyer to do the following:

- Review your contract of purchase and sale with you.
- Examine the conditions of sale and the "subject to" clauses.
- Discuss the completion (closing) date and the anticipated subject (conditions) removals.
- Answer any questions or concerns you may have.

Your lawyer needs to know how you and your partner (if you have one) have agreed to hold title. If you're buying a house alone, then you'll have, of course, *sole ownership*. With co-ownership, however, you have two options:

✔ **Joint tenancy:** The most important feature of *joint tenancy* is "right of survivorship." If your partner dies, title to the home will be transferred over to you automatically.

✔ **Tenancy in common:** Unless *joint tenancy* is specifically chosen, all co-ownership situations (whether spouses, family, or friends) are deemed to be *tenancy in common*. Under *tenancy in common,* each owner's share of the home's worth is passed on to that person's heirs. Tenants in common can have unequal interest in a property (for example, two-thirds versus one-third), and can specify who will inherit their interest in the property on their death.

Your lawyer not only acts as a legal guide for your contract but also oversees the entire process of transferring the property from the seller to you. Your lawyer will interact with many of the professionals you're seeing, so make sure she has all their contact info. Your lawyer will

✔ Arrange with your lender to transfer money from your mortgage to the seller. In most cases, your lawyer also drafts your mortgage document, double-checking that all the terms and conditions of your mortgage are properly met.

✔ Contact your insurance agent to verify for the lender that your home insurance is in place on the closing date. (Most lenders won't finalize your mortgage until you have home insurance.)

✔ Calculate the amount of money you owe the seller because of prepaid rents (if applicable), utilities, and taxes (these are known as *adjustments*). Often, your lawyer will also transfer the utilities to your name. (More on adjustments later in this section.)

✔ Check out the background of the property to ensure that it's legally owned by the seller (called a *title search*) and that there are no debts or claims against it (called *liens*).

✔ Arrange with the seller's lawyer to transfer the deed from the seller to you on the closing date. The balance of the purchase price — the agreed price, minus the deposit, plus any adjustments — and the keys will also be exchanged. Review the condominium certificate with your lawyer, if you're buying a condo. Condominium certificates are discussed in Chapter 5 also.

Because condominiums are regulated provincially, different documents, regulations, and procedures are used in every province. What we refer to generally as the condominium certificate may comprise more than one document and may go by a variety of aliases in different provinces, including, but not limited to, these: estoppel certificate, status certificate, information certificate, and declaration document. Ask your real estate agent which documentation applies in your situation.

At the end of all this, your lawyer draws up a *statement of adjustments,* which is a summary of the financial transactions among you, your lawyer, your lender, and the seller. A statement of adjustments lists the following dollar amounts:

- Purchase price of the home (owed to the seller)
- Adjustments owed to the seller
- Buyer's deposit
- Mortgage money from the lender
- GST/HST or land transfer tax, if applicable (to be paid through the lawyer)
- Lawyer's fees, including disbursements (costs the lawyer has taken for the buyer; for example, couriers and photocopying) and GST/HST

You then get a final sum of the money you owe, which should essentially be your down payment (minus deposit) plus your lawyer's total fees and applicable taxes. This money must be given to your lawyer by the closing date.

Getting that mortgage

Most mortgages won't be finalized until after the seller has accepted your offer. Hopefully, you got your mortgage pre-approved before you started home hunting (refer to Chapter 2). After your offer is accepted, all you have to do is go back to your lender with the details about the home and sign lots of paper. Taking the MLS listing or feature sheet is a good idea because it should have all the information about your home that your lender will need. Many lenders will also require an appraisal; they may have their own appraisers to do the job, but the appraiser or the listing agent will make an appointment with the seller (refer to Chapter 6 for more information about appraisals). If you're buying in a rural area, you also have to present certificates from the government that verify the location of your well and septic tank.

Some mortgages are more flexible than others in terms of missing payments, doubling up payments, and the like (refer to Chapter 3), so review your specific mortgage with your lender to remember what you can and can't do.

You may be a little too short on cash after you've bought the home, paid the lawyer, redecorated, and purchased that antique armoire, so many lenders are happy to also provide a line of credit to keep you afloat for the first few months. After your lender finalizes and approves your mortgage, your lawyer will receive a cheque in trust to be given over to the seller's lawyer on closing day. Before the lender will give over all this money, however, you have to verify that you have home insurance covering the home from the day of possession.

Insuring Your Home

"Mortgage" is just a fancy term for one whopping loan. And your collateral for this loan is your home — so it needs to be protected from anything or anyone that may cause damage (this includes *you*). Suppose one groggy morning you nod off while supervising the bacon and drop your newspaper onto the burner. Within minutes, your kitchen is a sea of flames and you can't remember where the heck that fire extinguisher went. Anything can happen in that pre-coffee stupor. In short — insurance is an absolute must. (Don't confuse this with *mortgage life insurance,* which we discuss in Chapter 3.) Because you can choose from different items to protect and different ways to protect your home, talk to your insurance broker to make sure you get the coverage you need.

Knowing what to protect

Home insurance has two parts: *property coverage* and *liability coverage*. Property coverage protects both your dwelling and its contents; liability coverage protects *you*. Although most policies cover all three aspects (your dwelling, your dwelling's contents, and you), you can tailor your insurance to fit the coverage you need. For example, if you're renting your home, you may simply need your dwelling protected and not its contents.

Protecting your dwelling

A dwelling is considered to be the home's structure and all permanent attached components. This definition can include different elements depending on the specific policy you have, so confirm what is covered with your insurance provider, especially if you get a different type of insurance for your contents than for your dwelling. The insurance provider will most likely insure you for the amount of money it will take to rebuild your house, rather than the price you paid for it.

Be aware that your policy likely covers the replacement cost of your home *exactly as it was*. Suppose a horrible fire burned your 75-year-old house to the ground. When building codes and regulations are changed, they generally exempt existing homes. Now suppose that current building regulations don't allow houses to be built in the same way, with the same materials, or even in the same place on your lot (suppose current regulations no longer allow waterfront homes to be so close to the shoreline)! If new building standards require an upgrade when you rebuild, the extra cost will most likely *not* be covered by your insurance policy. Ask your insurance agent about a *rider* (an add-on policy that lets you specify additional items to be covered) or extended coverage, if you have any concerns.

When insuring your home or renewing your insurance policy, getting bylaw insurance is a good idea. Bylaw (or compliance) insurance ensures that any repairs your house may require will comply with the current building code, and any extra cost to bring your home repairs/restoration up to the current building code will be the responsibility of your insurer. Many insurance policies include bylaw insurance in their standard policy, but check to make sure. Otherwise, your insurance company will rebuild your home only to the way it was before a fire, not to the extra, updated current standards for wiring, plumbing, and fire protection (sprinkler systems are expensive!) that are now required by the building code in some Canadian provinces.

Protecting your contents

Homeowners need to insure both the permanent structure (the dwelling) *and* the contents of their homes. In contrast, condo buildings are generally insured by the condominium corporation, so most condo owners need only worry about insuring the contents of their homes. If you're a condo owner, you need to find out exactly where the condo corporation's policy ends and yours should begin. Sometimes the corporation's policy will cover only the bare walls, leaving you to provide coverage for fixtures like kitchen cabinets. Two forms of content insurance exist:

- **Actual cash value:** When you make a claim (assuming it's approved), you receive cash for the current value of the item. This value is *not* the value of buying the same item new, but rather the cost of buying the item minus the depreciation in value due to age, wear, or obsolescence.

- **Replacement cost:** The lost or damaged item is covered for the cost of replacing the item with one of comparable quality. Obviously, because a replacement cost policy costs your insurance provider more than a depreciated-value cash payout, this kind of coverage comes with a heftier price tag.

Protecting yourself

Liability insurance protects you in the event that you, or your property, damage either someone else's property or someone else's person. This type of coverage covers you anywhere in the world. So, if while staying at a lovely B & B in the Welsh countryside you knock over a lamp and burn down the building, liability insurance will cover any damage or medical or legal fees that become your responsibility. This insurance also covers you if a flowerpot on your railing flies through the air and hits your mail carrier on the head during a windstorm. How much coverage you require is up to you. If you buy a new home with a swimming pool at the edge of a sea cliff and you know the neighbours' kids will be hanging around your place, you may want more liability coverage than if you buy a basic bungalow.

Understanding how you're protected

You can be covered by insurance in two general ways. Both policies work on an *exclusion principle:* Either the insurance provider will cover an event only if it's specifically named in your policy (standard), or the provider will cover all events *with the exception* of those specifically named in your policy (all-risks). Because an all-risks approach covers many more situations (such as your dog causing significant water damage by knocking over your 400-litre fish tank), all-risks policies are more expensive.

- **Standard (or basic):** *Standard* policies generally cover most "acts of God" damage, such as fire, lightning, wind or hail, theft, vandalism, and other incidents that are inherently beyond your control. Standard policies work on a *named perils* basis. A *peril* is what insurance companies call potentially damaging events, like the ones just mentioned. To work on a "named-peril basis" means that an event is covered only if it's specifically named in your policy.

- **All-risks:** *All-risks* coverage typically involves some *exclusions* —specific events named in the policy contract that will *not* be covered under the policy. Exclusions may include faulty workmanship, wear due to regular use, or damage that would have been prevented with proper maintenance. Any event not specifically listed in your policy is covered, so if unfortunate things seem to just happen to you, consider getting an all-risks policy.

Although the term *standard* is also applied to dwelling and content coverage at a standard level, insurers usually use the term *comprehensive* to describe insurance that protects both your dwelling and your contents in an all-risks policy. (Be aware that even under a comprehensive policy, limits will be imposed on the value of your claims for some items of personal property.) Homeowners wanting to protect both their dwelling and their contents don't necessarily have to protect both parts with the same kind of policy. They can also get protection known as *broad coverage.* Broad coverage works partly on an all-risks basis and partly on a named-perils basis. A broad policy covers "all risks," meaning anything that may cause loss or damage to your *dwelling.* A broad policy covers named perils when it comes to the *contents* of your home.

Read your home insurance policy carefully! Make sure you understand exactly what is covered and what is not. Insurance providers can differ greatly on their coverage of certain types of damage — coverage for water damage, in particular, ranges all across the board. Note the deductibles for various categories.

We can't offer any ballpark figures here on what home insurance costs. Your *premiums* (annual fees) depend on a large number of individual factors. For example, home size, modernity, and features, as well as neighbourhood, proximity to fire stations and hydrants, type of coverage, coverage provider, and your track record can all play a part in determining your premiums. The value of your home will also come into play, but that isn't necessarily the same as its sticker price. The important price for an insurance provider isn't how much you paid for your home, or what its current market value is, but how much it would cost to rebuild it. This amount may not be equivalent to what you paid for your house.

Extending your coverage

If you want particular items covered, or you're worried about particular events, you can introduce *riders* to your insurance. Riders are add-on policies that allow you to customize (as much as possible) your policy by specifying that particular additional items or perils are covered. However, your insurance provider has to agree to provide coverage for these items or events, which isn't a given, and they will adjust your premiums — upwards! — to pay for the extended coverage. You can also choose *endorsements,* which are similar in purpose to riders but are simply add-on statements or amendments to your current policy, as opposed to whole additional policies.

Again, the more you ask to be covered, the more expensive your premiums typically will be, but if you want your $10,000 painting fully protected, your peace of mind will be worth a rider or endorsement. Ask your insurer about the various extended coverage packages offered.

Home office owners beware

Home insurance isn't business insurance. If you run a small business out of your home, have a home office, or have property in your home that you use for business purposes, chances are this property is *not* covered by your home insurance policy. Furthermore, if a client is injured while visiting your home office, your liability insurance may not cover the accident. Many insurance providers offer home business packages as either riders or endorsements. If you use your home for business purposes at all, ask specifically what is covered and what is not under your home insurance policy.

In this information age, your home office's data may be more valuable than the computer you use to access it. Although you may be reimbursed for hardware, and perhaps software under some policies, you won't be reimbursed for lost data. Similarly, if your Web site inspires a liability claim against you, your insurance may not protect you. Find out before you upload that sensitive classified document! Ask your insurance provider exactly what is and isn't covered.

Are you covered?

If you take nothing else away from this section, take this single piece of advice — assume nothing; question everything. Make sure you ask *at least* the following questions when you investigate different insurance providers:

✔ Whom does the policy cover?

✔ Exactly what property is covered? (For example, does the policy include the backyard shed?)

✔ What perils/items are included, and what perils/items are excluded?

✔ What discounts do you offer?

✔ What are my responsibilities as a policyholder? Under what conditions are you allowed to terminate my coverage?

✔ Are riders or endorsements available? How will they affect my premiums? How will they affect my responsibilities as a policyholder?

✔ What is the procedure for making a claim?

✔ How and when can I contact a representative with questions about my policy or a claim? (For example, is there a 24-hour toll-free hotline for policyholders?)

✔ How long does it usually take to process claims? What is the maximum time limit, upon your approval of my claim, for providing me with due compensation?

Getting the best deal

After you know what sort of policy you want, and which particular riders and endorsements suit your needs, you can start comparing prices. Here are some things you can do to make sure you're getting the best deal:

✔ **First and foremost, shop around.** Different insurance providers offer a variety of packages and prices. The cheapest isn't always your best option — ensure that the insurance you're buying meets your requirements as closely as possible.

✔ **Ask all the providers you investigate about special discounts.** For example, some insurance providers may give discounts to non-smokers, or for houses that have good safety and security systems.

✔ **Find out what the reduction in your premiums will be if you increase your deductible.** The *deductible* is the amount that you, the policyholder, have to pay toward replacement costs. For example, if your $2,000 stereo is stolen, you pay the $500 deductible and your insurance company pays the remaining $1,500 to replace the system. You can usually save a lot of money in the long run by increasing your deductible. Standard minimum deductibles are anywhere from $200 to $500, but if you increase it to $1,000, you should be able to reduce your premiums significantly.

Picking up the tab on less expensive accidents or damages, even if they're covered by your home insurance policy, can save you money over the long haul. The fewer claims you make, the less your premiums increase. If you make numerous small claims, you may even be branded a "potential risk," and not only will your premiums increase, but you'll also run the risk of other insurance providers rejecting you in the future.

Last, but not least, make sure your home insurance kicks in on the very same day you take legal ownership of the property — whether or not you actually move in on that day. But, if you're building your home you should be aware that damage or loss during the building process is often not covered by home insurance policies. Once again, and we can't repeat it enough, ask providers exactly what is covered and what is not.

Chapter 12

Closing Time: Inspections, Surveys, and Warranties

The next two chapters cover the "before" and "after" picture of closing the deal on your new home. Yes — there is light at the end of the tunnel! In this chapter, we tell you all about home inspections for houses and condominiums, land surveys, and new home warranties (if you're buying a newly built home) — all-important parts of finalizing your deal that shouldn't be overlooked. Then, Chapter 13 takes a look at closing-day events and moving tips. And what's next? Why, you celebrate of course!

The Ins and Outs of Inspections

We can't stress this enough: Make sure your offer is subject to an inspection. You may think everything looks like it's in tip-top condition, but we don't know anyone (besides superheroes) that has x-ray vision and can see hidden issues, so get a professional inspection anyway. Every real estate agent and home inspector has stories of the unexpected results that come from a seemingly straightforward home inspection. We've even included a couple of stories here, to show you just how important getting an inspection is. Some sellers have inspections done before they put their homes on the market (a pre-sale inspection), but as a buyer you should have your own professional home inspection done. Occasionally lenders require an inspection before approving a mortgage, so unless you're Mr. or Mrs. Moneybuckets and have the cash in your back pocket, getting financing may require you to carry out a property inspection. The same goes for condominiums. In the Vancouver market, for example, lenders may request a copy of an inspection report if they're unsure about a building's soundness before giving final approval for a mortgage.

Even if you're planning to radically renovate or tear down the home in question, you still need to do an inspection. What if asbestos is found in the attic? Removal is expensive, and can be avoided if you discover the problem in advance.

If you are not able to do an inspection before submitting your offer (for example, if multiple offers are required on a pre-set date), include a *"subject to inspection"* clause in your contract of purchase and sale. (Refer to Chapter 10 for more information on "subject to" clauses.) In effect, a "subject to inspection" clause acts as a safety mechanism: It releases a buyer from the obligation to purchase a home if an inspector finds major faults in the building.

After the seller accepts your offer, have the house inspected as soon as possible. If the inspector spots any problems, you'll want as much time as possible to resolve them and make some decisions. You may be able to renegotiate the price of the property in question if some serious deficiencies are discovered — or you may decide to walk away. Even if the home is sound, the inspector can share a lot of good information about your new house with you and tip you off to anything you'll want to keep an eye on.

Knowing what to expect when you're inspecting

Building inspectors look at the structural elements of a home, including the basement, the roof, and the heating, plumbing, and electrical systems. He usually goes systematically through the home and gives you a full, written report when finished. A good inspector also makes recommendations on what should be improved (for example, installing GFCI outlets and a vent in the bathroom, or adding a handrail to the basement stairs).

If any problems are uncovered — and these problems can be anything from a leaky gutter to a leaky basement — it's decision time. One option is to *collapse* (cancel) your offer, because the condition of a positive inspection was not met. Your other option is to write a new term into the contract (if the seller agrees) that requires the seller to fix the leaky basement and any other problem areas. You are now renegotiating the contract, and adding new terms requires consent from both the seller and the buyer (refer to Chapter 10 for more on the negotiating process). If the seller refuses to accept a new conditional clause or an added term, your next option is to propose a price reduction to cover the costs you'll incur to fix the problem. If you and the seller can't reach an agreement, you can collapse the offer and look for another house.

Keep in mind that the seller is under no obligation to renegotiate. In fact, she may have priced the house acknowledging there was work to be done, and in her mind she has already discounted the price to cover the repairs.

Inspection costs can vary greatly if you're buying a very large or unusual property. In most cases, however, you'll find inspectors charge a fee in the range of $250 to $1,000. No one set price applies, because some inspectors base their charge on the complexity of the property, while others charge using a sliding scale based on the size of the property. A typical building inspection takes at least two or three hours. On completion, you receive a full, written inspection report that's signed and dated by the inspector.

In the event you're buying a larger, custom-built house (lucky you!) or a multifamily property, you may want to have a more comprehensive inspection conducted to inspect and analyze complex systems within the house. In this case, you may want to pay extra for a comprehensive inspection that will produce a technical audit report. This type of inspection typically takes 20 hours or more to perform, and includes the disassembly and disruption of the home's systems and components. You will need to get the owner's permission before conducting a technical audit, because the inspector will be dismantling key components of the owner's home. If you're interested in a technical audit, check to make sure your inspector is capable of performing this type of inspection and then get a price estimate before proceeding.

Choosing a good inspector

Find an inspector with a good reputation and a membership in the *Canadian Association of Home and Property Inspectors* (CAHPI). CAHPI maintains minimum standards for home inspectors regarding education and professional conduct. If you know any people who have recently bought (or possibly sold) their home, ask if they had an inspection and if they were happy with the inspector. If not, you can try a number of resources. Ask your real estate agent, friends, relatives, or people in the neighbourhood if they can recommend some good inspectors, or call your provincial or regional association of home inspectors.

You can also access CAHPI on the Web at www.cahpi.ca. The Web site has a "Hire a Registered Home Inspector (RHI)" section that provides links to the Web sites of CAHPI's provincial chapters. (Or, see the Appendix for a list of the CAHPI offices across the country.)

Your local CAHPI office can provide the names of home inspectors in good standing who work in your neighbourhood. Check to see if the inspectors you call are members of a local association of home inspectors, have an office you can visit (rather than only a cell phone number), and have a current business licence.

In many provinces, home inspectors are not regulated, so in those provinces anyone can hang their shingle out and call themselves a home inspector. Some inspectors may band together and form their own association. If they are not members of CAHPI, make sure they have the background, experience, liability insurance, and continuing education that members of CAHPI have as a condition of membership.

Inspecting a newly built home

Even if you're buying a newly built home, you should have an inspection done before you accept the home. You can make this part of your pre-completion inspection, before the completion of the sale. In new construction contracts, you can usually find a provision for a pre-completion deficiency inspection of the property. You can write into your contract that a professional building inspector will accompany you when you're doing your *deficiency inspection*. Before you agree to the terms of the sale contract, talk to your agent or lawyer to ensure that you're entitled to a deficiency inspection.

Unless you know enough about construction to recognize potential problems or faulty work, you should bring along a professional home inspector. After the visual inspection is completed, you'll be asked to sign a *certificate of completion* (sometimes also referred to as a *certificate of completion and possession*), stating that everything you paid for is complete. You can have the certificate drawn up by your lawyer and a representative of the builder, although many New Home Warranty Program–registered builders will already have professionally prepared documents for this purpose. Any apparent omissions or defects discovered during your inspection should be noted on the certificate of completion, because this certificate is registered at your local NHWP office. Filing the certificate is necessary for your warranty coverage to commence. More on New Home Warranty Programs later in this chapter.

If you've purchased a newly built condominium as a pre-sale (the building and unit were still under construction when you bought it from the developer), developers don't accept offers subject to home inspection after the unit is finished, but you can bring your home inspector along on the deficiency walk-through. This walk-through isn't an official home inspection, and by this time you've already committed to buying the suite, but this is your chance to get the inspector to check out the unit just before you move in so that you'll be aware of any problems. Your province's New Home Warranty Program (which we discuss later in this chapter) can protect you against any serious construction defects.

Your inspector should double-check that the materials the builders used are the same as what you requested or expected, that new appliances are properly installed, and that fittings and equipment are located as specified. Look at many of the same things you would investigate if you bought a resale home: Make sure the *gradient,* the angles of the land around the foundation, will direct water away from the house, and look for any signs of leaking in the basement and from the roof. Check the metal flashings around windows and the chimney to make sure they're properly caulked, and check that all the toilets flush properly. You wouldn't believe what gets thrown down the toilet during the construction process! Look into whether your province has a New Home Warranty Program (see the Appendix).

Most home inspectors, especially if they're affiliated with CAHPI or their provincial home inspectors association, are honest and pride themselves on thorough work. If, however, you've had a home inspection and you feel dissatisfied with the results, you have the right to have a second inspection performed (like a second doctor's opinion). To go further, if you feel the inspector was incompetent, report him to his local professional association.

Inspecting an inspection

A professional inspector knows what to look for to ensure that a resale home is up to snuff — that it meets modern requirements and has a sound structure. An average inspection takes at least two or three hours, depending on the size of the home. A good inspector will have you accompany her and will encourage lots of questions. Sometimes the inspector will start when you're not in the home — you won't have much to do when the inspector is poking through the attic. You should definitely be present for the last hour or two of the inspection so that the inspector can go over the good, the bad, and the ugly with you.

A good inspector won't offer to do home repairs for you — it would be a huge conflict of interest. Your inspector shouldn't recommend contractors to do the repairs unless they're very specialized repairs that require highly skilled trades. Your inspector is hired to investigate your home — not to give work to his buddies in the building trades.

An inspection is a visual walk-through to report on the elements of the home. It's not meant to be a picky this-doorknob-won't-turn-fully kind of examination, but an overall report of whether the home is sound. Of course, you don't get any guarantees, because a home may have problems even the inspector can't find. If the sewer system (which belongs to the city) under your new house is about to collapse, causing the bottom to literally fall out of your home, an inspector can't anticipate that.

The inspector completes most of the inspection report while touring the property, so the report is usually organized into locations starting with the site itself, and then working through the exterior and interior of the house. Your inspection report should cover all categories of concern relevant to each part of the house and property, including structural, exterior, interior, plumbing, electrical, and heating and ventilation components. A rough list of the kinds of problems an inspection report will alert you to follows.

What you see isn't always what you get

Say you make an offer on a beautiful detached two-storey house in Toronto's Little Italy. Elsie and Peter, the older couple who've lived there for 45 years, have lovingly maintained the home. You arrange an inspection to cover one of the conditions of the sale. You and your partner are both present when the inspector does a routine check behind a three-prong electrical outlet, and she discovers that it still has the old two-wire, ungrounded system. Local building code requires that every three-prong outlet be connected to a grounded system. When you look behind an electrical outlet, you should see three conductor wires: a black "hot" wire, a white neutral wire, and a green ground wire. Elsie and Peter's outlets have only a hot wire and a neutral wire. The "grounded" outlets weren't grounded at all.

Peter and Elsie, the owners, are devastated. They had paid thousands of dollars to have the house rewired with a grounded system. It turns out that the contractor had only changed the two-prong outlets to three-prong outlets, nothing more. Behind the walls, the original, ungrounded system remains. When you go back to the negotiating table, you can ask for a significant price cut to cover the costs of getting the house properly rewired. But Peter and Elsie are still horrified that the contractor has duped them, and they can't bring themselves to cut the price on their house, which represents the bulk of their retirement fund.

At this point, you can break off negotiations by choosing not to remove the subject to inspection clause, thereby collapsing your offer. Or you can go with your agent's suggestion to keep the deal alive: The original electrician should be contacted and forced to deliver the grounded electrical system he was hired to install in the first place. You can remedy a few unpleasant surprises that are discovered during a home inspection, but you need to uncover the problems in order to address them.

Home exterior

A building inspector examines the following exterior components of the house:

- **Roof surface:** The roof should be in at least *visibly* good condition. An unacceptably aged roof surface is obvious, but in the early stages roof degeneration can be quite subtle, and virtually invisible to the untrained eye. A roof surface in poor condition can mean water leakage or poor insulation, and in extreme cases can even lead to roof collapse.

- **Eaves:** The eaves should be in good condition, with no holes and minimal rust. Eaves in poor condition mean rain and snow will not drain appropriately, and this can cause serious difficulties if water accumulates on your roof or near your home's foundation.

✔ **Chimney(s):** The chimney(s) should be free from cracks or loose sections in the masonry, and should have a chimney cap. Chimneys in poor shape can cause ventilation problems.

✔ **Chimney flue(s):** The chimney flue is the exhaust vent over the fireplace. An unused fireplace can quickly have its flue blocked by debris, or even a bird nest or two. Flues that aren't in good condition may signal a malfunctioning or improperly maintained chimney.

✔ **Windows:** The windows shouldn't show any signs of wood or water damage. Damaged windows are sure indications of water and air penetration into the interior of the home. Double-paned windows shouldn't be fogged — a sign that the vapour seal has failed.

✔ **Siding/exterior walls:** Whether brick or siding, the house's exterior walls should be free of cracks, gaps, or signs of water damage. These are possible indications of damage to *interior materials,* rot, or moulds inside walls. Watch out! Also, look for possible rot on window trim and shutters, as well as any wooden decks and patios or external stairs.

✔ **Gradient:** The gradient, or slope of the ground, should be properly angled away from the home. An incorrect gradient will allow water drainage into the basement or foundation, causing water damage, rot, or even fungus growth.

✔ **Foundation:** The house's foundation should be free of cracks, bulges, or deformities. These abnormalities can indicate an extremely serious structural problem. Also, termite tubes or other signs of infestation may manifest themselves in this area.

✔ **Septic system/cesspool:** Septic tanks and cesspools should be tested for possible leaching. You can request a dye test if the inspector doesn't plan to run one.

Basic home interior

You can expect your inspector to check for these problems on the inside:

✔ **Flooding/leaks:** The inspector notes these and other visible signs of water damage inside the home. The inspector is also able to tell you if any waterproofing measures, a sump pump, or other additions have been installed. A *sump pump* is an electric pump installed in a recess in the basement (or occasionally outside the house) that will kick into action if the level of water in the drainage system starts to rise. The pump will mechanically aid the gravitational flow of the water away from the house. Waterproofing a home is extremely expensive, and this makes it important for buyers to be aware of measures already in place.

✔ **Insulation/ventilation:** Insulation and the ventilation system become problematic if the home leaks or doesn't allow moisture to evaporate, putting pretty much all of the major structural components at risk. Excessive moisture can cause rotting, rust, electrical shorts, and fungal growth. Furthermore, good insulation and ventilation will keep heating and cooling costs to a minimum.

✔ **Other unsafe components:** The other problems inspectors watch out for are largely dependent on the age of the house. For example, paint may be old enough to contain lead, some railings on staircases may be missing, or urea formaldehyde foam insulation (UFFI) or asbestos-laced Zonolite/vermiculite insulation may be throughout the home (refer to Chapter 8 for information on UFFI and Zonolite/vermiculite). Building materials change over the years, and so do safety standards. A qualified inspector has up-to-date information and can recognize potentially dangerous components in the interior systems/mechanics.

A fire sale (literally)

Bob and Shirley's offer on a 65-year-old home that seemed to be in good shape was accepted. Bob had owned five or six houses before, but because the couple was recently married, this was their first big purchase together. At first, Bob didn't feel a home inspection was necessary. He's a fairly handy guy and can handle lots of small repairs around the house. But Shirley had some concerns about a couple of things, particularly the mixture of old and new wiring, so they decided to make their offer subject to inspection and to do a full home inspection.

Good thing. They were stunned to find out that not only was the wiring not up to code, but it was also an extreme fire hazard. A previous owner (not the current seller) rewired an extension to the family room, and mixed two different types of wiring that were twisted together with a little electrical tape that had since fallen off. The home inspector couldn't figure out why a light was flickering in the family room, and he couldn't figure out how the newer wiring was routed through the wall cavity. With the owner's permission, the inspector removed one 1¼-x-2½-metre piece of wall panelling. Burn marks were on the back of the panelling where

the wires were connected, and it was still very hot — a disaster waiting to happen.

When the seller had bought the house three years before, she didn't do a home inspection. Therefore, she was completely unaware of the danger in the family room where her two small children always played. After Bob and Shirley's inspection, she immediately called an electrician. Bob and Shirley bought the house, with the written understanding that the seller would pay for the professional rewiring as necessary to bring it up to code and pass inspection from the city inspector.

The home inspection not only saved Bob and Shirley the cost of rewiring, but it also may have saved their lives. When you get an inspector's full report, you're able to evaluate whether the home in question is as good as it looks. The inspection report should list any substandard or failing elements, and the inspector should make suggestions regarding necessary repairs and how those jobs should be prioritized. Your inspector may also be able to furnish some rough estimates of the repair costs.

Your inspector examines these systems:

- **Plumbing:** Plumbing systems and pipes may no longer be up to scratch. The inspector is on the lookout for rust and leaking or water stains that warrant further examination. Checking water pressure and the condition of drains and pipes is also part of the job.

- **Heating:** Heating systems may be outdated or inefficient. For example, the valve that controls the flow of hot water into radiators can rust away, leaving you with no way to turn down the heat in that individual unit. Other problems may be unsafe exhaust venting, or chimneys that are blocked. The inspector looks for all of these problems, as well as for indications that the furnace, including the motor and burners, is functioning properly.

- **Electrical:** Electrical systems may be potential fire hazards or simply not dependable. Wiring always warrants extra attention. Your inspector should check any exposed wiring and its condition.

  If your home or condominium was built in the 1970s, it may have aluminum wiring that isn't reliable. In aluminum wires, electricity actually flows away from the screws used to hold the wiring in place at the back of an electrical outlet. Air pockets form between the wires and the screws, letting electricity arc between them, ultimately burning the wire away and deadening the outlet.

  Your inspector checks for signs of unreliable wiring, and also for problems such as reverse polarity outlets and two-prong convenience outlets. Also, older knob and tube wiring or old 60-amp systems are very difficult to insure. Remember, these issues aren't just about saving money on expensive repairs; they're about you and your family's safety.

Checking out condominium inspections

If you're buying a condominium, you may think you don't need an inspection. Obviously the place is well maintained by the residents or management company, and if it's new, how can there be anything wrong with it, right? Actually, those aren't safe assumptions (just read Yvonne's story a bit later on in this chapter in the sidebar "A river runs through it"). Home inspections don't apply strictly to detached homes — condominiums should get inspected too! In fact, during a condo inspection, many of the issues similar to those of a house get checked out.

Outside the condo

The inspector usually starts with the outside of the building. He will check to make sure all exterior components are well designed, well maintained, and functioning properly. He will examine the caulking and sealing around the windows, doors, and building details to be sure they're in good shape. If the building has a brick facade, the inspector will check the brickwork for loose bricks and to see if the mortar is holding the bricks properly and not deteriorating and leaking. If the building has a stucco exterior, the inspector will check to make sure there are no hints of water ingress and staining, especially in leaky-condo-prone British Columbia. (Changes in building codes in the late '90s have, for the most part, addressed leaky condo issues. However, a good inspector will be on the lookout for water issues regardless.) The inspector also walks through the parking garage and checks for any leaks or water ingress into the underground parkade.

B.C.'s leaky condo crisis affects more than just condos

One of the first things they teach budding architects is "Water is your worst enemy." Homeowners in British Columbia's coastal climate learned this lesson the hard way. After the building explosion from the mid-1980s to the late 1990s, it was clear that something was very, very wrong. Buildings were leaking all over the lower Mainland and Vancouver Island, and protective tarps became a standard part of the streetscape. Condos were singled out as the problem at first, but it quickly became clear that *building envelope problems,* structural flaws that permit water to penetrate a building, don't affect condos exclusively.

In 1998 the B.C. government passed the *Homeowner Protection Act* and opened the Homeowner Protection Office (HPO), a provincial Crown corporation, to license builders and conduct research and education programs for the construction industry and the public.

Home builders in B.C. and contractors who repair the leaky condos must be licensed through the HPO, and the HPO sets terms of the warranty coverage that will cover new construction and condo repairs. When buying or selling a new home or a rebuilt condominium in B.C., determine the warranty coverage of the construction and find out exactly what's covered by the warranty and when the warranty terminates. You'll also want to make sure the builder/contractor is registered with the HPO — all the registered builders/contractors are listed on the HPO Web site.

For more information, contact the HPO:

2270 – 1055 West Georgia Street

P.O. Box 11132, Royal Centre

Vancouver, B.C. V6E 3P3

Telephone: (604) 646-7055

Toll-Free: (800) 407-7757

Fax: (604) 646-7051

Web site: www.hpo.bc.ca

E-mail: hpo@hpo.bc.ca

A river runs through it

Yvonne finally paid off her student loans, got a great job, and was going to be a homeowner. With a little help from her parents, she would buy her first condominium. Having been around the block a few times, her parents placed one condition on their financial assistance: that Yvonne have a full inspection done before she bought anything.

After looking for a couple of months, Yvonne found a nice top-floor, one-bedroom suite in a very nice and seemingly well-maintained building, just one block off the bus route she used to go to work. The building was recently painted and looked great. Best of all, it was within her price range. The minutes of the building's meetings looked clean and "uneventful," if somewhat skimpy with details. The building had only 12 suites altogether, too small for most management companies to handle, and so it was self-managed. The 12 owners did their best to maintain the building, manage the finances, and take notes during their condominium meetings. Because it all seemed so perfect, Yvonne wasn't prepared for the results of her home inspection.

Her unit's balcony had substantial dry rot under the membrane and needed immediate repair.

The inspector poked around on a couple of other balconies and found that they all needed repair or replacement. The minutes of the condo meetings didn't indicate that the roof had actually been patched continually during the last couple of years. The inspector found that the roof was near the end of its lifespan and needed to be completely replaced very shortly. She also found numerous and substantial water leaks into the underground parkade.

The inspector estimated the repairs could total up to a minimum of $500,000 to $600,000 if resealing the parkade and the foundation would be necessary, a cost that was confirmed by a drainage company the next day. Because the building had so few residents and a very small reserve fund (they had spent all their money painting the building), Yvonne's portion of the future repairs could have ended up in the $40,000 to $50,000 range at least . . . and probably more. Although Yvonne loved the unit, she passed and bought another, slightly more expensive suite in a professionally managed building that her inspector said was one of the best she'd ever seen.

The inspector checks out the roof of the building to make sure the roof and drainage system are being well maintained and serviced. He may also check out any vents and skylights and make sure they were properly installed and are being maintained. If the building has a central boiler supplying hot water (as opposed to individual in-suite hot water tanks), most inspectors look in the boiler room to make sure the system is up to date and working properly. As for balconies or patios, the inspector also checks to make sure they have adequate drains and that no water is pooling on them, which can lead to rot in balconies that have a membrane over a wood frame.

Inside the condo

Inside the suite, the inspector checks the wiring throughout. He checks the electrical panel and makes sure the wiring is up to snuff, and checks the electrical outlets to see that they're all grounded and working properly. The inspector also checks all plumbing fixtures and checks the suite for leaks. Most inspectors also check the appliances that are included in the sale, but some focus more on the structure of the building and the condition of the systems within the suite.

Before booking an inspection for a condominium, ask the inspector if he wants access to the roof, the boiler room, or any other common areas. These places are usually locked, so the property manager or a resident of the building may need to be there to give the inspector access.

You Are the Owner of All You Survey

Once upon a time, kings and queens built their castles on hills because they could rule over all they could see. In today's smaller kingdoms, you can rule over all you survey. These days, homebuyers have a choice: You can request an updated survey from the seller, or you can purchase title insurance, which is increasingly more common.

Title insurance is another approach to property sale closing, widely accepted by lenders instead of a survey. This insurance provides protection against problems you may encounter with the title of your property: It covers expenses associated with repairing the title, or compensates you if your property's title comes under dispute. Lenders require either a survey or title insurance in order to finance your purchase, and your lawyer will incorporate it into your title documents. However, many reasons exist for getting an up-to-date survey as well as title insurance (though you don't need a survey when buying a condominium).

Land surveys are also known as building location certificates, mortgage certificates, surveyor's certificates, real property reports, plot plans, and certificates of non-encroachment.

Figuring out why you need a survey

A land survey is a legal map of a property's boundaries. In the best-case scenario, the seller will provide you with an up-to-date survey that's perfectly legal — in other words, one that's copyrighted and valid only if the original is signed and sealed. If the survey the seller hands you is old, unsealed, or otherwise fishy in any way, get your own done. When it's performed by a professional who is familiar with your region, a land survey

✔ Gives you certified, accurate measurements of the property and the exact location of the house, garden shed, garage, and any other buildings on it

> ✔ Lets you know of environmental or contamination problems on your site, such as whether your well draws on runoff from a nearby major road, or whether the site is in an area proven to contain dangerous levels of lead in the soil
>
> ✔ States who may review the survey (because a land survey, contrary to popular belief, isn't a public document)

If no up-to-date survey is available, you may want to write "subject to survey" into your offer — doing this will allow enough time for a proper and thorough survey to be done. A slipshod, cheap, hurried survey won't do you any good if a boundary dispute comes up, or if you decide to subdivide, build an addition, or remortgage. But again, you may find that title insurance for the type of property you're purchasing is adequate. Every jurisdiction is different, so consult with your agent.

Finding a professional surveyor

Like finding a good doctor or mechanic, the first step in the hunt for a professional surveyor is to ask around. Ask the previous owners of the home for the company they used. Or if your lender has requested a survey, they'll often recommend one. Your lender may provide you with an excellent surveyor who is familiar with your locality — and all the environmental, archaeological, and regulatory quirks that may go along with it. Your agent, banker, or lawyer may also be able to recommend a surveyor.

Parking problems

Toronto is famous for its lack of parking, so Bert and Ernie decided they really needed parking when they went to buy a home. They found a wonderful home that didn't have parking, but were encouraged by the other homes on the street, most of which had either front-yard parking or garages accessible by a laneway. The sellers had a survey from when they bought the home ten years ago, and Bert and Ernie didn't notice anything different about it: The deck and shed hadn't changed. They decided, against their lawyer's recommendation, that this survey was fine.

After they bought the home, however, Bert and Ernie were appalled to find that a Toronto bylaw prohibits the installation of front-yard parking in their neighbourhood, a bylaw enacted after the survey was done. Street parking was hard to come by, so instead of putting a garden in their backyard, they decided to put a parking spot there.

Given the size of their backyard, Bert and Ernie ended up with a small open parking spot, and the survey revealed they wouldn't be able to build a garage because it would encroach on their neighbour's property. The survey may not have shown the change in parking bylaws, but it would have shown the poor parking arrangement available in the backyard.

Failing this approach, hit the Yellow Pages. You may also be able to surf the Net for a good surveyor. Many provincial land surveyors' associations have Web sites, complete with member lists and other helpful information. Look for long-established companies, or those that are members of your provincial land surveyors association. Call three of them, describing the job you need done, and be ready to supply them with a legal description of the property as well as the civic address. Record how each company proposes to do the job and approximately how much they would charge to do it. Finally, ask to see samples of their work. Compare the companies' methods, estimates, and samples, and you'll find the surveyor who is right for you.

Does This Come with a Warranty?

A $30 clock radio comes with a warranty, but what about your house? If you're buying a newly built home, you may be covered by something called a *New Home Warranty*. But this warranty is nothing like the piece of paper that came with your new coffee maker. A New Home Warranty is actually a type of third-party insurance. And it may or may not come with your home, depending on whether or not your builder has bought into a plan.

Complicated? Well, yes. Basically, a New Home Warranty is insurance for your builder while the home is being built. Then, after the *certificate of completion* is transferred over to you, it becomes a kind of consumer warranty. Unlike home-owner's insurance (which you'll also need, and which we discuss in Chapter 11), the builder rather than the homebuyer buys the policy. Of course, just because you don't buy it doesn't mean you won't end up paying for it: The builder will likely tack the cost of the warranty on to the purchase price.

Legislation concerning new home warranties varies across the country, and not all provinces require them. In other words, not all homes come with them, and not all homes are covered in the same way. You'll have to ask your builder whether your home is protected by one. Your builder should be able to provide you with a registration, enrollment, or membership number for the warranty plan. That way, you can check with the issuer of the warranty to ensure that everything is in order.

If you do have a warranty for your house, keep it. Keep all documentation and policy information, registration confirmation, and contact numbers somewhere safe, where you can access them if you ever need to.

Note that in order to be covered under a province's *New Home Warranty Program* (NHWP), you may have to pay a registration fee, although generally the builder pays all associated fees. Pay attention to the timing and schedule of the warranty. Some coverage is good for only one year after you take possession of the house, and coverage of different problems may expire at different times. If you do have any problems or questions, call your provincial NHWP office. They can answer your questions and give you a list of builders that are registered with them as members of the NHWP. Some provincial

NHWP offices provide ratings of the local registered builders based on track record for both creating and solving problems. Others supply you with a list of criteria that builders have to meet in order to be registered members. Either way, you get the security of knowing you're choosing a builder that has been evaluated on a regular basis and meets high standards for quality and service. The New Home Warranty Program should be listed in your local phone book, or your provincial government's Consumer Affairs ministry can direct you to the warranty program specific to your province.

What's covered

So what does your New Home Warranty cover? The details vary across the country. Most include protection for some (but not necessarily all) of the following, with different items covered for different lengths of time:

✔ Defects in workmanship and materials

✔ Down payment protection

✔ Settling cracks in drywall (usually for the first year or two)

✔ Structural defects

✔ Violations of building and safety codes

✔ Water penetration

Timelines on the coverage also vary from sea to shining sea, so you'll have to check your specific policy for the details. You need to know what you're covered for as well as what you're *not* covered for.

With a warranty, you're in the driver's seat

A warranty can come in handy when things go wrong. If your "unobstructed view of the lake" is seen through a gaping hole in the wall, you'll want to have that certificate to turn to. In the best of worlds, you let your builder know of the problem and then he builds you a new bay window where you can relax and enjoy the vista. In the worst of worlds, he may argue that the hole isn't really a hole, but a great alternative to a cat door. Without another person there to arbitrate — except for the courts — things can get ugly pretty quickly.

In the event that you and your builder disagree over needed repairs, or what exactly qualifies as a defect, a New Home Warranty can come in handy. Because a New Home Warranty is backed up by a third party, someone else can step in to settle disputes, keeping both your interests and the builder's interests in mind.

You may want to think twice about your purchase if your builder isn't offering a warranty as part of the bargain. If you're buying a condo, make sure you get a warranty for the unit and that the condominium board has a separate warranty that covers the common elements.

Put it in writing

Verbal agreements don't usually hold much clout. If you notice any defects and want to make a claim, you *must* put the complaint in writing to your builder and keep a copy for your records. You should also send a copy to the issuer of the warranty to keep on file in case of a dispute. Taking photographs is also a good way to document problems. Many builders will give you a form to fill out; otherwise, organize your concerns room by room and include as much detail as possible about the nature of the problem. These documents should always include the plan number, lot number, and address of the residence in question. Oh, and of course, you have to file before the end of the warranty period.

When things go awry

Your warranty should outline a "reasonable time frame" in which builders must fix any problems that have been brought to their attention. "Reasonable," unfortunately, can mean a lot of things. One plan, for instance, gives builders up to a year to rectify defects. So if the light fixture in your bathroom doesn't work, you may be sitting in the dark for a long, long time. Getting your brother to rewire may not be a good idea: Most plans won't automatically reimburse you if you go ahead and get someone else to do the work, and some repairs may void the warranty altogether.

If you're considering buying a converted condominium, you may not qualify for the New Home Warranty Program, because although the individual units are new, the outside of the building isn't. Check with your provincial NHWP (see the Appendix) to see if the unit you're considering qualifies, and always get the details of the developer's warranty in writing.

Pre-closing Walk-Through

Taking a pre-closing walk-through is more common in some parts of Canada than in others. In some provinces, this walk-through is a term of the contract that allows you to inspect the property and to be sure that the seller hasn't neglected any contractual obligations before handing over the home. Your agent will arrange a time that is suitable for you and the seller, and will accompany you on the walk-through; an hour should be sufficient. Try to schedule your final walk-through a day or two before your scheduled closing date. Leaving little time between your final check and the actual closing ensures that you'll definitely take possession of the home in exactly the condition you want. Hopefully, the home will be empty of all the seller's possessions, so you'll find it easier to imagine where you'll put the grand piano, but chances are the home will be waiting for a final packing. This is a perfect time to take measurements for curtains and blinds, carpets, and large pieces of furniture. You may also want to bring in paint chips or wallpaper samples — or your decorator — if you plan to change the decor.

When you take your final pre-closing walk-through, check that all the *chattels* are in place — that everything the sellers agreed to leave with the house is still there. Things like the fridge and stove are commonly indicated as chattel in a contract of purchase and sale. Besides confirming that the home contains all the chattels agreed on contractually, your pre-closing walk-through gives you a chance to check that everything you *expected* would stay with the house is still there. Some people, for reasons yet to be determined, take fixtures with them: They cut off phone jacks, remove light switch panels, towel racks, cupboard doors, toilet roll dispensers, and sometimes fridges. If you find out early, you can discuss new problems with your lawyer before your final exchange with the seller.

The walk-through can also be a good opportunity to talk to the seller, if she happens to be home. You may be able to find out the neighbourhood gossip and such helpful tidbits like what time the mailman shows up, which neighbourhood kids are reliable and responsible babysitters, and other pieces of information that can help you adjust to life in your new home.

Chapter 13

Closing Time: Closing Events and Moving Day

*W*hat happens on closing day depends on what you do before closing day.

Stripped to its bare bones, the *closing day,* sometimes called *completion day,* is when you must have the papers signed (usually, you do this a day or two before), pay for your new home, and transfer the title.

If your real estate team is well organized, you may just have to sit by the phone and wait for your lawyer or agent to call to congratulate you that your new home is now registered in your name and you can come get the keys.

All the professionals on your team — your real estate agent, your lawyer, and your lender — will be able to give you an idea of what remains to be done on the closing day and which elements will involve you. You probably don't need us to remind you to read all documents and raise any concerns you have *before* you sign.

What You Sign

How does closing work? First of all, you have to read, clarify, and sign the following:

- ✔ **Mortgage:** Also called a *deed of trust,* this includes all the details of the mortgage agreement and, typically, allows that the lender can take possession of your property if you default on the loan.

- ✔ **Mortgage note:** Also known as a *commitment letter,* this guarantees you'll pay your mortgage and lays out the terms of the loan, when and how it must be paid, any penalties that may apply, and so on.

- ✔ **Affidavits:** Depending on the laws of your province or the requirements of your lender, you may sign several of these. Your lawyer can explain the implications of each. For example, often buyers are asked to confirm that the property will be their primary residence.

- ✔ **Down payment cheque:** To seal the deal, you have to sign away a very large amount.

- ✔ **Title:** The transfer of title (registration of change of ownership) is done at the land titles office. The seller must sign a warranty deed stating that no new loans have been taken out against the title and it is clear for the new owners. This deed must be notarized by a lawyer or notary and registered at the land titles office.

What You Pay

We explain closing costs in Chapter 2, but here is a reminder of the costs you're expected to pay on closing day.

- ✔ **Down payment:** You pay the portion not covered by the deposit that accompanied the offer.

- ✔ **Mortgage costs:** You may pay some or all of the following: application fee (usually waived), assumption fee, processing fee, prepaid interest, mortgage insurance, CMHC insurance, application fee, the GST/HST on the insurance if you have a high-ratio mortgage, and so on.

- ✔ **Insurance:** You pay for insurance on your property. Purchasing this insurance before closing is necessary.

- ✔ **Lawyer's fee:** You usually pay between $300 and $800, not including disbursements. Discuss this fee with your lawyer early in the process.

- ✔ **Lawyer's disbursements:** You usually pay between $250 and $600 in addition to the lawyer's fee. This amount not only covers the cost of more complicated procedures your lawyer performs on your behalf, such as the title search, but also covers miscellaneous everyday tasks like courier fees and photocopies.

✔ **Adjustments:** You pay money due to the seller for prepaid taxes and utilities.

✔ **Land transfer taxes:** You pay provincial tax on a home purchase, ranging from 0.5 to 4 percent and beyond. The city of Toronto has a municipal land transfer tax on top of that. Check with your lawyer, banker, or agent to see which taxes are charged in your city and province.

✔ **GST or HST:** You pay GST or HST (depending on which province you live in) on a newly built home as well as on a home that has been substantially renovated. You may be eligible for a rebate depending on the purchase price of the property. Note that you will also be charged GST or HST on the services of your lawyer. (Refer to Chapter 2 for more information.)

Lawyers offer packages that include all disbursements, which means you know all the costs from the get-go. When you're collecting quotes from different lawyers, make sure you ask whether disbursements can be included in the prices quoted.

If you ever thought opening a suitcase and unloading packets of bills like they do in the movies would be really fun, this may just be the one transaction where you can fulfill that fantasy. Most people, however, settle for paying their closing costs with a simple, pocket-sized certified cheque or bank draft.

In some cases, the *possession date,* the day you get the keys, is the same as the completion or closing date. If so, the seller's lawyer or agent gives your lawyer or agent the keys when the title is transferred, and she will bring them back to you. Never count on getting your keys very early in the day!

Give yourself enough time to collect all your funds into one account. If you're wiring substantial amounts of money from investments or from a partner's account, you may need a couple of days to process the transfers. Ask your lawyer for a chance to review all the closing charges at least one business day before closing. Keep funds ready in case the costs total more than you expected, and keep credit card balances low so you can access additional funds quickly if necessary. Most lawyers will let you know well in advance how much money you'll need.

A Moving Experience

Hopefully you had a good party when you got possession — because your life is about to turn upside down. Moving ranks as one of the top ten most stressful events in a person's life. Why? Well, technically, moving means transporting all your worldly possessions from one place to another. What it really means is moving your life. From finding a new school for your children to figuring out where the best place is to get pizza in the middle of the night, moving involves more than packing tape and a loaded van. Moving your stuff may take as little as a few hours. Moving your life will take a lot longer.

A wealth of relocation resources is just a few clicks of the mouse away. Have a look at the Appendix for some great Web sites to get you started.

Moving day versus closing day

Although it may seem like the logical choice, moving day shouldn't necessarily be closing day. The actual closing involves many different players, can take a long time, and doesn't always go as planned. What if you've got movers sitting on your front porch at dawn, clocking time on closing day?

It gets worse. If the land titles office happens to be busy on the date you planned to close, the title may not even be transferred by day's end, and you'll have to wait to take possession. This situation doesn't happen all that often, but when it does, it tends to be on a Friday. A lot of people close their houses on Friday, thinking they can move in on Saturday, which makes for a very busy land titles office. If the office closes before your house does, you'll be stuck waiting around until Monday for the deal to be done. The good news is that in this world of computers, many title transfers can now be done by your lawyer online. However, glitches happen!

So you'll be wise not to plan to have your closing day coincide with moving day, especially if it's at the end of the week, or at the beginning or end of a month, when city clerks are busiest. Schedule your closing the day before your moving day to cause as little stress as possible.

Timing is everything

When you move can have as much of an impact on your wallet as what you move and how you move it. You can sometimes save a lot of money by choosing your moving date strategically.

Keep in mind that, like hotels, rental and moving companies often have "off-season" rates geared to times when demand is at its lowest. Pricing rates generally revolve around renters' patterns. For instance, a truck rental company may charge you less if you're not moving within the first or last week of a month.

Less is more

Jim and Sue had been living together in a one-bedroom rental ever since university. Their furniture was a curious amalgam of hand-me-downs, most of which had seen better days back in the late '70s. The orange and brown colour scheme wasn't dreamy, but the couple had decided to wait until they moved into their first home before investing in "real" furniture. When the day came to move, however, the moving truck was filled with their outdated collection of clunky chesterfields and armchairs. They had forgotten that these pieces didn't fit into their new life and didn't have to come along for the ride.

One big way to save on moving costs — and hassle — is to move only what you'd really like to keep. Not only will you save the cost of moving these articles, you'll also save the chore of packing and unpacking them. If you're moving a long distance away, you may want to sell furniture instead of taking it with you: The cost of moving it may be greater than purchasing new furniture when you arrive at your destination. You can make some money by holding a garage sale and selling what you don't want to take along. Or you can do a good deed and give what you don't want to local charities like the Sally Ann or Goodwill.

If you live in Quebec or you'll be living there soon, be extra careful about choosing your moving date. Although it's not the law, it's tradition for many Quebec leases to begin on July 1 and end on June 30, so that's a time you should try to avoid. If you're absolutely stuck moving along with everyone else, book everything you need for the big day well in advance, because you won't find a truck or a strong set of arms to spare.

People also want to move when it's most convenient. Generally, this means that rates get hiked from Thursday to Sunday, because most people want to move sometime around the weekend. Consumer demand also drops dramatically during snow season. After all, what dummy would want to move in the middle of a snowstorm? (Answer: a dummy who wants to save money!) Accordingly, May to September is high time for moving, while October to April can land you a deal. You should be able to negotiate a discount if you

- ✔ Move during an off-peak time (October to April).
- ✔ Choose a day that falls early in the week (Monday to Wednesday).
- ✔ Pick a date that falls outside of the roving-renter period (first and last week of each month).

Whatever you do, try your very best to avoid moving from June 30 to July 2. In most provinces, and overwhelmingly so in many major cities such as Montreal, Canada Day is the busiest moving day of the year. Why? Well, for most families, the kids have finished the school year, and summer holidays are just starting — what better time to move? Unfortunately, movers will book up sooner and many will charge higher rates. Worst of all, we've heard of people being forced by crooked movers into forking out additional cash on top of the amount stipulated in their contract, just because those villains know that all other movers are fully booked and their victims have no choice after their boxes, furniture, and assorted bottle cap collections are in the truck.

Moving your life

Be prepared for the long haul. When you start trying to take care of all the little details, you'll realize that your life is a lot more complicated than you thought it was. If you're moving to a new city, for instance, medical, dental, and even veterinary records for every member of your household will have to be sent on. You'll also want to track down a qualified provider for each of these services. A simple task like redirecting your magazine subscriptions can require a month's notice or more, even if you're just moving down the block. Your lawyer may take care of some of these details, like water and property taxes. The rest is up to you.

If you're being relocated, and you're moving at least 40 kilometres closer to your new school or job, your moving and selling expenses (we're talking meals, travel costs, real estate fees, the works) are tax deductible. These expenses include the cost of shipping and storing your belongings and up to 15 days' temporary accommodation near either your current or future home. Contact the Canada Revenue Agency for details, any eligibility requirements, and the necessary claim forms, or visit their Web site using the search words "moving" and "principal residence."

Even though moving may be the furthest thing from your mind as you run around finding an inspector and otherwise arranging for your grand purchase, the more organized you are about moving, the less stress you'll have as the closing date approaches (besides, you want to save all that worrying for real problems that may arise). The best way to tackle the workload is to create a list of tasks that need to get done and a calendar that sets deadlines for accomplishing them. The list that follows gives you a head start, but keep in mind that every situation is unique. We suggest carrying around a notebook where you can jot down extra to-do's as you think of them.

Moving your stuff

Before you start rooting through your home, keep in mind that one person's trash is another's treasure. If you can, have everyone in your household participate in the weeding process. That way, you won't end up accidentally discarding a beloved object. Children need to be part of this process so that they'll understand why old favourite sweaters have suddenly disappeared. You may want to encourage small children to keep a memento, like a prized teddy bear. Soon they'll have to adjust to a strange new environment and may find themselves hankering for an old friend.

Keep the following tips in mind as you go through your belongings:

✔ Get rid of anything you've outgrown, especially bulky items like that old pair of skis with size-five boots and bindings.

✔ Be honest with yourself about what you use and what you don't use. There's no time like the present to be ruthless. If your sweater shaver hasn't seen the light of day in over five years, it's time to get rid of it — no matter what you paid for it originally. Same goes for the carrot juicer that's gone untouched ever since you moved on from your macrobiotic diet.

✔ Look at your new home's floor plans to evaluate what will fit in and what won't. You may discover that you're not truly wedded to the loveseat Sparky the cat has been using as a scratching post for the past five years. Or that your grandmother's old kitchen table doesn't look good in your new stainless steel kitchen.

✔ Get rid of clutter. Take a serious look at your attic, basement, closets, and other storage spaces. You may be surprised (or scared) by what you find there. We have some decluttering tips for you in Chapter 20.

✔ Use the two-year rule. Unless it's a vintage piece, if you haven't worn something within the past two years, part with it. Nobody needs to see anyone in electric blue sprayed-on spandex disco pants ever again!

✔ Don't forget the garden shed and garage. These places are chock full of items you *can't* take with you, including flammable, explosive, or other hazardous materials.

You may also want to start thinking about your storehouse of food. Generally, transporting food isn't worth the hassle, especially perishables like cheese and meat that can spoil en route. If you've got hundreds of dollars' worth of ham hocks in a deep-freezer, you'll want to be sure to eat them before moving day. You may well find that you have two months' worth of food in the home — and it all has to disappear by the time the last box is loaded into the van. In fact, planning on eating takeout the night before moving day is a good idea — or better yet, go to a restaurant and celebrate.

Packing it all in

Admit it: Packing is a loathsome chore. It always takes longer than you think it will, and you'll always need more packing supplies than you planned on. That said, we know some ways to make packing — and unpacking — a lot less painful.

If you can, give yourself plenty of time to pack. Otherwise, you'll end up throwing things haphazardly into boxes or, worse, not packing them at all. Count on packing being a big job, not a last-minute chore. Trust us: You're sure to find that you have more stuff than you thought you did.

Here are some essential supplies:

- ✔ **Boxes:** Big boxes, little boxes, picture boxes, and bike boxes. Boxes are far easier to pack into a van than irregular shapes, and will save you and your movers space and time. Use new materials, even though you may be tempted to pick up some discards at your local grocer. These used boxes may not be clean or sturdy enough for the job.

- ✔ **Tissue paper or old newsprint and bubble wrap:** Lots of it. Tissue paper is ideal for wrapping small objects, like coffee mugs, to prevent breakage. Although newspaper may seem like a good, cheap, and environmentally friendly alternative, it blackens whatever's wrapped inside. A friend of ours packed her china in last week's news, only to find out she had to rewash all her dishes at the other end.

- ✔ **Packing tape with a tape dispenser and extra rolls:** This puts the final seal on every box. Jake, who works in the shipping department at a local bookstore, recommends a criss-cross pattern around the box for added strength.

- ✔ **Big markers:** Indicate the destination and an abbreviated list of the contents of each box.

Before the packing begins, photocopy the floor plans of your new home, clearly marking each room with labels like Bedroom A, Bedroom B, Bathroom A, Bathroom B, and so on. Give everyone a copy, and arm your crew with markers. Then, pack the boxes by room, labelling each box appropriately when it's full. You may also want to micro-label, indicating which kitchen cupboard or dresser drawer the contents belong to. The movers will (or at least, they should) use these labels as directions, putting each box in its rightful place. If you keep a running list of the boxes and what's inside, you'll have a full inventory by the time the job is complete. When it comes time to unpack, everything will magically end up where it belongs. You won't have to move heavy boxes from room to room, nor will you have to guess what's in each one. This is a simple trick that will save you a lot of headaches.

Pack with care. After you're all packed up, you'll have very little control over what happens to your boxes en route: They may get jostled around in the truck, stacked one on top of the other, or (worse still!) accidentally dropped. Packing in bubble wrap or tissue paper cradles your belongings. Towels and other linens can also double as padding. Large appliances, like refrigerators, often require special handling before and after a move. And a computer may need to readjust to its surroundings for a day before being plugged in. Read your owner's manual, contact the manufacturer, or speak to your movers for instructions.

Beware the random packer. If your partner or children are helping you, make sure they understand your system. Deciding you need to redo their work will probably create tension you'd all be better off without!

After everything's packed into the truck, resist the urge to flee the scene without one last walk-through. Check every closet, shelf, and cupboard to make sure you've left nothing behind. Kids are natural snoops and are great at this sort of thing. Pretend it's a treasure hunt, and they'll most certainly find the antique ornaments you hid away five years ago and forgot about.

Moving it yourself versus hiring professional movers

Figuring out the best way to move into your new place depends on a few things:

- How much stuff you have
- The size of your budget
- The time you have to spend
- The distance you're moving
- The number of large friends with strong backs who enjoy heavy lifting that you have at your disposal

If you're moving from a one-bedroom apartment to a house, or if you're a minimalist, you may be able to save a few bucks and move it all yourself. Well, not completely by yourself — unless you're a professional wrestler — but with the help of a few strong, not clumsy, friends and family members. Get on the phone and start calling in those favours. (Keep in mind, if you call on your friends for help moving, be prepared to return the favour.) If you decide to take this route, understand that it's a big responsibility and you'll be in charge of the packing, loading, driving, and unloading, not to mention making sure that any valuables arrive unbroken. Depending on the load, you can rent a small trailer or a large truck (which you'll pay for either by the hour or by the day), but if you're nervous about manoeuvring a beast of a vehicle, some companies will provide a driver. Remember: Bend your knees when you lift those heavy boxes.

Be good to your friends and family, especially when they're helping you move. Make sure you have a cooler stocked with plenty of cold pop and beer for when you arrive at the new house. If someone starts to get cranky from all the heavy lifting, tell him to take a break and send him out to pick up the pizza.

Convenience and less stress are good reasons to hire a team of professional movers. Also, if you're relocating from Dartmouth to Iqaluit and you don't have time to drive the truck cross-country, then your only choice is professional movers. Moving costs more this way, but if your budget permits, you may be happy to leave it to the pros. They're experienced and know where to place your antiques in the truck so they don't break. And because you won't have to spend all your time saying "One, two, three, lift!" you can focus on other things, like making sure you haven't forgotten one of your kids, or your dog. Some companies charge on an hourly basis if the move is small, and others charge based on a combination of things, like how many movers you need, the type of furniture you have (a piano and a marble-topped dining table will up the price), and the number of boxes you've packed. The travel time and distance are always factored into the cost as well. Call or e-mail a couple of different moving companies for quotes, and ask your real estate agent for recommendations.

Keep in mind that you can really move in style by having the moving company do all the packing for you too! Though this will add significantly to your costs, you will be able to take advantage of insurance if anything they have packed breaks during transport. However, if you have heirloom china or anything irreplaceable, make sure that the movers pay special attention when wrapping, packing, and transporting your possessions.

The Canadian Association of Movers (www.mover.net) has a searchable online directory of its members. The goal of this group is to help the buying public access credible, professional moving services. The association expects its members to adhere to its system of professional ethics and standards — so check the database for members that are approved. While you're online, check with the Better Business Bureau for any complaints that may have been filed against the movers on your short list. Do a Better Business Bureau search by typing "Better Business Bureau" plus your city into your search engine.

Although some moving companies are small operations, you'll find some online with fairly sophisticated Web sites that let you plug in your information (how far you're moving, how many rooms' worth of stuff you have, whether or not you have a baby grand piano) and receive a price quote by e-mail. These online tools are great for budgeting for the big day, but we recommend that you also talk to someone from the moving company so that you can get the closest estimation of the cost before you sign anything.

Again, as with most things associated with a real estate transaction, getting a recommendation from satisfied friends is often extremely helpful. Ask questions. The national moving chain you decide on may have a sterling reputation in general, but the local franchisee may give disappointing service.

When dealing with movers (well, heck, when dealing with any professional), always get a proper written contract before any work begins. You're bound to find some operators whom you can trust only as far as you can throw them (and for those of you who haven't tried, this is not very far). Some movers may offer you a terrific deal, such as a very low price, as long as you agree to forgo a written contract and you pay in cash. Agree to this deal, and you'll be open to serious risks when the work begins. You may encounter poor service quality, no warranties, and extra costs that keep piling on. Without a contract, you won't have any course of action to deal with those cheaters.

Moving companies range from small and local — one-person operations run with a small truck and a cell phone — to huge operations with fleets of vehicles. But before booking any movers, always ask questions. Find out how long they've been in business, if they belong to the Better Business Bureau, and if they're fully bonded and insured. Working with a reputable, experienced company may cost a couple of extra bucks per hour, but you'll gain peace of mind. Moving is stressful enough without worrying about damage to your valuables, or your stuff ending up in Chicoutimi instead of Chibougamau.

The Moving Timeline

Trust us, you want to be as organized as possible as you work toward your move. Use this moving timeline as a reference while you pack, make calls, wrangle with your movers, and generally tear your hair out.

Two months and counting

Hey, it's never too early to get things rolling! Did we mention now is a good time to start packing?

- ✔ Start saving! Moving is a huge expense. If you start budgeting in advance for movers, insurance, supplies, utility transfers, child (and pet) care, and the bevy of incidental costs, your wallet won't be so hard hit when the bills come in. Remember, too, to factor in the costs after you arrive: Painting, housekeeping, and carpentry work should all be taken into account.

- ✔ Begin the pick-and-choose process: Decide what you want to take with you and what you want to leave behind. Plan to sell any discards — at a garage sale, for instance, or through the classifieds — at least a month and a half in advance.

- ✔ Start scouting out your new neighbourhood. Speak to the principal of your children's new school to take care of transfer details and find out about important dates. While you're there, find a neighbourhood restaurant where you can feast after the big move. You won't be in any mood to cook.

- ✔ Book the movers, van, or truck. You don't want to get stuck with your things all packed up and no way to move them. We suggest making your reservation as soon as you have a firm purchase agreement on your new home, especially if you're moving around the first of the month, when the rest of the world is doing the same.

One month to moving day

The number of people who apparently care that you're moving is amazing. Here's what to do to keep them in the know. Oh yeah, and keep filling those boxes.

✔ Ask your doctor, dentist, and veterinarian for referrals, and arrange for the transfer of records.

✔ Contact the phone company. While you'll technically have a lot of leeway in hooking up your phone service — it usually takes only a few days — getting in touch with the phone company in advance is a good idea. That way, you'll have your new number handy to give out along with your new address.

✔ Contact the subscription office of any magazines you subscribe to and inform them of your new address, letting them know which issue should be delivered to the new location. If you receive any catalogues that you'd like to continue to receive, don't forget to let the mail-order company know of your change of address.

✔ Visit your local post office at least two weeks in advance to request a redirection of mail service. For a period of six months, any mail that is sent to you at your old residence will be redirected to your new address, and you'll pay only about $30 for the convenience.

✔ Start packing non-essential items (like trinkets and knick-knacks, off-season sports equipment, books). This really eases the packing load as the big day gets nearer.

One week before

Now the countdown's really begun. Take deep breaths. Keep packing.

✔ Pick up any dry cleaning, shoe repairs, or other items left with local businesses. Return any outstanding library books (and that glue gun you borrowed from your neighbour three months ago).

✔ Call a locksmith to arrange to have your locks changed after you have possession of the house.

✔ Get boxes if you need more, and keep packing. You'll find tips to make the process easier in the section "Packing it all in" earlier in this chapter.

✔ Get rid of your kids! Having children and pets underfoot can slow down movers and increase the chances of an accident. If possible, make arrangements to send young children to a best friend's for a sleepover on the evening before moving day. You should also board pets for the few days around the move. (The last thing you want to do is hold up the moving process because Sparky the cat escaped and is nowhere to be found.)

The day before

You may feel like a contestant on *Survivor* at this point. Look at all those boxes!

✔ Stock up on snack food and bottled water to keep you going through moving day. Consider preparing some sandwiches, too.

✔ Buy paper plates and plastic cutlery and cups to use until you can unearth the real things.

✔ Deliver Sparky to the kennel or to a generous friend so that the fur doesn't fly on moving day. At the same time, drive the kids over to a best friend's house for their sleepover.

✔ Confirm your movers.

✔ Designate a box or bag for items that will be thrown in at the last minute, including bedding and pillows.

The big day

This is it — the day you've been working toward for the past two months. You probably wish you could just go away somewhere and leave it to the movers. Bad idea. We suggest you stick around — 'til the bitter end.

✔ Be there when the trucks arrive so you're available to give instructions to the movers and to point out any items that need special handling.

✔ Stay out of the way. A good moving team works like clockwork: They have a coordinated way of moving as a group and an efficient method for packing a truck. Although you may think carrying boxes out to the truck will speed things up and save you money, lending a hand may actually impede progress.

✔ Count the boxes as they're loaded onto the truck to make sure everything makes it on board.

✔ Do a final check around the house after everything is loaded. Look inside cupboards, closets, and the garage.

✔ Collect your children and pets after the move is complete.

After the move

That is, after you've slept. You should consider the following:

✔ Different provinces have different regulations regarding change of address notification. In Ontario, for instance, you're obliged to change your driver's licence and health card within ten days of moving. Some provinces provide automatic kiosks where you can make the change yourself — which may save you the time and frustration of standing in a long line. Or, you may be able to go online and make the necessary changes on your provincial government's Web site.

✔ If you're a first-time homeowner, stock up on some of the basics before you need them: a mop, stepladder, drill, hammer, screwdriver set, wrench, snow shovel, rake, hedge clippers, garden hose, outdoor broom, light bulbs. . . . You get the idea. Otherwise, you'll end up going to the local hardware shop every other day for a month. If you're planning a housewarming party, make the most of your friends' generosity and ask them to bring an item on your "stuff needed" list. If you're planning a painting party, make sure your friends bring brushes, sandpaper, and paint. When Marcus first moved into his new home, his friends put together a cooler full of stuff they thought he would need, including duct tape, band-aids, a flashlight, and slippers.

Getting Possessed — We Mean, Getting Possession

When you have the keys in your hand, at the open door of your new home — *now* you can celebrate! The drapes, appliances, and any other chattels that were specified in the contract should be right where you last saw them. But really, this is the fun part: The home is legally, officially, and absolutely yours, so do what you will. Enjoy.

Try not to second-guess yourself. Chances are, after you've bought your home you'll start seeing "For Sale" signs on all sorts of other dream homes. You'll begin to wonder, Should we have waited longer to buy? Did we make a hasty decision? Was this the right choice for us? This is normal. Don't regret your choice. Lots of hard work, careful consideration, and late-night debate went into your purchase. Remember what you discovered throughout your search: The outside of a house gives no reliable indication of its interior.

Accept that every new place you move to will cause you to feel a bit unsettled at first. The rooms may seem smaller (empty homes often do, with no furniture to give them a sense of scale), or the room colours may seem different than you remembered. Often this feeling will pass as you start to put up your own pictures, get your furniture where you want it, and put your favourite sheets on your bed. You'll need some adjustment time before you can move about the house in the dark without bumping into anything.

You've been in decision mode for so long that you may just be in shock now that you're sitting comfortably in your living room with no more papers to sign or bank hours to contemplate. So your mind starts to wander, and you start to think that maybe you should have tried harder for that house with the brand new turquoise and orange kitchen . . . it was kind of funky, after all . . .

Instead of wondering "What if?" concentrate on the "What now?" Nothing's stopping you from painting your kitchen turquoise and orange. It's your home now — and you can personalize it the way you want. Congratulations!

Part IV
Deciding to Sell

The 5th Wave   By Rich Tennant

I JUST THOUGHT IT WAS TIME TO SELL. THE LACES KEPT COMING UNTIED, THERE'S A LEAK IN THE HEEL, AND IT NEEDS ALL NEW ODOUR-EATERS.

FOR SALE BY OWNER

In this part . . .

Decisions, decisions, decisions . . . Should you stay or should you go? Should you buy, then sell, or vice versa? Can you afford to move? Can you find something better or more suitable than what you have?

If you're thinking about putting your home on the market, this is the section for you. Just like buyers using the first section, you won't find pat answers to these questions here, but you will find help on how to answer them yourself.

Chapter 14

To Sell or to Stay

*F*ew decisions have a bigger impact on your life — at every level — than deciding to sell your house. In fact, moving is one of the three most stressful life events (after death and divorce). A major change is scary, but as our lives develop, change may be necessary and even welcome. How much change you're ready for is up to you. You may decide you don't really need to move — you need to tear down some walls and finally renovate that bathroom.

In this chapter, we explain how to sort your priorities so you can be sure that you really do want to sell your home and that you know what you want to gain from the sale. Taking the time to consider how selling your home affects your life helps you avoid costly and unnecessary mistakes, and ensures that you'll be satisfied with your choices. Thinking it through and deciding what you really need gives you incredible peace of mind.

Making the Big Decision

Your house shapes your lifestyle. The amount you spend on housing determines how much money you can save for things like vacations, your retirement, or your kids' education. The location of your home dictates how much time you spend getting to work, school, and shopping — and how much money you spend on transportation, utilities, taxes, and maintenance. Your home also affects your social life and leisure time. Are you close to friends and relatives? Can you entertain easily at home or meet conveniently? Can you go for walks in the nearby park or putter in the garden when you need some time to yourself?

Now is the time to take stock of what you have and what you need. Don't try to keep track of all the reasons you want to sell in your head. Sit down and get everything out on paper (if it's been ages since you've written anything by hand, use your computer and just print it off).

Not all of your reasons to move carry equal weight. After you've made your list of likes, dislikes, needs, and wants, start thinking about what your priorities are and which factors are most important. When you feel you've got a handle on the issues, organize your list according to your priorities.

Organize your likes and dislikes for your current home, as well as your needs and wants for your future home, into three categories: property, location, and finances. We use these categories to discuss weighing out your decision to stay or sell.

Home sweet home: Your property

What makes your house a great place to live? Consider aesthetics like style, decor, and view, as well as practicalities like an eat-in kitchen, a two-car garage, room sizes and total area, and plenty of natural light. What's lacking in your living space? Do you find yourself coveting your neighbour's stunning stone fireplace, big backyard, sunny solarium, and well-stocked wet bar? Does the open loft with a rope railing that once appealed to your minimalist sensibilities now terrify you as a parent?

Often, we change homes because our needs change. Room for a patio and garden may be an absolute must when you're retiring and finally have daylight time to spend outside. Perhaps your home office has to expand beyond the corner under the stairs.

Make a list with two columns: one for all the benefits of your current home, and the other for all your dislikes concerning your living situation. Then make a second two-column list of the items that you and your family may need now or in the future, and all the things you don't absolutely *need* but would still give an arm and a leg for.

How significant a change do you need to make? Look at your lists, and think about whether your home can grow with your needs. If you build the sunroom that you've always wanted, or finish the attic to add an extra bedroom, keeping the home you have makes sense. But adding one extra bedroom may not be sufficient if you're planning to have three more children. Be realistic about how much renovation your home can accommodate.

Location, location, location: Your neighbourhood

Look at the logistics: Is your home located in a good area that suits your needs and tastes? Location is the seller's mantra, and it was probably a big factor when you chose your current house. Consider what sets your neighbourhood apart. Are the streets nice, safe, and quiet? Are good schools, public transit, and shopping in the area? Are there job opportunities for you and your family members? Is your extended family nearby?

Just as your housing needs may change over the years, so, too, may your priorities concerning location. Maybe you don't want to live next to your favourite dance club anymore, but you do want to be near good schools for your kids. In addition to the basic physical features of your location, don't forget the intangibles. The personality of your neighbourhood may be a big factor in your happiness or dissatisfaction with where you live. Over the years, communities change as people move in and out of neighbourhoods.

Remember why you moved to your neighbourhood in the first place. Ask yourself if those reasons are still valid. Are the people still as friendly as when you first moved in? Is the crime rate still low? Are the surrounding woodlands still unspoiled? Is the air quality good? Do your neighbours still show incredible enthusiasm for Hallowe'en festivities? Make sure your list of likes and dislikes concerning your current home includes mention of the surroundings.

Don't overlook commuting time when you consider the merits of your location. Although you may stand to earn a lot of money by selling your house in a premium location and moving farther out, it may not be worth it when the new hour-and-a-half commute takes its toll on you and your family. And with the rapidly rising cost of gasoline, the extra 45 minutes on the road ends up costing a mint. On the flip side, you may decide that the driving time is worth having more space and a large garden. You have to weigh the merits to make the right decision.

You may want to sell your home because you want to make a *big* change in location. From the big city to the suburbs, from the West Coast to the East — even though the grass may be greener or the salmon tastier on the other side, you may find the climate really isn't for you. Refer to Chapter 7 for advice on researching new neighbourhoods.

Dollars and sense: Your finances

Think about your budget. You know whether you're straining to meet financial obligations or whether you've got a nice fat nest egg in the bank. In addition to paying the mortgage on your home, you also pay for utilities, insurance, taxes, repairs, and basic maintenance (you can use the budget worksheet in Chapter 2 for a detailed examination of your current financial picture).

Doing the math

If you're looking to reduce your expenses, then downsizing to a smaller, less expensive home or area may be the smartest thing to do. However, if you're a prosperous business owner who was once a struggling entrepreneur, you may be ready to leave the cramped starter home behind and spend some money to get yourself a big house with a two-car garage and heated indoor swimming pool. Include your financial outlook in your list of pros and cons about the home you have now. Is it too costly? Or is it very affordable but simply not big enough for you, your spouse, the twins, and Doug the pug?

Don't forget that selling your house costs time and *money*. The transaction costs of selling a house can easily total 3 to 6 percent of the price at which you sell your property. In addition, be aware that unless you have paid off your mortgage, interest payments and discharge fees can take up an even larger percentage of the money you have invested in your home.

Get a good idea of what the market offers in your price range. If you're considering selling your $250,000 townhouse to invest in a $500,000 detached house, go to open houses and compare whether the houses in that price range have all the features that you expect. You may discover that the benefits of buying a house in that price range aren't as great as you think.

The money you have tied up in your house is the money you *don't* have for other financial goals. Determine the minimum you'd like to have to set aside for holidays, your retirement, and your children's education. Then decide how much you have to spend on your next home. See Chapter 15 for more details about the financial aspects of selling your home.

Saving your home and your sanity

James and Jenny bought their home eight years ago, right after they got married. The home was perfect for them back then, and it's still great for them now — even though they now have two small children. But, as with any growing family, the cost of living grows with them, and with car payments, day care costs, and the fact that Jenny has gone back to school to get her MBA and won't be working for a year, those monthly payments are starting to stress this family out.

James thinks they should sell the place and move somewhere more affordable — or maybe even consider renting — but Jenny is dead set against moving from the neighbourhood they live in and love. Luckily, they also have 70 percent equity in their home and a good mortgage broker.

By refinancing their home, they were able to pay off the minivan, pay Jenny's tuition, get rid of their credit card balances, and even top up their RRSPs. The good news is they still have 30 percent equity in their home and a better interest rate, and aren't being nickel-and-dimed by all their bill payments. In fact, they're saving $1,200 a month!

Refinancing

If the main reason you're thinking of moving is monetary, you may want to look into refinancing your current home. Currently, you can refinance a principle residence and take up to 90 percent of the equity. But remember, after the 80 percent mark, you'll need high-ratio mortgage insurance (refer to Chapter 3), most often provided by the Canadian Mortgage and Housing Corporation (CMHC).

Refinancing can make substantially reducing your monthly payments possible. If you're drowning in credit card debts or car payments, by taking the equity in your home, paying off debt, and perhaps even getting a more favourable interest rate, you may find that you don't have to move after all.

A complete refinance may not have to be the answer, though. Your mortgage broker or lender may be able to provide you with a secured line of credit against your current home. (The loan is secured by the home itself.) You may be able to use that money any way you want — and in many cases just pay the minimum interest on the line of credit each month. So, if you have a big-ticket item that needs attending to, like a new roof, you can use your line of credit to pay for it, and not have to worry about the roof over your head (literally).

Whatever you decide, make sure that you discuss all your financial options with your mortgage broker or lender. You may be surprised by the options that you have.

Refinancing your home can have fees or penalties associated with it. Make sure all of these are outlined to you by your banker or mortgage broker before you proceed.

Good Reasons to Stay Put

Examine your lists of likes, dislikes, needs, wants, and priorities (we provide guidelines for such a list in Chapter 7). Pay particular attention to the physical features you want or need in a home and your financial status and goals. Both of these considerations may be reasons for you to stay in your current home.

✔ **Renovating is a viable option**: If you're after more space, a new look, modernization, or greater efficiency, renovating your home may be the wisest course of action. If you live in a great neighbourhood, consider building an addition. Renovations may be a steal compared to the transaction costs of selling, and they may also add to the resale value of your house. See Chapter 20 for more details on which home renovation projects add the most value when you do decide to sell your house.

If you want to move because your house needs some costly repairs, investigate your options carefully. You may end up paying for the repairs anyway when your house doesn't sell because of them, or when the buyers insist on deducting the repair cost from the price they'll pay for the house. Buyers often overestimate the cost of repairs in order to protect themselves from the worst-case scenario.

✔ **Your finances are shaky:** If you're already having trouble living within your means, it may be wise to delay buying your dream home. As we mention earlier in this chapter, you may want to look into refinancing the home you currently own to try to get your balance sheet a bit more balanced. Even if you're thinking about moving to a less expensive house, keep in mind that you'll incur plenty of one-time expenses when you sell your house, buy a new one, and then move. Factoring in these expenses may mean you have to look for accommodation in a range several thousand dollars below what you initially thought you could afford. If you can possibly get your debts under control while staying in your current home, your financial and emotional state will be that much better off.

Nothing is more stressful than trying to move when you're strapped for cash, except perhaps trying to move when you are strapped for cash *and* time.

Good Reasons to Sell

Even if you love your home, there are times when it just won't be able to adapt to your ever-changing needs. Because you can't always build what you need or make the neighbourhood exactly how and where you'd like it, finding a new place to call home is often best. If any of the following conditions describe your situation, you're probably ready to sell.

✔ **The location of your home is unsuitable:** If you have a job offer in a great location with good long-term employment potential, or if you are ready to retire and look forward to the security and low maintenance of a retirement community, selling your house makes a lot of sense. (And if you're relocating for professional reasons, you may get a tax break on all your moving expenses — refer to Chapter 13 for more details.)

✔ **Your house is too small or too big:** If you and your family need more space and you don't want to renovate, or you can't get a building permit to put an extension on the back of the house, moving is probably your best bet. On the flip side, if the last of your six kids has finally moved out of your seven-bedroom home, it may be time to downsize — before any of them decide to move back!

✔ **Life throws you a curve ball:** After a traumatic event like a divorce or the death of a family member, you may simply want to leave bad memories behind. Take the time to review your financial situation and personal goals so that you make a move that is right for you.

✔ **Life is fine — but the neighbourhood isn't:** Maybe your life hasn't changed a bit, but somehow the neighbourhood has changed around you in ways you're not happy about. If you find yourself with the best house on the street — or the worst — it's a good time to move. If every other bungalow in your formerly sleepy neighbourhood has been replaced by a monster home, next time a real estate agent calls you, it's time to say, "Yes, as a matter of fact, I am interested in selling!"

Timing: Sell First and Then Buy, or Vice Versa?

Not a gambler? Even for people who enjoy moving from home to home, timing the move is really tricky. On the one hand, you can find yourself with no house, having sold your home before finding a new one of the appropriate size, style, or location. On the other hand, you can find yourself with no money as you carry two houses. You can avoid these pitfalls by basing your timing decisions on current real estate market trends and your own needs and priorities.

Riding the real estate cycle

Real estate goes through cycles. When there are a lot of buyers and not many homes available, it's a *seller's market*. This is also called a *hot market* because homes tend to sell more quickly and for higher prices. In a hot market, nail down the house you want — the tough part in this case — and then sell your house.

When there are more homes listed for sale than there are buyers shopping for new homes, it's a *buyer's market,* or a *slow market*. Prices tend to be lower and homes take longer to sell in a buyer's market. If the market is slow but there are lots of houses you can see yourself happy in, sell your house first — the hard part in a slow market — and then pick your next house from among your favourites.

Although trying to sell your home in a buyer's market means you may have to drop your asking price, chances are the next house you buy will also be at a reduced price, because market conditions tend to be similar within a particular region. Unfortunately, if you're moving cross-country, you can't count on being so lucky.

Market conditions within a city can be completely different, too. In any city, you'll find that one or two neighbourhoods are considered both trendy and family-oriented, and, regardless of the season, are always in high demand. Even in a recession, these neighbourhoods generate quick home sales just because of the sheer number of people who want to live within their borders. The trick is being able to identify the type of market that your present home and neighbourhood is facing:

✔ **Check out the "for sale" signs in the neighbourhood.** Are there lots of them, but none of them have sold stickers? That's not a good sign.

✔ **Look at recent sales.** Even if you do see a lot of sold stickers up, what a seller was asking for and what he got are two different things. If the market is hot, those properties may have received multiple offers and sold for above the asking price. However, if that house was on the market a while, there may have been numerous price reductions before the sold sticker went up.

✔ **Watch the news.** Nothing seems to interest people more these days than housing values and monthly statistic reports. But remember, these reports describe what has happened, not what will happen. Newscasts typically run a three-minute story that will cover what they believe is happening, but often it seems that potential home buyers and sellers are only hearing headlines such as "PRICES ARE FALLING" or "MULTIPLE OFFERS LEADS TO RECORD HIGH PRICES!" What should you believe? Your best bet is to ignore national trends, and stick to the neighbour-hood you are interested in. For instance, even in a down market, some areas of big cities like Vancouver, Calgary, or Toronto may still experi-ence bidding wars, while other neighbourhoods may see inventory languishing. That story will not make the news. Your agent will help you find out what's happening in your target area.

✔ **Speak with a knowledgeable neighbourhood agent.** After all, they are the ones who are living and breathing homes every day, and speaking to both buyers and sellers, as well as other agents. Local agents can see the nuanced changes in market conditions long before any statistical report can.

Real estate also goes through predictable highs and lows over the course of a year. Spring is usually a peak transaction time anywhere in the country. If you need to sell your house quickly during a slower time of the year, list your home at market value, or even a smidgen below actual market value. On the other hand, if you want to get the best price possible, put your house on the market at the beginning of the peak season. Price is an important marketing tool, so you want to get it right the first time. Chapter 15 gives you the low-down on pricing do's and don'ts.

Meeting your needs

Your needs form another important variable in the buying and selling equa-tion. Do you need to sell your home quickly? Do you want a certain price, and if so, are you willing to wait for it? Do you want to be in your next home by a particular date?

If you want to get your kids moved into a new house before the beginning of the school year, you may decide to buy that perfect house in the new neigh-bourhood before you have sold your current house. The way to prevent hanging on to two houses is to price your current home to sell. For example, if you have to sell and are facing the prospect of owning two homes in six weeks' time (carrying both would probably cost you an extra $2,000 to $3,000 per month), drop your asking price. Accepting an offer, albeit below your original asking price, meets two important needs: your kids start the new school year off on the right track, and you have only one home to carry — much more manageable. Examine your financial situation and determine your personal priorities early. But as a rule, selling before you buy is almost always better. In Chapter 16, we take a more detailed look at the financial consequences of both scenarios.

Determining how much you can get for your house

If you're going to sell your home, naturally you want to recoup the money you spent buying it and fixing it up, and you're thinking about how much money you *need* in order to buy your next home. Unfortunately, these factors don't determine the resale value of your home.

The cold, hard truth is that *buyers* determine the actual market value for your house through what they offer to *pay* for it. Truth be told, buyers don't care about how much money you need to get out of your home. If all the similar houses in your neighbourhood sell in a certain price range, buyers will likely offer a similar price for your home. Surveying the asking prices and recent sale prices of comparable homes in your neighbourhood gives you a basic idea of what price you can expect to get (we show you how in Chapter 15). In effect, timing is everything — being aware of the real estate market's trends makes you better prepared to get the price you really want or need.

If you're working with a real estate agent or broker, ask for a *comparative market analysis* (CMA), a report used to determine a home's market value. Your home is ranked next to similar homes in your neighbourhood based on details like size, condition, desirable features, and listing and sale prices. If you're selling on your own, you may be wise to get a professional appraisal to determine the actual market value of your home. See Chapter 15 for more on comparative market analyses.

Consider checking out the neighbourhood competition in person. You may think that the updates that you've done to your home are more than adequate, but your 5-year-old carpet may not be able to compete with the new hard-wood floors in the house listed two blocks away. Likewise, your kitchen may be light years ahead of the property that still has an avocado green refrigerator. Open houses are the perfect venue for this type of investigative reporting, so set aside a Sunday afternoon with pen and paper in hand to check out what's what in the 'hood.

Your house gets the most exposure to the buying market in its first few weeks of listing. The closer your house is priced to its actual market value, the more quickly it will sell. If you price your home too high and scare off buyers in the beginning, you may have to go through a few price reductions in order to sell. Pricing your house realistically from the get-go makes more sense — you'll sell it months earlier. See Chapter 15 for all the details on home appraisals and pricing your house accordingly.

Figuring out how much you can spend on your next house

Figuring out how much you can afford to pay for your next house is a long but relatively simple equation. It involves solely the basic math of addition and subtraction. You need to total your cash inflow and outflow, and then subtract the expenses from the income. The tricky part is taking inventory of all your sources of income and expenditure, and the exact amounts associated with each. Chapter 15 takes you through the cost assessments and calculations step by step.

Careful calculations help you be realistic about what you can afford. When you know how much you can spend, you need to investigate whether that amount really will get you the kind of house you want while allowing you to maintain your standard of living and save for long-term financial goals.

Never assume *anything* when investigating what you can get for your money. The perfect home may not be in the perfect neighbourhood. The perfect neighbourhood may have listings in your price range only for properties half the size you need. You may have to make sacrifices to make improvements, so you need to know what your priorities are. Even if you can make a decent profit on the sale of your current home, you have no guarantee that you'll be better off if you sell.

The safety net: Conditional "subject to sale" offers

One way to synchronize buying and selling is to find a house you like, make an offer "subject to" the sale of your current house, and, after the conditional offer is accepted, *then* put your house on the market. If the condition (selling your house) isn't met by the expiry date in the clause, then the offer you made for the other house becomes null and void if you and the seller don't extend the "subject to sale" clause's time frame. (Refer to Chapter 10 for other types of "subject to" clauses.)

By writing a "subject to sale" condition into your purchase offer, you don't have to buy the house you want until you've sold the house you're living in — giving you the peace of mind and the financial security that comes with not owning two homes *and* not being homeless.

You should know that a "subject to sale" conditional offer is less attractive to a home seller and therefore puts the buyer in a weak negotiating position. Because most sellers don't want to delay the sale of their home, they often are willing to accept a "clean offer" for less money. Most sellers who receive such an offer and are considering it will invoke the *time clause* (or *escape clause*), the amount of time the first buyer has to either remove all the conditions from their offer — including the "subject to sale" condition — or withdraw their offer altogether. Now it's time to hustle. If you put in a "subject to sale" offer and really want that house, you need to remove your conditions and firm up your offer, even if the second buyer's offer is several thousand dollars less. Some sellers won't even look at offers made subject to the sale of the buyer's current house, because they don't believe the buyer is serious. Ask your real estate agent how conditional offers are received in your local market.

Here's how it works. You write into your offer a "subject to sale" clause that essentially states, "This offer is subject to the sale of the buyers' current residence located at [address], on or before [expiry date of clause]. However, if another acceptable offer is received, the sellers will notify the buyers in writing and give the buyers 48 hours [24 or 72 hours is also common] to remove the 'subject to sale' condition as well as all other conditions from the offer, or the offer will be considered null and void." The *expiry date* of the clause indicates the amount of time you have to sell your house from the time the offer is accepted and therefore to remove the condition and make your offer firm, or withdraw your offer if the condition was not met. This date is usually negotiated to fall between four and six weeks after the offer is accepted, and it can be extended if both parties agree.

Don't confuse the expiry date of the "subject to sale" clause with the completion date of the offer itself. The *completion date* specifies the date you will close the deal if all the specified conditions are met. It is the day you become the legal owner of the property.

The *time clause,* which is negotiable, identifies how long you have to remove the "subject to sale" condition or withdraw your offer if the seller receives another acceptable offer before the expiry date on your clause. You see, even after the seller accepts your conditional purchase offer, she will still actively market her home, looking for a "clean offer" — an offer without conditions. If the seller receives another acceptable offer, she will *invoke the time clause* and notify you in writing that you have 24, or 48, or 72 hours (or whatever time period was written into the clause) to make a decision. At this point, you can remove the conditions and commit to buying the house — whether or not you have sold your own — or you can withdraw the offer.

If you've really found your dream home and your conditional offer has been accepted, you don't want your "subject to sale" clause to expire or the time clause to be invoked before you sell your current property. You must price your house to sell, which means being very realistic about its market value. The closer your house is listed to market value, the more quickly you will receive good offers.

For most people, it makes sense to put your house on the market *while* you look for your next home. Doing this gives you a good sense of what buyers are willing to pay for your house, and saves you from inflating the amount you think you can spend on your next home. If offers come rushing in, you can always accept the best, subject to the purchase of your next house.

Some buyers won't accept a seller's proposed counteroffer, especially if the counteroffer is conditional on the sellers' purchase of their next home. If you find yourself in this position, you have to decide what you're willing to risk. If you sell before you've found a new home, you risk becoming homeless — at least temporarily. On the other hand, if you reject the buyer's offer because you can't include the condition of buying your next house, you may wait a long time before receiving another one, depending on the market conditions and your pricing strategy.

If you have a lot of money, you can just buy your dream home and *then* put your current house on the market. Through *bridge financing,* you can use the equity in your first property to finance the purchase of the next. (See Chapter 16 to find out more about bridge financing.) It's the riskiest option financially, but it guarantees that you get the house you absolutely want.

Buying time with the closing dates

Getting the paperwork right is the next step in making a smooth transition. When you've found a buyer for your current home and a new house to move into, you'll need to schedule each *closing date,* the day you transfer ownership of a property and finalize the sale. Ideally, both the sale of your current home and the purchase of your new one should close one right after the other.

Scheduling both closing dates together affords you the most security financially — and emotionally. If it simply can't be done, the next best option is to try to extend the closing date on your purchase so that it follows the closing date of your home's sale. See Chapter 22 for details on negotiating deadlines that will work for you.

Try to avoid the last day of the month or year as a closing date. These times are particularly busy for the agencies that will be registering and filing paperwork for the transfer of ownership, termination of insurance, and the like, not to mention movers.

Chapter 15

The Price of Selling

*Y*ou may be thinking, "Great! I'm selling my house, there's a big cheque coming in, and I'm gonna be swimming in cash!" Although it's true that there *will* be a big cheque at some point, you ought to keep in mind some costs tied to selling your house. The idea is to provide for these costs in advance, because most of them must be paid before that cheque gets cashed. Careful and informed planning can help ensure that the process of selling your house goes smoothly.

Pricing Your House to Sell

If you price something too high, it won't sell. This rule is especially true for big-ticket items like houses. Potential buyers are skittish to begin with at the prospect of having to make such a big decision. If your price tag is too high, you'll scare them off right away. Worse still, your home may look shabby compared to the competition in that higher price range — never a good marketing plan. The key is finding the balance between reeling in the buyers at the start and getting your home's true value in the end (after negotiation, of course).

How much is your home worth?

The best way to find out how much your home is worth is to ask a professional. You can hire a professional appraiser to give you an appraisal, or you can ask your real estate agent to give you a *comparative market analysis* (CMA), sometimes also referred to as a *current market analysis* or a *competitive market analysis*. A sample CMA is shown in Figure 15-1.

COMPARATIVE MARKET ANALYSIS

COMPARABLE HOMES RECENTLY SOLD

Address	Age	Lot Size	Floor Area	Bdrms	Bthrms	Bsmt	Listed Date & Price	Selling Date & Price	Ass.Value ('10)
312 Elm St.	55	33 x 120	2000	3	3	Full	Jul.5/11 $580,000	Oct. 20/11 $570,000	$550,000
2525 Maple St.	48	33 x 120	1956	3	2	Part	Apr.17/11 $600,000	Apr.25/11 $605,000	$590,000
4323 Pine St.	51	33 x 120	1830	3	2	Full	Jun.28/11 $625,000	Sep.14/11 $610,000	$600,000

COMPARABLE HOMES FOR SALE NOW

Address	Age	Lot Size	Floor Area	Bdrms	Bthrms	Bsmt	Listed Date & Price	Ass.Value ('10)
3737 Chestnut St.	63	33 x 112	1860	3	3	Full	Aug.15/11 $599,000	$586,000
461 Maple St.	47	33 x 123	1750	3	2	Full	Jun.2/11 $600,000	$590,000
518 Birch St.	45	33 x 120	1905	4	2	Part	Sept.29/11 $630,000	$615,000
2431 Elm St.	55	35 x 115	2000	3	3	Full	Oct. 4/11 $650,000	$620,000

YOUR HOME

Address	Age	Lot Size	Floor Area	Bdrms	Bthrms	Bsmt	Recommended List Range	Recommended Sale Range
495 Pine St.	51	33 x 120	1850	3	2	Full	625,000/$635,000	$610,000/$620,000

MARKET VALUE DEFINED: ... the price expected when a reasonable time is allowed to find a purchaser when both sellers and prospective buyer are fully informed.

LISTING PRICE: ... the price asked for a property, as set by the vendor. The vendor is urged to take into account information supplied and market conditions.

Sales Representative: _____   Date: October 15/11

Figure 15-1:
Your real estate agent can give you a comparative market analysis that looks something like this.

As far as assessing the market value of your house, appraisals and CMAs are essentially the same. Both professionals consider all the factors influencing the worth of your property (such as location, total floor area, general condition of the home, and amenities). They research the recent sale prices and current asking prices of similar homes in your area, compare the finer details, and adjust up or down to determine your home's *fair market value* (FMV). If your home has, say, an attached double garage, then it may be worth a little bit more than someone else's down the street that, like yours, is a three-bedroom two-storey with four baths and a finished basement, but comes with only a carport.

Most real estate agents will prepare a CMA for you free of charge. You will always have to pay an appraiser. If you're selling without an agent, you should definitely hire an independent appraiser. The legal system, as well as most financial institutions, recognizes appraisals prepared by certified professional appraisers only. (You can read more about appraisals for sellers in Chapter 19.)

Your buyer can put a *clause* (a condition) into the offer stipulating that it is subject to the home's sale price being confirmed by an independent appraisal. If your buyer's appraisal reveals they have offered more than your home is worth, your buyer may retract the offer, or your buyer's mortgage lender may refuse to finance the purchase.

The three most common pricing mistakes

We know it's your home and you can ask whatever price you like for it, but we're here to tell you to proceed with caution. Your ego may tell you your home is worth $1 million, but the market may tell you something else altogether. Your listing price heavily influences your likelihood of selling success; it can determine whether your home is snapped up by eager buyers or languishes in the classifieds for months. Here are three pricing mistakes that sellers often make.

Trying to make a hefty profit

The reasoning for setting a high price goes something like this: "If someone buys it for the high price, great, I made some money. If I have to drop the price a little to sell, then I haven't really lost anything because I still got a fair price." The problem is, it doesn't work that way. Your home gets the most attention for the first few weeks it's on the market. If you set the price too high, you run the risk of buyers bypassing your home because of its high price. Simply put, if the value of your home is $450,000 but you insist on listing it at $525,000, all the potential buyers who should be looking at your home won't be, because your asking price doesn't line up with their budget. If your home isn't fairly priced for those crucial first few weeks, it may become stale by the time you do lower the price. Buyers see your listing and think, "If it's been on the market for this long and they have to keep lowering the price, there must be *something* wrong with it." That line of thinking may not be true, but that's the perception. Those buyers may then turn around and purchase something else by the time you lower your price.

Furthermore, if the initial asking price is too high, buyers won't feel that there is competition for the home — and this means they won't be in any hurry to make an offer. Either way, by the time you do lower the asking price, agents (and their buyers) have lost interest in your home and you may have to sell for less than you would have gotten had you priced your house realistically in the beginning.

We are Canadians, and because of that, we are polite. Typically in the first month of a listing, and even after that, buyers don't present offers that are substantially lower than a home's asking price, even if the offer is for fair market value. You may think that you can ask for a high price for your home so that someone will bring you a low offer and then negotiate a deal, but chances are, you won't get any offers (or interest) at all.

The only real circumstance where you can be "optimistic" in your asking price is in an overheated seller's market where there are few, if any, homes that directly compete with yours. In this dream-come-true scenario, you can ask a higher price than your CMA indicates. Better yet, you may get offers from competing buyers, driving the price higher than what recent sales indicate your house is worth.

Setting the sale price based on your needs

Many sellers have a new location (or even a new house) in mind and know how much money they need to make on the sale of their current home in order to purchase a new one. Other sellers may be planning to "trade down" as a way to make money they can then invest for retirement. Frankly, buyers don't care about your needs. Buyers have their own needs to worry about, one of which is paying fair market value for their new house. If you keep the sale price too high because you "need the money," you simply won't be able to sell your home.

Setting the sale price based on how much you have "put into" your home

Getting $30,000 in renovations done doesn't necessarily equal an extra $30,000 on the sale price of your home. Some improvements to your home will increase its value (for example, kitchens and bathrooms are often the best places for renovations that add to the resale value of a home), but others will not. However, if the improvements that you have made are overly personalized (are you the one with that turquoise and orange kitchen we heard about?), they may actually cost you money.

Cosmetic improvements, such as fresh (neutral) paint, are always good investments. Although they won't increase the value of your home by a significant margin, basic home touch-ups are relatively cheap and extremely important for making a good first impression on buyers. A good agent knows what counts and what doesn't, and so do most buyers — you can also see Chapter 20 to find out which renovations are most valuable for sellers.

Sum Fun: The Math of Selling Your Home

With home prices rising year after year, you may think you're going to make a bundle off your bungalow. But a whole lot of expenses go into selling your home, so we recommend doing some simple math with us before you start counting your cash.

Estimating the costs of selling

On the surface, the economics of selling your home seem pretty simple. You sell your home, and hopefully, you make enough money to cover the purchase of another one. If the sale price of your current home is greater than what you pay for your new home, "I save money" appears to be the logical conclusion. Unfortunately, a few steps in the middle of the process may shrink your profits from the sale. With proper planning, you can accurately estimate the proceeds of the sale to find out for sure. This section takes you through the expenses you're responsible for as a seller.

Agent's commission

Unless you have time and energy to burn, chances are you'll hire an agent to help with the sale of your home. Your agent receives a commission when you sell — usually a percentage of the sale price — as does your buyer's agent. And guess what, you're responsible for both! A typical total commission expense may be between 2.5 and 6 percent of the selling price, but rates are negotiable. Some agents will charge you a flat fee for listing your home: these tend to be discount agents, so you may find that you will have to handle some responsibilities yourself, such as showing the home. Many flat-fee agents will not pay for local advertising, or hold open houses. If you decide to sell privately, you'll probably still deal with buyers who are using an agent, so you may get stuck with some commission fees no matter what.

Legal fees

The sale of a home requires complex legal documentation. You may need a lawyer to draw up or check over all paperwork and documents. Depending on the amount of work to be done, your legal fees will vary. Talk to several lawyers to get an idea of how much your case may cost, but budget at least $600 to $1,200, including *conveyance* (the transfer of the title to the property), and more if you need documents to be drafted by your lawyer.

Repairs or renovations

Most homes will *not* require major renovations to ensure a sale. If you've kept your home in good shape or if your home is relatively new, you may need to do only minor repairs. First impressions go a long way — no matter how new your home is, pay attention to cosmetic details (chipped paint, leaky faucets, loose doorknobs, and so on). The better your home looks, the quicker it will sell. In preparation to sell, you should always consult with your agent about the best way to present your home and what details need to be attended to.

Your buyer will have a home inspection (for plumbing and structural problems, and so on) to find out what improvements (if any!) are necessary. Whatever repairs are needed may be deducted from the selling price, likely with a margin of error that will benefit your buyer. In some circumstances you may wish to have your home inspected, like if you suspect there is a serious problem, or if you live in an area where properties, often condos, are commonly listed as having a "positive inspection" available to potential buyers. Other sellers use their inspections as a marketing tool to demonstrate how "good" their homes are and thereby to get top dollar for them. If you're selling a condominium and the building has a *positive engineering report,* you have an excellent selling point — use it. A glowing inspection report from a reputable agency provides an incentive to potential buyers. However, if the inspection reveals any serious liabilities, you're legally obligated to disclose that information to potential buyers.

No right answer to whether or not you should absorb the cost of the building inspection exists. You may be wasting your money, because the buyers will probably have their own inspection done anyway. On the other hand, you may see some benefits at the negotiating table. Talk to your agent (if you have one), and take a look at Chapter 19 for more information about inspections for sellers. If you choose to have your home inspected, remember to include the inspection fees when totalling the cost of repairs and renovations.

Discharge of your mortgage

If you don't have a mortgage, give yourself a pat on the back and skip ahead to the next point; otherwise, read on! Most lenders have a few options available for handling your mortgage when you sell, depending on the specifics of your current mortgage agreement. You may be allowed to take your mortgage with you to your new home, you may be able to let the buyer assume it, or you may be able to pay it off early. (We cover all the options in Chapter 16.)

Lenders often charge legal and/or penalty fees when you discharge your mortgage when you sell. Remember, these fees can go into the thousands of dollars. Check your mortgage agreement to see what is permitted, and talk to your lender to find out what fees you may incur. Fees are sometimes negotiable. If you have been a loyal client of your lender for many years, you may be able to "talk down" a prepayment penalty, but don't hold your breath. Many lenders have a policy against renegotiating. Whatever arrangements you make with your lender, be sure to get a copy in writing.

Property taxes and prepaid utilities

The day you usually pay your property taxes is not likely to coincide with the day you sell your home (if Fate loves you that much, skip ahead to the next point). In the sale contract, there will be an *adjustment date* (the day the buyer assumes all responsibility for paying property taxes, and so on). Usually the adjustment date is the same day as the *possession date,* or the day you hand the buyer the keys. In effect, your buyer may owe you a refund on a portion of your annual property tax (or you may owe the buyer some money if you don't prepay your property taxes). Likewise, any prepaid utilities, condo fees, or assessments need to be reviewed. Your lawyer can work out exactly how much is owed to whom and adjust the taxes as part of the conveyance or statement of adjustment. (The *statement of adjustment* shows the net result for the vendor [seller] or purchaser of the home, taking into account the purchase price, deposit, real estate commissions, legal fees, property purchase tax, property taxes, and all other adjustments.)

Moving costs

Obviously, how much it costs to move depends on how much stuff you're moving, how far you're moving it, and what moving company you hire. Other factors may enter into the tally, including the time of year and any "special care" items you may be moving (such as your baby grand piano). Do your research. Find out exactly how much stuff you've accumulated over the years and how much getting it to your new home is really going to cost. An extra few hours assessing the contents of your basement and garage, plus a phone call or four, are a lot less hassle than under-budgeting your moving costs by several thousand dollars, or finding out too late that your one-bedroom home has three bedrooms' worth of memorabilia (two-thirds of which will not fit into the moving truck).

Survey fees or title insurance premiums

Some banks require a survey in order to approve a mortgage on a house. (No surveys are required for condos; most condo buildings have a building or strata plan that shares the total floor area of the unit in lieu of a survey.) Usually, this cost is absorbed by the buyer (as you probably already know), but sometimes sellers have an existing survey certificate from when they purchased the house. If no alterations or additions have been made to the property, the seller's survey may still be acceptable to the bank. The fee for having a survey done depends on the size and particularities of the property (but be warned, it can cost up to $1,000). In lieu of a survey, some lenders will accept title insurance, which basically insures the title of the property against any disagreement about property lines, or even against fraud. The cost of this insurance usually depends on the size and/or value of the property. Your mortgage broker or lender can provide details.

Appraisal fees

You need to know the value of your home before you set the selling price. If you're not using an agent, you may want to hire a professional appraiser for an expert opinion of how much your home is worth. (Your buyers will probably still have a second appraisal done — their mortgage lender may require it, or they may simply want to be certain they're getting a good deal.) If you're using a reputable and experienced agent, you may not bother with a pre-listing appraisal. (For more information on appraisals, see Chapter 19.)

Don't confuse an inspection with an appraisal. An inspection reveals any major structural or systems-related problems with your home that will need to be fixed before you sell; an appraisal investigates what the market value of your home is. The appraiser may take into account any of the same problems that the inspector looks for, but is really only interested in the dollar value on the bottom line.

Location-specific expenses

Some geographic regions come with their own unique set of housing issues. As a seller, you may be responsible for extra costs associated with your particular region.

Believe it or not, Canada has termite hot spots. If you know you live in a hot spot, you may want to have a termite inspection performed. Insects and other pest problems may be part of a standard home inspection. If you live in a region notorious for pest infestations, you may have to pay for a separate inspection. In some cases, getting a termite warranty is possible. If you have one, and keep it active, it may cover the cost of the inspection.

If you're a rural dweller, you may want to have the well water tested or a modern filtration system installed. If you're a resident of Nova Scotia, you may want to have the results of a recent ground test for radon handy for showings. Maybe you live on a fault line, or maybe you live on a flood plain. Wherever you live, be aware of the extra expenses you'll incur because of your location (and see Chapter 23 for more on regional concerns).

GST/HST

Regardless of whether the sale of your home is GST or HST exempt (see "Some Good News about Taxes" later in this chapter), one of these taxes applies to most services you'll use in selling your home, depending on the province or territory you live in. So expect that real estate agents, lawyers, appraisers, building inspectors, surveyors, and anyone else you hire to help sell your home will charge GST or HST on top of their service fees.

Selling your home is an expensive endeavour. Unfortunately, money isn't the only currency associated with selling. You're also going to spend time — lots of it. We can't supply you with the numbers in discussing all the expenses you'll encounter when selling your home; you need to figure them out for yourself. This is because each situation is different and each requires investigation, which will eat up many hours. The old saying that "time is money" certainly applies when it comes to selling your home. Many aspects of home selling can't be done on your own, and there are many other tasks that you must take on yourself. Anything you pass off to someone else will cost you money; anything you don't will cost you time.

Tallying it up

When you have an idea how much selling your home will cost, you can estimate how much money you will make (we assume the best) on the sale of your home.

If you have investigated the anticipated market value of your home and each of the costs we outline earlier in this chapter, then you've already done the hard part. Just fill in Table 15-1 to determine the net proceeds you'll realize from selling your home. Start with your home's estimated sale price and then subtract whichever associated costs apply. What you're left with are the net proceeds from the sale.

Table 15-1	Calculating the Net Proceeds from the Sale
Item	*Amount*
Estimated sale price	_____
– Agent's commission/and or flat fees	_____
– Legal fees	_____
– Repairs or renovations	_____
– Discharge of your mortgage	_____
– Property taxes and prepaid utilities +/–	_____
– Moving costs	_____
– Survey fees (if applicable)	_____
– Appraisal fees (if applicable)	_____
– Location-specific expenses (if applicable) (termite inspection, well water inspection)	_____
– GST/HST (if not already included)	_____
Net proceeds from sale =	_____

Some Good News about Taxes

The money you make on the sale of your home (remember, we're assuming the best) and the money you spend moving to your new home may be tax deductible (it's true!). Here's how it works.

Principal residence exemption

If you have lived in your home the entire time you have owned it, *all* proceeds of the sale are tax exempt — this is known as the *principal residence exemption*. If this is true for you, skip ahead to the next section. If, however, you bought a residential lot and waited a while to build on it, or if you rented your house out for a few years while you hunted truffles in the French countryside, or if for some other reason your home was not your principal residence for a period of time while you owned it, read on.

If the final sale price is less than what you paid originally for your home, that money is non-taxable. Isn't that generous? You, too, get to skip ahead to the next section. However, if the sale price is greater than what you paid for your home in the first place, a portion of that money may be taxable. You'll probably want to talk to your accountant about the particulars of your situation, but the approach outlined here gives you a good idea of how much of the proceeds you'll be taxed on.

Consider the case of the Rosen family. In 1994, Chris and Pat Rosen bought a beautiful lot just outside the growing city of Barrie, Ontario. They already had one daughter, but were hoping to have more children after they settled in their new house. They spent three years renting while they built their dream home, which was finally completed in 1997. The Rosens lived happily in their new home, and as the city quickly expanded, so did their family. They had twins. They decided to sell and move to a more rural community in 2004, where Chris could work from a home office, Pat could have a huge garden, and the children would have more property to play on. Owing to the large influx of new residents in their area, housing prices had skyrocketed. They managed to sell their home for $450,000, more than double the $200,000 they had initially paid for its construction between 1994 and 1997. Chris and Pat figured out their taxable gain on the sale when they filed their tax returns for 2005 using the *principal residence exemption formula*:

> 7 years as principal residence (1997 to 2004) + 1 year (current taxation year) = 8 years
>
> 8 years ÷ 10 years that they owned the property (1994 to 2004) = 0.8
>
> 0.8 × proceeds of sale (calculated as the net proceeds from the sale of their home minus the amount they originally paid for it). Therefore, 0.8 × ($450,000 − $200,000) = $200,000

Therefore, $200,000 isn't taxable!

So, if $200,000 of the proceeds of the sale isn't taxable, Chris and Pat owe tax on just $50,000 ($450,000 − $200,000) − $200,000, which is the difference between the proceeds of the sale and the non-taxable portion of the sale as calculated using the principal resident exemption formula.

If you've owned your principal residence since before 1982, you need to use a slightly more complex formula than the principal resident exemption formula — due to a change in the taxation policy in 1981. The procedure for long-time homeowners is the same, only you have to calculate the exempt portion twice, under the hypothetical assumption that you sold your home on December 31, 1981, at its FMV for that year, and reacquired it on January 1, 1982.

Moving tax credits

If you're an employee relocating for a new job (or being transferred), if you're self-employed and relocating for professional reasons, or if you're moving to become a full-time post-secondary student, your moving and selling expenses are tax deductible! These expenses include all the selling costs listed in Table 15-1, except repairs or renovations, and your personal travel costs, including food and lodging. They also include the cost of shipping and storing your belongings, and up to 15 days of temporary room and board near either your current home or your new home. Even legal fees and transfer taxes (affectionately known as "the welcome tax") incurred on the purchase of your new home count as moving expenses. The only catch is that your new home has to be at least 40 kilometres closer to your new school or place of business (so if you're moving from one part of the city to another, it probably doesn't count).

As with any tax breaks, some eligibility restrictions exist — contact the Canada Revenue Agency for details and claims forms. (Visit the Web site at www.cra-arc.gc.ca, and use the search terms "moving" and "principal residence.") Or ask your accountant or financial adviser for assistance.

Chapter 16

Balancing Selling and Buying

. . . .

In This Chapter

▶ Investigating financing options for mortgage holders

▶ Exploring the options involved in trading up

▶ Choosing to trade down

▶ Getting a reverse mortgage

▶ Timing your buying and selling properly

▶ Deciding not to sell

. . . .

So you've weighed the pros and cons, and after careful deliberation, it looks as if both you and your finances can handle the stress of selling your current home. Now it's time to sit back and let the buyers come rushing in, right? Not so fast. You've got a few more details to work out — like where your next home will be and how you're going to pay for it.

Remember all the work and hassle that went into buying your current home? Well, here's the bad news: You have to go through the hassle of selling *and* buying now. The good news is this: Buying is easier the second (or third, or fourth) time around. If this is your second sell, you've already become acquainted with the fine points of coordinating the sale of your house with the purchase of another — probably the hard way. For you lucky first-time sellers, this chapter helps you figure out how to balance selling with buying *before* you get into trouble.

What to Do with Your Current Mortgage

What happens to your current mortgage if you decide to sell your home? You have three choices:

✔ Pay off your mortgage.

✔ Let your buyer take over your mortgage along with your home.

✔ Take your mortgage with you to your new home.

When your parents were buying their first house, they probably had to beg and pray for a mortgage. Times have changed. Today's mortgage market is buyer-driven. Instead of crawling into the bank on your hands and knees to plead for your mortgage, you can stand tall and ask potential lenders, "What can *you* do for *me*?" Here are a couple of items a lender may offer you:

✔ A discount off the current posted interest rate if you're looking for a new *first* mortgage on a property. (The number of mortgages you've had in the past on other properties doesn't matter — only the home you're looking to buy now is in question here.)

✔ A legal package that allows you to use the lender's lawyers, at a discount, for the *conveyance* of the title and preparation of the mortgage documents. The conveyance of title is the transfer of ownership, the registration of the new owners, and the registration of the mortgage at the appropriate land titles office. (See Chapter 21 for more information on conveyancing.)

✔ A free appraisal. This can save you several hundred dollars if your lender absorbs this cost.

As we mention in Chapter 3, the financing world is much more competitive than it was just a few years ago. Speaking to a mortgage broker can help you get the best interest rate and terms possible, with the least amount of effort.

Paying off your mortgage early

If you've owned your home for a long time, you may have built up substantial *equity*. Equity is the difference between the value of your property and the outstanding debts against it — for example, if your home is worth $250,000 and you have paid off all but $12,000 of your mortgage, you have accumulated $238,000 worth of equity in your home. If you have only a small portion of your mortgage to pay off, you may want to consider *discharging* it (paying it off early).

Most lenders offer financing plans to help you discharge your mortgage faster while avoiding high penalty fees. A financing plan may allow you to do one of the following to help discharge your mortgage more quickly:

✔ Increase the amount of your mortgage payments.

✔ Make mortgage payments more often.

✔ Exercise *prepayment* options. (You can pay a certain amount of the principal each month or each year in addition to your regular payments, or a percentage of the principal can be paid down each time you renew your mortgage terms.)

Using any of the above options decreases the length of time required to pay off your mortgage. (We discuss mortgages in detail in Chapter 3.)

If you're a long-range planner and you're considering selling your home in the next five years, talk to your lender to see about renegotiating your terms. You may be able to modify your payment schedule or negotiate a mortgage renewal that permits you to discharge your mortgage as soon as possible, without paying a *penalty fee* (you pay this fee to your lender as compensation for paying off your mortgage early).

If you want to pay off your mortgage with a single cheque, you'll likely pay a penalty fee. The amount of the penalty fee may vary greatly, depending on the original mortgage terms and interest rate that you negotiated. Make sure to read the fine print, and ask your mortgage broker or lender to explain the ramifications of paying off your mortgage early.

Some financial institutions may negotiate the mortgage penalty fees if your buyer also takes out a mortgage with them, or if you use the same lender for your next mortgage, but don't hold your breath. Whatever arrangement you make with your lender, get a copy *in writing*.

Letting your buyer take over your mortgage

If you're trying to sweeten the deal for a potential buyer, and your mortgage rate is lower than the current rate, consider taking advantage of the *assumability* option. Basically, you allow your buyer to assume your mortgage at its existing rate when purchasing your home. Assumability is often restricted to fixed rate mortgages. (Refer to Chapter 3 for a discussion of fixed rate and other types of mortgages.)

Assuming a seller's mortgage is rare, however. Generally, if circumstances make your mortgage look attractive to a buyer, it's probably a mortgage you want to hang on to, rather than having to approach a lender for a new mortgage at the higher current interest rate. The only scenarios that truly warrant considering the assumability option occur either when you've got a great mortgage and your highest priority is selling *fast* (and you can afford not to take that great mortgage with you) or if you're in a tough buyer's market and the incentive of a below-market mortgage rate will help you sell your home.

Here's how the assumability option works. Your buyer must meet your lender's credit requirements before your lender approves the mortgage transfer from you to your buyer. Fees (which can be hefty) for the legal work and paper shuffling may also be required. Fortunately, because most lenders now require your buyer to meet their credit and income standards, you no longer risk taking financial responsibility if your buyer fails to pay the mortgage in the future, as was the case in the past in some provinces.

If your buyer assumes your mortgage, you benefit in three ways:

✔ An assumable mortgage is a marketing tool; it may be just the enticement a buyer needs — the lure of a lower interest rate.

✔ Because your lender is already familiar with your home, the home appraisal requirement may be waived, saving the buyer a few hundred dollars, and by doing that your house may be more enticing to the buyer.

✔ If the buyer assumes your mortgage, you're no longer responsible for the discharge penalty fees, which saves you even more money.

When letting the buyer assume your mortgage, don't take it for granted that you'll be absolved of all responsibility if the new owner defaults on mortgage payments! Make absolutely sure to indemnify yourself — get it *in writing* — that you have no further financial obligations with regard to the mortgage after your buyer assumes it, and that you are *fully discharged* from the mortgage.

Taking your mortgage with you to your new home

Most mortgage agreements have a *portability* option that allows you to apply your current mortgage to a new home if you decide to sell. "Porting" your mortgage may be your best alternative if there's too much still owing on your mortgage for you to consider paying it off immediately, and if your existing mortgage rate is lower than the current rate.

Often, only fixed rate mortgages are portable. If your new home requires extra financing, you can usually borrow additional funds at the current rate — your new mortgage rate will be a blend of your mortgage's existing interest rate and the current interest rate. For example, if you have three years left on a five-year mortgage term, you may be able to borrow the extra money at the current three-year rate. (So the additional $20,000 you borrow to finance your new home will fit into your existing mortgage at the current three-year rate.) The additional mortgage you just took out to finance your new home has the same expiry date as your original mortgage. When the time comes to renew them, you renew them as one mortgage.

Should you keep the mortgage you already have?

If you're wondering about the benefits of porting your existing mortgage to a new home, you can check out the financial consequences online. Surf the Internet — find a Canadian online mortgage calculator (try `www.canadamortgage.com` or `www.canequity.com`), and pretend you're going to port your existing mortgage and borrow a bit more at the current rate. The calculator will determine your new blended interest rate, and tell you what your payments will be. You can simply multiply your monthly payments by the number of months in the mortgage term to get the total amount that you will pay if you port your mortgage.

Use the mortgage calculator a second time to figure out the total amount you would pay on a new mortgage at whatever the current interest rate happens to be. If the total amount payable for a new mortgage is less than you would pay by keeping your current mortgage with a new blended interest rate, then you stand to save if you pay off the current mortgage rather than porting it to your new home. Just be sure that the savings you will make with the new mortgage are greater than the penalty fee you'll be charged for paying off your current mortgage early.

Porting mortgages has become quite common due to the low interest rates of recent years, but choosing what's best for you always depends on your unique financial situation and how much risk you're willing to take. If you've taken to following the rise and fall of mortgage rates religiously in the past few years, you may feel confident in allowing your buyer to assume your current mortgage so that you can take out a new variable-rate or short-term open mortgage on your new home. (Refer to Chapter 3 for details on variable rates and open and closed mortgages.) If you can stand the headache of renegotiating your mortgage every six months, you'll probably end up saving money in the long run.

If you're not a risk-taker and can't be bothered to scour the financial section of the newspaper every morning for the latest trends in mortgage rates, the bit of extra money you may pay to port your fixed rate mortgage is worth it, just for the peace of mind.

Trading Up: Your Options

What's a trading-up situation? When your grand plans for the future involve investing in a home bigger and better than the tiny one-bedroom condo you currently own, you're in a trading-up position. Like any other home seller with a mortgage, you have three kinds of financing options (discharge it, let your buyer assume it, or port it). Which one is best for someone in your shoes? The most economical option depends on the current state of the mortgage market.

✔ **If the current interest rate is equal to or lower than the rate on your existing mortgage:** You may want to discharge your current mortgage and take out a new one with the same lender. Because lenders usually offer a discount on the current mortgage rate to keep your business, you're guaranteed to get a lower rate. But bear in mind the cost of prepayment penalties for discharging that we discuss earlier in this chapter.

When considering whether to discharge your mortgage, don't sacrifice important options for that extra one-half- to one-point discount on your mortgage rate. For example, if your current mortgage allows you to prepay as much as you want every six months, you may end up saving *more* by sticking with your current mortgage and paying it off faster — even though it has a higher interest rate.

The mortgage market is highly competitive these days, making discharging an existing mortgage favourable for many sellers. Lenders want your business, and they'll bend over backwards to get it. The rate that is posted and the rate you can negotiate are often very different — you may be able to get a rate one point or more below what is published. With all the tools available on the Internet, it isn't difficult to figure out if you'll save money — even if you're charged a penalty fee for paying off your mortgage early.

Trading-down dilemma: To buy or rent your next home?

Renting does allow greater flexibility than simply trading down. If you think that it won't be long after selling your home that you may need to move to a nursing home or some other residence where personal assistance and medical attention are close at hand, you may want to rent for that short time. If you're in perfect health, renting may allow you to spend your retirement years living a few months here and a few months there — experiencing life in all those little towns you always wanted to visit but didn't have the time to while you were working.

If you're no longer interested in, or capable of, dealing with the responsibilities of home ownership and you don't mind letting a landlord call some of the shots, renting may be a viable option. Keep in mind, however, that many of the freedoms afforded by renting are also available to condo owners. Condo upkeep is a shared responsibility, plus you have a smaller likelihood of break-ins if you decide to spend a few winter months somewhere sunny.

Renting involves three big pitfalls you should be aware of: You will be vulnerable to rent inflation, you will have to deal with a landlord (who may decide to sell your rental — which may leave you with nowhere to live), and each time you move there is a chance that your new landlord will not be compassionate and fair. If you have many independent years ahead of you and would prefer to settle in one place, buying may be the safest course.

✔ **If the current mortgage interest rate is higher than your existing rate:** You may want to port your mortgage and borrow a little extra at the higher rate — your new rate will then be a blend of the two rates. As a previous *mortgager* (someone who's taken out a mortgage), you may have some extra bargaining power. Your existing mortgage lender may cut you a deal on a new mortgage in light of your loyalty and good credit history. Or a new lender may sweeten the pot by offering you better terms to lure your business away from your existing lender.

If you're thinking about porting your mortgage, talk to your mortgage broker or lender about any fees or restrictions that may apply to your case. If you know you're going to be taking out a new mortgage, shop around for the best deal and get pre-approval. Most major lenders now offer online pre-approval services, as we discuss in Chapter 3.

✔ **In times of drastic changes — if interest rates skyrocket or house prices drop catastrophically:** You may want to let your buyer assume your mortgage to make your house as attractive as possible. However, in most cases, letting a buyer assume your mortgage is probably not going to be in your best interest. If you're trading up, you may not be on an extremely tight sale deadline. You can afford to wait for a buyer who is willing to pay a fair price, so there's no need to sell at a loss or give up a great mortgage rate. That flexibility makes the assumable option unfavourable. But if your back is to the wall and you need to move fast, you may be willing to give up a great mortgage rate to facilitate a quick sale. Even if you need to sell quickly, lowering the asking price can be more economical than giving up a great mortgage rate.

Trading Down: Your Options

The kids have all moved out, it's too quiet, and you have more space than you need. Besides, you can always use some extra money for those approaching retirement years. Turning Sally's bedroom into the other half of your home office may be nice — but maybe now is the time to trade in your home for something smaller and less expensive.

Consult Chapter 15 to find out how to determine the net proceeds of your home's sale. Decide how much you want to spend on your next home. If you can afford it after paying the costs of selling your home, go ahead and sell. Depending on your plans for retirement (and your health), you may want to rent instead of buying your next home. If (now that you've *really* thought about it) you can't imagine living anywhere else, or you're not sure you'll be able to find something suitable in your price range, you may consider taking out a *reverse mortgage* (we explain reverse mortgages in the next section).

A home that is your principal residence is a tax-free investment. By using the money you made on the sale of your previous home to purchase another one, you're putting your money into an investment that will (hopefully!) grow tax-free. If you decide to rent from the time of your home sale onward, any interest subsequently made on the money you received from the sale of your previous home will likely be taxable (assuming the money is invested outside of an RRSP) — and can potentially bring you into a higher tax bracket! Real estate appreciation is tax-free growth, but it is generally *slow and steady* growth, in contrast to mutual funds or stocks that generate taxable income but can increase or decrease dramatically depending on the stock market.

Reversing Your Mortgage

If you need extra income to help maintain your current standard of living after you retire, or if you need extra income for personal care expenses, you may want a *reverse mortgage*. A reverse mortgage is an agreement between you and a lender that allows you to "tap into" the equity built up in your home. You can do this in a few different ways: Your lender may give you a lump-sum payment, send you monthly payments, offer a line of credit, or offer some combination of these options.

Some standard restrictions on who can enter into a reverse mortgage agreement exist — usually, you must be at least 60 years old and have no outstanding debts against your home. However, you don't need to meet credit or income requirements to be eligible for a reverse mortgage. In Canada, reverse mortgages are offered through the *Canadian Home Income Plan*. (See the Appendix for contact information, or consult the Web site at www.chip.ca.)

The amount of money that you can access ranges from 10 to 48 percent of the value of your home. The total funds you can access is determined by

- The value of your home
- Your age
- Current interest rates
- The type of reverse mortgage you choose

Unlike a conventional mortgage, a reverse mortgage doesn't have to be repaid right away — repayment starts when your home ceases to be your principal residence (a home is no longer considered a principal residence if the borrower moves elsewhere, dies, or sells the home). When you do begin to repay the mortgage, you are responsible for the borrowed principal plus interest and any other legal or administrative fees associated with the agreement.

The amount that you must repay for a reverse mortgage *cannot* exceed the value of your home, and you *cannot* be forced to sell your home to repay the mortgage if you still reside there. When lenders determine the amount a borrower can receive, they're betting that the home won't depreciate significantly and that the borrower won't reside there so long that the payout exceeds the value of the home.

Repayment can be made by you, your family, or your estate, and need not involve the sale of your home. If you do decide to sell your home, whatever profit you make over the market value of your home is yours (or your family's, or estate's) to keep. If the sale generates less than the value of the reverse mortgage on your home, usually a third party, such as an insurance provider, is responsible for making up the difference.

Although not many homeowners have taken out reverse mortgages, the popularity of this option is growing. If you feel passing down your home to children or grandchildren is important, you may not want to experiment with a reverse mortgage.

Many seniors consider a reverse mortgage because they cannot pay all the bills required to maintain their home. Seniors should investigate whether or not they can *defer* their property taxes, which would mean one less hefty bill to pay each year, and may allow them to postpone or eliminate the need for a reverse mortgage. If property taxes are deferred, they are generally repaid when the homeowner moves out of the property or when the home is sold.

Interest rates for reverse mortgages are generally as much as 1.5 to 2 percent higher than a typical mortgage rate. You may decide that getting a line of credit that's secured by your home is a better option, though you'll have to prove that you have a monthly income (shown on your income tax return, which can include pensions and investment income), and then make monthly interest payments on any money you borrow. Before settling on a reverse mortgage, make sure you discuss your options in detail with your financial adviser and your lawyer.

To Sell Before 1 Buy, or Buy Before 1 Sell?

Deciding whether to buy first and then sell, or to sell first and then buy, can be challenging. Carrying the costs of two homes, or having to move out without having a place to go to, may cause panic. Do not despair — you are not the first to face these scenarios, and options exist.

242 Part IV: Deciding to Sell

Selling before you buy

Selling your current home before you buy your next one certainly does eliminate some of the financial uncertainty. At least you know you have enough money to buy another home. If dear Auntie Edna would love to take you and your six children in for five months while you search for a new home, then don't worry about selling first (and consider yourself lucky for having such generous relatives). But, if you don't have anywhere to stay in the time between selling and buying, you may be in dire straits both emotionally and financially.

If you're trading up, you may be counting on all the money you made on the sale of your home to go toward the purchase of a new one. Renting a space large enough for an entire family can cost thousands of dollars per month, and renting for several months will put a significant dent in your buying power. And then there's the stress that goes along with residing in limbo for extended periods of time. If you're trading down, the proceeds of the sale may be enough to cover the cost of renting for a few months. You need to work out the financial implications *beforehand*.

Whether you decide to sell before you buy or buy before you sell, do not underestimate how long finding a new home will take. A longer closing period (the timeline between the firming up of your purchase or sale contract and the completion date) may make the process easier for you.

Buying before you sell and bridge (interim) financing

So you've found the most amazing new home — it's only 20 minutes south of your new job; it's surrounded by parkland to the west; there's a gym, a huge grocery store, and a local fruit and vegetable market to the north; and the best theatre, restaurants, and shopping in town are to the east. The home is even in your price range. You know that if you wait to make an offer, someone else will snatch your dream home up, but you haven't sold your current home yet, you still owe $125,000 on it, and you don't have a spare $50,000 to make the down payment. What can you do?

Rest assured, you're not the first home seller who has been caught in the middle of buying and selling. Mortgage lenders have developed a plan for precisely this situation — it's called *bridge financing*, or *interim financing*. With bridge financing, your lender lets you borrow the money you need to bridge the gap between buying a new home and selling your old one. This type of financing usually involves a personal fixed rate loan, often one lump sum that can be repaid at maturity or prepaid at any time without penalty. Bridge financing doesn't have standard maximum or minimum amounts; your lender will decide how much they are willing to give you based on how much they think you'll be able to repay. Because you have already worked out the proceeds of sale and your cash flow for before and after the move, you can make an educated guess about how much your lender will be willing to give you.

Buying first and then selling has a downside if you require bridge financing. (If owning two homes simultaneously won't put a crimp in your style, buy to your heart's content!) The downside to bridge financing is that you're paying interest on a relatively large sum of money for however long selling your current home and repaying the loan takes. With stricter lending requirements in recent years, you'll want to make sure that all your financial ducks are in a row and that you have everything in place with your lender before you tackle interim financing. No one wants to be caught owning two properties and then have their financing fall apart. Remember our earlier warning: Don't underestimate how long selling your home may take. If market conditions are favourable for sellers in your area, your home may sell in a week. If conditions aren't so favourable, selling can take many months (or even a few years, if the government just tore down the school across the street to build a biohazardous materials–testing facility). What if your home's value takes a nosedive? What if you simply can't sell your home at all? Murphy's Law will govern the sale of your home to some degree. Bridge financing usually generates some small hassles only, but the worst case scenario can leave you in the bottomless pit of debt. Buying first in a slow market is extremely dangerous. Talk to a local real estate agent about the current market conditions in your area as they relate to your home specifically.

Timing it right: The ideal selling and buying scenario

If you must be stuck in either position, selling first is the less risky of the two. Unless you're moving just because you see a home you like better, you have (hopefully) put considerable thought into where and when you will move. Assuming that you've done your homework, you'll know what to expect when shopping for a home in your new area. Even if it takes a little longer than expected to find the perfect home, you know exactly how much you can afford and have the security of knowing that you're in a financial position to buy.

The ideal situation is that you sell your current home and buy a new one *at the same time*. This entails stipulating in your offer on a new home that the offer is conditional on the sale of your previous home. Usually this "subject to sale" clause specifies a time limit — like 30 days — for the condition to be met. (The "subject to sale" clause is discussed in detail in Chapter 14.) Adding this clause isn't an uncommon practice, but it may make some sellers reluctant to accept your offer.

If it's a seller's market in your neck of the woods and a buyer's market in your new area, you may have enough leeway to make such stipulations. But if you're moving into a seller's market, you may not have this option. Would you accept a conditional offer on your home if you thought you could get an unconditional offer easily? If you're moving into a seller's market, you may be competing with others making offers on the same home. Making a conditional offer may be just enough to tip the balance in someone else's favour. On the other hand, if you think the seller may be receptive to a conditional offer, it's a great way to buy first without taking a huge financial risk.

Changed Your Mind about Selling?

Selling your home is scary business. After researching your new area, maybe you've realized that you've been taking your current location for granted — it's really not so bad; perhaps staying put and making some renovations is the best plan. (If you have already listed your house and then change your mind, you can always cancel the listing.) If you've come to this conclusion, you have some financing options to help foot the bill.

Home equity loans and homeowner lines of credit

Most major lenders offer home equity loans (also known as second mortgages and home equity lines of credit) for homeowners. These options allow you to access whatever equity you have built up in your home. If you have paid off your mortgage in full, you may be able to borrow up to 80 percent of the value of your home to put toward renovations. Home equity loans (exactly like mortgages) are often fixed rate loans with long repayment periods. Lines of credit for homeowners usually have variable interest rates and are available as long as you like after only one application.

If you're undertaking large renovations all at one time, a home equity loan may be the best option. If you know exactly how much the renovation will cost and are planning to pay for it all up front, a home equity loan gives you the security of knowing precisely how much your regular payments will be. If you intend to make smaller renovations over many years, or if you're unsure how much renovations will cost, a line of credit may be better suited to your needs. After all, you have to pay interest only when, and if, you use the line of credit.

Many financial institutions allow you to combine home equity loans and lines of credit (for example, you may start off with a line of credit, borrowing only small amounts over a longer period, and then decide to borrow a large chunk of money for a bigger renovation project at a later date — as a home equity loan). Most financial institutions will allow you to structure your payments to suit your financial situation. Home equity plans are a great advantage to those of you who decide that renovating makes more sense than selling — they allow you to borrow large amounts of money at lower interest rates than those of regular personal loans or lines of credit.

Refinancing your mortgage

Another option to pay for renovations is mortgage refinancing. If it's time to renew your mortgage and interest rates are relatively low, refinancing may be the preferred option. Some lenders will allow you to borrow up to 90 percent of the value of your home, less whatever you still owe on your current mortgage. (Refer to Chapter 14 for more details.) To figure out the most economical route, talk to your lender about the products they offer for home renovators.

Part V
Preparing Yourself and Your House to Sell

The 5th Wave   By Rich Tennant

The salesman convinced us that a security system would really increase our home's resale value.

In this part . . .

This part contains the most "for sale by owner" information, since it not only outlines the steps in putting your home on the market, but also contains lots of useful information for everyone. From choosing an agent (if you want one) and a lawyer, to getting an appraisal or inspection, as well as all the contracts, statements, and steps in between, this section gets you from the decision to sell to the point where you're ready to talk to potential buyers.

Chapter 17

Selecting Your Selling Team

In This Chapter

▶ Finding an agent

▶ Deciding to sell your house yourself

▶ Hiring a lawyer

*U*nless you've got a hidden stash of Van Gogh paintings, your home is probably the most expensive thing you'll ever have to sell. And because of the enormity of the task at hand, most sellers seek professional help from a real estate agent. You, however, may be a take-charge kind of person with some time on your hands who's considering selling your home privately. In this chapter, we tell you what to expect when you sell your home with an agent or on your own.

Whether or not you're using an agent, you'll need a real estate lawyer. An experienced lawyer who specializes in real estate will ensure everything goes smoothly. Your lawyer will be so handy, you may even regret telling all those lawyer jokes.

Identifying the Right Real Estate Agent

Most people approach the task of selling their homes as a team sport. Make things easy for yourself by picking the best players to back you up. The most important positions on your selling team are your real estate agent and your real estate lawyer. Choose both individuals with care. In this section, we take you through the ins and outs of finding the best agent. We do the same for lawyers a little later on. Another potential member of your selling team is your real estate agent's broker. Refer to Chapter 6 for more on the relationships among you, your agent, and your agent's broker.

If you aren't sure who you want to use as a real estate agent, make sure you ask everyone you know and trust who they have used as an agent recently. A recommendation from someone you trust is a great starting point, but you'll still want to get more names and referrals before choosing an agent. Ask family members, co-workers, and neighbours if they have the name of an agent they used. And more important, were they happy with the agent's service and professionalism? (Remember, you want to pick someone local.)

Real estate agents, also known as *salespeople, representatives,* or *registrants* in some provinces, can use the term *Realtor,* provided they are registered members of their local real estate boards or associations. The word "Realtor" is actually a registered trademark of the Canadian Real Estate Association (CREA), and only members in good standing with CREA can use the term "Realtor." This means they are licensed professionals and are legally bound to protect and promote your interests as they would their own.

Picking the perfect real estate agent for you is partially luck and partially knowing what to look for. We recommend you interview several candidates before you make a decision.

What to look for in your agent

The best real estate agents score high on the list of qualities below. Keep these in mind when you're asking more targeted questions during your interview (we give you a list for that as well, later on in the chapter). Your agent should

- ✔ **Be a full-time professional:** When you sell your property, you hand over a sizeable amount of money to your real estate agent — probably anywhere between 2.5 and 6 percent of the price, and up to 10 percent on small recreational properties. A good agent earns a commission by giving you good advice, promoting and marketing your property, skillfully closing the deal, and taking care of the details. To do the job right, you need a full-time professional. A big part of selling a house is being in contact with many buyers and understanding what they respond to. Don't settle for anything less than a dedicated, full-time real estate agent.

- ✔ **Charge a reasonable commission rate:** Find out what commission the agent charges on a sale. Is the agent's commission rate in keeping with the range you have been quoted by other agents? A range of commissions is charged across the country, and commissions are calculated differently in different areas and by different companies. In Toronto, a seller may pay a 4 to 6 percent commission. By comparison, in Vancouver, many companies charge a 7 percent commission on the first $100,000 of a sale and 2.5 percent on the balance. Some discount companies work for a flat fee commission ($5,000 or $10,000) or a flat percentage (as low as 1 or 2 percent). Although the market for most recreational properties is very active, more-remote properties have traditionally been more difficult to sell than conventional, more-accessible properties, so commissions may be as high as 10 percent of the sale price for that remote cabin in the woods with water or float plane access only.

The agent willing to accept the lowest commission likely isn't going to do the best job of selling your home. Occasionally a company that charges a lower commission requires homeowners to pay for all advertising (including buying a sign from the agent in some cases!), as well as doing all their own showings and even hosting the open houses. The agent may require you to be responsible for home measurements and a host of other issues, and a misrepresentation can leave you open to legal action from a disgruntled buyer. What you thought was going to save you money can cost you extra in out-of-pocket expenses, and you may not receive the regular feedback, contact, and advice that you'd get from a full-service agent. Sometimes a company quotes a low commission to secure a listing, and after the house has been on the market for a month or so, recommends that you pay a higher commission for more services. Suddenly the commission looks pretty much like all the other quotes you found. Also make sure that the commission quoted allows for a commission to be paid to a buyer's agent. Make sure the total commission quoted is all you will be paying . . . you don't want any surprises.

✔ **Inform you how she handles holdover clauses as they apply to commission:** In some rare cases, you may still owe your agent the commission even if your home doesn't sell while you have it listed with her agency. Your agent can use a *holdover clause* to claim a commission even if your home's sale happens after the listing expires. An average holdover period may last 60 to 90 days from the expiration of the contract. Occasionally, a buyer who made an unacceptable offer on your house while it was listed may approach you again after the listing has expired, this time with an acceptable offer. Depending on the timing of the offer and the wording of the listing contract, you may still have to pay your agent the commission. Check the fine print of the listing contract to see if it includes a holdover period, and ask your agent if her company has ever enforced the holdover period.

If a real estate agent doesn't negotiate a fair and equitable commission for himself, will he negotiate a good price for your house when dealing with buyers? If you're looking for a good deal overall, the commission may not be the best place to cut corners. Like everything in life, you get what you pay for — make sure you compare the value of the services offered versus the commission rate charged by the agency, and make sure you're getting a satisfactory level of service in relation to the commission structure being charged.

✔ **Quote a reasonable listing price for your home:** Beware the agent who quotes the highest listing price. Is she trying to "buy" your listing? Telling you what you want to hear instead of suggesting a realistic listing price can cost you in the long run. When you interview real estate agents, ask them what listing price they think they'd assign to your house, and ask how they determined this price. You can do this as a casual conversation at the first meeting with an agent, or you can ask her to prepare a complete Comparative Market Analysis (CMA) and discuss pricing in more detail after she has viewed the property and returned with the complete CMA. You'll quickly sense how knowledgeable the agent is about houses in your neighbourhood, as well as the real estate market in your price range. Take a look at Chapter 15 for more about CMAs and to find out how you can get a pretty good idea of what's reasonable . . . and why pricing your home too high initially is a big mistake.

✔ **Have a good track record:** Ask the agent how many years he's been working as a real estate agent. Ask for references — get the names and numbers of at least three people whose homes he's sold in the past year or two. Call the references the agent provides. If the people you speak to have mixed feelings about the way the sale was handled, find out what went wrong and how, looking back, they would have prevented it. Hindsight is always 20/20. (However, if their biggest complaint is that the agent acted ethically and wouldn't lie about the crack in their home's foundation — well, you may want to rethink whom you turn to for advice!)

✔ **Be local:** If you're selling a starter home in the suburbs, the best real estate agent in the neighbouring city isn't the right choice for you. You want an agent who works full-time in your area. Your agent's networking and connections are, in fact, very valuable marketing tools available to you. The more local agents (and therefore buyers) your agent works with, the larger the pool of potential buyers for your home.

Working with your local real estate star, you'll see that the agent knows your neighbourhood inside and out. A well-versed local agent knows what homebuyers are after, and how to showcase your neighbourhood and community. Chances are, the agent has a good idea how to sell your house from the moment she pulls up to the curb.

✔ **Sell houses like yours:** The agent who sold the largest number of local monster homes last month isn't the best candidate to sell your starter home. Hire an agent who lists and *sells* lots of other starter homes — someone who's constantly working with people in the market for a home like yours, and who understands which buyers will be interested and what features those buyers are looking for in a home like yours.

✔ **Make selling your home a priority:** Be alert to signs that the real estate agent won't have time to personally work on marketing your house. Some top-selling agents just have too many listings to take care of your property personally. Their assistants take care of the legwork, attend open houses, and schedule showings. You don't want to find out partway through the process that the agent you so carefully selected has delegated your listing to an assistant.

A busy agent is busy for a reason, however. If your real estate agent has many listings, that means many phone calls to show and sell all his listings. If your agent is in demand, he's probably a good one.

Similarly, you don't want to list your house with an agent whom you'll never see again until the listing is ready to expire and she swings by to renew the contract. If an agent is planning an extended vacation in the near future, don't use that agent! Sometimes selling your house takes longer than you think it will, even when the price is right. For all the work you're doing to keep your property looking its best, you don't want to let buyers slip through your fingers while your agent is cavorting with the locals in Bora-Bora.

✔ **Stay in touch:** Nothing is worse than feeling as if you don't matter or count, so you want to deal with an agent who responds to your calls or e-mails in a timely manner. (Within reason, of course. Don't expect your agent to answer your 11:30 p.m. phone call — he needs to sleep, too!) Better yet, find an agent that reports back often to you without you having to call them!

✔ **Be Web-proficient:** The Internet is a great tool and is constantly changing how the real estate market works both in Canada and internationally. An agent who has been inspired to be proficient on the Web is an agent who can adapt and innovate along with the times. Look for an agent who has an up-to-date Web site that is user-friendly.

✔ **Have specific ideas for marketing your home:** You can even request a written marketing plan from each of the real estate agents you interview. The marketing plan should include the listing price for your home, a list of comparable properties on the market, recommendations for making your home more marketable, plans to advertise and promote the property, and details on how the agent intends to manage agents opens, or open houses. Will there be a virtual tour and professional floor plans? What about pictures? Staging?

✔ **Be enthusiastic about the prospect of working with you to sell your home — from start to finish:** If your agent isn't excited about selling your home, how enthusiastic will she be when she's showing the house to potential buyers . . . and how thrilled will potential buyers be when she shows the house in a very lackadaisical and lazy manner?

Build a list of real estate agents to interview. After you decide to sell your house, you'll start to notice "For Sale" signs and "Sold" signs posted on people's lawns. Take a walk around the neighbourhood, and write down the names and phone numbers of the agents who have the most signs up. The more "Sold" signs, the better. Presto! You have a list of agents who are clearly active in your neighbourhood and skilled at closing deals. If you find some open houses, take the opportunity to meet the agents. Interview them. Talk to people you know who have bought and sold houses recently. Add to your list the names and numbers of local real estate agents who come with good recommendations.

"I pledge to you . . .": The agency relationship

Realtors work within a legal relationship called *agency.* The agency relationship exists between you, the principal, and your brokerage, the company under which the individual who is representing you is licensed. The essence of the agency relationship is that the brokerage has the authority to represent the principal in dealings with others. Here, the relationship is expressed by the British Columbia Real Estate Association (BCREA):

Brokerages and their Licensees are legally obligated to protect and promote the interest of their principals as they would their own.

Specifically, the Brokerage has the following duties:

✔ To show **undivided loyalty.** The Brokerage must protect the principal's negotiating position at all times, and disclose all known facts which may affect or influence the principal's decision.

✔ To **obey all lawful instructions** of the principal.

✔ An obligation to **keep the confidences** of the principal.

✔ The responsibility to **exercise reasonable care and skill** in performing all assigned duties.

✔ The duty to **account for all money and property** placed in a Brokerage's hands while acting for the principal.

You can expect competent service from your brokerage, knowing that the company is bound by ethics and the law to be honest and thorough in representing a property listed for sale or lease.

What to ask your agent

When you've got a healthy list of agents to interview, consider some of the following questions that will quickly narrow it down:

✔ Are you a full-time real estate agent?

✔ How long have you been in the business?

✔ What area do you work in primarily?

✔ Do you use the Internet as a sales tool? And how?

✔ Do you have a Web site?

✔ Do you access real estate portals such as www.realtor.ca?

✔ Do you take colour digital photographs of homes to post online?

✔ Do you typically sell houses in any specific price range?

✔ What asking price would you recommend for my house?

✔ How did you determine the asking price for my house?

✔ What specific ideas do you have for marketing my house?

✔ Would you be present at all showings of my house?

✔ Do you use lock boxes? If so, how do you log visits? (See Chapter 20 for more on lock boxes.)

✔ How many local homes in my price range did you sell last year?

✔ Can I get the names and numbers of three people whose homes you sold in the past two years?

✔ How will you keep me informed after my home goes on the market?

Choosing to Go It Alone

If you decide to sell your home without a real estate agent, your greatest asset is recognizing what you know and what you don't — what you can do yourself and what you should delegate.

Realize that selling a home privately is an extreme sport; if it was as easy as slapping a "For Sale" sign out front and calling it a day, everyone would be an agent! In between answering the phone, scheduling appointments, verifying potential buyers' identities, confirming their qualifications with financial institutions, and showing off your home, you need to maintain a perfectly groomed house and lawn. Chances are, you'll be trying to raise a family and hold down a job at the same time. Your lawyer is indispensable when it comes to arranging a title search, negotiating with buyers, and reviewing legal contracts. (More about your lawyer later in this chapter.) Fair warning: Selling your home yourself is a time-intensive undertaking.

Listless and lost

Beware of a breed of agent referred to as *listers* because of their "list 'em and leave 'em" attitude. These agents agree to an unreasonably high asking price, just to get your listing. If the market is really hot, then nothing else is done until another agent brings buyers to your door, at which point your *lister* shows up to collect his part of the commission. Most of the time, however, your house just languishes on the market, and your lister ultimately convinces you to lower your price . . . to where it should have been to sell your house in the first place. Dealing with an agent like this can be extremely frustrating, especially if you actually believed that you'd achieve that high list price and started mentally spending those extra dollars in your head. Having to readjust your expectations can be a bit depressing — especially if it means having to rethink your budget for the purchase of your next home . . . and that budget is going downward.

Getting connected

One dedicated downtown real estate agent we know tirelessly promotes her listings and her business to the 8,000 households in her *farm area*, that is, the downtown neighbourhoods she works in constantly. At peak periods, she may have dozens of "For Sale" signs up. Every time she gets a new listing, she advertises it in local papers and features the home in a flyer sent to every home in the area.

As a result of her high profile in the area, she finds a buyer for 45 percent of local homes she lists. She believes it's not the specific listing advertisement that sells the home, it's her contacts. Because so many people call her first when they want to sell or buy in the neighbourhood, she can quickly match sellers and buyers.

We're not suggesting that you track down this agent (or one like her — they're out there) and hire her at all costs. But keep in mind the agent's profile in the neighbourhood you want to buy into.

And the stakes are high. Selling your home is a business transaction and a legal transaction — involving your largest single investment. When it comes to marketing your home, negotiating with sellers, and dealing with contracts, you have to make a lot of decisions and do a lot of work that most people rely on their agents to do.

Recent changes have made it possible for "For Sale by Owner" properties to be listed on the Multiple Listing Service (MLS). The seller must retain an agent (at an agreed-upon flat fee) to "list" the property, but then the seller handles all responsibilities in regard to the sale — a sort of à la carte approach to agent services. This ability for private sellers to use agents' tools is still a grey area at the time of publication, however, and more changes may be to come.

We want you to be realistic and prepared to deal with all the complexities of making a private sale. In this section, we help you determine your limits so that you know which aspects of home selling you can handle, and how to find a lawyer or agent to take care of the home-selling processes that you can't.

Saving the commission

The big reason people like the idea of selling their homes privately is the money savings they anticipate. By selling privately, you don't pay a *commission* (the percentage of the sale amount that goes to the agent who made the sale). Commissions vary across Canada and from agent to agent, but they tally in the thousands. (For details on commissions, see Chapter 15.) We describe the ranges of commissions agents make across the country in "What to look for in your agent," earlier in this chapter — and don't forget the additional GST or HST payable on the total gross commission.

Selling your home yourself will probably cost less than a tenth of what you will pay if you hire a real estate agent to make the sale. However, if your buyer has an agent, then your savings won't be as great because the buyer's real estate agent will want a commission to assist in the sale.

If you want to sell your home yourself to save commission on the sale, you have to work hard. The closer you can match a real estate agent's professionalism, the more realistically you price your home for the current market, and the more you focus on getting the property sold, the more savings you make. Just remember that during private sales, often the seller and buyer both want to save the commission money, which may lead to some interesting negotiations.

Working out the costs of selling it yourself

We know you're visualizing what you can do with all that commission money you save by selling your home yourself. Well, take those dollar signs out of your eyes! Here are the expensive and troublesome realities you face if you plan to sell your home privately:

- ✔ **You may have to lower the asking price for your home.** If a buyer is considering two identical properties with the same asking price, one being sold by you, the owner, and the other by an agent, unless you can offer your buyer a better price, chances are he'll take advantage of the expertise and facilitation provided by a real estate agent.

- ✔ **You incur the cost and hassle of advertising that your home is for sale.** You'll have to actually sell your house before you can cash in on your saved commission. If you opt to engage a flat-rate Realtor to list your home on MLS, you are responsible for all measurements of the property and the home, and for all intents and purposes, will handle everything — including fielding phone calls, making appointments, taking pictures, and negotiating the sale of the property.

Some agents are offering *à la carte* services: for example, you might have the agent handle phone calls and booking appointments, but you handle all showings.

Also, you can choose from several "For Sale by Owner" sites on which you can post your home for a fee. The trick is to make sure you end up at the site with the most online traffic. You'll also have to try to keep track of what similar homes are selling for in your area — make sure you can keep track of selling prices on any Web sites you choose. You may also want to advertise in local and regional newspapers, but the cost for print advertisements quickly adds up.

✔ **You're responsible for researching and accurately determining the right price for your home.** Pricing your home is very important. (Refer to Chapter 15 regarding comparative market analysis and potential pit-falls when setting the price for your home.) If you hire an appraiser to assess the current market value of your home, expect to pay between $150 and $300 for this service. A real estate agent may offer you a *comparative market analysis* (CMA) free of charge to try to get you to list with them. A CMA states what your home is worth (its *fair market value,* or FMV) based on comparisons to similar homes currently for sale and recently sold in your area. (We compare appraisals and CMAs in Chapter 15.)

✔ **Selling your house on your own isn't going to fit neatly into a schedule.** You must be very accessible — by phone and online — if you're going to sell your home privately. Expect prospective buyers to knock at your door at all times of the day and night . . . regardless of how large the words "By Appointment Only" appear on the "For Sale" sign in front of your house. You'll have to accommodate the needs of prospective buyers' schedules in order to show the home, and if you have a family, you also face juggling their schedules. When you sell privately, you don't have the luxury of a real estate agent who organizes and administrates the showings of your home.

✔ **The legalities involved in selling a home are considerable.** You may not be aware of special legal considerations when selling your home, and you can risk being held liable by the buyer. An experienced agent is on the lookout for any possible legal issues — after all, her commission and her reputation are at stake if something goes wrong with the sale of your home. And if she by chance overlooks a legality, she has errors and omissions insurance to cover her — you don't! (Refer to Chapter 6 regarding an agent's roles and responsibilities.)

✔ **Emotions may cloud your judgment.** You need to be professional and objective during negotiations with your buyer. Your personal attachment to the property may prevent you from being an effective negotiator. If you don't have experience at a bargaining table, you're probably not the best person to haggle with a potential buyer's experienced and well-informed real estate agent.

✔ **Real estate agents will see your "private sale" advertisements in the newspaper, and they'll be calling you, too.** Like any ambitious business people, real estate agents look to expand their businesses, and they're in touch with the market. When your house appears available, agents will solicit you, hoping that you're tired of dealing with the headaches of trying to sell your home yourself and will hire them instead.

Setting aside your emotions as a homeowner to be an effective home seller

In Chapter 20 we talk about making your house look its best to sell more quickly. A big part of that process is putting away the most personal items in your house — your extensive china doll figurine collection, the pipe cleaner crafts your kids have been bringing home since kindergarten, and so on. The goal is to depersonalize the house so buyers can immediately imagine themselves living there.

In addition to depersonalizing your home, you'll also want to put away your emotional connections when preparing to sell. The house is no longer your home; it's a product you're selling. Try to stay detached and objective, even though you may feel the prospective buyer is insulting your personal tastes. You'll need to give yourself little reminders about emotionally disconnecting as you do research into the current market value of your home and when you're dealing with buyers face to face.

If you weren't selling your home, would you open your home up to a perfect stranger? Of course you wouldn't, so make sure you have some background information on your buyers before you let them into your property. Ask each prospective buyer for a home phone number and a work number, and then call the numbers to confirm that they belong to that buyer. Meet buyers in front of your home instead of opening the door to them directly. You don't want to be caught unaware if a buyer who was supposed to be a little old lady turns out to be two burly men with baseball bats! And, if at all possible (especially if you're female), try not to show your property alone or in the evening. At the very least, make sure a friend or family member knows when you're meeting a buyer, and then check in with that person afterwards to confirm you're okay. We don't give you this information to scare you: Any agent meeting a buyer who called directly from the number on a listing sign will take the same precautions — and you should too.

Not all buyers will like your house, and not all will have the nicest manners. Try to take negative comments in stride. At the very least, they reveal that the prospective buyers are imagining themselves living in the house. Don't get defensive. Because any purchase is a matter of balancing the pros and cons, just make sure you show prospective buyers all the selling features as well. If they hate the broadloom, point out that hardwood floors are underneath. If they complain the house is too far from town, let them know it's only a five-minute walk to the lakeshore, and anyway, a well-stocked convenience store is just a kilometre farther down the road.

Find out as much as you can about buyers so that you can demonstrate all the benefits your house has to offer them. Also, look at every potential buyer as part of your test market. If enough people comment that the house seems dark and gloomy, for example, replace 60-watt light bulbs with 100-watt ones. Your house will seem bigger, brighter, and more inviting to the next buyers who visit.

Remember, you don't have to like potential buyers, you just have to get along with them well enough to keep them interested in your house, allow as few factors as possible to turn them off, and negotiate a deal.

Although you'll want to set aside your emotional connection to the house when you're dealing with buyers, understanding your motivations to sell and the impact it has on your life are important tools in keeping the process moving forward. Develop a plan to get what you need out of the sale, and review it regularly to see if anything needs to be changed.

Do you need to get a certain amount of money out of the sale in order to retire comfortably? Does your market research support this selling price? Do you need to move quickly? Price is the biggest selling feature of a house. What is the lowest price you can live with to expedite the sale? Are enough people hearing about your house? Are there any good advertising venues you haven't tried?

Your goal is to sell your house and get on with your life. If you're determined to sell your home yourself, be honest about what you do know and what you don't know, and be realistic about what you can do and what you can't do. Do your research, and hire the necessary experts.

Getting some help

Selling a home is a lot of hard work, and that's why it's a full-time job for so many professional agents. If you're feeling a bit overwhelmed by your decision to do it yourself and think you may need help after all, you don't necessarily have to go for the total range of services offered by a real estate agent — and the fees that go with it. Some companies offer different packages, each with a different level of service, depending on how much help you want.

In Chapter 8, we discuss MLS, the Multiple Listing Service, which is a great tool for selling your home. At this point only licensed agents can list properties on this Web site, but changes have been made recently that may open up www.realtor.ca to "For Sale by Owner" homes in a kind of "pick and choose your service" system, as we mention earlier in this chapter. Some real estate companies offer an MLS package, and a licensed agent will list your home on the site for a discounted price. These companies can also help you with marketing tools like newspaper ads and lawn signs.

Don't forget about the Web sites made specifically for private sellers to list their properties. They may not have as many listings as MLS, but they'll help you get the word out. There are lots out there — just google "private real estate sale" or "sale by owner" and you'll get more info about advertising and other issues you may face. (Check out www.privatelist.com, where you can advertise online and get more information on selling privately.) See the Appendix for a handy list of some other great Web sites.

Maybe you're a natural promoter and you've found a buyer all on your own (go on, give yourself a pat on the back!). You feel like an immense weight has been lifted, and that the hardest part is now behind you. That is, until you wake up in a cold sweat, thinking about the tonne of paperwork you'll have to take care of (and you were never very enthusiastic about numbers or contracts or those other pesky things). Some local companies offer a paper-work-only option, and for a flat fee an agent will take care of the purchase agreement and be sure the transaction goes smoothly right up until closing day. Most of these companies (if available in your area) advertise in the local real estate papers. Don't forget that you'll still need a lawyer (or notary) to handle your sale, and you can have the lawyer review your paperwork if you have any questions.

Don't Let Your House Come Back to Haunt You . . . Hire a Good Real Estate Lawyer

In case you're wondering whether you need a real estate lawyer to help with the sale of your home, the answer is yes. Emphatically, *yes!* Law school takes *years* to get through for a reason — because laws are complex and sophisticated. No matter how smart you are, you need a professional. Period. Your lawyer performs a number of necessary tasks to cement your home's sale, tasks that you don't have the knowledge or resources to accomplish — unless maybe you're a lawyer yourself.

You risk losing hundreds of thousands of dollars if you try to put the sale through yourself and get it wrong. If you can spare hundreds of thousands of dollars and you really want to represent yourself, you can go ahead and gamble — it's legal. But for 99 percent of home sellers, selling their homes without a lawyer's involvement simply isn't worth the risk. Remember, even lawyers use this old adage: "The lawyer who represents himself has a fool for a client."

At the very least, you require a lawyer (or a notary public, especially in Quebec) to handle the change of ownership for your home, even if you're selling the home privately. Don't forget, a real estate lawyer has liability insurance as a safeguard in case any problems arise with transferring the title for your home.

Picking the right real estate lawyer

Recommendations from friends, family, and business associates give you the best place to start your search for a top-notch real estate lawyer. Often banks work with real estate lawyers, and your local bank manager may be able to give you the names of some of the lawyers they use.

Your provincial law society also has names of local real estate lawyers — get a list of names and telephone numbers so that you can make further inquiries. When you call the lawyers on your list, ask them to estimate how much work will be required for your particular circumstances, and what the approximate costs will be. Also see the Appendix for our suggestions on locating legal counsel across Canada.

Cost out lawyer's fees

When you call a lawyer to make an appointment, ask how much it will cost (as if you need to be reminded), what approximate amount you'll have to bring into the lawyer's office, and the preferred method of payment. Make sure that you specifically ask for the *"all in"* cost, which will include all your legal fees, any applicable taxes and adjustments for property taxes, and other pro-rated fees. Ideally, you'd be able to sit down and chat with the lawyer about her fee structure and her level of service and expertise. But be prepared — many busy lawyers will be happy to provide a quote for their fees over the phone, but may not be available for an interview or consultation just to explain their fee structure.

Lawyers usually charge a flat fee for the service required (the handling of the sales transaction, for example). These flat service fees are often around $300 to $500, but that's not the total cost of their legal services. You also pay disbursements and taxes. *Disbursements* are any fees that your lawyer encounters while working for you. (Disbursement fees can include, for example, courier fees, registration fees, long distance phone calls, reproduction costs for documents, and any other costs your lawyer pays on your behalf.) And, of course, you're responsible for the tax on any goods or services provided. An average "all in" cost for the straightforward sale of a residential property with a single mortgage, which can be discharged using the proceeds of sale, may be $500 to $1,500. The cost varies, however, depending on the complexity of your case.

When contacting a real estate lawyer about flat fees or "all in" costs, you should also ask what the lawyer's rates are, in the event that something goes wrong and you need extra services. Most of the time, extra services can be obtained on an hourly-rate basis.

Know when to contact your lawyer

Most home sellers go to their lawyers *after* they have signed the sale contract. For simple, straightforward sales done through a real estate agent, you can safely wait to see your lawyer until you have the accepted conditional offer in hand. But if you're selling privately or if yours is a complicated sale, ideally your lawyer reviews the conditions of sale prior to you signing any agreement of purchase and sale.

Definitely make the offer subject to review by your lawyer if your buyer stipulates conditions that your agent views as strange, or if you have a rental unit on your property and the tenants will remain after the new owners take possession. If your lawyer is also your brother and he's willing to get out of bed at 1:00 a.m. to come over and review the offer on the spot, by all means take advantage of your connections. Getting a professional opinion is always helpful. But if the timing doesn't allow for a trip to your lawyer's office and you're selling a fully residential property with a real estate agent, you have one mortgage, you're using a standard contract, and there are no unusual encumbrances or conditions, don't be afraid to go ahead and sign — that is, if you're happy with the offer.

If you have an agent

If you're selling through an agent, a typical scenario might run something like this: Your agent comes over to your home at 7:00 p.m. with the buyer's offer. The buyer will pay the price you want, but there are a few *conditions* (refer to Chapter 10 for a discussion of conditions). Your agent thinks the conditions are typical and shouldn't evolve into any problems, but you want a second opinion from your lawyer. You need to make up your mind quickly and want to jump on that great price. Unfortunately, your lawyer closed up shop at 5:00 p.m. So you write in a clause making the contract or agreement of purchase and sale subject to your lawyer's approval within 24 hours, and you go ahead and sign. If you have an experienced and reputable agent and reasonable buyers, there shouldn't be any problems with this strategy.

If you fear your home's sale is going to get complicated, talk to your agent to get an idea of the *likely* conditions before you see any buyers' offers. Your agent can help you compile a list of possible scenarios to present to your lawyer for an expert legal opinion. Armed with the advice of your agent and your lawyer, you're as ready as you'll ever be to evaluate an offer that comes in late on a Saturday night.

Preparing for the worst

When you're buying or selling a house, your will is probably the furthest thing from your mind. However, everyone who owns real estate should have a will, and selling or buying a home is an excellent time to write your will or revise the one you have:

✔ You're acquiring or disposing of a major asset that may affect the distribution of the assets of your estate.

✔ At conveyance time, you're already using the services of a lawyer or notary public who will necessarily become acquainted with your personal financial situation.

As you shop around for a lawyer or notary public to handle your conveyance, you can negotiate the extra cost of your will into the conveyance package — and you should pay less than the stand-alone cost of the drafting or review of a will.

If you're going it alone

In a private sale, the smart course of action is to review the conditions of the offer with your lawyer before signing anything. Because you don't have a real estate agent to review the conditions of the sale agreement, you take a significant risk if you accept the offer unadvised. Most buyers' offers are not made and sealed in a slam-dunk time frame. At a minimum, the "subject to lawyer's review" clause allows you to sign the contract and still have a safety hatch in the event that your lawyer subsequently discovers problems. The buyer may have an agent who's drawn up the offer, and if you don't have an agent you should make sure your lawyer reviews the contract before you sign anything — the buyer's agent may have added clauses to the contract that are overly beneficial to her client, the buyer. Remember, this is a legal document. Don't be embarrassed to ask your lawyer questions. Better to find out now — you may feel a lot more foolish if you don't.

Provincial real estate associations across Canada (see the list of contact information in the Appendix) have standard forms for their contracts of purchase and sale, which have been created by lawyers and committees of real estate professionals who review the form and content of the contracts on a regular basis. If your buyer uses one of the appropriate standard provincial forms, chances are your lawyer won't uncover any problems with the paperwork involved. However, the content of the offer may still need to be reviewed.

Preparing to visit your lawyer

Give your lawyer all the necessary information right off the bat. When you call to make an appointment, ask what documentation you should bring. Your lawyer will probably ask for the following:

✔ Legible copy of the accepted offer, although if you're using a real estate agent, the agency has already forwarded a copy of the contract plus other documents to the lawyer's office

✔ Latest property tax bill

✔ Utility bills for the past year

✔ All mortgage information, or your mortgage discharge statement if you no longer have a mortgage or if you intend to discharge your mortgage with the proceeds of your home's sale

✔ Any transfer or conveyance documents from when you purchased the home (if you still have copies)

✔ Documentation for any chattels (any items you agree to leave in the house for the new owners) that are to be included in the sale and that have their own title or lease, such as a leased security system

✔ Any additional information relevant to the condition of your property or the title (ownership) of your property

You may be able to fax or e-mail the necessary documents, saving yourself a trip to the lawyer's office.

Taking care of business: What your real estate lawyer does for you

When your real estate lawyer has all the relevant information, things get cracking. The role of your lawyer and the role of your buyer's lawyer aren't set in stone. Although some tasks are commonly relegated to the buyer's or the seller's lawyer, if you want to arrange with your buyer to do things differently, nothing's stopping you. As the seller, your lawyer's traditional role involves the following tasks:

✔ Reviewing the sale contract

✔ Ensuring that the titles and documentation for any chattels that are included in the sale are in order

✔ Reviewing your mortgage information and performing or verifying calculations

✔ Reviewing your property tax bills

✔ Pro-rating to the adjustment date any annual utility costs, condominium fees, and municipality fees

✔ Determining if any refunds are owed to either you or your buyer, and the amount of these refunds

✔ Preparing a statement of adjustments

✔ Preparing the transfer deed

✔ Making sure you are in position to deliver a clear title to the buyer on the completion date

Performing a title search and verifying that there are no encumbrances (or other adverse conditions) against the property are typically the domain of the buyer's lawyer, and will be performed by the buyer's lawyer prior to the completion date.

Chapter 18

Listings and Disclosures

. . . .

. . . .

*I*f getting ready to sell your house meant only painting the fence and wait-ing for your agent's call, the process would be a lot less stressful. But like so many other major events in life, selling your home involves lots and lots of papers. In this chapter, we tell you how to wade through all this paperwork, and before you know it, you'll be breathing easy again.

Listing Contracts

If your home is going to have any chance of selling, then buyers are going to have to know that it's for sale in the first place. Marketing your home involves listing it either on your own or through an agent. If you're listing through an agent, you'll need to fill out and sign a *listing contract*. The list-ing contract gives authorization to one (or more) agency to sell your home, and specifies how much you'll pay for its services. The contract is a legally binding agreement that places obligations on both you and your chosen real estate agency. You have some options for listing your home.

Selecting your listing type

Three kinds of listings exist: MLS (or multiple) listings, open listings, and exclusive listings. MLS listings are the most common.

✔ **Multiple Listing Service (MLS) listings authorize your selling agent to work with other agencies' salespeople.** An MLS listing markets your home across Canada, reaching a huge network of real estate agents.

Your agent is free to cooperate with all other agencies, and gives them all full cooperation and access to your home's listing. The MLS system, along with the local real estate boards that maintain it, has very specific requirements regarding cooperation between real estate agents. MLS listings are often in the best interest of the seller, because they can give your home maximum exposure to the market. The listing contract and the MLS data indicate what portion of the total commission is payable to the buyer's agent — that is, the agent who brings along a ready and willing buyer for the property.

If you need to sell quickly, you'll want to take out an MLS listing —it's the best possible way for your home to get maximum market exposure. If you want the best possible price for your home, the surest way to get the right bid is to advertise to as many people as possible that your home is for sale. An MLS listing ensures that your home quickly reaches the right network of real estate agents. The Canadian Real Estate Association's MLS Web site (www.realtor.ca) allows access to nearly all the MLS listings in Canada through its links to local real estate boards across the country.

✔ **An *open listing* authorizes one or more agents to sell your home while protecting your right to sell it yourself.** Open listings are rarely if ever used in residential real estate, but are frequently found in commercial real estate where properties or businesses are made available without being actively listed through an agent. The owner may sell the property without an agent or entertain offers that come through any agent. You, the seller, don't have to deal personally with any of the agents who are working on your behalf, and if you find a buyer, you aren't obligated to pay any commission fees. Often, the buyer will pay the buyer's agent a finder's fee for locating the property, and the seller doesn't have to pay commission. (The buyer's agent has an agency relationship with the buyer, but the seller has no agency representation.)

✔ **An *exclusive* listing authorizes an agency to market your home for a specified period of time.** Exclusive listings are rare. Generally exclusive listing contracts don't allow you to sell your home yourself during the listing period, and often involve a *reduced* commission fee, which is a benefit to you. By bypassing the MLS system, an exclusive listing means your agent's not under any obligation to show your property to other agents. Your listing agent has more control over the marketing of your home. Usually the listing agent cooperates with other real estate agents, but the listing *broker* calls the shots. (Refer to Chapter 6 for an explanation of the role of a real estate broker.) As an exclusive listing, the property doesn't appear on the MLS system and doesn't get the exposure provided by the MLS database. Most sellers, however, want the extra exposure and agent cooperation guaranteed by the MLS system, and therefore sign an MLS listing.

When choosing the kind of listing that's right for you, consider all the variables. What are the general market conditions? How well are other homes of the same size, price, and location selling? Do you have the time to be searching for buyers on your own? And exactly how easy should it be for buyers to find you? When you know what your needs are, and you know the market conditions for homes like yours, you're in a good position to decide on your listing strategy. And when you have a listing strategy squared away, you'll need to know what to expect when it comes to signing the listing contract, which we discuss in the next section.

People who are serious about selling their homes list their homes via the MLS system because it gives their homes maximum exposure on the market. Because of this, many buyer's agents don't consider open or exclusive listings to be serious efforts to sell the property.

Detailing your listing contract

A *listing contract* is a legal document that must be signed by both you and your agent, usually via standard forms that are supplied by your local real estate board. All the particulars about your home appear on the listing contract; it also states under what conditions you're willing to sell, and you and your agent's obligations. Make sure you obtain a copy of your listing contract and that you put it somewhere safe (not the same safe place you put that spare house key you haven't been able to find in five years).

If it makes you more comfortable, or if you're concerned or confused about something in your contract, you can have your lawyer review it before you sign. Remember that although you're listing with an individual salesperson, the listing contract is with the salesperson's *agency*. (So if Suzanne Smith, your real estate agent, works for Sell That House Realty, your listing contract is with Sell That House, not with Suzanne.)

A listing contract deals with three sets of issues:

- **The exact details of the property for sale:** Your home's lot specification, size, building materials, heating and air conditioning systems, number and descriptions of rooms, and other details are presented in the listing contract. Any extra items (movable things, such as appliances or furniture) or chattels included in the sale are also shown on the listing contract. (The contract also specifies if any items are *excluded* from the sale of the home; for example, the chandelier in the dining room, or the hot tub.)

- **The financial particulars relating to your home:** The listing contract establishes the asking price for your home, and may (depending on your jurisdiction) disclose information concerning your mortgage (such as the balance, payment schedule, or maturity date), as well as the property taxes and any legal claims on your property.

✔ **The precise terms of employment for your agent(s):** Your listing contract specifies who's allowed to market your home and in what manner, as well as stating the time period in which your home can be marketed by the agent, and what you will pay the agent for marketing your home.

Multiple Listing Service (MLS) listings all come with a standard disclosure statement so that you can reveal all your deep, dark secrets . . . just kidding! We discuss disclosure statements in detail a little later in this chapter.

If you ever think of selling, would you let us know?

If a neighbour or friend expresses an interest in your home, you can add an exclusion to the listing contract (in exclusive and MLS listings only) that states that you don't have to pay your agent a commission if that neighbour or friend (they must be specifically named in the contract) buys your house. After all, it was you who got them thinking about your home in the first place — not your agent!

Before signing the listing contract, notify your agent that your neighbour or your rich cousin Aubrey may want to buy your property and that you don't want to pay commission if either one of them follows through. Put the exclusion in writing before you sign the listing. Give the names of the excluded parties to your real estate agent before he comes to list your house. Your agent will prepare a letter stating the exclusion, which is signed by his manager. The letter should read something like this:

"This letter is to confirm that XYZ Realty acknowledges that the following parties are excluded from the listing contract dated May 1, 20__, and should either party purchase the property at 123 Main Street, Kamloops, there will be no commission payable to XYZ Realty.

Mr. and Mrs. Neighbour,

125 Main Street, Kamloops

Aubrey McCousin,

18 Showoff Lane, Moneysville

Signed by both the agent and the agent's manager"

In some cases, an exclusion may have a time frame attached. For example, "No commission paid if either party purchases the property by May 30, 20__." Your agent may want this time frame included, because he will be investing his time in the listing, so if the excluded parties don't make a move until four months into the listing contract, his efforts won't go unrewarded. Not to mention the fact that the time frame usually encourages the excluded parties to make a decision sooner rather than later.

Keep in mind that additional clauses such as this may slow down your home's sale. The existence of exclusions may show on your home's listing and can discourage agents and buyers who don't want to deal with any possible complications to the sale.

Your listing contract does *not* obligate you to accept any offers on your home, even if the buyer fully meets the conditions of sale stipulated in the contract. Conditions change: You may receive what seems like the perfect offer on your home on the same day that a major family issue crops up. It's called life, and it happens. A listing contract creates an agency relationship between you, the seller, and your selling agent. Throughout the selling process, your real estate agent acts in your best interests to sell the home, without misleading or making any misrepresentations to potential buyers. Refer to Chapter 6 for more information on agency relationships.

Disclosure Statements

When you sign the listing contract, you'll likely be required to fill out a *disclosure statement,* also known as a *property disclosure statement,* or in Ontario, a *seller property information sheet (SPIS).* The disclosure statement is a legal document in which you describe your property and all other items included in the sale to the best of your knowledge. Depending on where you live, the disclosure statement may be viewed by the buyer prior to making an offer, or be provided to the buyer after you accept the offer. Regardless, the disclosure statement is usually incorporated into the contract (signed and acknowledged by the buyer) and becomes part of the contract. For MLS listings in Canada, disclosure is usually mandatory; for *most* exclusive listings, disclosure is recommended.

Basically, the disclosure statement informs the buyer and your agent about the condition of your home, and protects you and your agent from any litigation in the event that a buyer discovers some dreadful problem with your property that you weren't aware of. By providing detailed information on the condition of your home, you ensure that your agent accurately represents your property to potential buyers. You *are* responsible, however, if deliberately concealed information about your property comes to light after you have signed and submitted the disclosure statement.

Who sees my disclosure statement?

Disclosure statements are designed for the benefit of all parties in the transaction. You disclose what you know about your property, and the buyer receives the disclosure statement, often using it as a starting point for a professional home inspection. Both the buyer's and seller's agents refer to the disclosure statement while viewing your home, and they may point to any disclosed deficiencies when negotiating the contract.

The disclosure statement puts the onus of accuracy on you, the seller, and any misrepresentation is potentially dangerous. As the seller, you must disclose everything you know about your home, and you're obligated to disclose anything that *you should have been reasonably expected to know*. For example, if there's a minor water leak in your basement that appears only once a year under heavy rains, you should disclose that there's potentially a problem with the drain tile or foundation. Buyers will inevitably find small problems you try to hide. We put it this way: If you're not sure whether to disclose, disclose.

By signing a legal document that states you have disclosed all knowledge of the condition of your property, *you* (the seller) are responsible for any concealment — usually *not* your agent — if a buyer pursues legal action after becoming aware of some previously undisclosed information. You are liable, however, only if you *intentionally* conceal information. If you don't disclose information because you aren't aware of the issue, it's simply a case of bad luck for your buyer. Your agent would be liable if *she* fraudulently misrepresented any details that are contrary to the information represented by you, the seller.

Bear in mind that most buyers will do a building inspection, and by doing so, the buyer assumes some responsibility for the condition of the house. Buyers will do their due diligence as they inspect and investigate a house. If you complete a disclosure statement to the best of your ability, and a problem surfaces that you were unaware of and the home inspector missed, the buyer's dispute will likely be with the home inspector, not you.

In many areas, sellers may have the option to simply draw a line through the disclosure statement and state on the disclosure form that "the seller makes no representations regarding the subject property, and the buyer is to do their own due diligence." This option is common in several instances. The seller may have owned the property as an investment and rented it out, perhaps never having lived in it. Or it may be an estate sale, in which case the estate has no direct knowledge of the condition of the property. Or the seller may be unable to fill out the disclosure statement because of health issues or age. In these cases, the buyer should make every effort to be especially diligent with the home inspection, knowing that the seller hasn't provided any information.

What do I need to disclose?

The disclosure statement deals with all aspects of your property. It asks you about both land and structures. A typical disclosure statement deals with three categories of information.

General information

This section is geared toward the land areas surrounding your property. You include information about the following, if applicable:

- **Public systems:** Is your home connected to public water and sewage systems, and are you aware of problems with either of these systems?

- **Rental units:** Do you have rental units, and are they authorized?

- **Encroachments, easements, and rights-of-way:** Are there any that aren't registered in your title?

- **Ownership issues:** For example, have you received any notices of claims on the property?

Structural information

Here, you disclose information specific to your home itself. You may include any or all of the following:

- **Insulation and ventilation:** What kind of insulation and ventilation do you have, and are there any problems with it?

- **Electrical, plumbing, heating/cooling systems:** Again, are there any problems you are aware of?

- **Structural damage:** Is there any (unrepaired) flooding, fire, or wind damage to your home?

- **Pests:** Have you had any insect or rodent infestations? Have they been addressed? How and when?

- **Inspections:** Has your home passed a full inspection? Do fireplaces, security systems, and safety devices meet local standards?

Additional information

This section provides blank space for any extra information that is relevant to the condition of your property, or for explanations of any problems or conditions that have previously been mentioned, or repaired in the past.

If you're selling a condominium, you need to include information about current restrictions (regarding pets, children, rentals, or use of the condominium unit) and any future restrictions you're aware of (for example, new bylaws or proposals). You also need to disclose information about anticipated repairs or major construction projects planned for the building.

Being dishonest when filling out the disclosure statement won't help you. Even though your buyer will be relying on the word of your agent, he will also read the sale contract carefully — and you're legally obligated to disclose any known adverse conditions in the disclosure statement that forms part of the sale contract. If you lure an unwitting buyer into making an offer by misrepresenting your property in the disclosure statement, you look foolish when the buyer does his inspection and shows you to be ignorant, at best (or a liar, at worst). You don't want to lose a ready, willing, and able buyer because you didn't disclose all the necessary facts on the disclosure statement. And you definitely don't want to face a legal battle if your buyer later sues you for not properly disclosing the condition of your home.

Chapter 19

Inspections and Appraisals for Sellers

In This Chapter

▶ Deciding whether to get a pre-listing inspection

▶ Determining your need for an appraisal

*W*hen you're purchasing a new home, you need to make sure you know what you're buying. This is why home inspectors and appraisers are so important to house hunting — they help you make sure your home is a good investment.

And now that you've decided to sell your house, making sure you know what you're selling is just as important. Having an inspection and appraisal done isn't just something buyers do — you should consider it as well. Maybe an inspector will tell you that the leak in the basement is actually just a tiny tear in a water pipe, rather than the massive problem you assumed it was (and were willing to lower your home's price for). Or, perhaps an appraiser will alert you to a new bylaw that prevents you from making that improvement that was going to raise your asking price. Without an appraiser's advice, you may have had to tear down the potentially illegal renovation.

Inspections for Sellers

We know what you're thinking: "Why would I want to pay hundreds of dollars for an inspection when my buyer will have one done anyway?" You're right, your buyer will, almost certainly, have an inspection performed on your home. Some lenders will approve a buyer's mortgage only subject to the home passing a full inspection, and most buyers' offers are also contingent on the seller's home passing a full inspection.

If your house is well maintained, then an inspection is generally not necessary — don't waste your money. However, if the real estate in your vicinity is affected by common problems — like radon in the Maritimes, contaminated well water in rural areas, or leaky condos in British Columbia — having an inspection done may be advisable. A positive inspection report is a great marketing tool to relieve buyers' concerns. Refer to Chapter 12 for tips on how to choose an inspector.

Why you should have your home inspected

If you have your home inspected before you put it on the market, you realize the following benefits:

- ✔ An inspection alerts you to any defects that require repair. You may want to do the repairs to help raise the value of your home, as well as to prevent haggling with buyers over the cost of repairs that, in turn, affect the asking price for your home. Also, by doing the necessary repairs before you list the home, you cut down on the amount of time your home may spend on the market — an important consideration when trying to interest prospective buyers. Remember, many buyers don't have the interest, the energy, or the excess cash to make repairs. You may save a sale by doing what your buyer isn't interested in undertaking herself.

- ✔ Having a professional home inspection performed before you list may save you from having to redo any cosmetic improvements. For example, if an inspection reveals you have to take out part of the walls of your home office to update the wiring, then you want to find this out before you add a fresh coat of paint.

- ✔ Providing a full inspection report to potential buyers gains their respect and fosters trust in both you and your home.

- ✔ If you're selling your home privately, a professional home inspection may help you determine the value of your home, and in turn enable you to set the right list price for your property.

Why not to have your home inspected

We have to point out the two main drawbacks to having your home inspected before putting it on the market:

- ✔ If your inspection reveals any serious problems, you're legally obligated to disclose that information to potential buyers (and to your agent, if you're required to sign a disclosure statement — refer to Chapter 18 for details on disclosures). You may prefer the "ignorance is bliss"

> approach, but chances are your buyers (and their lawyers) won't share this point of view.
>
> ✔ The inspection costs you hundreds of dollars, and any buyers who make you an offer will have their own inspection performed, regardless of whether you have already done so.

If you don't feel you need an inspection report to inspire buyer confidence, and you're certain that your property meets safety standards, don't waste your money on an inspection. If you just want to make sure that your plumbing and wiring are in good condition, you may just want to get a plumber or an electrician to take a look around. Ditto for a roof: Knowing how much life is left in your roof can be very important when selling a home. Having your home inspected before putting it on the market can eliminate one more uncertainty from the selling process, and that means one less thing you have to worry about. The real benefit of a pre-listing inspection is *peace of mind*.

What your inspector looks at

An inspector examines closely all the major functional systems in your home, including the following:

> ✔ **Structural components:** Roofing, foundations, floors, walls, columns, and ceilings
>
> ✔ **Exterior components:** Exterior wall cladding, doors, windows, eaves, balconies/decks, and vegetation
>
> ✔ **Interior components:** Walls, stairways, counters, cabinets
>
> ✔ **Heating and cooling systems:** Furnace, air conditioning
>
> ✔ **Electrical systems:** Wiring, outlets, and GFCIs
>
> ✔ **Plumbing:** Condition of pipes, faucets, and drains
>
> ✔ **Insulation and ventilation:** Insulating materials, ductwork

Refer to Chapter 12 for more information on inspections.

How to prepare for the inspector

Your inspector isn't authorized to turn on any systems that aren't already operative in your home. So you need to have all your home's systems turned on and ready for the inspector's visit, including gas, water, electrical, heating, cooling, and plumbing systems. Be on hand to help if the inspector needs to rearrange your personal property in order to gain access to blocked-off areas. You can take a few steps to make sure the inspector can do the job easily and thoroughly:

✔ Make sure electrical panel boxes are unblocked.

✔ Remove clutter blocking access to electrical panels, the attic, basement crawl spaces, the foundation, heating and cooling systems, water heaters, and pipes.

✔ Restrain your pets and watch your children so they don't interfere with the inspection.

✔ Have a copy of each of the following:

- Any service records, warranties, or information on age and performance for appliances that will come with the home

- A written list with the age of all major structural components and systems components, and any service records and warranties

- Your utility bills for integrated systems (for example, electric or gas)

What common problems to expect

No matter how conscientious a homeowner you are, some things are simply beyond your control. Your inspector will likely uncover a few common problems — most will be simply the effects of age and improvements in standards for home safety and efficiency.

Exterior

Here's where you (somewhat sheepishly) admit to ignoring for years that tiny river of a crack beside one of your basement windows. Guess what? It's growing — fast — and may cause serious structural problems down the road. This is one exterior problem your inspector may dig up. Some others include the following:

✔ **Aging roof surface:** If the problem is advanced it will be obvious, but in the early stages it can be quite subtle and easily overlooked.

✔ **Defective windows:** Are seals broken and the windows fogged? Are there breaks or crack? Do they shut properly?

✔ **Wear on siding:** If it's wood, are there signs of rot? Is the vinyl siding cracking or warping at all, or is it loose? If it's a brick exterior, how is it holding up? Bricks cracked? Crumbling brick mortar?

✔ **Ground that isn't properly sloped away from the home:** A proper gradient prevents water drainage into the basement or foundation.

✔ **Cracks, bulges, or deformities in the foundation:** These abnormalities can indicate a more serious structural problem.

Interior

The insides of people's homes can hide a multitude of sins. Here are a few that your inspector may unearth:

- **Signs of flooding or leakage into the basement:** Waterproofing a home is extremely expensive (as you already know if you looked into it after your basement flooded). If you installed any waterproofing measures, a sump pump, or other additions, make sure the inspector takes note.

- **Improper insulation or ventilation:** If air can get in, water can get in. One of the first things they teach budding architects is that *water* is your *worst enemy*. If your home leaks or doesn't allow moisture to evaporate, all your major structural components are at risk. And to mention the obvious, if your insulation is shoddy, heating and cooling will be inefficient and expensive.

- **Interior components that no longer meet safety standards:** For example, old paint that contains lead, or missing railings on staircases.

- **Outdated electrical, heating, or plumbing systems:** If your home is very old, be especially observant of these systems, as they may be both inefficient and unsafe. For example, some insurance companies (and, for that matter, finance companies) won't take on some older types of wiring, like knob and tube.

A final note: If you're handy and have done work over the years on any of the major operating systems in your home, have them looked at thoroughly. Unless you're a professional electrician, plumber, or HVAC installer, you should be aware that just because "it works" doesn't mean you've fixed things properly or safely.

The inspector doesn't evaluate your home — if you want an evaluation, hire an appraiser. An inspector merely reports. For example, your house may be of the "they don't make 'em like they used to" persuasion, but the inspection report states only that your furnace is 48 years old and is functional and presently operational, not how well it heats. If you want a report that includes how well your systems function, hire the necessary heating or plumbing contractors to evaluate these systems.

Appraisals for Sellers

If you're selling privately — that is, without an agent — an appraisal makes a lot of sense. You obtain a professional, objective assessment of what your house is worth on the current real estate market. Based on your appraisal, you can realistically set the price for your home. (See Chapter 15 for the perils of pricing.) And if you're selling your home through an agent, having an appraisal done makes sense under certain circumstances.

Unlicensed appraisers are out there. Whatever identification is presented to you should show the appraiser to be AACI (Accredited Appraiser Canadian Institute) or CRA (Canadian Residential Appraiser) designated. If you have any friends who have recently hired an appraiser, ask if they were satisfied that they received a fair appraisal, and if so, ask for the appraiser's phone number. Work only with an appraiser you trust. Refer to Chapter 6 for tips on finding an appraiser.

Considering if a home seller needs an appraisal

Whether or not you have your home appraised, buyers almost always need to have an appraisal when they apply for a mortgage. If your buyer doesn't need a new mortgage — for example, if your buyer is assuming your mortgage — then you don't need to worry about appraisals.

However, under some conditions having your home appraised before you put it on the market can be a good idea. The chief benefit of having a professional appraisal performed before you list your home for sale is that you eliminate uncertainty and get a realistic price range for your home. This is especially important if you require a certain amount of money out of your house to plan your next move. An appraisal lets you know if your plans are financially viable. Although you may not be required to get an appraisal on your property, the assurance it gives you means one less thing to worry about. In addition, if your home is special or unique in some capacity that makes it difficult for you and your agent to compare and gauge its value, you should probably hire a professional appraiser.

The majority of home sellers don't hire an independent appraiser before listing their homes for sale, unless they're selling privately. Most real estate agents are well versed in the factors that influence the market value of a home, and can provide you with an accurate estimate of your home's worth. What's more, your agent uses the same process (and database) as an appraiser to judge your home's value — a comparative market analysis (CMA) — and the agent does it free of charge.

Even though a real estate agent and an appraiser use the same process to appraise a home, there are differences. You hire an appraiser for the specific task of supplying you with an expert, unbiased opinion. A real estate agent, however, is a professional *sales* agent, and the opinion of an experienced and reputable agent may take into account intangibles — the "Wow!" factor — because the agent knows a certain type of buyer will pay big bucks for your home. An appraiser may not be aware of the perceived value of the restored stained glass windows by the front door, or the mature landscaping in the front and back gardens.

Hopefully, you've done a little investigation on your own and have some idea of what comparable homes are selling for in your neighbourhood. If your agent's suggested price is wildly out of whack with what you've seen on the market, or you're willing to pay the few hundred dollars for greater peace of mind, you should contact an appraiser.

Exploring how an appraisal is performed

The first thing you'll want to know about an appraisal is how much to budget for it. A standard home appraisal (say, a bungalow in a neighbourhood with a fair amount of owner turnover) can run you anywhere from $200 to $500, depending on the size and location of the property and the depth of the assessment. Basically, the rate is determined by how much work the appraiser has to do to figure out the value of your property. If there have been a lot of comparable sales in the recent past, it's a fairly easy job. If the last time a house sold in your neighbourhood was in 1957 and it was nothing like yours, an appraisal will be a little more complicated, and thus more expensive.

What will I get for my money?

Appraisers will be very quick to tell you that they aren't home inspectors. Having said that, they do look at a lot of the same things. Here's a list of some of the things an appraiser notes about your home:

- ✔ **Size:** What is the total square footage of the home, including basement, if there is one? What are the lot dimensions?

- ✔ **Age:** What is the age of the home? The roof?

- ✔ **Condition:** Does the home need repairs that will affect its value?

- ✔ **Upgrades, finishing:** What work have you put into the home recently that will increase its value? Bathrooms and kitchens are usually the focus here.

- ✔ **Infrastructure:** Heating, plumbing, and electricity. Do they all function properly? Or are there costly repairs needed?

- ✔ **Amenities:** Especially in condos, but in houses too — sauna, pool, hot tub, deck, garage, and so on.

- ✔ **Neighbourhood:** Schools, shopping, transportation, safety, and so on.

- ✔ **Immediate surroundings:** What does your yard back onto, a park or a high-rise apartment? Which way does your condo face, south for the best light, or east for the morning sun?

- ✔ **Anything that makes your home special:** Unique features can boost the value of your home.

The appraiser is required to do a visual-only inspection of all the items on the above list — but may investigate more closely by measuring the property and probably taking photos. Any signs of problems or potential problems, like cracks in the walls that can indicate excessive settling, will be documented.

If you live in, say, a Victorian neighbourhood, don't hire an appraiser who specializes in suburban homes built after 1980. Choose an appraiser who's familiar with the special attractions a home like yours offers prospective buyers.

An appraiser may use one of three methods to evaluate the subject property:

- **A comparative market analysis (CMA):** This evaluation is based on a comparison of your home to the recent sale prices and current asking prices of comparable homes in your neighbourhood, taking the condition, amenities, and other particulars associated with your home into account to adjust that figure up or down. See Chapter 15 for an example of a real estate agent's comparative market analysis.

- **A replacement cost approach:** This method determines the value of your home based on how much it would cost today to rebuild your exact home. This approach is used less frequently than the CMA because it provides a less accurate picture of how much buyers are willing to pay for your home.

- **A rental income approach:** This is used for homes that include rental units, and is essentially a CMA that factors in the income and expenses generated by those units.

Regardless of the method employed by your appraiser, the value she determines is a professional opinion. The nature of an appraisal is such that two different appraisers, for example, yours and your buyer's, may come to different conclusions about the value of your home. If your buyer's appraiser (or the appraiser sent by your buyer's mortgage lender) determines the value of your home to be less than the offered amount, you may lose the offer. The buyer may no longer be willing to pay the offered price, or the buyer's mortgage lender may refuse to finance the offered amount. In this case, the buyer and/or seller may want to get a second appraisal if the first is not satisfactory — even appraisers make mistakes sometimes.

How long will an appraisal take?

Believe it or not, an appraisal doesn't take much time. For an ordinary home, it should take 10 to 15 minutes. But the more unique features your home has, the longer noting all the items takes.

After the visit to your home, the appraiser researches other sales in your area in the recent past to compare what other homes similar to yours have sold for. This helps put a market value on your home and will also highlight any unique features of your property. The research process takes a little longer, but again, for a standard home, you can expect the report in a day or two. If your home is in an old money, leave-it-to-the-grandkids neighbourhood where sales are uncommon, the research will be harder and will definitely take longer.

Investigating appraisals for condominiums

The appraisal process is almost identical for condominiums and houses (go back and read the preceding section if you skipped on to this one). The costs are the same, although a really posh condo may run you a little more. One thing that does make a difference in condos is the maintenance fee. A very high monthly fee that clearly supports extras like a concierge, swimming pool, and meticulously maintained property won't detract from the value assigned to a condo. However, a high monthly fee on a condo without a lot of frills reduces the price that a buyer is willing to pay.

Be aware that the appraisal may not take into account the status of the condominium corporation — and this is a factor that significantly affects how much a buyer offers for your home. (Refer to Chapter 5 for more information on condominium corporations.) Even though the state of the building management's finances has a bearing on the value of each unit, appraisers don't usually have access to this information. For example, if there's no money in the building's reserve fund, underground parking upkeep or security may be neglected, possibly decreasing the value of the property. If you want a more accurate estimate, you can provide your appraiser with a copy of your condominium's documentation, which will include all the relevant information about maintenance, finances, and the legal obligations of the condo corporation. In some provinces, this documentation is referred to as the estoppel certificate, condominium certificate, status certificate, or information certificate.

Preparing for an appraisal

You can take a few steps to make a favourable impression on any appraiser:

✓ **Showcase your home.** Although, technically, cleanliness and tidiness (or lack thereof) shouldn't affect the appraiser's "objective" opinion, appraisers are human, so showing off your home for the appraisal never hurts. If the appraiser thinks you're a conscientious homeowner, he may give you the benefit of the doubt and place your home at the upper end of a range of values.

✓ **Make sure the appraiser has all the relevant information about your home.** Everything from appliance warranties and inspection reports to receipts for any recent work done on structural, electrical, heating/cooling, or plumbing systems should be available. Feel free to give the appraiser any information you have on recent asking prices or sale prices in your area, especially any private sales that may not show in sales statistics. Even though the appraiser will research the most up-to-date information, making sure she has all the information she needs never hurts.

✔ **Be available while the appraiser tours your home.** Be on hand for questions, but don't interfere. Feel free to discuss factors that you, or the appraiser, feel influence the value of your home, and make notes. This will help you understand why the appraiser may or may not agree with your own assessment of the value of your home.

Get a written copy of the appraisal if you can. Remember that if you're the seller, you won't have access to the buyer's appraisal. If you disagree with any of the factual information that is reported, you can argue to have the report adjusted. But if you don't have a copy of the appraisal, you won't be aware of any errors. If a certified appraiser refuses to correct factual errors, you can report him to the appropriate authority, the Appraisal Institute of Canada (www.aicanada.ca). Note that if a bank is doing an appraisal for the buyer, the buyer may not get a copy of it, especially if the bank is paying for the appraisal. If, as the buyer, you're paying for the appraisal (and you couldn't negotiate for the bank to pick up the cost), you may be in a stronger position to get a copy of the appraisal from the bank.

Be sure the appraiser knows why you need her services. The purpose of the appraisal may have an effect on the final cost and on the amount of time it will take. Homeowners also get appraisals done when they're considering refinancing or renegotiating their mortgages, dividing property after a divorce, or in connection with other legal concerns. The fees for a home appraisal for litigation purposes are far higher; they can go well into the thousands of dollars because the report is more comprehensive and includes more detailed and slightly different material, and it may have to be presented in court.

Chapter 20

Making Your House Shine

In This Chapter

▶ Deciding what renovations, if any, to make

▶ Using successful marketing strategies

▶ Ensuring your home makes a lasting first impression

*A*fter you're sure about selling your old place and finding a new place to call home, you'll start to notice a big change in your attitude. Your *home* — the place where you relaxed, slept, worked, ate, raised kids, and cuddled pets (and maybe let dust bunnies accumulate in the corner) — will slowly become a commodity, a *house*. And if you get top dollar for this house, you'll be in a better position to buy a great new home.

In this chapter, we walk you through a good, hard look at your house, to help you determine what needs to be done to improve it, and what improvements are unnecessary. After you've decided what needs to be done, we give you tips on how to roll up your sleeves and make your house the shiniest on the block.

Undertaking Home Improvements

You can admit that you're addicted to those renovation television shows that have become so popular — and you're not alone. Just stroll down the aisle of any Rona or Home Depot, and you'll run into do-it-yourselfers as well as contractors shopping for their clients.

As a seller, renovations mean more to you than just making the place look great. Hopefully you're increasing the resale value of your home, right? Lots of people feel that way. However, one of the most common selling mistakes is to make major renovations before a sale. Pouring thousands of dollars into renovations doesn't result in an equivalent increase in the market value of your home. Some renovations are "good" and others are "bad" in terms of a return on your investment, and you need to know which is which before jumping in with both feet. And renovations that would have fallen into the good category or the bad category can, if poorly executed or done outside of the price point that buyers expect in your neighbourhood, fall into the "ugly" category and knock money off your sale price.

Improvements that save your buyer money as the new owner of your home do increase the value of your home to some degree and increase the desirability of your home. For example, making your home more energy efficient means your buyer saves on heating and cooling costs. However, this renovation probably won't return more than 30 to 50 percent on your investment. In fact, there are few, if any, renovations for which you'll get back all of what you put in. Here are some guidelines to follow as you spruce up your home to sell it:

- ✔ **Inexpensive cosmetic improvements, such as repainting, are always your best bet.** Select colours from a neutral, conservative palette to repaint your house inside and out. (You may think that a magenta living room is warm and inviting, but most buyers will not.) These colours will make your house look brighter, larger, and well maintained. Statistics show that when you sell your house, you'll recuperate at least 60 to 65 percent of the money you spent on painting.

- ✔ **If interior or exterior structures of your home need improvement to make it saleable, then larger renovations may be worth the time, money, and hassle.** For example, if you neglected to add an extra bathroom to go with those two extra bedrooms you built back in 2005, and your daughters have grown up having to run across the house when nature calls, then adding one now makes sense. As a general rule, kitchens and bathrooms are good places for renovations. Upgraded features of kitchens and bathrooms make good selling points, and on average, home sellers get about 65 to 75 percent back on the money they put into modernizing.

But if you'll never make back the money you spend, why would you even consider renovations? The fact is, if buyers recognize your home needs work, they'll factor into their offering price a large margin of error for the cost of renovations. You can either sell your home "as is," which means the buyers will pay a lower price and undertake renovations and improvements themselves, or you can undertake some good renovations yourself before you sell. Although you may never get a 100 percent return on the money you spend renovating, you may *lose less* than if you were forced to drop the sale price into the "as is" category.

Remember all those people you saw in the aisles at Home Depot and Rona? Well, a lot of them are attempting to do home renovations by themselves. Although many of these home improvement stores now offer in-house classes on how to do things like tiling, a level of skill and patience is still required. Are you really up to the task of replacing the bathroom plumbing, or doing some major rewiring? You may end up having the job done twice: the first time when you mess it up, and a second time when a professional has to come in to fix what you've done. Shoddy renovations can end up costing more money in the long run and will be detected when the home inspector pays you a visit. They also make potential buyers suspicious. If buyers notice that the new dimmer switches you installed don't work (or spark when you turn them), they'll wonder what else wasn't done properly.

If your timeline for selling your home is a few years down the road, you may want to make a major addition to your home. That way, you get to enjoy the new features, plus they'll add value to your home when you eventually sell. But if you're looking to sell immediately, leave well enough alone — significant renovations are just a bad idea.

Lose a little, or lose a lot . . .

When Ken and Barbi decided to sell their dream home after 20 years, they listed it at $250,000. Along came Shelley, who loved the house but could see that the bathrooms — which had never been upgraded — were due for some major renovations. This was a common complaint from everyone who viewed the house. The contractor Shelley called said it would cost $7,000 for all the renovations, but just to be on the safe side, she budgeted $10,000 — so she made an offer of $240,000. Ken and Barbi weren't thrilled at the idea of knocking $10,000 off the price of their biggest asset. So Ken phoned a contractor friend who said he could do it for $6,500. They went ahead with the renovations and re-priced their house at $255,000 (original price of $250,000, plus $5,000, approximately 70 percent of the renovation cost). In a perfect world, a new buyer would have come along, seen the beautiful new bathrooms, and have been willing to pay the full asking price. No such buyer appeared, however, but the house did eventually sell for $246,000. By renovating the bathrooms, Ken and Barbi overcame buyers' objections to the bathrooms and ended up recovering all but $500 of the renovation cost. They may have been better off selling as is — it would have saved them a lot of energy, and they could have moved on to their new dream home a lot sooner.

A few streets over, Flo and Harry couldn't resist adding a purple porcelain bathtub and fuchsia tiles imported from Italy — to the tune of $12,000. Like Ken and Barbi, they'd been in their house for 20 years and had also priced it at $250,000, the standard market value for the neighbourhood. Predictably enough, few buyers shared Harry and Flo's taste for pink and purple porcelain, so the highest offer they received was $240,000. Everyone was factoring in the cost of ripping out that crazy purple bathtub. So Flo and Harry were out the $12,000 they initially spent installing those vibrant-coloured fixtures *plus* the $10,000 that got knocked off their asking price by the potential buyers. Remember, you're selling the home to someone else, not decorating according to your own personal flair. Try to make sure your home improvements appeal to mainstream tastes, and you'll have better luck with your investments.

Sometimes renovations are simply not warranted. Even though your 50-year-old bungalow could badly do with fixing up, it may not be worthwhile if you notice that all the houses that have sold on your street have been torn down to build brand-spanking-new monster homes. If people are buying into the neighbourhood for the land, rather than the house that sits on the land, don't waste effort and money on what will become demolition debris.

If you've renovated parts of the home you're selling and you're curious about how much (or how little) it'll add to the resale price, the Appraisal Institute of Canada (www.aicanada.ca) has a cool feature on its Web site that you should check out. The tool is called Renova, and it's a guide to the possible returns of the 20 most popular home renovations in Canada. Just choose the type of home improvement, such as building a new deck, enter the amount you spent or anticipate spending, and Renova will provide you with a range of how much the improvement adds to your home's value. The numbers aren't exact, and in no way is the guide meant to replace a professional appraisal, but you'll get a rough idea of the value of your renovations.

If you're thinking about renovating, talk to your real estate agent. If you aren't using an agent, good places to go for information are the Canada Mortgage and Housing Corporation (CMHC) or the Canadian Home Builder's Association. Both organizations offer many products that deal with home renovations, and have plenty of free information available on their Web sites (www.cmhc-schl.gc.ca and www.chba.ca).

Creating curb appeal

Making a good first impression is crucial to selling your home. Potential buyers don't walk up your driveway blindfolded; their first view of your property is from the street. Your home has to look good outside as well — this is often called *curb appeal*. You never know who's going to drive by your front yard, so consider it part of the marketing strategy.

A big "For Sale" sign in front can go a long way to getting your home noticed, but you want to make sure the next reaction will be "And it looks great!" You have to draw buyers in before you can dazzle them with the stunning reclaimed hardwood floors and huge master bedroom with ensuite bathroom. Getting the right kind of attention requires a plan of attack.

Take a cold, hard look around the exterior of your home. Is the hedge overgrown, and are the shutters peeling paint? Is your garage jam-packed to the rafters with ten years' worth of outgrown hockey equipment and broken toys? Take the time to trim those hedges, sort out those shutters, and clean out that garage. If you don't have room to park your cars, your potential buyer will assume you don't have enough storage space — not a good impression, and that can cost you a sale.

Pretty on the outside

In case you're wondering where to begin, here's a checklist of tasks to help enhance the exterior of your home and yard:

- Clean out the garage, and move any large, infrequently used items into storage elsewhere.

- Clean windows, shutters, eaves, doors, and mailboxes.

- Replace damaged window or door screens.

- Do any necessary repairs, and touch up paint.

- Get out the gardening gloves: Trim hedges, trees, and shrubs; rake leaves; mow the lawn; weed gardens; tend to flowers.

- Clean oil marks and stains off the driveway.

- Ensure the garage door opener is working properly.

- Clear and clean paths, patios, and patio furniture.

- Make sure your house number is visible from the street.

- Do last-minute tidying to get rid of any clutter that's accumulated over the past week.

- Pick up all junk mail regularly.

If you're planning to have an inspection or appraisal performed, the best time to do it is when you're cleaning up and making cosmetic improvements in preparation to sell (refer to Chapter 19 for more on both inspections and appraisals for sellers). As part of the spiffing-up process, you'll want to make any repairs suggested by your inspector or appraiser.

Alluring interiors

So, your home positively sparkles outside in the sunshine — great. But after a buyer moves beyond the exterior, you need to back up that great first impression with something even better inside. Just clean and tidy is fine for the outside, but inside your home you must be concerned about two extra qualities: neutrality and ambience.

Being organized and spotless isn't enough. Buyers who are touring your home need to be able to see themselves living in it, and that means you have to erase, as much as possible, your personality from the interior. A neutral setting lets buyers start to think seriously about your house as "my new home," and this is the first step toward an offer. This neutrality doesn't just mean toning down personal touches: It also means removing family photos from the mantle, and all the finger-painted masterpieces from the refrigerator. After you've visibly neutralized your house, you need to take care of all the other senses that create ambience — the smells, sounds, and feels that make your home comfortable and inviting. Use the list in the sidebar "An inviting inside" to make sure you've covered all your bases.

If you plan to repaint, or if you're replacing countertops or fixtures, choose light, neutral colours. Painting is better than wallpaper — it's much easier for a buyer who doesn't share your design sense to repaint than to strip wallpaper. Light, neutral paint will make rooms brighter and feel larger, and will remove some of your personality from the decor. Simple cosmetic improvements are relatively inexpensive and make a big difference to the appearance of your home. Make sure all light fixtures are operational and have the highest-rated bulbs (although some houses may benefit from dim lighting!).

Be prepared to show at any time of day or night, and on short notice. Keep things clean, and have a contingency plan for your family and pets in case you get an unexpected call from your agent.

Clearing out your clutter

You may think that your classic beer can collection is a work in progress, but chances are your prospective buyer thinks of it as junk. If you can't find your kitchen table because of all the newspapers strewn across it, or opening the hall closet can result in a small avalanche, it's time to get cracking. After all, you're planning on moving, so you may as well start packing up and tossing what you don't want or need anymore.

An inviting inside

Hardly know where to begin? Take a look at this list, and plan to perfect your home's interior appeal:

✔ Make renovations that you were planning on (see the beginning of this chapter for information on "good" and "bad" renovations).

✔ Repaint or touch up paint, and repair cracking plaster.

✔ Fix or replace leaky faucets, wobbly doorknobs, loose cupboard handles, and squeaky hinges or floorboards.

✔ Clean draperies and upholstery; shampoo carpeting.

✔ Move excess furniture and belongings (especially toys) into storage — buyers will have an easier time walking around, and the rooms will appear larger.

✔ Get rid of any unwelcome visitors (like those cute little squirrels that live in your chimney, and the family of mice in the crawl space) — call an exterminator if you must.

✔ Wash inside windows, walls, panelling, and any other surface that may have smudges or fingerprints.

✔ Put away all small appliances on kitchen countertops, and clean any large appliances that are included in the sale.

✔ Lock away jewellery and valuables.

✔ Add comforting touches like candles or flowers; light the fireplace (if you have one, if it's clean and functional, and if it isn't August).

✔ Have fresh towels in bathrooms.

✔ Empty all garbage cans, and make sure that all sinks are clean and all toilets are flushed.

✔ Purge closets

✔ Clean inside kitchen and bathroom cabinets, especially under sinks.

Be aware of odours (especially those you may have become accustomed to, such as cigarette smoke or pets), and take countermeasures (try baking bread or putting a few drops of vanilla in a warm oven just before a showing). If you're a smoker, or have one living in your home, you may want to refrain from the habit (inside your home at least) while your property is on the market. Ask a non-smoking friend to be honest about the smell. A good solution to eradicating heavy smoke smells in the walls can be washing them down with a mix of water and ammonia.

✔ Weather permitting, open windows to let in as much fresh air as possible.

✔ Place any inspection reports, records, or information sheets outlining the features of your home in plain view, with enough copies so that buyers can take one with them.

Decluttering is a combination of cleaning, clearing, and organizing before showing your house. With each item, ask yourself, "Do I really need this?" Be honest. If you don't need it, get rid of it. If you do, figure out exactly where the item should go and then keep it there. Clutter-free rooms look more spacious and make the house more appealing to interested buyers. Plus, you'll have less stuff to pack up, move, and unpack.

Here are some tips for clearing clutter:

✔ **Work your way up.** Instead of doing a bit in every room in the house, approach the job one room at a time. Start in the basement, then move on to the main floor and keep going (or start on the top floor and work your way down — whatever works best for you). You'll have a better sense of accomplishment if you see the house getting organized step by step.

✔ **Face the skeletons in your closet.** The first place we put things that have no place is in the closet. Realistically, you probably don't need eight sets of yellow sheets and that collection of plastic shopping bags. Many of us keep clothes we haven't worn in two or three years. So unless you're serious about weight loss (and not too concerned about fashion), you may want to donate your old sweaters and pants.

✔ **Scrap it, but not literally.** Some things you'll want to keep — just keep them organized. Put photographs, important newspaper clippings, or your children's artwork in albums, or create a scrapbook.

✔ **Recycle all that paper.** Even in the age of the Internet, paper clutter is almost inevitable. Put old newspapers in the recycling box, donate your paperback mystery novels to charity, and invest in a small filing cabinet to store what you absolutely need.

✔ **Clear off surfaces.** Colognes, sunscreens, and cosmetics on the bathroom counter make it look small and crowded. In the kitchen, decide whether or not you need to display the mixer, the blender, and the jars of multicoloured pasta, or if they can be stored in the cupboard.

✔ **Put your toys away.** Your knick-knacks and collectibles may be very cool, but they also take up a lot of space. Pack them in advance, and rent a cheap storage space to keep nonessential stuff until moving day.

✔ **Keep it up.** Unfortunately, you can't just do this once and then be done with it. Your hard work will be wasted if you don't make an effort to keep your house clutter-free. Try spending 15 minutes a day putting things where they belong. It's not a fun 15 minutes, but it's well worth it.

Having a garage sale is a great way to get rid of closet clutter. It not only improves the look of your house for showings but also makes moving that much easier. Anything that doesn't sell and is still useable can be donated to your local Goodwill.

Home staging: Cue the professionals

You've seen them on all sorts of TV shows as of late, and you may want to take advantage of one yourself. Home staging professionals prepare your home to be shown, making sure to show all its finest qualities in the best possible light. And the better your house looks, the better price you'll get. If the market is a little slow when you list your home, home staging can speed up the selling process by making your home the star attraction among the others on the market. If your home has languished on the market for a couple of months, you may want to call the home stagers and let them work their magic instead of reducing the asking price.

The process enhances your home's best features with appropriate colours, furnishings, and props to make it all the more alluring to potential buyers. You may find it difficult to see your home — the place where you've created so many memories — as a product. But when it's up for sale, it is indeed a product. You need to figure out ways to show that it's better than all the other products out there. Sometimes doing this requires professional help, even if you think you have a real flair for decorating.

Home staging (also called *house fluffing*) involves more than a fresh coat of paint. A home staging professional will evaluate every room in your house (yes, even the back area where you keep your lava lamps) and make recommendations on how to make the rooms look bigger and better, highlighting the good and hiding the bad and the ugly. The home staging service will then do the same thing for your yard. Home staging can also be a good option for vacant homes. A fully furnished home usually looks more attractive than a vacant space, so a properly staged vacant property will often sell more quickly — and hopefully at a higher price — than a vacant property that looks empty and neglected. The staging service will actually bring in furnishings, artwork, and plants (temporarily, of course) to give the home a polished look and accentuate the good stuff. Better still, if you're busy and a bit stressed, like most people selling their homes, they'll come in and do all the work for you. If you're on a tight budget, however, be warned: Home staging can get fairly expensive. Depending on whether you want a simple consultation, major rearranging, or a complete staging, you'll need to think about how much you can afford to spend. Most staging companies will offer an "à la carte" range of services, ranging from a quick rearranging of furniture to a total redo with rented furniture and accessories. Many staging companies have a minimum term of contract (60 days or 90 days, for example), and at the end of that term, you can decide if you want to keep the staging furniture or pay for the decorating and consulting done to date and move on . . . hopefully, your home has sold in the initial staging period.

Should you hire a home staging professional? That depends on your budget, the type and current condition of your home, and your neighbourhood, as well as how quickly you need to sell. It's definitely worth a bit of Web research. Although you aren't guaranteed that staging your home will help you get more than your asking price, it can give you a huge advantage over homes that are only so-so in appearance.

Ask your real estate agent to recommend a reliable home staging service, or find out more by searching for "home staging" on the Internet.

Going to Market

So your home sparkles inside and out and you're ready to get the word out that you want to sell. From the sign on your front lawn to your open house, your marketing techniques are a key part of the home-selling process. Although you may be able to advertise a garage sale with a flyer posted at the end of your street, we suspect selling your home will take a bit more effort. To sell your home with the least amount of hassle — and for the highest price — you need to have a marketing plan.

The more professional you are about your advertising, the more trusting your buyer is likely to be. If you're selling with the help of a real estate agent, you automatically benefit from the image and credibility of the company your agent works for, and their marketing expertise.

If you're selling your house on your own, take a page from the real estate agent's book: A coordinated effort is better than a haphazard one. An agent explores all avenues for sale and *acts* like a salesperson. You should, too. Make the most of the resources available to you, type any information sheets instead of handwriting them, use professional signage, and be polite to buyers.

Your basic "For Sale" sign

If you have a yard, posting a "For Sale" sign in it is one of the best ways to attract buyers. If they're interested in your neighbourhood, buyers will tour the area looking for potential homes. Don't let them miss yours. Your sign should be prominently displayed (perpendicular to the road) and list a number where your real estate agent or you, the homeowner, can be reached. If your house is on a corner lot, maximize your exposure by putting a sign facing each road, providing local bylaws allow more than one sign.

Consider yourself warned: Unless you put the words "shown by appointment only," your buyers may come knocking at any time of the day or night. In fact, they may come knocking at any time, regardless.

If you're selling on your own, give yourself an edge by investing in a quality "For Sale" sign. Make sure that the sign will withstand weather conditions and has a solid post or spike so that it can be easily secured out front of your home. A quick scan on the Net or in your local Yellow Pages should help you find a quality sign maker at a reasonable price. The sign should say "Private Sale" or "For Sale by Owner" and include a phone number where you can be reached easily.

Advertise, advertise, advertise

The purpose of placing an advertisement is to get people to phone and book an appointment. You want to give the basic information — like the number of bedrooms, general location, kind of house (bungalow, split-level), and key selling features. Make sure you include the price, which will encourage only serious buyers to call. A good ad will tempt, but not give it all away: After all, you want to entice buyers to actually come by and see your home.

When people phone you, ask them how they heard about your house, so that when it comes time to review your progress, you can stop advertising in places that aren't producing any results. Advertising will cost money, but missed buyers will cost you more.

Listing in the newspaper

If you're selling with the help of an agent, you won't have to take care of writing and placing ads in local newspapers and real estate weeklies. However, you can help out your agent by identifying the key selling features of your home. Make a list of the top five or ten reasons you bought the place, and your agent will incorporate these key factors in the ads if they help increase your home's appeal.

Weekend ads generally have a greater readership, but the best coverage is achieved by taking out both a weekend and a daily ad. Note that many "real estate only" papers are run by the real estate agencies in the area, and don't accept "For Sale by Owner" advertisements.

Check out the competition. How can you make your house stand out in comparison? Buyers read through real estate advertisements with their own criteria in mind, so put front and centre the amenities that will capture the attention of your target market. Your home's proximity to great schools, its waterfront location, the award-winning design, its open floor plan, or its unbeatable view deserves mention in your print advertisements.

If you're selling privately, use the words "Private Sale" or "For Sale by Owner" in your ad. The potential to get a good deal through shared savings on the commission is an excellent selling feature. If you're willing to cooperate with buyers' real estate agents, put "courtesy to agents" or "will cooperate with agents" in your ad. Some buyers won't deal directly with a seller and prefer to have their agent contact you to coordinate a showing. Some agents will call with prospective buyers for your house, and others will be interested in listing your house. Whether or not you decide to use an agent's assistance in selling your home, take the time to talk with them. An agent can offer you great advice on competitively pricing your home, and potentially assist in the sale of your home.

Many real estate agents will be pleased to work with you. If an agent brings you a buyer and you can negotiate a commission fee, you may just have a deal. And because the point here is getting your house sold, cooperating is definitely worth considering.

Real estate agents are a home seller's best marketing tool because they're constantly in touch with potential buyers and other agents. The majority of home sales are completed through agent-to-agent contact, not by advertisements or "For Sale" signs.

Reaching beyond your local newspaper

Where else should you advertise? Specialty real estate publications are the most targeted, but you should also advertise regularly in the newspapers, particularly the issues that run the most house listings. You may also want to advertise in national or city-specific papers, as some buyers may be relocating.

Buying a home is a serious business, so you will be wise to treat it as such. Buyers will be wary of giveaways, gimmicks, or anything else that smells of double-dealing. In any advertising, be flattering but sincere when you describe your home. In the end, your home will speak for itself.

These days, virtually everyone starts their home-buying search on the Net. If you're working with a selling agent and have an MLS listing, you already have the advantage of reaching a wide audience. If you're selling on your own, you'll want to try to get as much online attention for your home as possible. Many Web sites cater to people who want to sell their homes privately; just do a search with the words "For Sale by Owner," and you'll get a wide selection to choose from. And don't forget sites like Craigslist, either.

Creating your own Web site

If you're selling your home yourself and you're relatively tech savvy, a great use for all your digital toys is to create your own Web site. If you don't have the gadgets, your local Web design company can help you out, or just ask your favourite techno-geek. Include your Web site address in newspaper ads, put it on your lawn sign, and use it as a link on your listing on another site.

If you're a professional Web site designer, you can do whatever you want. But if you're not, try to keep things simple. At first, an animated introduction, icons featuring that cartoon character you created (and think is so cute), and flashing graphics may seem like great ideas. We're here to warn you: They're not. Think of what you'd want to get out of the Web site if you were a home-buyer. Would you want entertainment, or straightforward information about the house? Most likely the latter. Plus, having too many bells and whistles will look tacky or cheap, and if people are turned off right away by your Web site's appearance, they probably won't give a darn about your house.

You can even send potential buyers on a virtual tour, a "mini-movie" where you give them a 360-degree view of each room. But be sure to keep your tour professional, and make your home look as good as it would if someone was doing an in-person walk-through. Avoid fancy camera tricks, no matter how fun the zoom and the fade-out features are — they'll just distract, or worse, annoy viewers. If you're including narration, write a script, don't improvise.

Always, always check for spelling mistakes or typos in your advertisement or Web site. People may be frightened to see you've got a "1,000-square-foot mouse for sale."

Making sexy feature sheets

A *feature sheet* is the classy, showy older sister to the newspaper ad. Essentially a flyer that you or your agent distributes to potential buyers when they come to view your home, a feature sheet includes the same basic information — type of house, number of bedrooms and bathrooms, total floor area, neighbourhood, price, and contact telephone number — but it also uses colour and strong design elements to make an impressive pitch for your house.

Selling with the help of an agent? If so, chances are your agent will prepare the feature sheet for you. If you're selling privately, here are some suggestions for making up your own feature sheet:

- ✔ **Attend some open houses and ask for their feature sheets.** If you see a well-designed form, model your own in the same manner. Of course, you can't use any copyrighted text or illustrations, so don't plagiarize, but do take note of what information is specifically outlined and how it's presented most effectively.

- ✔ **Put a great photograph of your house looking its very best on your feature sheet.** If you don't already have the right shot, hire a photographer or get a talented friend to take photos using a wide-angle lens and a film type that allows for multiple prints. You may even want to use pictures of your house at different times of the year, so that prospective buyers can see how cozy your home looks with a dusting of snow, and how magnificent the gardens are in the summertime.

- ✔ **Ensure the pages of the feature sheet are detailed, but also readable.** Don't feel you have to fill the page completely — white space allows people to focus on the important elements of your feature sheet without feeling overwhelmed, and leaves room for note taking. Stick to a standard, easy-to-read font for the text and a simple, bold headline. If the elements of good typography are beyond you, ask a design-savvy friend to help you, or look for a professional you can pay to create the feature sheet for you.

If you have a scanner and a colour printer, you can create your own brochure. If you don't, waltz down to the nearest photocopy place; many copy shops have computer, scanner, and quality colour photocopying facilities.

Keep a stack of feature sheets handy to give to prospective buyers who visit. You may even want to attach an information box to your lawn sign so that prospective buyers can pick up a copy when they drive by. The feature sheet provides a good reference when buyers are comparing homes and gives them a reminder of all the features your house offers. The feature sheet is a marketing tool that will keep selling your house even while you're on the golf green or taking a nap.

Showing (Off) Your Home

Remember that a house showing can be a painful experience for any home seller. If the reality of moving out of the beloved family home hasn't hit yet, it certainly will now. Try to focus on the excitement of finding a new place to live. If you're selling on your own, find a balance between showing all the features of your house and letting people move through it at their leisure. Nothing annoys a buyer more than a seller hovering nervously over her shoulder.

If you're working with a real estate agent, he'll show your home to potential buyers for you. If you're selling privately, you may still allow other agents to show your home.

Some agents will use a *lock box system* to facilitate showings when you can't be around. A lock box contains your key and is secured with a coded lock system. If a buyer's agent wants to bring prospective buyers into your home, she can access the lock box and then return the key to it when the buyer leaves. All entries may be recorded so that you know who has gained access to your home, and when. In areas that do not have such systems, a numbered "punch code" might be used. If this is the case in your area, make sure the code is changed frequently by your agent, to avoid unexpected or unscheduled appointments.

If you're selling privately, make getting in touch with you easy for buyers. You may want to put your cell phone number on your sign, and then make sure to keep the phone with you so you can receive and return calls promptly; otherwise, check your messages often. If your voice mail greets callers with the singing efforts of your 3-year-old, it's time for a change! Your outgoing message should state that the house is for sale and that you'll return calls as soon as possible.

Handle phone calls as professionally as you can. Explain to your kids that if prospective buyers call when you're not available, they should simply take down a name and phone number, and tell the person that you'll return the call as soon as possible. Get back to buyers as quickly as you can, and have all the information they may request on hand so that you can let them know you're serious about selling your home.

Fielding the calls

If you're selling privately, you take all the calls from people interested in your home. Many people, both buyers and sellers, find the initial phone call a bit awkward. You'll quickly find ways of putting yourself and your callers at ease, so don't be annoyed or defensive if the caller sounds wary at first.

Lock boxing — no punching involved

The lock box system makes life infinitely easier for you. You don't have to automatically drop what you're doing as soon as you get wind of someone else who wants to see your house. Let your agent take care of the showing — that's one of the reasons you hired her. Your agent will leave a key to your house in an outdoor lock box. This allows other agents to show your house when your own agent can't be there. Now, pluses and minuses to this setup exist. On the one hand, your house may get shown to more buyers because the lock box is really convenient. However, it also means that your agent won't be there to point out the fantastic features your house has to offer and draw buyers' attention to the built-in bookcases in the study, the breakfast nook that gets the morning sun, and the short walk to the local school and shopping centre.

Nevertheless, buyers often want to look at homes with their own agent, not the seller's. A good agent chooses the right buyers to show the home to and doesn't need to go over each feature point by point with an overeager listing agent.

If your agent recommends a lock box, find out what security precautions are taken. Most companies verify the identity of the agents who want to show your house before giving them an access code to the lock box. Many lock box systems used in major metropolitan areas rely on a lock box "key" (which may be like a swipe card) that is issued only to agents, has a code known only to that agent, and must be updated daily. This means that if the key is lost, it's useless to anyone else, ensuring the safety and security of your home.

Nevertheless, you aren't obliged to use a lock box if you prefer to have your agent present at every showing. In fact, you can make it a condition of the listing that your agent is present at every showing of your house. Remember, you pay the commission, and you call the shots.

Always, always have a pen and paper by the phone. Try to engage callers in a regular conversation so they don't feel as if they're being grilled. Respond to their questions frankly, and ask them questions as well. Find out as much as you can about your callers. Open-ended questions work best. What are they looking for in a house and neighbourhood? How familiar are they with the neighbourhood? Do they have school-aged children? Will they have to sell their own house before they buy?

As you find out more about the callers, you'll be able to demonstrate some of the ways your house may fit their needs as you answer their questions. For example, if they have children, you'll want to emphasize the excellent reputation of the local schools, the recreational facilities in the nearby park, and the polite, well-adjusted teenagers down the road.

You want to find out where they work and if they can give you a number you to reach them at there. This is useful for checking the identity of callers, and if you need to reschedule at the last minute, you know where to find them. Also, ask how they heard about your house, and make a note for when you review your marketing plan.

Don't negotiate with buyers over the phone. If they say the price is too high, urge them to come and look at the house. If you think they are serious buyers, ask them *when* they want to come to see your house. Make the time specific: "Would Thursday evening or Saturday morning be better for you?" Try to line up successive appointments, maybe 45 minutes apart, so that as one set of prospective buyers is arriving, the earlier one is leaving. This way, buyers get a sense that there is a fair bit of interest in your property . . . and you have to get your house ready only once.

Call to confirm all appointments. People are less likely to stand you up if you have called to confirm.

Be prepared for a potential buyer to walk through the door on short notice. One of the joys of cell phones is that someone may be standing on your front lawn asking when she can see your house. If you're working with an agent, he will schedule the appointment at a convenient time. If you're selling on your own, you'll have to get buyers to come back when it's convenient for you, or let them in on short notice. You'll also have to keep your home in tip-top shape on a full-time basis. Even though all this may seem inconvenient (it is!), it'll all be worth it when you close the sale.

Staying secure

Real estate agents work with buyers all the time, and become very good at screening people who either aren't serious about buying or are genuinely creepy. Likewise, if your home's showing is with another agent, that buyer's agent will have prequalified the buyers to make sure they can afford the house and ensure that they are ready to buy the right house if it comes along at the right time.

When you're selling privately, you do have to talk to strangers, but you don't have to let them into your home. Trust your instincts. For your own safety, don't allow anyone who just knocks on your door to tour your home right away. If someone shows up without an appointment, speak to them at the door, and cover the same topics you'd discuss if they called to arrange to see your home. Take their names, phone numbers, and any other details. Explain that you can't show your home immediately, but can make an appointment with them later. You may want to leave a list with a friend or neighbour of the names and phone numbers of everyone who schedules appointments. Likewise, you may want to establish a safety system with a family member or friend. Notify the person before an appointment, and make sure you check in again after the prospective buyer leaves. Conversely, you may want to have that other person present with you for showings. In almost no other situation would you let a stranger in your home. Watch for your own personal safety.

Make sure to take precautions against being robbed. Ask people to sign a visitor information sheet so that you know exactly who has been in your home, when they came in, and how long they stayed. This list will be useful for assessing the amount of interest in your house and for keeping track of prospective buyers with whom you'll want to follow up. However, in the event of theft or damage, you'll also have some information about everyone who has been through your home.

Holding an open house

The open house is your home's big day. The basic idea is that your home is open for showing on certain designated days (usually during the weekend). An open house may cut down on the number of private showings you have to give, thereby reducing the disruption to your daily life. Also, many buyers feel more comfortable and leisurely being "one of the crowd" rather than touring on their own.

The more people who see your home, the more chance there is that someone will fall in love with it. Someone who wasn't even thinking of moving may wander in and fall in love with your property! Your home should be at its best on the day of the open house, so follow our preparation tips in this chapter. If you haven't already overhauled your home, before the open house is the time to do it.

If you're selling privately, announce the times and dates of your open houses in the classifieds, and post an "Open House" sticker on your "For Sale" sign with the appropriate hours showing. Buyers who happen to drive by and see the notice will think it's their lucky day. Make sure everyone who comes to the open house gets a copy of your feature sheet. Plan ahead so that you don't book an open house on a long weekend — it will probably be a waste of time. If you're not selling privately, you can rely on your agent to take care of all the organizational details of your open house.

All your neighbours — and your neighbours' friends — may troop through your home during your open house. Maybe they *are* just being nosy, but remember that word of mouth can be a great marketing tool, too. So let them talk. Give them a reason to talk! The more people who know about your fabulous home, the more potential buyers you may attract.

But nothing seems to be working!

If you've taken all of your real estate agent's expert advice, had plenty of open houses, and still haven't received any offers, you must be wondering, what's gone wrong? The problem can be one of many things, but the following are the most common:

✔ The asking price for your home is too high.

✔ Your home's in poor condition.

✔ Your home's located in a less desirable neighbourhood.

✔ Buyers don't know about your home.

Don't give up. Get feedback from potential buyers, either directly or through your agent.

If you've heard from several buyers that they love your home and it's in great shape, but it's just a bit beyond their budget, you may consider lowering the price. If the general feeling among buyers is that the price and location are great, but the property feels dated, you may want to get out the paint and spruce up your home's appearance.

Make sure you talk to your agent about how many buyers have come through your home and what they're saying. You can drop your asking price, refresh your advertisements, or do some home improvements, but whatever the problem is, you can fix it only if you take the time to figure out what's stopping your home from selling.

Whatever you do at the open house, here are four basic rules to observe:

✔ **Don't negotiate the price verbally.** Be firm that you'll seriously consider all *written* offers.

✔ **Don't give a particular reason why you're selling your home.** A good standard response is, "We've enjoyed this house, but it's time to move on."

✔ **Don't indicate you're under time pressure to leave.** This gives potential buyers an edge when negotiating.

✔ **Don't take things personally.** You want to sell your home, not defend your love of avocado-coloured appliances. Don't lose your cool; you may lose a sale.

Part VI
Sealing the Deal

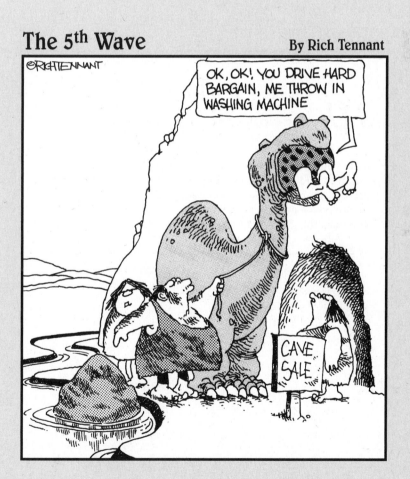

In this part . . .

When the curtain rises on your market-ready home, we want you to be prepared. So we're going to be your coaching and cheerleading team to help you transform your home into an open house. We'll also give you pointers on how to handle buyers once you've wowed them into making offers. And finally, we'll walk you through sale contracts and negotiations, right up to when you pass the keys on to the new owners.

Chapter 21

The Legal Stuff

After you find a buyer, you need to take care of all the legal stuff. And though sale contracts, deeds, and titles may just seem like "stuff" to you, taking them very seriously is vitally important, because one slip-up can send your sale sideways. Selling your home is a great accomplishment — now it's time to see it through to the finish line.

Recipe for a Successful Contract

Unless your current house was picked up off an abandoned lot by a tornado, carried hundreds of kilometres, and plopped onto your land, you already know about sale contracts. (Take a look at Chapter 10 to see the *contract of purchase and sale* from a buyer's perspective.) Here, we review the contract from a seller's point of view.

If you've made any radical changes to your home since you bought it, or if new developments in the community may complicate the sale of your home, certain aspects of the contract of purchase and sale may take priority that didn't in the past. (In some provinces, you use *an agreement of purchase and sale*, and in others, you use *a contract of purchase and sale*; the term may be different from place to place, but the results are the same.) If you didn't buy your current home, or if it's been so long since you bought your home that you can't remember a single thing about signing the contract, pay very close attention — because the paperwork has changed, agency relationships have changed, and disclosure requirements have changed as well.

When the excited and happy buyer decides that she wants to buy your home, she fills out a contract of purchase and sale that includes

> ✔ The price the buyer is offering
>
> ✔ All conditions the buyer wants on the contract
>
> ✔ The date when the buyer wants to take possession of your home

The buyer's agent may give the contract to your agent, and you'll review the offer with your agent (or lawyer, if you're not using an agent). The buyer's agent may also choose to present the offer to you and your agent in person and give you some background information about the buyer, including how she arrived at the starting point of her initial offer. At this stage, the contract is called an *offer,* and if you and the buyer can agree on all terms and conditions, you'll have an accepted offer, *subject to* the agreed terms on the offer (refer to Chapter 10 for info on "subject to" clauses). If the offer is subject to the buyer receiving and approving an inspection report on your home by a certain date, your home won't be sold until the buyer has had a chance to review and approve the inspection report by that given date.

The offer can be presented anywhere, but doing it at the seller's house is customary. If you have too many distractions at your house (kids, pets, in-laws), you may want to meet at your agent's office, or at the buyer's agent's office if it's closer. Wherever you meet, you should feel comfortable and relaxed as you review the offer.

Your agent will take you through the offer step by step and point out the key features, while the buyer's agent explains how or why the buyer made the offer subject to various terms and conditions. All conditions (or "subject to" clauses) must be removed from the contract before your house is considered *sold* — that is, sold unconditionally with a firm and binding contract in place.

When you're selling your home and receive an offer, regardless of whether you're selling with the help of an agent or by yourself, always keep a poker face if the buyer's agent is presenting the offer in person. Losing your temper and screaming about a low offer, or jumping around giddily because you can't believe the buyer came in so high, won't do you any favours in the negotiating process. You don't want to show the other side your cards.

Reading the Recipe: Basic Contract Know-How

Sale contracts are a bit like pancakes. Basic pancakes need flour, eggs, and milk, but beyond that you can add blueberries, bananas, cinnamon, maple syrup, and anything else you like, whether it's in the batter itself or on top.

Great pancakes have no set recipe, but they all use some common ingredients. The same goes for real estate sale contracts. The bulk of the recipe depends on the particulars of your situation. Because we can't tell you exactly what your recipe should be, in this section we tell you what sorts of things will be of particular concern to you, the seller, in some key areas. After all, when you cook with quality ingredients, you're much more likely to end up satisfied.

Many real estate agents use computer software packages that contain standard forms for contracts of purchase and sale, as well as certain phrases that can be inserted into the contract. So you may receive a completely computer-generated document, though receiving a handwritten contract isn't uncommon.

Real estate laws differ from province to province. Consequently, no single standard contract for all of Canada exists. Provincial real estate boards or associations each have their own standard contracts that they make available to agents. However, most *local* real estate boards or associations have their own contracts, too — which are generally variations on the provincial forms.

Most home sales use a contract supplied by the local real estate board. Be prepared to receive a lengthy document: The offer — the partially completed contract you receive from the buyers — may be six or seven pages (or longer).

Don't worry if your sale is particularly complex or unique. The standard forms are only a guide — they can be modified to suit the particulars of your sale, and you can add as many schedules, also known as *addendums,* as you need. These add-on forms specify all the clauses and conditions of sale that simply don't fit in the space allotted on the standard agreement. Some come with pre-printed clauses; others require you and your agent to fill in the particulars.

A contract of purchase and sale has a typical structure with three main sections: First it lays out the legal property description and terms of the offer, then the conditions of sale and any restrictions or obligations involved in the ownership of the property (known as *covenants*), and finally the signatures for acceptance. In the next sections, we explain all these contract components in detail.

A dash of offer

The offer to purchase is prepared by the buyer's agent, and will usually resemble the copy of the Ontario Real Estate Association's contract of purchase and sale. The "Offer to Purchase" section has a threefold function. First, it identifies the parties involved in the transaction:

✔ You (the seller)

✔ Your buyer

✔ The agent(s) acting on behalf of the buyer and seller

If your home is owned jointly by both you and another party (perhaps your spouse or partner), both owners are identified in the seller section. Second, the offer identifies the home as it's registered with the local land registry office, the lot and plan numbers, and sometimes the approximate dimensions of the lot. All this information is taken from the listing contract or from the title search that either you or the buyer (or your agents) have obtained. Last, the offer sets out the major financial details — usually consisting of the offered price and amount of the deposit.

Every offer has some common elements. Make sure that all this information is supplied in the buyer's written offer:

✔ The name and address of the buyer (in some provinces, supplied only upon acceptance of the offer)

✔ The amount of the initial deposit accompanying the offer, or payable on acceptance of the offer

✔ The civic and legal address of the property being sold

✔ The amount of the buyer's initial offer

✔ Subjects and terms and conditions of the offer

✔ Items included and excluded from the sale

✔ Completion, possession, and adjustment dates (which may be the same day in some provinces or circumstances)

✔ Time that the offer is open for acceptance (also referred to as "irrevocable time" in some provinces)

✔ The buyer's signature (witnessed, where necessary)

Name and address of the buyer

The buyer or buyers supply their names and addresses, so you know whom you're dealing with (although in some provinces, the buyer's address is obtained only upon acceptance of the offer). If the offer is made in a company's name, you'll need to know the position the buyer holds in the company and whether or not the buyer has signing authority on behalf of the company.

Be very careful if the buyer's name is followed by "and/or nominee" in the offer to purchase. The buyer may intend to assign the contract to a third party (maybe the daughter who's graduating from medical school in the spring, maybe the money-laundering subsidiary of Crooked Mile Inc.), and ideally the buyer should specify who that third party (or nominee) is on the contract. If the name of the third party isn't specified in writing, it may create ambiguity in the contract and possibly make the contract unenforceable. In British Columbia, for example, the contract of purchase and sale is assignable unless explicitly stated otherwise. Your agent or lawyer can explain the proper way to assign the contract and deal with any potential problems.

Initial deposit and deposits in general

A deposit is an initial amount of money to confirm that the buyer is serious about the offer to purchase your home. A deposit that accompanies your buyer's offer forms part of the down payment when the sale is completed. We recommend that the deposit be made by certified cheque or bank draft. Indeed, in some parts of Canada, the deposit *must* be presented in this fashion.

No standard figure for the deposit exists, but from the seller's perspective, the bigger, the better. If the deposit is substantial (a reasonable and substantial deposit is about 5 to 10 percent of the purchase price, depending on price range), your buyer will be less likely to consider walking away before the sale is completed. If you're buying another house based on the sale of your current home, the deposit gives you assurance that your buyer is committed to the purchase of your current home. You don't want to commit to buying a new house unless you feel secure that your buyer's offer is sincere and the sale of your home will be completed on schedule.

Initially, the offer may be presented with a small deposit ($500 or $1,000) that the buyer will increase when all the conditions are removed from the contract. In some provinces, no initial deposit is required; the buyer makes only one deposit of about 5 percent. If the buyer doesn't make a sincere effort to satisfy and remove the conditions, thereby collapsing the offer, he risks forfeiting his deposit. By making a small deposit, the buyer risks losing less money if he changes his mind about buying your home. If the buyer breaches the contract after conditions have been removed, litigation may follow and things can get messy.

The buyer's deposit can be placed in an interest-bearing trust account, so that at least the buyer will earn interest on the money until the completion of the sale. Real estate agents will have a company trust account in most cases, and there may be a small surcharge involved for holding the deposit in trust.

Civic and legal address of the subject property

Your home's address is included to make sure you're selling the right property. The legal address isn't that much of an issue in towns and cities, but if you're selling vacant land you should always check legal descriptions at the land registry office, especially where there may not be a street number and address. If you're unsure about your home's legal description, check your property tax notices or contact the land registry office in your area. You can find a listing in the Blue Pages of your telephone book.

Price of the initial offer

The price is your starting point for negotiations, and probably the first thing you'll want to look at when the offer comes in. If the initial price the buyer offers is at least reasonable, you can probably negotiate an acceptable price for you and the buyer. In an ideal world, the initial offer will be at exactly the price you asked for or better, and you can skip to the part where you negotiate the other terms of your sale contract. If the offer isn't everything you hoped for, see our negotiating tips in Chapter 22.

A handful of covenants, a sprinkle of conditions

One of the most important parts of the agreement is the "conditions" of the sale. We know what you're thinking: "Of greater concern than the price?" Yes. The financial details contained in the "Offer to Purchase" portion of the sale contract are easily and quickly verified. The conditions of sale may be much more complex and can be treacherous if you don't review them carefully.

In Chapter 10 of this book, we discuss the various conditions (or "subject to" clauses, or subjects) that are common in contracts of purchase and sale. Most "subject to" clauses require the buyer to do some work to satisfy the subjects, such as the buyer approving an inspection report or obtaining a mortgage. All of these subjects must be satisfied within a reasonable time frame. The subjects are noted in the body of the contract, and in essence, the buyer is saying that she will buy your house if it passes an inspection and if she can get a mortgage. Other "subject to" clauses or conditions of the contract require the seller to do some work. These clauses may require that you remove the junked car in the garage, or repair a loose handrail by a specific time, before the buyer will commit to buying the house.

Remember that all terms and conditions included in an offer to purchase your home are negotiable; both parties (you and your buyer) must agree to them. You'll almost never see an offer that doesn't contain any "subject to" clauses. Sometimes, in a very active market with competing offers, buyers keep the "subject to" clauses to a minimum to make their offers as attractive as possible to sellers. Even with a plethora of competing offers, you'll usually find a quick "subject to inspection" clause inserted in an offer. You can choose to reject one or all the "subject to" clauses the buyer has attached to the offer, but if you do, you risk losing the offer altogether. Use good judgment; if you think the buyer's requests are reasonable, then accept them and let the buyer go about fulfilling the conditions. If one or two of them seem completely ridiculous, talk to your agent about making a *counteroffer* that excludes the conditions that you find unacceptable. Of course, if you're selling privately, you have to take care of this yourself, but do consult your lawyer for help so that you can state your terms clearly in a counteroffer.

Assuming that you do accept a few of the buyer's conditions specified in the "subject to" clauses of the offer, you must confirm that the items have been addressed. In effect, you're saying that yes, the buyer has arranged his mortgage or approved the inspection report in accordance with "subject to" clauses in your contract. You and the buyer must acknowledge that these conditions have been met so they can be removed from the offer.

Procedures vary from province to province for removing "subject to" clauses from an offer. In Nova Scotia, for example, clauses are typically worded so that if no written notice from the buyer to the contrary is received by the seller, the seller can assume the buyer is satisfied. In most provinces, a standard form is attached to the offer stating that X, Y, or Z condition has been satisfied; in Ontario, you attach a *waiver;* in Saskatchewan, you attach a *condition removal form.* In British Columbia, "subject to" clauses are removed using a separate *amendment.* "Subject to" removal documents are usually prepared by the agents on the applicable standard forms. Standard contracts and add-on forms are suitable for about 99.9 percent of home sales and are mandatory in some provinces. These standard forms are supplied by your real estate agent. If you aren't using an agent, your lawyer will have these forms available.

We go over some of the most common "subject to" clauses so that you have an idea of what your buyer may include in the offer.

Subject to financing

This is the condition that the buyer includes in the offer basically as a safeguard until obtaining proper mortgage financing. In some cases, the buyer's financing can require that the home be appraised at an equivalent or greater value than the purchase price. With mortgage pre-approval offered by most lenders, many of today's buyers come to the negotiating table with the security of financial backing. Even if they have a pre-approved mortgage, most buyers should make their offer subject to financing for a short period (a couple of days) to allow the lender to do an appraisal and confirm that the accepted offer is fair market value. If your buyer doesn't have a pre-approved mortgage, five to seven business days should be adequate for a bank to arrange a new first mortgage. Like all "subject to" clauses, the "subject to financing" clause must include a date by which it must be removed. A commonly worded "subject to financing" clause reads like this:

> "Subject to new first mortgage being made available to the buyer by_____, in the amount of $_____ at an interest rate not to exceed ____% per annum calculated semi-annually, not in advance, with a ____-year amortization period, ____-year term and repayable in blended payments of approximately $_____ per month including principal and interest (plus ½ of the annual taxes, if required by the mortgagee). This condition is for the sole benefit of the buyer."

"Subject to financing" clauses require the buyer to make a true effort to arrange the required financing. The buyer isn't permitted to just sit at home and say, "I couldn't get it." If you think that a buyer didn't make a good-faith effort to get financing, and can prove it, you may be in a position to refuse to return the initial deposit if the offer falls apart because this condition hasn't been met. This type of situation is where lawyers get involved, but keep in mind that a clearly worded "subject to financing" clause and a true concerted effort by the buyer eliminates the need for lawyers and disputes related to financing subjects.

Subject to inspection

Most offers these days have a "subject to inspection" clause, a condition that the home passes a full inspection. No matter how well you've maintained your home, be prepared to have an inspection conducted by the buyer. If you had your home inspected prior to listing, you shouldn't have any surprises with your buyer's inspection. If your home is relatively new and it passed an inspection before you purchased it, and you haven't seen any evidence of problems, you probably don't need to worry about an inspection turning up anything significant. If you own an older home in which the major operating systems and structural components haven't been updated or replaced in decades, this condition may become an issue. Even if your home seems to be running smoothly, you may be in for some unpleasant surprises come inspection time. Typically, the clause will read something like this:

> "Subject to the buyer, at their own expense, receiving and being satisfied with an inspection report from a certified building inspector of their choice on or before _____. This condition is for the sole benefit of the buyer."

Chapter 19 discusses the main reason against having a pre-listing inspection: If it reveals any problems, you, the seller, are legally obligated to disclose that information. Disclose everything in writing to prevent future problems.

Subject to sale

Buyers often make an offer conditional on the sale of their previous home prior to an agreed-on date. Possibly your buyer doesn't expect to have any problems selling her home, but is simply playing it safe. But perhaps the buyer is in a position to make only a conditional offer because she thinks she'll encounter difficulties in unloading her own property, and she has to sell her home to be able to buy your house. (We discuss in Chapter 16 why buying before you sell is dangerous.) It's your call whether you should accept an offer with this sort of condition. If you're confident in your buyer's ability to sell her previous home, or if you feel you aren't in a position to be rejecting reasonably priced offers (conditional or otherwise), then accepting may be the best course of action. But if you're in a seller's dream market (such as downtown Toronto or Vancouver) and you have no doubt that another, unconditional offer will be forthcoming, you may wish to hold out for the better offer. Talk to your agent about market conditions in your area and how they should influence your perception of a "good" offer. The sale clause can be written as follows:

> "Subject to the buyer entering into an unconditional agreement to sell the buyer's property at 123 Main Street, Anywhere, Saskatchewan, by _____. This condition is for the sole benefit of the buyer.

> However, the seller may, upon receipt of another acceptable offer, deliver a written notice to the buyer or the buyer's agent [enter name of the buyer's agent and company name] requiring the buyer to remove all conditions from the contract within 12/24/48/72 hours [choose one] of the delivery of the notice. Should the buyer fail to remove all conditions before the expiry of the notice period, the contract will terminate, and all deposit monies will be returned in accordance with the Real Estate Act."

The portion of this clause from the word *However* on is known as the *time clause* (or *escape clause*). This clause is extremely important if you think that you may receive other offers while this buyer is trying to sell her home. The length of the notice period is negotiable and can be as short as 12 hours, but this puts a lot of pressure on the buyer, and you will find that many buyers won't agree to this. If you're in a seller's market, you'll want to keep the notice period as short as possible, because this will allow you to deal with a backup offer relatively quickly, if one comes in. From the buyer's point of view, the longer the notice period, the longer she'll have to arrange interim or bridge financing. And the longer she'll have to consider all her options, and the longer she'll have to sell her house.

If you need to invoke the time clause, you may want to get confirmation that the notice was actually delivered at a certain time. Although technically this isn't necessary to make the notice valid and enforceable, it helps keep everyone clear on the process. The delivery can be witnessed by someone, or the buyer or the buyer's agent can sign a copy of the notice to acknowledge receiving it. At this point, there is no negotiating and you're just waiting to see who will buy your home. The notice to invoke the time clause will look like this:

> "This notice constitutes written notice from the seller to the buyer requiring the removal of all conditions (or condition) from this contract within (24/48/72) hours or this contract will terminate at the end of the (24/48/72) hour period and the deposit will be returned to the buyer. This time clause will start running on delivery of this notice to the buyer or [the buyer's real estate agency], which will be at _____ o'clock a.m./p.m. on (date), 20__. Therefore, the [24/48/72] hours will terminate at _____ o'clock a.m./p.m. on [date], 20__."

In some provinces, you may have to exclude Saturdays, Sundays, and statutory holidays from the time clause. In this case, the clause will read "24/48/72 hours, excluding Saturdays, Sundays, and statutory holidays." Your agent or lawyer will know local provincial regulations.

Escape clauses

Another category of "subject to" clauses depends on a third party or requires the approval of one party to the contract. These *third party subject clauses* are often called *escape clauses* or *whim and fancy clauses,* because either party can simply withhold approval and walk away from the contract.

One of the most obvious escape clauses is *subject to a relative or friend reviewing the contract.* This is very ambiguous and hard to enforce, and you should do everything you can to avoid such a condition. Another escape clause is *subject to the buyer obtaining financial advice.* The buyer should have received financial advice before writing the contract — this is an extremely obvious escape hatch, and may indicate a buyer who isn't serious.

You or your agent should recognize escape clauses and try to keep them to a minimum, and where they're necessary, keep the timeframe as short as possible. Generally, a contract with an escape clause is unenforceable until the subject is removed.

Clauses introduced by the seller

Few vendors are concerned with what happens to the property after it has been sold. However, in some cases the vendor may want to place restrictions or obligations on the new owners of the property. For example, when history buffs and activists Pierre and Marie decided to sell their Vieux Quebec home, which had narrowly missed being designated a Canadian heritage site, they wanted to stipulate in the contract of purchase and sale that the new owners respect the home's historical significance. So they introduced a clause stating that the new owners were forbidden to undertake any major additions or renovations to the original structure other than restorative projects to preserve the character and historical importance of the building. However, most covenants of this sort come with the land and aren't the prerogative of the seller to introduce. Remember, too, that a clause of this nature will in many cases severely limit the number of interested buyers who will consider purchasing your home.

If your property has municipal or provincial conditions restricting the use of the property, they should be clearly outlined in the contract to protect you from any future actions by the buyer. If you aren't in an unusual position like the one mentioned above, and there were no restrictions or obligations placed on you when you bought the property, you shouldn't attempt to introduce these sorts of clauses.

Subject to seller's purchase

A clause that you as a seller may need to include is a *subject to purchase* clause. This condition stipulates that the buyer's offer to purchase will be accepted only if the seller's offer to purchase another home is in turn accepted.

For example, Lars and Jorge wanted to sell their house, but only if they could get the house of their dreams. They did find one house that fit the bill, but their offer, subject to the sale of their own house, was rejected. The couple decided that in such a busy market, they had better list their house and keep an eye on their dream home. After a couple of weeks, Lars and Jorge got an offer on their house, and notified the prospective buyers that they would sell only if they could come to an agreement on their dream house. The buyers appreciated the advance warning and were in no rush, so they accepted the "subject to purchase" clause. It was written into the contract of purchase and sale as follows:

> "Subject to the seller entering into an unconditional agreement to purchase the property at _____ by _____. This condition is for the sole benefit of the seller."

"Subject to purchase" clauses aren't very common, and in a situation like Lars and Jorge's, letting the buyer know the seller's plans in advance is always a good idea so that the buyer won't be surprised to see a seller's condition added to the contract.

What's included — fixtures and chattels

Anything that is fixed to the structure of your home (known as a *fixture*) is assumed to be included in the purchase price unless otherwise stated. Anything movable — appliances, furniture, and the like, known as *chattels* — is assumed to be excluded from the sale. Nonetheless, in some provinces, appliances are typically included in the sale price. Find out early in the process what the conventions are for your area. Now is the time to exclude from the sale anything buyers may think they'll be getting, whether it's your fabulous new and astonishingly silent dishwasher, or the antique chandelier from your great-grandmother. Conversely, removing that beautiful chandelier and replacing it with something suitable may prevent a lot of squabbling later.

The contract of purchase and sale will list exactly what is, and what is not, included in the sale. How would you like to buy a home in Moose Jaw and take possession in February only to discover the furnace had been ripped out of the basement? These kinds of events aren't common, but they have been known to happen. Clearly this section of the contract is of greater importance to the purchaser — the one likely to get the short end of the stick. But you need to do a quick review of this section as well, just to ensure that everything you want to take with you will still be yours come moving day.

Time frame of the offer, or "irrevocable date"

The time frame of the offer is one of the most important elements of your contract of purchase and sale. This element states that the offer is valid only for a certain length of time. If this length of time expires before the offer is accepted, the offer is null and void and the deposit is returned to the purchaser unless both parties agree to extend the time for acceptance.

The *completion date* is the date on which the buyer pays his money and has the house registered in his name. The *possession date* is the date the buyer assumes possession of the property. If all conditions have not been met by the *subject removal date,* the offer can be withdrawn and the transaction terminated.

Pay extremely close attention to these dates. Most contracts hold the vendor responsible for the property until the completion date. If a fire ravages your home the day before the completion date, it's *your* problem. From 12:01 a.m. on the completion date, the property and all included items are at the risk of the buyer. The buyer will actually have insurance on the house hours before the house is registered in his name.

Arrange to have your insurance policies terminated on the closing date, and not before. If possible, avoid the last day of a month or year as a closing date. These are busy days for banks, creditors, insurance providers, and most administrative staff that will be involved in processing the new information generated by the sale. This means you're at an increased risk of otherwise avoidable delays in registering the sale of your home.

If you have rental units

The contract of purchase and sale becomes considerably more complex if your home has rental units and your buyer intends to continue renting out these parts of your property. This aspect is typically a larger headache for the buyer than for the seller. However, if you have tenants at the time of sale, be prepared for some extra hassle. For example, if you live in Ontario, you'll have to sign a statement to the effect that you're charging a legal rent. If it turns out you aren't charging a legal rent, you're in trouble not only with your tenants but also with your buyer. The possible obstacles are far too case-specific for us to deal with here — so all we can do is give you some general advice.

If you have a rental unit and are selling to a buyer who intends to continue the tradition, speak to your agent or lawyer about the legal and contractual consequences *before* signing the contract of purchase and sale. If you're getting close to an agreement on price and you want to keep negotiating, you can go ahead and accept the offer, but make it subject to consulting with your lawyer if you have concerns. In many parts of the country, a copy of the rental agreement may become an addendum or schedule to the contract. If the buyer wants to terminate the tenancy, the buyer will request in the contract that the seller give legal and binding termination notice to the tenants in accordance with the provincial tenancy legislation.

A pinch of acceptance

This final section of the contract is quite simple. When the contract has been negotiated to your and the buyer's satisfaction, all that remains is to sign on the dotted line (as well as fill in the appropriate dates and seals), and accept the offer subject to the terms and conditions outlined. You must make sure that both parties have initialled any changes made to the contract and that all signatures have been witnessed where necessary.

Especially for Condo Owners

The legal workings of selling a condominium are slightly different than those for selling a house. First of all, condos may have separate standard legal forms. In essence, these forms are similar to the standard contract of purchase and sale for a house — both kinds of forms cover the details of the offer, the conditions of sale, and the acceptance. But two very important elements are specific to condominium sale contracts: the financial status of the condominium corporation and its bylaws. In many areas you use the standard forms, and then add the condo clauses just as you would add financing clauses to the contract.

In most provinces, these details are included in a document known as the *condominium certificate, estoppel certificate, information certificate,* or *status certificate*. It lists the expenses for a specified unit, discusses the status of the complex in its entirety, explains the regulations and procedures for the administration of the complex, outlines the rules governing the behaviour of residents and the corporation, and stipulates all financial obligations. Refer to Chapter 5 for more on this important document.

Making sure your buyer has had a chance to carefully review the condominium certificate or equivalent documentation before removing the subjects from the offer is extremely important. The buyer's lawyer can also review any aspect of the information package that concerns the buyer. The lawyer may also want a copy of the building's insurance policy to make sure the building has adequate coverage.

Is everything in order?

In B.C., under the Strata Property Act, the strata corporation (the condominium corporation) prepares a package for the seller or the seller's agent to give to potential buyers. This package, usually put together by the property manager of the condominium, includes

✔ An information certificate

✔ Current financial statements and bylaws for the building

✔ Minutes from the building's meetings for the past year or two

✔ Any rules or regulations regarding the use of the suite

All of these items are specified in the contract, and the offer is subject to the buyer receiving and approving all of these documents.

Check with your province's Condominium Act, or ask your agent, to see what the condominium corporation must provide for the seller in your province.

As a vendor, you can anticipate your buyer's request to see the condominium certificate by ensuring your agent has a copy of all relevant papers, and by providing copies to potential buyers at showings. You must make all these documents available to the buyer, and if you can provide everything promptly, it may help to solidify a trusting relationship with potential buyers and speed up the process. The condominium corporation must provide you with a copy, but it often takes quite a while to process requests. The moral of the story is, send in your written request for all the required documents well in advance. Keep in mind that fees may be attached when ordering these documents, if in fact they're coming from a building management company.

Your buyer will also be interested in the state of the condominium corporation's *reserve fund*. This is the fund that supplies money for structural repairs and any renovations or work needed on the complex. This information is generally contained in the condominium certificate or the financial statements for the building. Your agent will need this information as she presents your suite to potential buyers. You can win points with potential buyers by being knowledgeable about the status of the corporation and the procedure if repairs are needed on the building.

Deeds and Titles

You've got some great buyers lined up who plan to keep feeding the hummingbirds that hang out in your garden. Oh, and they've also offered you a great price for your home. Time to call the moving truck, right? Well, before you sign the contract and hand them the keys (and the bird feeders), you have to prove to them what it is you really own — and then legally transfer this ownership to them. You may think of that gurgling stream out back as yours, but is it your property? Do you owe anything to anyone in relation to your house? You're not off on the road to your fabulous new home yet — but read this section, and you soon will be.

Conveyance

The process of transferring ownership is known as *conveyance*. When you sell your home, whether it's a house or a condo, your lawyer prepares a legal document called a *deed*. The deed certifies that all the conditions of sale have been met, and transfers ownership of the property to your buyer. A deed may not always transfer full ownership; it may transfer partial ownership, or any other specified interest in the land.

We found *Duhaime's Law Dictionary* to be an indispensable online source of legal terminology — the definitions are reader-friendly, and it's free! Visit the Web site (`www.duhaime.org`) to look up any legal terms you find baffling.

Any claims or encumbrances against a property, such as Crown grants or rights-of-way, can also be transferred along with ownership. The term *conveyance* also applies to the transfer of these encumbrances. When your lawyer has dealt with all aspects of conveyance, the information becomes collectively known as the *title* to the property. The title identifies the property and the owner of the property, and lists any debts or claims against the property.

All the transfer of title information has to be registered with your province (generally at a provincial land titles office) in order to guarantee that you will no longer be held responsible for that property. The drafting of the conveyance documents is the responsibility of the buyer. When the documents are submitted for registration, the buyer is issued a *certificate of title,* and you no longer have any claim to the property.

Usually the buyer (or, more precisely, the buyer's lawyer) is responsible for doing the title search. The title search ensures that you do, legally, own the property and that no debts or claims exist against it that you haven't disclosed. Many provincial registry offices are now automated and keep original documents only on microfilm. Those that still keep paper documentation don't allow original documents to be removed from the registry office. If your property is more than 100 years old, the original documents may have been archived. Restricted access to documents means that your lawyer and your buyer's lawyer may have to meet in the local registry office to perform some of the necessary tasks.

Land registries

Just as the various provinces and territories support distinct real estate laws, they also support many different systems of land registration across the country. It is not always the same department or division of government that is responsible for registering land titles. For example, in Alberta, Land Registries is a division of Alberta Municipal Affairs, and in Saskatchewan it is the newly formed Saskatchewan Land Information Services Corporation that is the registration agency. In the Northwest Territories it's the Legal Registries division of the Department of Justice, and in Newfoundland and Labrador it is the Commercial Registrations division of Government Services and Lands.

Different provinces and territories have divided the land differently. This means that the identification information for your property will take a form dictated by your provincial government. If you desperately want to know exactly how it works in your area, you can contact your provincial or territorial government, or the land surveyors' association, but there's no pressing need to be an expert on systems of land registration.

You do, however, need to know about the documents that are typically required for registration. In all cases, these include the *transfer deed* (prepared to change the registered ownership of the home) and your *mortgage discharge statement* (instructing your lawyer regarding the paying of applicable funds back to the bank). If your buyer is assuming your mortgage, you must register the conveyance and your buyer must register the new mortgage on the property, as well as any new rights-of-way or minor easements for utilities. In those cases involving properties with outstanding debts or claims, these must be registered or *discharged* as well (if they have not been already). And should an up-to-date survey be required, it may be registered too.

Almost every registration or service provided by your local registry office comes with a separate charge. Registering the transfer of land usually entails a base fee plus $1 or $2 per every $1,000 of the value of your home. For example, if your home sold for $250,000, you may have to pay a $35 base charge plus $250 to register the transfer deed. Registration of a mortgage discharge will carry a separate fee, as will the survey plan and any other documents. If you need to obtain copies of official documents, you'll have to purchase them, usually for around $10 a copy. The cost of any registrations that your lawyer makes on your behalf will filter down to you as disbursements — in other words, you'll pay for them as part of your legal bill. When you get a quote from a lawyer for your conveyance, make sure the price includes all fees and disbursements.

Clearly, the registration of some of these documents falls to your buyer. However, they may become of interest to you if the documentation for your title to the land was not registered properly.

Western Canada primarily uses the Torrens System of land registration. This system holds that regardless of the existence or status of any previous titles, the certificate of title that you possess is *indefeasible*. This means that so long as you have a certificate of title, ownership of your land can't be taken away from you under any circumstances. Claims, debts, or other ownership issues not spelled out in your certificate are irrelevant to your title.

In other parts of the country, your title must be validated before you can transfer it to another party. If there happen to be any previous titles with unresolved ownership issues, these can affect your right to ownership. The Torrens System was adopted to make the validation of titles unnecessary, and therefore to make transfers of titles simpler and easier to record. But even under the Torrens System, there can be hindrances to a smooth title transfer.

Chapter 22

Negotiating Tricks and Bargaining Chips

*H*ammering out a final deal with the buyer of your home involves several elements. Yes, price will be the first thing on your mind, but pay attention to other key details, such as the possession date, conditional clauses and their expiry dates, the extras you'll include in the sale (chattels like your washer and dryer), and the amount of the buyer's cash deposit (we discuss all of these items in Chapter 21). Everything is negotiable, so have a clear idea of what is most important to you and be flexible in everything else.

Set the Stage to Negotiate the Offer

Ideally, all property owners should be present when you're negotiating an offer to purchase because all signatures are required to seal the deal. If you and your spouse (or your sibling, or parent, or other partner) jointly hold the title to your home, then both of you should be at the negotiations. Turn the ringers off the phones, and keep children and pets out of the way.

Make yourselves comfortable for the negotiation; it may take a while. You may want to have some snacks handy, but you'll want to steer clear of alcohol entirely. Believe it or not, the contract of purchase and sale may be deemed null and void if the buyer is under the influence of drugs or alcohol when signing it (likewise, if your buyer's proven to be insane, coerced with force, or underage!).

Keep Your Eye on the Prize: What's Really Important

You love your home. You may have raised your kids there and decorated it to your taste and style, making it a reflection of you. And we know you're a wonderful person, so who in their right mind won't love your home too? Imagine your horror when you find out that the couple making an offer on your home want to rip out everything — the red velvet wallpaper and even the orange shag carpet! You may feel so offended that you want to throw their offer in the garbage, but if the dates are perfect, the offer is subject only to inspection, and their initial deposit is a fair starting point, you'd better give the negotiations a try.

Remember that the point here is to sell your home — for a fair value, as quickly and simply as possible. Just because your potential buyer doesn't appreciate your retro tastes doesn't mean that a deal can't be reached. No one-size-fits-all negotiating strategy exists, but you should have an unemotional, businesslike game plan that allows you to make rational decisions as you go through the buying and selling process. Unfortunately, your buyer may not share your negotiating style and approach. Try not to take the proceedings personally. You're working on a business deal, and you share a common goal — the buyer wants to have your home, and you want her to buy it, at least if the price is right. If you've received a fair offer from the buyer, put personalities aside and deal with the terms of the offer!

Work out your strategy in advance, taking into account whether you're in a buyer's or a seller's market, and therefore whether you're negotiating from a position of relative weakness or strength. (Refer to Chapter 14 for market definitions.) If you're negotiating in a buyer's market, purchase offers can be scarce and you may have to take a lower price for your home than you had hoped for. In a seller's market, you may be able to capitalize on the competitive conditions and hold out for a bigger and better offer if your negotiations go poorly.

Even the most stoic of sellers may find themselves getting worked up at the negotiating table. Stay cool, and act calm. You're making big decisions here, and you don't want to do anything rash. This is particularly important if you're selling privately, because you won't have an agent at your side to help you stay unflustered and objective. Try to keep in mind that if you're selling in a buyer's market, you may have to accept less than what you hoped for. But when you turn around and buy, you'll likely be able to take advantage of the same conditions.

The Negotiating Process

In reality, the first step you'll take as a seller in the negotiating process is setting the asking price for your home. (Refer to Chapter 15 for more on setting the price.) Whether or not you're using a real estate agent, your asking price lays the groundwork for the selling process. The asking price can affect how many offers you receive and how long your home remains on the market, and is the springboard from which you'll dive into the deep and murky waters of conditions, terms, and clauses.

Don't negotiate until you get a written offer. And don't sign *anything* until you've consulted with your real estate agent or your real estate lawyer (or notary public, if you live in Quebec). You need a professional to make sure the contract is legally binding and the terms and conditions represent you properly. This is tricky stuff. If you have even a signature in the wrong spot, the contract may be null and void.

Don't dismiss early offers. Houses often generate the best offers earliest in the process when they're fresh on the market . . . and you never know when, or if, the next serious offer will come. Sometimes your first offer is your best offer. Remember that an offer represents an opening bid to start negotiations. Both the buyer and the seller want the same thing: the best possible price and terms of sale. Each party can make certain concessions and certain gains.

The offer may seem to be overly detailed and specific, but to ensure you have a binding contract with no misunderstandings, every detail should be written into your purchase agreement. Including little things like remote garage door openers in the contract may seem silly, but it's those little things that can drive you crazy if they're not clearly specified in writing.

When you get an offer, your options are to accept it, reject it, or *sign it back,* that is, return it to the buyer with a counteroffer proposing a different price or different terms. Review the offer with respect to each of the following considerations.

Count on the counteroffer

After her husband passed away, Mary realized that she didn't need the large family home that they had lived in for the last 20 years. In a buyer's market in Vancouver, she listed the home for $1,695,000 (not outrageous in Vancouver, by any means).

About a month later, a couple who had visited the home several times submitted an offer that was more than $300,000 below the asking price.

Infuriated and insulted, Mary told her agent that there was no sense in responding to the offer. But her agent convinced her that she shouldn't take the number on the contract personally, and that she should counter. Sure enough, the buyer came up in price by almost $250,000. After some more negotiating, with concessions made on both sides, the final sale price was $50,000 below the list price, a substantial difference from the initial offer.

Knowing how low you will go

First and foremost, we're all interested in the prices we pay for our purchases. Your home isn't just a purchase, though; it's an investment — and if you've cared well for your home, you should hopefully be able to make a profit when it comes time to sell the place. Determining what your home is worth in the current housing market takes a bit of analysis. In Chapter 15 we provide you with detailed information on estimating a realistic sale price for your home. But after you've figured out your listing price, you also need to decide what is the lowest offer you'll accept.

Remember that the initial offer is the buyer's starting point, just as the list price is your initial bargaining position.

Entertain any and every offer you receive. Don't reject anything out of hand, unless your lawyer or real estate agent strongly advises you to do so; make a few changes to the agreement and counter your buyer's offered price. If a buyer is interested enough to write up the paperwork, you have a better-than-decent chance of negotiating a price you're willing to accept.

Remember that negotiating requires give and take. If you don't give buyers an idea of your flexibility, they won't take the time or effort to pursue an agreement. A buyer may be truly interested in getting your house, but may put in an offer that cuts $25,000 off the asking price. Don't tear it up; he may be following the "You can't blame a guy for trying" philosophy. The response to your counteroffer may surprise you by being, "Yeah, okay."

Negotiating the "subject to" clauses: "Only if you promise to . . ."

"Subject to" clauses are a buyer's safety hatch — a way to escape the contract of purchase and sale if something goes wrong. If a buyer needs to sell her home before she can afford to buy yours, she may make her offer "subject to sale," meaning that her offer to buy your home will be confirmed only when she's been able to secure the sale of her own current residence. (Refer to Chapter 21 for details.) Here are three of the most common clauses on an offer to purchase:

- ✔ **"Subject to financing" clause:** This type of clause doesn't offer much room for negotiation. A buyer can't remove this subject clause during the offer/counteroffer process, unless perhaps he has a lot of equity and doesn't really need a mortgage, or requires a small and easy-to-get fast mortgage. Remember, if the buyer didn't need a mortgage, he likely wouldn't have made the offer subject to financing in the first place. You can try to negotiate a shorter time limit for the buyer to arrange his mortgage, however. Often too, a buyer who uses this clause will have a pre-approved mortgage — it's usually only a matter of an appraisal to have the mortgage finalized. If this is the case, then allowing the buyer this clause may put you in a better position to negotiate other things.

- ✔ **"Subject to inspection" clause:** This clause is commonly included in a buyer's offer to purchase a home. Because it should take no more than two or three days to arrange an inspection, this is an easy clause to negotiate. As with the "subject to financing" clause, though, you can try to negotiate a shorter time period for the inspection's completion to speed things up. Most inspectors can deliver a copy of the inspection report at the end of the inspection. (Keep in mind that most buyers won't want to pay for an inspection until they have their financing in place. Why inspect something if it turns out that you can't buy it?)

- ✔ **"Subject to sale" clause:** This clause can be negotiated with regard to the length of time you give your buyer to sell her current home. Any buyer who already owns a home probably can't afford to carry the expense of two homes at once. You have to be reasonable here. No matter how anxious you are to move, allow the buyer a decent amount of time to list and sell her home. Usually four to six weeks is considered fair, and (depending on how badly you want to sell to this particular buyer) you can agree to extend the time period if she can't meet the original deadline.

In conjunction with the "subject to sale" clause, also include a time clause to keep your options open. If you're waiting for your buyer to secure financing or sell his residence, your time clause can release you to pursue another offer that arrives in the meantime.

The time clause gives the first buyer a specified time period to remove all the "subject to" conditions from the contract and close the sale. If the first buyer can't remove all the subjects in time, your time clause releases you from the contract and allows you to pursue other offers. Refer to Chapter 21 for more about the time clause.

If you extend the "subject to sale" clause, you'll probably have to extend the completion and possession dates stated on the contract of purchase and sale. Whatever dates you choose, they'll probably change when your buyer has a buyer for her own house. Your closing date for the sale may depend on your buyer's yet-to-be-negotiated closing dates on the sale of her house.

If you've found a house you really want to purchase after selling your own, you can try to add a *subject to purchase* clause that makes your home's sale conditional on whether you can still get the house you want. But be prepared: Your buyer may not be happy with this condition and may not accept its inclusion in the contract. This clause isn't at all common, but in some situations it can give you peace of mind that you won't be homeless if your dream house was snatched up before you had a chance to sell.

If you're selling a condominium, you may encounter a *subject to viewing condominium bylaws and financial statements* clause. In many provinces, the law requires that a condominium corporation provide the buyer with full information on the condo complex and its regulations. Your buyer must acknowledge in writing that the information's been received and approved. You won't have too many negotiating points here, except for the time frame and how far back into the building's history the buyer wants to go.

Expect some regional differences and extra information to be required in different parts of the country. For example, around Vancouver (where there have been a number of leaky condominiums), the buyer may ask for any engineering reports or building envelope studies that are available (or for rainscreen warranty information if the building has been repaired), and the seller must provide the information to the buyer.

In most provinces, when a "subject to" condition in the contract of purchase and sale has been met, it's formally removed from the contract with a written *waiver, amendment,* or *condition removal form*. These legal documents are usually signed by both parties (the buyer and the seller) to confirm that a condition has been fulfilled and is no longer part of the offer.

Including appliances and household decor: "I never liked those drapes anyway"

Anything permanently attached to the property is considered to be part of the package. So any built-in cabinets, built-in appliances, or wall decorations — legally considered *fixtures* — are things you'll be leaving behind for the next owners. Anything portable (*chattels*), on the other hand, is yours to keep, if you want it. Under this logic, the drapes are still yours, but the tracks they hang from aren't; Grandma Bertha's bedside lamp comes with you to your new home, but the beautiful chandelier in the entrance hall belongs to the new owners.

Anything portable that you *do* want to leave behind (the drapes, the refrigerator, the pool-cleaning accessories you won't need in your new condo) must be written into the contract specifically and listed item by item. Something else to keep in mind, though: Anything you *don't* want to leave behind is best removed before showing the house at all. If you can't do that, be sure to make it clear to everyone who walks through the door that those items are not part of the deal. You don't want prospective buyers to fall in love with an antique light fixture that you'd never consider parting with and make an offer that turns on whether or not it's included in the sale. And build *everything* (exceptions and inclusions) into the property section of the contract. If you include a built-in vacuum system, make sure you also include the attachments and powerhead for the system.

Even if you plan to include portable items in the sale of your home, do it at the last minute. If the portable items are listed in the contract right from the start, they don't seem like bonuses when you're negotiating, because potential buyers will try to talk down your price anyway. If you wait until *after* a buyer tries to talk you down, including the washer and dryer may appease him as much as lowering the price.

Don't include any leased items as part of the sale. Many companies lease security systems and water filtration systems, and if they're left with the house, the buyer will be charged. The last thing the buyer wants is to get a bill for a security system she thought she'd bought outright with the house. Specify in writing that the buyer agrees to assume the lease on the security system if there is a lease.

Buyers may also specify that certain items be *removed* as a condition of the offer. Some people just don't want the brown and gold linoleum and faux-wood panelling greeting them on moving day. Some buyers make big requests. For example, you may receive an offer $5,000 below your asking price and with the condition that you remove the shag carpeting. Part of your negotiations will include figuring out the buyer's priorities. Is he just looking for any excuse to cut the price? Is he willing to budge on the rug? As a concession, you may agree to remove the rug but cut less off the price. Or you can try dropping your price and leaving the rug with the property. Your agent or lawyer won't recommend any substantial changes to your home before closing — just in case your home doesn't close for some reason — but, hey, if your buyer insists that if you remove all the tacky light fixtures, he'll agree with the price of your counteroffer, you can probably agree to remove those lights.

Deciding on the closing date

After having spent a couple of hours reviewing the price, the subjects, and all the inclusions and exclusions, the dates may seem relatively minor. Give yourself a breather from the contract, and then refocus. The dates will be the most important factor when moving time comes around. If you can negotiate a sensible and relaxed set of dates now, your move will be much easier at a time when stress will be at an all-time high. Again, if you can get ideal dates scheduled, you may drop a little bit off the price in return for the buyer's flexibility.

The *closing date* (or *completion date*) is the day when the money changes hands and the title is conveyed to the buyer. The *possession date* is the day you receive (or give) the keys to the other party. The *adjustment date* is the day that property taxes, condominium fees, and any other annual municipal fees and utility bills are adjusted to. These last two dates should be one and the same: You get the keys, you start paying the bills.

Of course, sometimes people surprise you

Jed and Daisy were being relocated to the southern U.S. and needed to list and sell their home fast. They didn't have a chance to clean up the really big problems around their house, like the car-on-cinder-block flower planters in the front yard. So they trimmed, weeded, watered, and crossed their fingers. Most of the prospective buyers turned around without even getting out of their cars, and Jed and Daisy were just about ready to give up. But — surprise! — the next couple to view the house weren't put off by the dead car museum out front. In fact, they asked that it be included in the sale contract! You just never know when someone like Spyder and the missus will want to keep what you can't bear to take with you.

Ideally, give yourself a one- or two-day overlap where you have the keys for your new house as well as the keys for the house you've sold. The following would be a perfect scenario, starting on a hypothetical Monday:

- **Monday:** Completion date on your present house (that you are selling).

- **Tuesday:** Completion date on the house you're buying.

- **Wednesday:** This is the possession and adjustment date for the house you're buying. You get the keys for the house you're buying at noon (the usual time of key transfer) unless you negotiated an earlier time.

- **Thursday:** This is the possession and adjustment date for the buyers of your house. You give the keys to the buyers of your old house at noon.

This scenario gives you a chance to have a relaxing move, and still go back to clean up your old house Thursday morning before you give the keys to the buyers of your old home. The downside is that the buyers pay their money on Monday but don't get their keys until Thursday noon. This is fairly common in some provinces, and for the right price, the buyers will accept the dates after they have negotiated with you on all the terms of the agreement. In other provinces such as Ontario, it's common to have the closing date and the possession date as the same day. If this is the case, it may be worth arranging interim/bridge financing to close the house you're buying a couple of days before your present home's closing date so that you don't have to store all your possessions, especially if something is delayed.

Discuss with your real estate agent or your lawyer how many days you'll need for the closing. If you're working with a real estate agent, you may still want one or two days to run the contract by a lawyer. In some provinces, legal documents can't be signed on Sundays or statutory holidays.

The *transfer of title* officially closes the contract when you file the paperwork at the land titles office. These offices are typically open from 9:00 a.m. to 3:00 p.m. weekdays, though in some provinces they keep longer hours and filing can be done electronically. If at all possible, don't even try to officially close two contracts on the same day. (If you must, make sure both sides of the transaction are aware of the situation, and have a contingency plan discussed with your legal team.) Leave at least one day to close the sale of your current house and transfer money before you go back down to the land titles office to close the purchase of your next house. (Refer to Chapter 13.)

Racing against the clock: Open for acceptance until . . .

When you realize how many changes can be made to the contract, you may find you'll need more time to reach an agreement. If both you and the buyer agree, the offer can be extended until an agreement is reached on all the terms. If the offer expires before you reach full agreement with the buyer, it should be rewritten with a new time frame for acceptance.

Signing on the dotted lines

Both the buyer and the seller have to sign the contract, and usually have their signatures witnessed on each page. In some jurisdictions, having one page of the contract signed and witnessed (such as the first page or third page), and then having both parties initial the bottom of every page, is sufficient. Your agent or lawyer can advise you on the proper way to sign or initial the contract.

Multiple Offers

If you're lucky enough to be selling your home in a red-hot seller's market, you may get competing offers on your home. This embarrassment of riches has to be treated carefully to ensure you get the offer you want in place without selling the house to two different people.

Keep these guidelines and practices in mind to ensure everything goes smoothly:

- ✔ **Keep everyone informed.** If more than one buyer is interested in your home, making sure everyone is kept up to date when offers are starting to be written is in your best interest. In the ideal scenario for the seller, the buyers enter into a bidding contest and pay up to, or more than, the asking price.

- ✔ **Act in good faith.** Many buyers won't compete with another buyer when making an offer. Remember that what's good for the seller isn't always good for the buyer. If a seller tries to get greedy and delay one offer hoping to get a second competitive offer and cause a bidding war, this plan may backfire and both potential buyers may cancel their offers.

Imagine Ken and Sue list their fabulous heritage house for sale. It's a hot seller's market, meaning buyers outnumber sellers, and the low inventory of homes means Ken and Sue should get close to their $499,000 asking price.

Buyers A, B, and C all see the house the first day it's listed for sale, and all come to the same conclusion: The house is gorgeous, the house is well priced, and they want it.

Ken, Sue, and their agent get together to review the offers. Buyer A is the first to notify the listing agent that she has an offer, so her offer is presented first, followed by the offers from B and C. Before making changes to any offer, Ken and Sue discuss all three offers with their agent and decide which offer has the most potential. Buyer C is offering $475,000, which is all he can afford. Both A and B are offering the full price of $499,000, with similar terms and conditions.

Ken and Sue decide to deal with offers A and B. A's offer is $499,000 and subject only to inspection. The dates are perfect, and the $50,000 deposit is attractive. B's offer is $499,000, but it's subject to financing (with B stretching to afford the price) and inspection, with a $25,000 deposit.

Ken and Sue have a couple of options: They can choose to accept one offer as is, or with minor changes that both parties agree to, and hope that the conditions go through and the contract is fulfilled. Or, they can reject both offers as presented and ask A and B to present better offers and hope for an even more advantageous offer. In the end, Ken and Sue decide to accept A's offer. But they actually have a third option: Accept B's offer as a *backup offer*.

Backup offers

In some provinces, a second offer can be accepted as a backup offer, subject to the collapse of the first offer. Your agent or lawyer will advise you what is acceptable in your province. The offer is worded something like this:

> "This is a backup offer only and is subject to the seller being released by the buyer from all obligations under the previously accepted Contract of Purchase and Sale by _____, 20__. This condition is for the benefit of the seller."

Looking at Ken and Sue's situation again, they could accept B's offer as a backup offer subject to A's offer collapsing. B has nothing to lose by being a backup offer for a couple of days while A has an inspection done. If A isn't thrilled by the inspection, then B has the chance to purchase the house, subject to her own inspection and financing. If A buys the house, then B's offer won't proceed and B will get any initial deposit money returned to her.

The other common situation for a backup offer is when the buyer has added a "subject to sale" clause to the offer and a second offer comes in, subject to the collapse of the first offer. In this scenario, the first offer should have a time clause in it, giving the buyer 24, 48, or 72 hours (or whatever was negotiated) to remove all subjects from the contract. If the seller gets a second acceptable offer, the seller gives written notice to the buyer who placed the first offer to remove all subjects within the prescribed time frame, or step aside so that the backup offer will be the offer in effect. An example invoking the time clause can be found in Chapter 21.

In the best of both worlds, the seller wants to sell at the listing price and the buyer wants to buy at the originally offered price. Negotiating is what falls in between.

Part VII
The Part of Tens

The 5th Wave   By Rich Tennant

"Now, Rex. When the listing said 'Plenty of room for pet,' I think it was referring to the back yard."

In this part . . .

There are all sorts of folk traditions around setting up house. You'll find some entertaining lists here, as well as practical advice on making your new house a safe and well-maintained home. We've also compiled information on a host of regional issues that may affect you, depending on where you live.

Chapter 23

Ten Regional Concerns When Buying a Home

- -

In This Chapter

▶ Keeping abreast of developments in the big city

▶ Being aware of considerations for rural homeowners

- -

*F*or a country with a population smaller than the state of California's, Canada takes up a lot of space. Just think of all the differences in our provinces and territories, from the temperate climate of Vancouver, British Columbia, to the frigid conditions of Inuvik, Northwest Territories. The incredible variety in this huge country of ours can make homeownership very different from region to region. Moving to a new part of Canada can be the best thing you'll ever do. But before you peel off your "I Love Toronto" bumper sticker and head for Trout Creek, or ditch your one-horse town for the bright lights of Halifax, keep these tips in mind.

Check Transportation Routes in Cities

The fact that a city has a public transportation system doesn't necessarily mean that everyone in the city can get from point A to point B with ease. When researching an urban property, go online to check out the city's transit system. Finding out what times buses, trains, streetcars, and even ferries run can make a huge difference in where you plan to live. If the townhouse you've got your eye on has streetcar access only, realize that getting anywhere may take you longer than it would from a property with bus or subway access. If you move to a suburb outside of the city and have to be at your place of employment at 6:00 a.m., you can find yourself out of luck if the train or bus service doesn't start until 5:30 a.m.

Be Cautious about Industrial Sites

You've probably heard plenty of horror stories about people developing all kinds of illnesses that turn out to be directly related to emissions from the factory half a kilometre away, or to the pollutants contained in that dumping ground over the hill. If your new home is anywhere near large power generators, factories, or dump sites, or on reclaimed industrial land, start by doing some research in the back issues of the local paper. Have there been any articles, disputes, or series of letters to the editor about the industrial site? Next, seriously consider getting the soil and water of your new home tested, especially if you're going to be using well water. That's where pollutants leaching into your property will likely turn up.

Stay Away from Major Roads if You're Noise-Sensitive (Or Nose-Sensitive)

If you commute, buying into that new subdivision along the highway can be extremely tempting. But before you do, get the whole family to do a sound check. Stand in the yard, close your eyes, and listen. Can you handle the level of noise you hear on a daily basis? Repeat the check in all rooms of the house, with the windows open and closed. The same rule applies for a property on any major road in a town or city. Constant traffic can become extremely disruptive to your sleep and relaxation. If your idea of the perfect summer afternoon is lounging in the backyard reading a book, or having friends over for a barbecue, having to wear earplugs to concentrate or yell to be heard may ruin the fun. Also, try to check the noise at different times of the day, and if possible see how loud the noise is in the evening when you may be trying to go to sleep. Next, do a smell check in your new neighbourhood. Vehicles on highways and busy roads can emit a lot of stinky exhaust that can affect the air quality of your region. Keep in mind that you may get a deal on a home that is in a noisy or smelly area, but when the time comes to sell, it may be an issue that puts off potential buyers.

Steer Clear of Emergency Routes

If you're moving into a town or city, being near a hospital can seem like a plus at first. After the first week, however, you may have heard more than your fill of ambulance sirens. The same goes for fire routes. Making some phone calls or checking online to see if that semi-detached is on a designated fire truck or ambulance route doesn't hurt.

Very noisy routes aren't always necessarily around the corner from the fire station or hospital. If you're on the only road that leads to the bridge dividing the town, you may be in line for some serious siren wailing.

Be Certain Your Street's on the Level

Melody found a beautiful house in a good area of a major city. However, she noticed something very odd — all the houses across the street looked significantly shorter than those on the side where she wanted to buy. In fact, it looked as though they had sunk partially into the ground!

Melody called her municipal Building Department, and they confirmed her observation. The houses on one side of the street had been built over an improperly filled gravel pit, and they had begun to sink some 30 years ago. The Building Department had on file the exact perimeter of the gravel pit, and it turned out that Melody's new house was on solid ground.

Even if your street looks picture-perfect, calling the Building Department is a good idea. They can tell you what was on your property before your house, when your house was built, and by whom. Even if your house is on the level, having that information on file is always beneficial.

Make Sure You're in a Good School Region

If you have children or are planning to have them in the next little while, do some research into the school *catchment area* for your new home. The catchment area is the geographical boundary that determines which children go to what school. Catchment maps are available online from the local school board or district. If you're outside the catchment area of the school you want your children to attend, contact the school. Sometimes children are permitted to enroll in a school outside their catchment area — but they may be outside the bus route (if in fact there is one), making you responsible for getting them to school and home again every day.

The Fraser Institute publishes annual Report Cards that rank and rate Canada's primary and secondary schools in British Columbia, Alberta, and Ontario, and secondary schools in Yukon and Quebec. If you want to know more, visit www.fraserinstitute.org and click "Report Cards."

Avoid Rainy-Day Regions if You're a Sun Worshipper

Anyone who has lived in Vancouver can tell you stories about the interminable stretches of rain. On the upside, living in a coastal area can be mild; when that sun *does* come out, you can play golf in December. So a little rain may be a setback you need to learn to live with. At the same time, you may love the hot, humid summer in Toronto, but can't stand the long, snowy, grey winters. Obviously something needs to give, so you need to do some research. Go online to find out about the average temperatures and precipitation in the area you've chosen. This being Canada, you may have to decide between umbrellas or snow shovels in December!

Watch Out for Waterways

There's no doubt about it: Homes by a river, lake, or stream can be real showstoppers. But the waterway can spread with a serious spring thaw, and your rosebushes may quickly become underwater plants. In the case of extreme rainfall or storms, you, your partner, and Spike the hamster may have to vacate. Local authorities (or the seller) can tell you if the property you're interested in has historically been prone to flooding. Find out whether the property is in a flood plain, because it can affect your ability to get home insurance. Also check that local planning regulations don't restrict development or future renovations near a stream that runs through a property. Many provincial stream protection acts exist, and they may substantially affect where you can build on a property that has a stream running through it. Also, water safety will be an extremely vital lesson to teach your children; after all, a potentially dangerous element will be a part of their backyard.

Research Services in Rural Areas

That charming lakefront cottage out on Rural Route 12 may seem to you like a promise of pastoral bliss, but there's a chance it can leave you in no man's land. Check with the town hall or your region's public works office to find out exactly what municipal services are available to the property. How often is garbage pickup? Is there any recycling pickup? Do you have an emergency 911 locator on the property? Is there snow removal on your road in the winter? Will you have to get propane delivery, or pay through the nose for electricity to heat your house? Much of this info may be found online — even rural areas maintain Web sites now — so you'll be able to find out a lot without having to pick up the phone.

Think Twice about Lease Land

Many recreational areas across Canada are built on lease land held by a provincial government or First Nations peoples. Typically, cottages or summer homes are built on this land. It is possible that your lease may not be extended, and you may not receive any compensation if you build your cottage or summer home on lease land. (Although compensation may have been stipulated in the lease, you may walk away with no compensation after a court dispute.)

Another possibility is being forced to pay a huge increase in your annual lease payments. For example, in Vancouver in the late 1990s about 75 lease-holders who were leasing Musqueam Band land saw their annual rent jump from $375 to $23,000. Ultimately, they took their dispute to the Supreme Court of Canada. The court's ruling forced the leaseholders to pay an average yearly rent of $10,500.

If you want to buy a property on lease land, do your research well. Have a lawyer carefully review all aspects of the lease, paying special attention to any escalation in lease payments, what may happen to the land, and any improvements at the end of the lease. Because of the uncertainty related to lease land, the price of a summer home or cottage will generally be lower than on freehold property, and lease land will always be harder to sell and finance than freehold land. So, although that lakefront property may be stunning, lease land requires careful investigation before putting your money down. Make sure that your lawyer studies the many variables that can apply to your newfound dream cottage on leased provincial land or First Nations land.

Chapter 24

Ten Tips for Condo Buyers

· ·

· ·

*C*ondominium comes from two Latin words: *con,* which means "with," and *dominium,* which means "ownership." And when you think about it, the name really fits what you're about to invest in. A condominium lets you take advantage of owning your own home, but it also lets you share this ownership with others.

But before you sign that offer and run off to a cocktail party to flaunt your new Latin skills, think of this: If you make an ill-informed decision, a condominium can make you suffer the very worst of both worlds. You can get locked into owning a cramped, restrictive unit, and you can be stuck in a bad building with irresponsible owners you can't stand.

The whole reason you want a condo is to get the best of both worlds, and we don't want you to end up with a lemon. So read these tips, and do some research into your prospective new home.

Insist on Documentation, and Read It as if Your New Life Depended on It

When your offer has been accepted, you should very quickly have in your possession a *condominium certificate* (also known as a *strata documentation package*), which contains different documents given different names from province to province. However, whatever package you get should include variations of a sample deed, a strata plan (equivalent to a land survey), homeowners' bylaws, and a budget. Make and keep a copy, and get the originals to your lawyer ASAP if you're not using an agent. Then, dive into everything yourself. This stuff is so boring it'll guarantee you a good night's sleep, but you must persevere and read it! You may find out that your silverpoint

Persian cats, Mutt and Jeff, aren't invited (or worse yet, maybe only one pet can come, and who can make that kind of choice?), or that your much-loved giant barbecue isn't permitted.

The condominium's financial status is of the utmost importance to you. If you read the financials and the minutes of meetings and notice that the building is due for a new roof, yet nothing is in the contingency fund to pay for repairs, you'll know that if you buy in you may find yourself paying a big assessment down the line. A well-managed condominium will have a financial plan that takes into account the building's future maintenance and repair costs.

Put It under a Microscope: Condos Need Inspections, Too

Buying a condo can be as big a financial commitment as buying a house. For this reason, get an inspector on your team before you remove the subjects from your offer to buy. The inspection should cover most of the same things that a standard home inspection would cover (as we detail in Chapter 12): the exterior upkeep of the building, the basement, the heating, water, and ventilation systems, and interior problems such as possible leakage in your unit.

Use Your Measuring Tape if You Buy New

That condo development so wonderfully close to your workplace is already zooming into sold-out status. The catch? It's not built yet. To get the condo of your dreams, you may have to invest in an unfinished project. But if you do, make sure you figure out the differences between the spacious, pristine model unit and your unit — the one that will be built from the floor plan that the condo developers have shoved into your hands.

This floor plan is also called a *condominium plan* (or *strata plan*) — the owner's equivalent to a land survey. The strata plan will give you the exact dimensions of your condo, as well as its situation in the building, the number of condos on your floor, and whether that beautiful bay window you'll have in your living room has north or south exposure. You should also get the strata plans for the parking areas, basement, laundry, gym, and any other parts of the building that you'll partly own.

Keep in mind that buying a condo before it's built means that you can have a wait on your hands. What happens if your new condo won't be ready for up to two years? Will you be prepared to sit it out? What if market conditions or your financial situation has changed? You may have fallen in love with that condo and entered into a contract when you were footloose and fancy free, but that one-bedroom condo may now be too small for you, your new husband, and the Great Dane puppy you just adopted.

Take a thorough look at your strata plan before you buy. It's not uncommon to hear people raving about how well laid out the floor plan of their new condo is — until they realize that they've bought a 900-square-foot two-bedroom that may be smaller than they expected. Figure out if the rooms in the unit will really be big enough for you. How does your prospective new condo's "spacious" master bedroom compare with your current, humble boudoir? You may be surprised to find that it may be significantly smaller.

Get to Know the Board of Directors

Taking the time to get in touch with your homeowners' association's board of directors will give you an idea of the kinds of people with whom you'll be sharing your new home. If the treasurer ran off to Maui last year with the funds for that upcoming renovation, you'd want to know, right?

Stay Away from High-Rental Developments

If you buy a house, you want to make sure your new neighbourhood is made up of people like you, who really make a commitment to the upkeep of their homes and the safety of their street. That's why it's not the best idea to move onto a street where most of the homes are rented. The same goes for condos.

New developments often have only the very basics in bylaws, which means that you may find that you're the only owner living in a building where the units were purchased mostly by investors to rent them out. You may find that you're more comfortable knowing exactly what the lay of the land will be before you buy.

When you're thinking of buying into a condo development, ask the condo corporation what percentage of units in the development are rented. The higher the percentage, the more concerned you should be. The more renters there are in the building, the fewer people you'll see raising their hands to pitch in for long-term improvements, like extensive roof repairs, landscaping, or plumbing.

Watch Out for Maintenance Fees That Are Too Good to Be True

If you're looking into a new building, don't jump to buy if you see low monthly maintenance fees. It's possible that your condo developers are keeping these costs artificially low to lure new buyers. When the developers are done and the homeowners' association takes over, the grim truth is uncovered as actual monthly costs are determined.

To prevent getting duped when buying a condo with unusually low maintenance fees, compare the developer's stated maintenance fees with the actual maintenance fees of an established building of a similar size. Make sure you know exactly what your maintenance fees cover, so you can make a fair assessment.

Ask about the Building's Commercial Property

Alyssa was overjoyed when the salesman in the condo showroom told her that there would be a convenience store, dry cleaner, and dental clinic on the first floor of the building. However, her joy turned to anger at a homeowners' meeting six months later, when she discovered that these properties paid ludicrously low maintenance fees and were given extra parking places for free. If you're thinking of buying into a new building, ask how many commercial properties there will be, if any. Then, ask to see documentation of how much in maintenance fees these businesses pay, as well as any other perks they may be getting, such as extra parking. The nature of the businesses will be important to you as well . . . having a busy, noisy salsa bar and a pawn shop in the building may change the way you feel about commercial space.

Share as Few Walls as Possible, Especially if You Crave Quiet

A good rule when looking at condos is that the more walls you share with other units, the greater your chance is of hearing the odd voice or thump. The same goes for the floor and ceiling: It will be quieter to just have someone below you than to have people above and below you. (Anyone who's lived underneath a Tae Bo video addict can attest to this.) This is one reason why corner suites are usually more expensive, and why top-floor corner suites are the *crème de la crème*.

Own Your Locker and Parking Space

When you're told that you'll have a big storage locker and a parking place, make sure you determine whether you own them or are given exclusive use of them. If they're for exclusive use, you don't own them, you can't sell them, and you may not be able to transfer use of them to someone else. If you own them, you can make a little side money by renting them out or selling them if you decide to give up your car or have a big garage sale.

Check for Signs of Aging

Condominiums built in old apartment buildings can be really charming, especially if the modern, cement-block ones look like big warts on the skyline to you. But make sure that the old-fashioned vibe you get from the building won't put you in the Middle Ages after you move in. If you're looking at a condo in an old apartment building, check for signs of dilapidation, such as crumbling walls or roof. Also, check to see whether the heating, cooling, ventilation, and security systems are up to date. If they're not, you may soon be paying extra maintenance fees to fix a big breakdown.

Chapter 25

Ten Tips for Condo Sellers

. . . .

. . . .

When selling a condominium, you need to go through the same procedures and checklists a homeowner goes through, but some differences do exist. You obviously want to get the best price possible and appeal to as many people as possible, so the trick is to make the unit look bright and attractive. Here are our ten tips to making your condo as attractive to buyers as possible.

Wait Until Your Building Is at Its Peak

You can't do too much with the building itself, but if you know the building is due to be painted in the next month or so, you may want to wait until then so that your suite looks its best before putting it on the market. And if any noisy or messy work is planned in the building (such as replacing hallway carpets or retiling the lobby), ideally you'd like to wait until that work is done too. The better the building and complex looks, the better price you'll get for your suite.

Prepare the Suite for Sale

If a house looks cramped and small due to unnecessary clutter, you can only imagine how small a condominium can look when it's crammed with tonnes of stuff. A good idea is to go through the suite and clean out the clutter (see our decluttering tips in Chapter 20). Having a yard sale in a condominium isn't easy (you probably don't have a yard, and the balcony simply won't do!), so throw out what you can. Many condominiums have small closets, so you may need to go through and take out clothes you're not wearing right now — for example, if you're selling the suite in summer, remove the space-eating bulky winter jackets and boots. Now is the time to pack everything away that you aren't using. Some stuff can go in your storage locker (if you have one), but that should be kept tidy, too, so we recommend renting a storage unit nearby and throwing your extra furniture and boxes into it — anything to make your suite look larger and less cluttered. If you have family or friends who live in a nice house nearby, now is the time to call in a favour and ask if you can throw some boxes into their basement.

Let Your Neighbours Know

If you live in a very desirable building with a low turnover of suites, let your neighbours know you're thinking of selling. You may be able to sell the suite privately to someone who has a friend who's always wanted to live in the building (we discuss private sales in Chapter 17). If you list with an agent and your building doesn't allow "For Sale" signs, make sure you get a feature sheet up in the building's bulletin board ASAP to let everyone in the building know your suite is for sale. In great buildings, a lot of suites will sell by word of mouth from neighbours within the building.

Whether you're selling privately or working with an agent, you may want to consider doing a mail-out with a feature postcard of your condo, including the basics like total floor area, number of bedrooms and bathrooms, and of course, the asking price. Doing this lets people in the immediate area know that you have listed your condo, and they can tell their friends, too!

Know Where to Advertise

You're not just selling your condominium (come on, remember how nothing is ever as simple as you think it is?), you're selling a lifestyle as well. If you don't have an agent to help you out, the first thing you need to figure out is what type of person would be happy living in your building. Then you need to figure out how to reach that person.

Is your condo building full of active seniors who play miniature golf and have cocktail parties a few times a week? Perhaps a local seniors' centre has a newsletter where you can place an ad. Are there many families with children, or single parents? Your community newspaper can be a lead to a good buyer, or check with your neighbours to see if they know like-minded people who may be interested. And if you need a buyer who has a well-paying job and who likes the quiet life, you're not going to advertise on the hydro pole by your city's university. You need to figure out how to target your market.

Prepare Documents

The buyer of your unit will need to see as many documents as possible, so if you have the minutes from the building's meetings for the last couple of years and recent copies of the rules and regulations, make sure you collect them all and set them aside. If you list with a real estate agent, she'll need these documents, and it will save her time, money, and paper to photocopy documents you already have instead of ordering another set from the management company. (We talk about rustling up the proper papers in Chapter 21.) However, you may want to order up all the proper documentation from the management company regardless. A chance always exists that through no fault of your own you haven't received a recent update on the building bylaws, or you've misplaced minutes from two years ago. Having complete and accurate documentation is essential, and will prevent problems for you down the road.

Fix the Little Things

If you're in a smaller suite, the little things that don't work properly will drive you crazy. The sound of a dripping tap can resonate throughout the entire suite, and one burnt-out light bulb can make the whole suite look dark and small. If the fridge is very noisy when it runs, it can sound like a dump truck idling in the corner. Now is the time to get around to doing the little things you've been putting off.

Don't Forget the Storage Areas

Your first impulse may be to just chuck everything in the closet, or better yet, keep it in your storage locker, if you have one. But these are important features of your condo that potential buyers really need to see, and they don't need to see them stuffed with, well, stuff. If you occupy the suite, you'll be moving anyway, so go through your storage locker and get rid of all those old clothes that no longer fit (congratulations — you look great!), as well as the boxes of cat toys that Fluffy no longer has interest in. Stack what remains in an orderly fashion, and give the locker a good sweeping while you're at it.

Familiarize Yourself with the Building

In most provinces, you'll be asked to fill out a seller's *disclosure statement* when you sell your suite. The disclosure statement will ask questions about the suite and the building that you answer to the best of your knowledge. If you're unsure about the status of the building, you'll probably have the option of answering "Do not know," but the more you know about the building, the better you can fill out any necessary disclosure forms. The buyer will also review all the minutes from meetings for the building, but you may want to review the minutes again before completing the disclosure statement to ensure that you're aware of any issues.

Make Notifications: My Dear Tenants . . .

If you're selling a suite that is tenanted, check with your provincial tenancy agency to ensure you comply with the rights of the tenant as you sell the suite. Make sure the tenant is aware the suite is for sale, and assure the tenant that his lease will be recognized and assumed by the new owner, if that's the case. Let the tenant know that any damage deposit and accrued interest owed to the tenant and being held by you will be forwarded to the new owner. Procedures will vary from province to province regarding giving notice to the tenant to show the suite, so make sure you're in compliance. If you're listing with an agent, the agent should be familiar with the local procedures and regulations.

If the tenant is messy and doesn't keep the suite clean and tidy, you can ask him to keep it as clean as possible. He may just need an incentive, in which case you can always offer a discount on the rent in return for a cleaner suite and a little extra accommodation for showings. You can't go into the suite and start cleaning up the tenant's stuff — but you can always ask him to keep things clean and help you out in other ways.

Of course, if your tenant is an out-and-out slob, you may have a bigger problem on your hands. Tenanted properties often sell for less than those occupied by owners. The tenant doesn't have a financial interest in the property, and may be worried that he'll be out of a home when the unit sells. Consequently, he doesn't have much interest in making sure your condo shows to the best of its ability.

Light It Up

Unless your nickname is Queen of the Night, chances are you're attracted by ads that begin with the words "Bright, spacious, one-bedroom . . ." Real estate ads often start by highlighting (pun intended) the amount of light a space gets. Even if you don't have a southern exposure or picture windows, you can still show off how bright your condo is, and it's pretty easy to do. A few strategically placed lamps (corners work well for spreading light) will help buyers feel the cheerful atmosphere, plus the brighter it is, the bigger it looks. Keep your curtains or shades open (unless it's the time of day the neighbour across the way practises his tap dancing), and use mirrors to reflect light and space.

Chapter 26

Ten Ways to Protect and Maintain Your Investment

In This Chapter

▶ Keeping an eye on your surrounding property

▶ Servicing your heating and cooling systems

▶ Safeguarding your home

Many people subscribe to the "if it ain't broke, don't fix it" view of home maintenance. But it will cost you so much more to repair water damage than it will to check the roof for loose or damaged shingles every six months. Just as you should change your car's oil every 5,000 or so kilometres, so should you change your furnace's air filter at least twice a year — you may dote on your car, but ultimately, your home is a much larger investment, so take care of it! Imagine selling your home for $50,000 less than you want because of water damage in the basement. And if you check your home's foundation regularly, you may be able to prevent the damage altogether. Whether it needs to be done monthly or yearly, take the time to inspect as well as repair your home's interior and exterior. We guarantee you'll enjoy living in your home much more, and you're likely to be very happy with its resale value.

Inspect the Exterior

Do an exterior inspection twice a year. Check your home's foundations for signs of cracking, bulges, or deterioration. If you have a brick home, you should watch for deteriorating bricks or masonry; aluminum siding should be checked for rot, dents, cracks, or warping. If you have any retaining walls, make sure that they're well maintained, with no signs of cracks or erosion.

Clean and check your eavestroughs at least once a year in the fall. Trim vegetation away from gutters and downspouts to prevent blockage. One of the best ways to examine your eavestroughs is to watch them when it rains. Do they drain properly, or do they overflow? Are there holes? Where does the water drain? Downspouts should direct water away from your home, not toward the basement. Water constantly pouring into the side of the house can eventually find its way into the house.

Don't force yourself to climb on your home's roof — you can just use a pair of binoculars to take a quick survey. Look for damaged or missing shingles, especially if water is leaking into the interior of the house. Check the flashings (the metal or plastic reinforcing the angles and edges on a roof), too, for deterioration. Call a roofing specialist in to do a full inspection if you notice anything. Watch chimneys for loose or deteriorated mortar, and examine the flashing around the chimney. Look for birds' nests in them, too.

Look at What Surrounds Your House: Landscaping, Yard, and Deck

Inspect the property around your house before and after winter. Have a look at the trees — are they healthy? If a branch has no leaves but others are in full bloom, that branch is probably dead and needs to be removed before it falls onto the new addition or onto an innocent passerby. Have a look at any exposed tree roots near the house; they can sometimes grow into your sewer system, or even lift up walkways or driveways around the home. Trim any shrubs around your doorways and windows so that prowlers can't hide behind them. Make sure tree branches don't brush against your house — trees are a great way for squirrels and other less savoury rodents to get into the attic and eaves of your home.

If you have a lawn sprinkler system, check it once a year in the spring for leaky valves or exposed lines. Get rid of any garden debris that can attract wood-eating insects — you don't want your home to be a termite hotel! Check out your pool and hot tub: Look for leaks or damage. Pool liners should be in good repair, and if water is in the pool, it should look like water you'd want to swim in, not a slimy, green science experiment. Look at your walkway for unevenness.

Finally, don't forget to inspect the garage: its foundation, roof, and walls. In the summer, if you have an asphalt driveway you should check it and patch up any cracks.

Maintain Heating and Cooling Systems

Service, service, service. That's all we have to say about your heating system. It's cleaner and also easier on your wallet if the system is working at its highest efficiency. Have your system inspected and serviced once a year — a good time to do it is just before you start using it for the winter. If you have a forced-air system, clean or change your furnace filters at least twice a year. Have the ducts cleaned out, too, so that the air can travel freely around the home without moving lots of dust around. If you have in-floor or radiant heat, make sure that those systems are checked on a regular basis, and baseboard heaters should be checked to make sure all wiring is up to snuff. Include the chimney on your "to clean" list: a blocked chimney is a big fire hazard.

A central air conditioning unit should also be serviced once a year. Remember to cover it before the winter when not in use. If you rely on window air conditioning units to keep you cool in the summer, make sure to store them in a safe place for the winter (not on your garage floor where de-icing salt can leak onto them) or protect them from snow with plastic sealed with duct tape. When window units are in place, make sure to fill any gaps between the window and the unit — gaps reduce the unit's efficiency and stability.

Stay Warm: Insulation

If you've ever had frozen pipes in the winter, you know the importance of having good insulation. Even if you're not worried about frozen pipes (you live in Victoria, don't you . . .), insulate your hot water pipes to keep them from losing heat when in use. If you notice small drafts around your home, you may be able to block them with the addition of spray foam insulation. Ask at your local hardware store for tips on convenient mini-insulation materials. Watch for drafts especially near electrical outlets and light switches on exterior walls, under baseboards, around window and exterior door casings, and around entrances to un-insulated areas in your home, like the cold storage room.

Speaking of un-insulated areas, you should think about insulating some of them: Your attic and your basement are two good places to start. Good insulation makes your home more efficient, keeping your heating and cooling costs low. Insulation can now be blown into hard-to-reach areas in attics and walls, creating that extra barrier your home may need.

Breathe Easy: Ventilation

Clean air is particularly important to create a healthy living space, especially if you or someone in your family suffers from allergies or asthma. Make sure your home breathes so there's an adequate exchange of air inside your home. Don't seal all your doors and windows so that they're absolutely air-tight, or you may have trouble with a buildup of moisture or harmful gases inside your home. Because modern homes are so airtight, some have built-in air exchange systems to keep clean air flowing through them. Ventilation options include attic fans, heat recovery ventilators, and balanced mechanical ventilation systems — or keeping windows open.

Again, like the heating/cooling systems in your home, have your ventilation system serviced yearly. Your home's ventilation includes kitchen exhaust hoods, bathroom fans, and dryer exhausts, so don't neglect these either. On the outside of your home, check around the ventilation openings for any cracks, leaks, or damage. On the inside, clean or replace ventilation screens or filters, and turn on your fans and fume hoods at all settings to make sure they work properly.

Sleep Soundly: Home Safety

Here are ten things to do regularly to safeguard your home:

- ✔ Replace batteries in smoke detectors at least twice a year.
- ✔ Test all your smoke detectors, fire alarms, and carbon monoxide detectors once a month.
- ✔ Don't leave any inflammables near the furnace, water heater, or space heaters.
- ✔ Pay attention to the condition of stairways and their railings; make repairs if they are unstable.
- ✔ Plan out fire escape routes for your home, and make sure your children know how to get out if they can't use regular doorways.
- ✔ Test locks on all the doors and windows, and change them if you've had a break-in or lost a key.
- ✔ Ensure extension cords are tucked away from people's feet and pets' teeth.
- ✔ Check any exposed wiring — including those extension cords, phone cords, cable lines, and appliance cords — for broken or frayed wires; replace them if you find anything.

✔ Test your circuit breakers every six months.

✔ Update that list of emergency numbers and information on your fridge, especially if you have a caregiver.

Keep an Eye on Your Doors and Windows

Inspect all window and door screens for rust, holes, and tears, and mend or replace them. Give the screens and windows a good wash. Replace any broken or cracked panes of glass. Open and close all doors and windows: Do they stick? Oil door hinges where they bind or squeak. Test window locks. Look at your windowsills for signs of water damage. If the wood framing feels damp or looks warped, rainwater may be getting through. Look for deterioration of window trim, seals, putty, caulking, and weather-stripping on both the exterior and interior. If you notice problems, fix them immediately. The longer you allow water damage to occur, the more expensive it becomes to repair. Test outdoor lighting to make sure your entrances are lit adequately at night.

Cook Up a Storm in a Safe, Sumptuous Kitchen

The kitchen is a fine place for water problems, so inspect it thoroughly. Check for leaks under the sink and around the dishwasher (if you're lucky enough to have one of the mechanical ones, that is). Watch around the sink and faucet for places that need resealing.

Every outlet near the sink should be a GFCI receptacle (ground fault circuit interrupter) that will protect you from being electrocuted if it comes in contact with water. You should test it every six months (press the little test button; it's that easy!).

Clean out that fridge and freezer. Get rid of the dust that builds up on the refrigerator coils — you know what dust we mean! Make sure the seal on the fridge door is tight. Give your stove and oven a thorough cleaning, especially if you use them often. You'll find the cooking elements produce less smoke and odours and have less chance of causing a grease fire if you keep them clean.

Check the burner operation on your stove to prevent fire hazards. Make sure your fire extinguisher still works and that it's within easy reach in case of an emergency. You should also have a kitchen exhaust hood above your stove that is properly vented outside to remove the smoke and odours while you cook. Change or clean the filter every month or two.

Get Away from It All in a Leak-Free Bathroom

Every six months, you should inspect your bathrooms. As in the kitchen, test the GFCI receptacles in your bathroom (see "Cook Up a Storm in a Safe, Sumptuous Kitchen" above). Check for water leaks around the faucets, toilets, and pipes. Watch for water damage (typical signs include brown patches, warped wood, and mould) in the flooring, walls, and ceiling. Re-grout what you need to, especially in the corners of your shower and where the tub meets the wall. Make sure that the toilet flushes properly, that the handle doesn't stick, and that it seals properly after a flush. For plumbing repairs, consult a professional; if you're a novice, you may make a minor problem into a major one.

Confront Your Childhood Fears: Visit Your Basement and Attic

You may not spend much time in either your basement or your attic, but don't ignore them altogether. Although you may use both areas for storage, go through them once a year and get rid of unnecessary clutter; if you've left paint, varnish, or oily rags about, make sure you properly dispose of them — they're a major fire hazard.

Basement and attic leaks are the major cause of water damage, so inspect these areas carefully. Watch for water leakage in crawl spaces, on ceilings, on walls, and around windows. A brown patch on a white wall is a bad sign. Use your nose: A damp, musty smell is a good indication of water leakage, even if you don't see anything.

Look for signs of termites or other pest infestations: hollow-sounding beams, holes in wood, droppings, and bite marks are a good indication that you're not living alone. In the summer, look in the attic for bigger freeloading visitors. You may be able to set a few mousetraps yourself, but if you discover a raccoon or some other large varmint, you're better off calling a professional pest remover.

Appendix

Where Can I Get More Information? Real Estate Resources

· ·

You're going to have lots of questions as you go through the home-buying or home-selling process. Fortunately, lots of people out there are ready to supply the information you need, through the ring of a telephone, the visit of a mail carrier, the click of a mouse, or the squeal of a fax.

Home Shopping or Selling

Nowadays, many house hunts and sales start on the Internet, and for good reason. Surfing for home listings helps you get an idea of the going rate on what you're looking for, and can tip you off to plum real estate before everybody else has had a chance to see that sign on the lawn.

Multiple Listing Service (MLS)

This Web site is an excellent place to start your search — it's the official site for MLS listings brought to you by the Canadian Real Estate Association. Search by region, price, or even number of bathrooms at www.realtor.ca.

Listing services

These sites, many of which feature a combination of agent-represented and private-sale listings, can provide you with hours of happy home hunting.

www.bchomesforsale.com (B.C. only)
www.crls.ca
www.homesalez.com

www.inthehouse.com (Alberta, B.C., and Ontario only)
www.virtual-agent.com (both U.S. and Canadian listings)

Private sales

Whether you're buying or selling, these sites all have one thing in common: They're about people taking real estate into their own hands through "For Sale by Owner," or FSBO, listings.

www.ab4sale.ca
www.assist2sell.com
www.bc4sale.ca
www.canadahomesforsale.ca
www.canadian-real-estate-for-sale.com
www.craigslist.org

www.ebay.ca
www.forsalebyowner
canada.com
www.homesellcanada.com
www.on4sale.ca
www.privatelist.com
www.propertyguys.com

Mortgages

The world of mortgages is complicated. No doubt, if you've already attempted doing some research, you've found a bewildering amount of information and advice out there. Buyers and sellers alike have a million questions to answer before deciding on the right financial plan for their individual needs. The following resources offer plenty of easy-to-understand and helpful information to prepare you for the world of mortgages.

Online mortgage calculators

Most Web sites devoted to mortgage information and those of major financial institutions offer online mortgage calculators. If you're having trouble navigating a site, try using links to "Calculators," "Tools," "Mortgage," "Mortgage Centre," or "Personal Banking." You can find online calculators at the following sites:

www.bmo.com
www.canadamortgage.com
www.cibc.com
www.citizensbank.ca
www.ingdirect.ca
www.laurentianbank.ca

www.nbc.ca
www.rbcroyalbank.com
www.scotiabank.com
www.tdcanadatrust.com

Canada Mortgage and Housing Corporation (CMHC)

The CMHC is Canada's national housing agency and serves many roles in the housing industry. The CMHC insures high-ratio mortgages to protect lenders from default, assists in public-private partnerships in housing, conducts and coordinates research into housing issues, and has Canada's largest database regarding homes and housing.

CMHC National Office
700 Montreal Rd.
Ottawa, ON K1A 0P7
Phone 613-748-2000 or 800-668-2642
Fax 613-748-2098
E-mail chic@cmhc-schl.gc.ca
Web site www.cmhc-schl.gc.ca

You can find addresses and contact information for all the regional offices at the CMHC Web site.

Canadian Housing Information Centre (CHIC)

This sub-organization of the CMHC, which provides a wealth of housing information, is also worth checking out.

CHIC Library
C1-200, 700 Montreal Rd.
Ottawa, ON K1A 0P7
Phone 613-748-2367 or 800-668-2642 (ask for the library)
Fax 613-748-4069
E-mail chic@cmhc-schl.gc.ca

Genworth Financial Canada

Genworth is a private sector supplier of mortgage default insurance in Canada.

Genworth Financial Canada, National Underwriting Centre
Phone 800-511-8888
E-mail mortgage.info@genworth.com
Web site www.genworth.ca

You can find regional offices' e-mail addresses and telephone numbers on the Web site.

Canadian Home Income Plan (CHIP)

CHIP is the major organization that currently offers reverse mortgages in Canada. Its address is:

CHIP Head Office
45 St. Clair Ave. W., Suite 600
Toronto, ON M4V 1K9
Phone 416-925-4757 or 866-522-2447
Fax 416-925-9938
E-mail info@chip.ca
Web site www.chip.ca

Canadian Association of Accredited Mortgage Professionals (CAAMP)

Membership with CAAMP is a good sign that a mortgage broker is an on-the-level business. CAAMP has members from every region of Canada, and their Web site is a great place to start when you're hunting for good general information on mortgages or a reputable broker in your area. Their site also offers online mortgage calculators and a detailed glossary of mortgage terms, if the many bank sites we mention earlier in this appendix left you high and dry.

CAAMP Corporate Office
2235 Sheppard Ave. E., Suite 1401
Toronto, ON M2J 5B5
Phone 416-385-2333 or 888-442-4625
Fax 416-385-1177 or 888-579-2840
E-mail info@caamp.org
Web site www.caamp.org

Mortgage brokers

The Web features some great Canadian mortgage brokers, helping you to shop around for the best deal. These Canuck corporations do the legwork for you, often getting lower rates from financial institutions than all us regular Joes ever could, no matter how many flowers and chocolates we may send.

CanEquity Mortgage
Phone 888-818-4262
Web site www.canequity.com

Dominion Lending Centres
Phone 888-806-8080
Web site www.dominionlending.ca

Invis
Phone 866-854-6847
Web site www.invis.ca

Credit Reporting

Your lending institution will perform a credit check when you apply for a mortgage.

Equifax Canada Inc.

Equifax Canada is one of the largest credit-checking agencies in Canada. You can contact them to confirm the status of your credit rating if you are curious.

Equifax Canada, Consumer Relations Department
Box 190 Jean Talon Station
Montreal, QC H1S 2Z2
Phone 514-493-2314 or 800-465-7166
Fax 514-355-8502
E-mail consumer.relations@equifax.com
Web site www.equifax.ca

Inspectors

Home inspectors are an integral part of most home sales in Canada. An inspector offers an educated and independent opinion about the overall condition of a home, and the systems within a home.

Canadian Association of Home and Property Inspectors (CAHPI)

Formed in 1982, CAHPI maintains and regulates national standards in home inspections, and offers a Code of Ethics that its members must adhere to. CAHPI offers education services to its members and interacts with government agencies and the public as a leading authority in the home inspection field.

CAHPI National Office
P.O. Box 13715
Ottawa, ON K2K 1X6
Phone 613-839-5344 or 888-748-2244
Fax 866-876-9877
E-mail info@cahpi.ca
Web site www.cahpi.ca

Contact information for CAHPI's regional offices changes annually. Consult the national Web site for more information.

Real Estate Associations

Provincial real estate associations are a good resource to answer any questions about specific provincial laws and regulations. These associations can often direct buyers and sellers who are searching for an agent to the applicable local real estate board. Here is a list of real estate associations across Canada:

Canadian Real Estate Association
Minto Place, The Canada Building
344 Slater St., Suite 1600
Ottawa, ON K1R 7Y3
Phone 613-237-7111
Fax 613-234-2567
E-mail info@crea.ca
Web site www.crea.ca

This site also has an internal search engine that gives you access to every individual real estate board in Canada.

New Brunswick Real Estate Association
22 Durelle St., Unit 1
Fredericton, NB E3C 1N8
Phone 506-459-8055
Fax 506-459-8057
E-mail info@nbrea.ca
Web site www.nbrea.ca

Newfoundland and Labrador Real Estate Association
28 Logy Bay Rd.
St. John's, NF A1A 1J4
Phone 709-726-5110
Fax 709-726-4221

Nova Scotia Association of Realtors
7 Scarfe Ct., Suite 100
Dartmouth, NS B3B 1W4
Phone 902-468-2515
Fax 902-468-2533
Web site www.nsar-mls.ca

Prince Edward Island Real Estate Association
75 St. Peter's Rd.
Charlottetown, PE C1A 5N7
Phone 902-368-8451
Fax 902-894-9487
E-mail office@peirea.com
Web site www.peirea.com

Chambre immobilières du Québec
990 av. Holland
Québec, QC G15 3T1
Phone 418-688-3362
Fax 418-688-3577 or 866-688-3362
Web site www.ciq.qc.ca

Ontario Real Estate Association
99 Duncan Mill Rd.
Don Mills, ON M3B 1Z2
Phone 416-445-9910
Fax 416-445-2644
E-mail info@orea.com
Web site www.orea.com

Manitoba Real Estate Association
1873 Inkster Blvd.
Winnipeg, MB R2R 2A6
Phone 204-772-0405
Fax 204-775-3781
Web site www.realestatemanitoba.com

Saskatchewan Real Estate Association
2811 Estey Dr.
Saskatoon, SK S7J 2V8
Phone 306-373-3350
Fax 306-373-5377
E-mail info@saskatchewanrealestate.com
Web site www.saskatchewanrealestate.com

Alberta Real Estate Association
300 – 4954 Richard Rd. S.W.
Calgary, AB T3E 6L1
Phone 403-228-6845
Fax 403-228-4360
E-mail info@areahub.ca
Web site www.abrea.ab.ca

British Columbia Real Estate Association
1420 – 701 Georgia St. W.
P.O. Box 10123, Pacific Centre
Vancouver, BC V7Y 1C6
Phone 604-683-7702
Fax 604-683-8601
E-mail bcrea@bcrea.bc.ca
Web site www.bcrea.bc.ca

Yukon Real Estate Association
49 Waterfront Pl.
Whitehorse, YK Y1A 6V1
Phone 867-667-5565
Fax 867-667-7005
Web site www.yrea.ca

Surveys

Here is a list of provincial associations of land surveyors:

Association of New Brunswick Land Surveyors
212 Queen St., Suite 312
Fredericton, NB E3B 1A8
Phone 506-458-8266
Fax 506-458-8267
E-mail anbls@nb.aibn.com
Web site www.anbls.nb.ca

Association of Newfoundland Land Surveyors
62 – 64 Pippy Pl., Suite 203
St. John's, NF A1B 4H7
Phone 709-722-2031
Fax 709-722-4104
E-mail anls@nf.aibn.com
Web site www.surveyors.nf.ca

Ordre des arpenteurs-géomètres du Québec
Iberville Quatre
2954 boul. Laurier, bureau 350
Québec, QC G1V 4T2
Phone 418-656-0730
Fax 418-656-6352
E-mail oagq@oagq.qc.ca
Web site www.oagq.qc.ca

Association of Ontario Land Surveyors
1043 McNicoll Ave.
Scarborough, ON M1W 3W6
Phone 416-491-9020 or 800-268-0718
Fax 416-491-2576
Web site www.aols.org

Saskatchewan Land Surveyors Association
408 Broad St., Suite 230
Regina, SK S4R 1X3
Phone 306-352-8999
Fax 306-352-8366
E-mail info@slsa.sk.ca
Web site www.slsa.sk.ca

Alberta Land Surveyors' Association
10020 – 101A Ave., Suite 1000
Edmonton, AB T5J 3G2
Phone 780-429-8805 or 800-665-2572
Fax 780-429-3374
E-mail info@alsa.ab.ca
Web site www.alsa.ab.ca

Association of British Columbia Land Surveyors
301 – 2400 Bevan Ave.
Sidney, BC V8L 1W1
Phone 250-655-7222
Fax 250-655-7223
Web site www.abcls.ca

Appraisers

Appraisals usually go hand in hand with mortgage approval, so sourcing out the professionals make sense. Here's where you can start your search:

Appraisal Institute Of Canada
403 – 200 Catherine St.
Ottawa, ON K2P 2K9
Phone 613-234-6533
Fax 613-234-7197
E-mail info@aicanada.ca
Web site www.aicanada.ca

This mailing address is for AIC's national office; for the provincial offices, just visit the Web site or call the office in Ottawa.

Lawyers

Lawyers are involved in most real estate transactions in Canada, except in Quebec, where notaries are the norm. The buyer and the seller should have their own lawyers to act in their best interest, to review the contract of purchase and sale, if necessary, and to complete the transfer of the property from the seller to the buyer.

Federation of Law Societies of Canada (FLSC)

This is the blanket organization for all provincial law societies. The FLSC Web site has a link to each provincial and territorial law society Web site and e-mail address for inquiries. Many provincial Web sites list local lawyers and their specialties, or provide links to provincial legal education associations or societies that provide this information. The Federation of Law Societies of Canada can be contacted at:

Federation of Law Societies of Canada
World Exchange Plaza
45 O'Connor St., Suite 1810
Ottawa, ON K1P 1A4
Phone 613-236-7272
Fax 613-236-7233
E-mail info@flsc.ca
Web site www.flsc.ca

Provincial lawyer referral services

For listings of lawyers and firms, www.canlaw.com is a great Web site. CanLaw's listing includes names, addresses, and areas of expertise. It is divided by province and then further divided into area or city. The site also has links to real estate pages!

Finding specific lawyers or firms

If a friend has given you the name of a lawyer or firm but you aren't sure how to find them or aren't sure if they even practise real estate law, www.canadian lawlist.com is worth a visit. This site contains a database of lawyers and their specialties that is searchable by lawyer name or firm name.

Warranties

Home warranties are essential to protect buyers of newly built or substantially renovated homes. Some provinces have provincial warranty programs, and other provinces have mandatory warranty coverage supplied by private companies. Check out the list of provincial New Home Warranty Programs for the one that applies to you.

Atlantic Home Warranty Program

Established in 1976, the Atlantic Home Warranty Program has backed more than 80,000 homes in the Atlantic region.

15 Oland Cres.
Halifax, NS B3S 1C6
Phone 902-450-9000 or 800-320-9880
Fax 902-450-5454
E-mail info@ahwp.org
Web site www.ahwp.org

La Garantie des maisons neuves de l'Association provinciale des constructeurs d'habitations du Québec

5930 boul. Louis-H. Lafontaine
Montreal, QC H1J 1S7
Phone 514-353-1120
Fax 514-353-4825
E-mail clientele@apchq.com
Web site www.apchq.com

Tarion Warranty Corporation (formerly Ontario New Home Warranty Program)

Phone 416-229-9200 or 877-982-7466
Fax 416-229-3800 or 877-664-9710
Web site www.tarion.com

For addresses of regional locations, visit the Web site.

New Home Warranty Program of Manitoba Inc.

200 – 675 Pembina Hwy.
Winnipeg, MB R3M 2L6
Phone 204-453-1155
Fax 204-287-8561
E-mail mbnhwp@mbnhwp.com
Web site www.mbnhwp.com

New Home Warranty Program of Saskatchewan Inc.

4 – 3012 Louise St. E.
Saskatoon, SK S7L 3L8
Phone 306-373-7833
Fax 306-373-7977
Web site www.nhwp.org

Alberta New Home Warranty Program

Incorporated in 1974, the Alberta New Home Warranty program was the first new home warranty program in Canada. It has offices in Calgary and Edmonton.

Calgary Office
301 – 30 Springborough Blvd. S.W.
Calgary, Alberta T3H 0N9
Phone 403-253-3636 or 800-352-8240
Fax 403-253-5062
E-mail ConsumerRep@anhwp.com
Web site www.anhwp.com

Edmonton Office
204 – 10464 Mayfield Rd. N.W.
Edmonton, AB T5P 4P4
Phone 780-484-0572 or 800-352-8240
Fax 780-486-7896
E-mail ConsumerRep@anhwp.com
Web site www.anhwp.com

Homeowner Protection Office in British Columbia

Since the collapse of the British Columbia New Home Warranty Program, the Homeowner Protection Office has established warranty guidelines to help re-establish and strengthen consumer confidence for buyers of new homes and condominiums. The HPO licenses builders, oversees mandatory third-party warranties on all new homes, offers reconstruction loans to owners of leaky condos, and offers education and research programs. The HPO Web site has great links to industry associations and information, warranty information, government links, and British Columbia's Better Business Bureaus, and outlines relief programs available to people with leaky condominiums in B.C.

Homeowner Protection Office, Licensing and Compliance
2270 – 1055 West Georgia St.
P.O. Box 11132, Royal Centre
Vancouver, BC V6E 3P3
Phone 604-646-7050 or 800-407-7757
Fax 604-646-7051
E-mail hpo@hpo.bc.ca
Web site www.hpo.bc.ca

National Home Warranty Programs

In many provinces, third-party warranties are required for new homes and condominiums. National Home Warranty Programs is one of the major companies that offers third-party warranty coverage for new construction across Canada. Their Web site, www.nationalhomewarranty.com, offers excellent information about warranty coverage across the country.

Builders

If you're buying a newly built home, finding out as much as you can about the various people associated with building it from the ground up is important. This broad category includes builders, renovators, trade contractors, product manufacturers, and lending institutions.

Canadian Home Builders' Association (CHBA)

The Canadian Home Builders' Association represents more than 6,000 firms in the residential construction industry across Canada. Its Web site contains links to provincial and local home builders' associations and provincial warranty program sites.

CHBA
150 Laurier Avenue W., Suite 500
Ottawa, ON K1P 5J4
Phone 613-230-3060
Fax 613-232-8214
E-mail chba@chba.ca
Web site www.chba.ca

GST/HST new housing rebate

The federal government's GST/HST rebate on new housing is complex enough to warrant a little time spent on the Canada Revenue Agency's Web site at www.cra-arc.gc.ca. Using the site's search function, type in "GST/HST new housing rebate" to find a wealth of helpful information on official requirements and eligibility.

Building resources and materials

Looking for a drywaller in North Bay, or roofing materials in Moose Jaw? Log on to www.constructioncanada.com. Whether you're building your new home or just renovating your old one before you sell it, and whether you need basic materials or a professional to come and do all the work, this Web site can help you find the assistance you need.

House plans and design

If you're reading this section, chances are you know your Tudor from your Colonial, so your best bet may simply be to type a specific search for house plans or design information into your favourite search engine. But if that's just not your style, we've come up with a couple of sites that you may find useful. At www.houseplans.ca, you can search for and purchase house plans that comply with the National Building Code of Canada. If you need an architect and don't know where to start, try www.architecture.ca and click on "Associations" to find a licensed architect in your area. Meanwhile, if you're

looking to jazz up the inside of your home, go to `www.interiordesign
canada.org` to find the association of interior designers closest to you.

Home Insurance

Insuring both the structure and contents of your home, as well as yourself in
the event that you cause damage to somebody else's home, is important. You
should purchase a policy that offers both property and liability coverage.

Insurance Bureau of Canada (IBC)

The Insurance Bureau of Canada can answer any questions regarding insurance matters in Canada, and direct you to the appropriate contact in your
area. You can get in touch with them at their head office:

IBC Head Office
777 Bay St., Suite 2400
P.O. Box 121
Toronto, ON M5G 2C8
Phone 416-362-2031
Fax 416-361-5952
Web site `www.ibc.ca`

Relocating

When you're moving a long distance, the Web can help you find out all the
little details about your new hometown that you'd normally find out at the
town hall, by talking to locals in the doughnut shop . . . you get the idea. The
Web site `www.relocatecanada.com` offers exhaustive information on most
cities in Canada, from a brief history to health services, transportation, and
even the weather. It's the first stop of all the Web surfers we know who fall in
love online with someone from a different city.

Movers

Hiring a reputable moving company is vital to get your earthly belongings
from point A to point B in one piece. But how do you know your above-
board mover from someone like those guys your brother-in-law once hired,
who refused to carry boxes of books because they were too heavy and took
smoke breaks every 15 minutes? A great place to start in your moving search
(and a good place to visit when you have a mover in mind) is this association:

Canadian Association of Movers
2200 Sherobee Rd., Suite 404
Mississauga, ON L5A 3Y3
Phone 905-848-6579 or 866-860-0065
Fax 905-848-8499 or 866-601-8499
E-mail admin@mover.net
Web site www.mover.net

But what if you're doing the move yourself? If your worldly possessions are few, if your budget is tight, or if you just have a whole bunch of well-muscled, reliable friends, you may be thinking you can handle this one. If that's the case, check out our list of Web sites below for truck and van rentals, as well as moving supplies and tips.

www.budget.ca
www.discountcar.com
www.hertztrucks.com
www.nationalcar.ca
www.thedrivingforce.com
www.uhaul.com

Packing supplies

When it seems you're already running around to a million places getting ready for your big move, knowing that most major moving companies will take orders over the phone, fax, or Internet for boxes and packing materials, and will ship them to your home, may take a load off. Talk to your moving company about purchasing supplies.

Condominiums

Owning a condominium isn't like owning a house. Though some similarities exist, there are more differences — like the role of the condominium corporation, maintenance fees, and commercial property. These are details you want to work out before you sign on the dotted line and gain possession of that condo of your dreams.

Canadian Condominium Institute (CCI)

The Canadian Condominium Institute is an independent, non-profit organization that assists all aspects of the condominium community through research, education, and information dissemination. You can contact their national office at:

CCI National Office
310 – 2175 Sheppard Ave. E.
Toronto, ON M2J 1W8
Phone 416-491-6216
Fax 416-491-1670
E-mail cci.national@taylorenterprises.com
Web site www.cci.ca

Index

mortgage *(continued)*
  signing, 192
  size of, calculating, 22–23
  term, 34, 37–38
  variable rate, 35, 39, 51
  vendor (seller) take-back mortgages
    (UTB), 40–41
mortgage broker
  discounts, 234
  fees, 26
  finding, 46–49
  interest rate updates from, 35
  line of credit from, 213
  obtaining a mortgage without, 47–49
  online, 46–47
  real estate agents as, 87
  resources, 362–363
  services provided, 45–46, 86–87
mortgage discharge statement, 321
mortgage insurance
  application fee, 26
  for high-ratio mortgage, 26, 32–33, 42, 43
  incentives and refunds, 43
  mortgage default, 361–362
  mortgage life, 44
mortgage note (commitment letter), 192
mortgage payments
  blended, 36–37, 238
  extra payments, 32, 34
  payment options, 38–39
  portable and blended payments, 39–40
  prepayment options, 32, 34, 38, 234
  prepayment penalty, 226, 235
  schedules, 36–37
  weekly or biweekly payments, 32
moving
  best time for, 194–196
  costs, 29, 201, 227
  getting possession of new home, 204–205
  mover discounts, 195
  moving your life, 196
  moving your stuff, 196–197
  moving yourself, 199–201
  overview, 193–194
  packing, 197–199
  packing supplies, 374
  professional movers, 199–201
  relocating for a new job, 231
  relocation expenses, 231
  resources, 373–374
  tax credits, 231
  timeline for, 201–204
  truck and van rentals, 374
Multiple Listing Service (MLS)
  about, 359
  assignment listings, 76
  listings of homes for sale, 121
  overview, 267–268, 269
  private sellers options, 260
  "For Sale by Owner" properties listed
    on, 256
  sample listing, 122
multiple offers, 160–162, 332–333

• N •

National Home Warranty Programs Web
    site, 371
natural gas heating, 129
negotiating the offer. *See also* contract of
    purchase and sale; offer to purchase
  backup offers, 333–334
  closing date, 330–331
  counteroffers, 326
  extending the offer, 331–332
  fixtures and chattels, 329–330
  focusing on what's important, 324–325
  leased items, 329
  lowest offer you'll accept, 326
  multiple offers, 332–333
  overview, 325–326
  preparation for, 323–324
  signing the contract, 332
  "subject to" clauses, 311, 327–328
neighbourhood
  appraisal, 95
  choosing, 64–65, 111–117
  looking for homes "For Sale," 120
  open houses, 217
  priorities list, 116–117
  proximity of neighbours, 70, 76
  as reason to sell, 214–215
  school considerations, 112, 113
  scouting out, 201
  up-and-coming, 114–115
net worth calculator, 48
new condominiums, 71–77, 176, 344–345

• S •